MW01166079

# "STALIN OVER WISCONSIN"

CLASS AND CULTURE

A series edited by

Milton Cantor and Bruce Laurie

# "STALIN OVER WISCONSIN"

## The Making and Unmaking of Militant Unionism, 1900–1950

## STEPHEN MEYER

RUTGERS UNIVERSITY PRESS
New Brunswick, New Jersey

**Library of Congress Cataloging-in-Publication Data**


Meyer, Stephen, 1942–
    "Stalin over Wisconsin" : the making and unmaking of militant
unionism, 1900–1950 / Stephen Meyer.
        p.      cm.
    Includes bibliographical references and index.
    ISBN 0-8135-1798-2
    1. Trade-unions—Wisconsin—History.    2. Trade-unions—Wisconsin—
Political activity—History.    3. Trade-unions and communism—
Wisconsin—History.    4. Allis Chalmers—History.    5. Industrial
relations—Wisconsin—History.    I. Title.
HD6517.W5M48    1992
322'.2'09775—dc20                                                91-32610
                                                                    CIP


British Cataloging-in-Publication information available

To Margo:

Finally done!

Let's get rid of the kids,

find some good music,

and go dancin'.

# CONTENTS

# PREFACE

*"Stalin Over Wisconsin"* is both similar to and different from my earlier work, *The Five Dollar Day*. Both are workplace studies that rest on my conviction that we still know too little about the hidden terrain of production and its connection to larger social and political issues. Both explore worker reactions to technical change, although one emphasizes the semiskilled workers' response to the rapid development of the Fordist mass production model and the other the skilled craftsmen's to the Allis-Chalmers evolution from batch production to a mix of batch and mass production. At Ford, workers mainly resisted covertly and quietly; at Allis-Chalmers, they did so openly and defiantly. Finally, both studies examine different forms of the corporate power that dominated and shaped attitudes and values of American workers. Although both firms used their considerable economic and technical powers to contain worker resistance, Ford relied on social and cultural forms of domination and Allis-Chalmers on more direct political ones.

The absence and the abundance of sources make doing the history of a modern corporation difficult. Allis-Chalmers was sensitive to public image and its available records are thin, mainly a large collection of public relations materials and a smaller one of corporate history. Nonetheless, Harold Story, the architect of the firm's labor relations policies in the 1930s and 1940s, did leave a small, but important, collection of personal papers that touched on his work at Allis-Chalmers. On the other hand, the union and government records are voluminous. The comprehensive union records include those of UAW Local 248, the national and regional machinists' union, and the state and local AFL and CIO councils. And, since the 1930s, federal agencies extensively monitored and oversaw the American industrial relations. The National Labor Relations Board, National Defense Mediation Board, National War Labor Board, and Federal Mediation and Conciliation Service also left a vast public record on labor-management relations at Allis-Chalmers.

This study originated in Bob Zieger's 1981 National Endowment for the Humanities Summer Seminar on Labor History at Wayne State University, where the Archives of Labor and Urban Affairs held the UAW Local 248 papers. At the time, I was seeking a research project located in my new hometown, Milwaukee, in order to have access to a rich mine of local sources. UAW Local 248 was important in local, state, and national labor history. In the mid-1930s, the UAW local organized Wisconsin's largest firm, the Allis-Chalmers Manufacturing Corporation. This local influenced the shape and character of the Milwaukee and Wisconsin labor movement, forming the foundation for industrial unionism in Wisconsin. Moreover, it also played an important role in the UAW's internal politics and in the formation of American labor policies through the 1930s and 1940s. Thus, the Allis-Chalmers UAW local both mirrored and influenced the national labor situation through the 1930s and 1940s.

As a local research project, this study rests on the extensive resources of local archives, notably the labor and other collections of Madison's State Historical Society of Wisconsin, its Milwaukee Area Research Center at the University of Wisconsin–Milwaukee, and the Milwaukee County Historical Society. Moreover, it also rests on the substantial public record of federal agencies in the National Archives in Washington, D.C., and Suitland, Md. Finally, in addition to research for an autoworkers and technology project, a resident Rockefeller fellowship at Wayne State University's Reuther Library allowed me to tie together some loose ends of UAW history.

A research project always incurs huge debts to the many archivists, historians, and others who shared their knowledge and skills. I especially want to thank Warner Pflug and the entire staff at the Reuther Library, who made a summer visit and a later yearlong visit friendly, comfortable, and productive. I also want to thank Harry Miller, Dale Treleven, and Jim Cavanaugh at the State Historical Society of Wisconsin, Chuck Cooney at the Milwaukee County Historical Society, Jerry Hess at the National Archives, and Stan Mallach at the University of Wisconsin–Milwaukee for their invaluable aid and assistance.

I am also indebted to the many historians who have shared their ideas, commented on various drafts, and offered encouragement. In many long and provocative discussions, Nelson Lichtenstein shared his important insights into the history of autoworkers, the shop floor, and American labor relations. Over many beers at different conferences, Steve Rosswurm shared his extensive knowledge about the history of labor and Communism. Darryl Holter frequently offered his informed views on the history of Wisconsin labor. Although he may not agree with many of my interpretations, I want to thank Bob Zieger for his generous reading and comments on a much too long earlier draft. With their considerable editorial skills, Bruce Laurie and Milton Cantor carefully read and commented on both long and short versions of the manuscript, greatly enhancing its style. I also want to thank Jim Cronin, Phil Scranton, Ava Baron, David Roediger, Ellen Schrecker, Toni Gilpin, and David Brody for their advice and encouragement.

I am also indebted to many Allis-Chalmers workers who shared their firsthand knowledge of the Milwaukee labor movement with me. The first two Local 248 presidents, Harold Christoffel and Robert Buse, endured many hours of my prying into their lives and experiences. Ralph Koenig and Ralph Amerling, two later Local 248 presidents, also added their perspectives from years of union experience. And special thanks to the last generation of Allis-Chalmers workers, especially union president Bob Russel and former bargaining committeemen Don Weimer and Frank Schanske, who shared their ideas and experiences.

Different incarnations of this project have been presented at sessions or panels of many academic conferences, including the NEH DeKalb conference on the Future of American Labor History, the Social Science History Association, the North American Labor History Conference, the Society for the History of Technology, the American Historical Association, the Wisconsin Labor History Society, and the Chicago Area Labor History Group. Thanks to the panelists and audience members for their critiques, thoughts, and comments.

Finally, a special tribute to Margo Anderson for her thoughtful readings, insightful critiques, endless prodding, remarkable patience, and, despite all this, enduring friendship. Stephen, Eric, Rachel, and Jennifer, thanks for the small and large pleasures of life.

# "STALIN OVER WISCONSIN"

# 1

## INTRODUCTION

On September 23, 1946, the *Milwaukee Sentinel*, the conservative Hearst newspaper, inaugurated an exposé on Communists in the American labor movement. The initial article prominently featured a political cartoon. Labeled "Stalin over Wisconsin," it vividly depicted a large drooling Stalin-headed spider overreaching a webbed globe, implanting a flag with the words "Wisconsin, District 18 on the Communist World Map." The accompanying article took the theme of "Red-Fascism" and elaborated on the Communist infiltration of the Wisconsin labor movement. "The Communist control of the CIO in Milwaukee and Wisconsin," the Hearst series began, "is a serious community problem. The cancer of Red-Fascism here is a national disease far greater than is obvious. For Milwaukee is important beyond its size to America's defense of democratic ideals at home and throughout the world."[1]

The "John Sentinel" series, written by a fictitious and anonymous reporter, ran for almost two months and targeted the officers and rank-and-file leaders of Wisconsin's largest industrial union, United Automobile Workers' (UAW) Local 248, at the Allis-Chalmers Manufacturing Company. Every day for two months, the *Milwaukee Sentinel* boldly headlined front-page stories on the world, national, and local Communist conspiracy, focusing on UAW Local 248's dominant role in the Milwaukee and Wisconsin Congress of Industrial Organizations (CIO). Six months after Winston Churchill's famous "Iron Curtain" speech in Fulton, Missouri, the John Sentinel series inaugurated the domestic Cold War against American labor.[2]

In the late 1940s, this Cold War campaign against the Left was successful. Centrist and rightist union leaders purged leftists from unions and left unions from the CIO. After that, the conventional wisdom maintained that the youthful and insurgent CIO unions "matured" into sober, respectable, and responsible ones. Often neglecting the motives and actions of ordinary workers, this institutional approach stressed the reasonable and rational bureaucratization of American unions. Nonetheless, the fundamental questions are why the CIO unions were so rebellious and, more important, why so many American workers accepted Communist or leftist union leaders through the 1930s and 1940s.

This study aims to explore the making and unmaking of militant industrial unionism during the depression and postwar eras. It is the tale of ordinary people who lived through extraordinary times. It features the officers, rank-and-file leaders, and members of UAW Local 248. Although it is a case study of the Allis-Chalmers plant in the Milwaukee suburb of West Allis, Wisconsin, this history of the workers there also constitutes a microcosm of American labor history for the twentieth century. Allis-Chalmers workers lived through economic booms and busts, through prosperous, lean, and turbulent years, and through eras of the open shop, conservative business unionism, militant industrial unionism, and conservative Cold War industrial unionism. They unionized, were deunionized, and reunionized. During two world wars, they labored long hours to fabricate the military goods for faraway European and Pacific battlefields. They confronted an obdurate, if not reactionary, firm that operated in highly competitive markets. They were skilled batch production craftsmen and semiskilled mass production workers. They came from a variety of ethnic backgrounds—Germans, native-born Americans, Poles, Slavs, Italians, and others. They were many men and a few women, many whites and a few blacks.

Most important, the varied experiences of Allis-Chalmers workers figured prominently in the history of Milwaukee, Wisconsin, and the United States. Through the twentieth century, the Allis-Chalmers Manufacturing Corporation was Wisconsin's largest industrial establishment; it manufactured capital goods for the national and international markets and agricultural equipment for the mechanization of American farms. Its West Allis plant, its corporate headquarters and Wisconsin's largest industrial complex, spawned the state's largest CIO union, which dominated and shaped Milwaukee and Wisconsin CIO councils. The making and the unmaking of this militant UAW local paralleled the national rise and ultimate taming of the CIO's militant mass movement of American industrial workers. Moreover, Wisconsin's legislative tradition established precedents for both progressive and retrogressive labor legislation. In the late 1930s, for instance, the Wisconsin Employment Relations Act provided a state model for the antilabor Taft-Hartley Act.

After World War II, events at Allis-Chalmers influenced and molded the national political climate. The 1946–1947 strike at Allis-Chalmers played a significant role in Walter Reuther's contest with R. J. Thomas for consolidation of power in the international UAW. Also during this strike, Harold W. Story, an Allis-Chalmers attorney and vice president, testified before both the Taft and Hartley committees and influenced the eventual shape of national labor legislation. After testifying before the Hartley committee and after the loss of the post–World War II Allis-Chalmers strike, Harold Christoffel, the young organizer and leader of UAW 248, was the first union leader indicted and eventually jailed in the Cold War Red Scare. Finally, the Allis-Chalmers strike's influential role in Milwaukee politics was a key factor in the 1946 congressional races and resulted in the election of Joseph McCarthy to the United States Senate. The history of Allis-Chalmers workers stretches far beyond the confines of West Allis; it shaped the contours of postwar America.

Through the 1930s and 1940s, two figures—Harold Story, the principal Allis-Chalmers labor strategist, and Harold Christoffel, the first Local 248 president—illustrate two divergent aspects of the theme of work, class, and power in twentieth-century America. Otto Falk, the Allis-Chalmers president in the 1930s, even referred to the two different Harolds—"our Harold and the union's Harold." As vice president in charge of industrial relations, the company's Harold possessed and used the significant economic and political power of Wisconsin's largest industrial firm. The union's Harold, with a strong commitment to worker solidarity and industrial unionism, led several thousand workers and organized them into Wisconsin's largest industrial union.[3]

Harold W. Story was American-born with roots that ran back to the American revolutionary era. Born in 1890, he was the son of Willis E. and Alice L. Story. He grew up in what is now Wauwatosa on his family homestead, near Story Hill and the current site of Milwaukee county stadium. In the 1890s, his father and uncle operated the Story Brothers and later the Wauwatosa Stone quarries from this location. The two family quarries continued into the 1920s and 1930s. As a young man, Harold Story served as secretary for the family firm and in the 1920s became its president. Story Brothers also sold real estate during the 1920s, an era of suburbanization. Despite the death of his father in the early 1900s, Harold Story retained a modest level of wealth and economic security from the family firm.[4]

As a youth, Story attended Milwaukee's West Division High School and then the University of Wisconsin where he received his B.S. in chemistry in 1910. From 1912 to 1915, he attended the University of Wisconsin Law School and obtained his law degree. From 1915 to 1917, he worked for Quarles, Spence, and Quarles, a prestigious Milwaukee law firm. In 1919, after seventeen months of service as an officer with the Allied Expeditionary Force in Europe, he returned to Milwaukee and became a partner in the law firm of Lenischek, Bossel, Wickham, and Story. Later that year, he accepted a position as attorney with the Allis-Chalmers Manufacturing Company, where he worked until the late 1950s. In 1920, he married Lina Duffy, his college sweetheart and sister of F. Ryan Duffy, later a prominent federal judge in Milwaukee.[5]

As the attorney for Wisconsin's largest industrial enterprise, Story gradually became an important figure in local and national affairs. In 1932, when Max Babb, the more senior attorney, rose to be Allis-Chalmers president, Story replaced him as the firm's general attorney. As the restive West Allis workers moved toward unionism in the early 1930s, Story, who had acquired some labor experience in the calmer 1920s, became the chief Allis-Chalmers labor strategist. The new state and federal labor legislation required an experienced legal mind to untangle the intricacies of labor policy. In 1934, Story became an Allis-Chalmers vice president. In the same year, he represented Allis-Chalmers interests as technical adviser for the Wisconsin Unemployment Compensation Act and as a member of the President's Conference on Unemployment Compensation. In 1939, he again represented his firm's interests as technical adviser for and drafter of the Wisconsin Employment Relations Act, a revision of Wisconsin's liberal labor legislation tailored to fit the unique Allis-Chalmers labor situation. This "Little Taft-Hartley law" served as a precursor of the 1947 revisions of the Wagner Act. Over the years, Story was an influential member of several prominent Milwaukee social clubs and of many local, state, and national organizations, including the legislative advisory committee of the Wisconsin Employment Relations Board, the Wisconsin State Board of Public Welfare, the Board of Vocational and Adult Education, the National Conference of Christians and Jews, and the Hoover Commission on Labor-Management Relations.[6]

Harold Christoffel's social experience was a world apart from Harold Story's. His family had the shallower roots typical of "old" immigrant stock. Its members were hardworking and socially mobile. Through the twentieth century's first decades, the family economy mirrored the national economy. His parents immigrated to the United States from Switzerland. After arriving in Milwaukee in the 1890s, his father, John M. Christoffel, practiced the carpenter's trade until 1910. Lena, Harold's mother, bore and raised nine children between their arrival and the 1920s. Except for occasional absences, most of the offspring lived in the family residence after they had grown up and entered the job market. As they matured, most of them had jobs as low-level clerks, craftsmen, or factory workers. During World War I, the senior Christoffel and his oldest son, John Jr., enjoyed steady work and high wages as unapprenticed machinists in the Milwaukee war economy.[7]

The postwar years' modest prosperity continued for the Christoffel family. In 1921, John M. Christoffel returned to the building trades and operated a small contracting firm, Universal Repairing and Manufacturing Company, from the family's new residence. The oldest son continued to work as a machinist until he also became a contractor of carpentry work and later cement work. By the mid-1920s, the Christoffel family was on the fragile road toward working-class economic security. The several working adult children lived at home. The Christoffel family seemed secure.[8]

But the death of John M. Christoffel meant a family economic crisis. A generation younger than Story, Harold Christoffel was born in 1912 and witnessed the illusory lower-middle-class prosperity, which easily fell apart. A young teenager when his father died, Christoffel later recalled telling shopkeepers that he bought stale bread for the "chickens" and poor cuts of meat for the "dog." Although he attended Milwaukee Technical High School, he quit at sixteen and worked as a messenger for Western Union. Then, for a while, he worked as a helper for an electrical contractor and later as shopworker for the Louis Allis Company, which manufactured electrical products. In 1929, he began an apprenticeship with the Allis-Chalmers Manufacturing Company. While an apprentice electrical worker, he continued his education at the Milwaukee Vocational School, studying electrical engineering four nights a week. His sudden fall to poverty seared his consciousness. He told a CIO reporter, "He wanted to know why, when his instructor said he was an electrical genius, he and his family were eating dog meat."[9]

The Allis-Chalmers apprenticeship started shortly before the onslaught of the Great Depression. Nonetheless, along with other Allis-Chalmers apprentices, he worked through the hard times since Wisconsin's strict apprenticeship laws prevented his dismissal or layoff from Allis-Chalmers. He did spend a short time bumming in the West in 1932. Schooled in economic hard times, a Milwaukee socialist tradition, and a family heritage of Swiss socialism, the bright apprentice became active in radical politics and involved in the Young People's Socialist League (YPSL). In fact, he served as the YPSL state educational director. The young socialist, the *CIO News* related, developed an interest in the "hot and heavy debates on economic problems, including craft vs. industrial unionism." In 1933, Christoffel was president of the Allis-Chalmers Apprentice Association and gained his first experience as a labor organizer. He drew up a petition that eventually resulted in a wage increase for all apprentices.[10]

Soon after he finished his apprenticeship, Christoffel learned from a Socialist West Allis sheriff about the National Recovery Act's section 7A, which guaranteed American workers the right to organize. With other young militants and more senior shop veterans in the Allis-Chalmers electrical department, he organized fellow tradesmen into the International Brotherhood of Electrical Workers. Workers from other West Allis shops also attempted to organize other AFL craft unions. Craft unionism, however, did not sufficiently attract Allis-Chalmers workers. In 1937, Christoffel and other union pioneers finally succeeded in organizing them into the CIO's automobile workers union. Christoffel, now a twenty-five-year-old skilled electrical tester, served as Local 248's first president until he entered the U.S. Army during World War II.[11]

Through the 1930s and 1940s, Harold Story and Harold Christoffel were bitter antagonists in a contentious struggle for the hearts and minds of Allis-Chalmers workers. From their different social positions, their different experiences in the worlds of work, class, and power, Story and Christoffel marshaled their respective resources and forces for the making and ultimately the breaking of Wisconsin's largest and most influential union.

Within the UAW, the Allis-Chalmers local had the solid reputation of a Red local in the late 1930s and early 1940s. Its left politics was an important dimension in the economic struggle over management or union control of the West Allis Works. The UAW local played a prominent role in several important controversies about Communism in the UAW and CIO. These controversies in turn became part of the official anti-Communist history of left unionism in the postwar era. The most important was a controversial 1941 strike, which Max Kampelman labeled "[p]robably the most serious Communist inspired defence [sic] strike." For the most part, this and similar "old" labor histories have been either top-down examinations of international unions or Cold War analyses of the labor and Communism issue. More recently, several "new" labor histories have begun to examine important left-wing unions, often at the local level and within a social context, without blatant Cold War biases.[12]

Despite UAW Local 248's prominent place in the pantheon of left unions, no Local 248 union officer ever publicly admitted actual Communist Party membership. In the 1940s and many years later, its two presidents in the 1930s and 1940s, Harold Christoffel (1937–1944) and Robert Buse (1944–1947) denied ever belonging to the Communist Party. Still, a considerable amount of material, including the testimony of ex-Communists, the reports of Allis-Chalmers officials and researchers, and the recollections of Communist Party members, suggests that

Christoffel and other union officers were either Communists or at least had a working relationship with the Milwaukee Communist Party. Most of the evidence of this surfaced during two Allis-Chalmers strikes, in 1939 and 1941, and especially during the fall and winter of 1946 and 1947, in the midst of a bitter eleven-month postwar walkout. After their orchestration of a widespread "Red-baiting" campaign to discredit the union leadership and to break the strike, Allis-Chalmers officials presented this evidence to Senate and House investigative committees in 1947.[13]

As part of this antiunion campaign, Allis-Chalmers officials, *Milwaukee Sentinel* officials and reporters, Federal Bureau of Investigation agents, and members of the House of Representatives cooperated to entrap Harold Christoffel on a perjury charge for his testimony before Congressman Fred Hartley's House Education and Labor Committee (HELC). In fact, two future American presidents, John F. Kennedy and Richard M. Nixon, then freshman congressman, interrogated Christoffel about his union activities and political beliefs. This effort also included attempts to create perjury cases against Robert Buse, then the Local 248 president, and R. J. Thomas, a vice president of the UAW. The corporate and governmental effort involved break-ins of the Wisconsin CIO Council and UAW regional offices, the publication of Allis-Chalmers research as neutral journalism, and the investigative hearings of the Hartley committee. After obtaining illegally gathered information about the union's pro-Communist activities and associations, HELC members, especially the conservative freshman Wisconsin congressmen Charles Kersten, questioned Christoffel about specific incidents, events, and associations. Ten days later, the HELC heard the testimony of Louis F. Budenz, who denounced Christoffel as a Communist. Four days later, an HELC subcommittee went to Milwaukee, heard more testimony, and subpoenaed actual union records. Ultimately, Christoffel was indicted, tried, convicted, and jailed for giving perjured testimony before the HELC. In the emerging Cold War climate, he was the first union leader indicted and subsequently jailed as a Communist.[14]

In the 1930s and 1940s, three ex-Communists specifically testified that Harold Christoffel was a Communist Party member. The most prominent was Louis Budenz, a former national Communist leader and managing editor of the *Daily Worker*. In February 1947, before he left New York for a Milwaukee speech, Budenz told a *Milwaukee Journal* reporter that it was "undeniably true" that a controversial 1941 Allis-Chalmers strike was "ordered by the [Communist Party's] national executive board after discussions with the political committee of the Communist party." In the interview, the ex-Communist said, "There were discussions with Harold Christoffel, then the president

of the union at Allis-Chalmers and he agreed that there were sufficient worker grievances to call a strike." The next day, Budenz repeated the charges in a Milwaukee speech at Mount St. Mary College.
Harold Story and several other Allis-Chalmers officials attended the
Budenz speech at the small Catholic college. When he spoke, Budenz
charged that Harold Christoffel was one of "the party's top flight
leaders in the American labor movement." He also claimed that Eugene Dennis, a national Communist leader, and Ned Sparks, a Wisconsin Communist leader, "undoubtedly engineered the 1941 strike."
One month later, before the House Committee on Education and
Labor, Budenz added that Christoffel attended a 1940 meeting with
Dennis and Fred Blair, a Milwaukee Communist leader, and agreed to
call the 1941 defense strike.[15]

Several years earlier, two former Wisconsin Communists had also
testified that Christoffel was a Communist Party member. In 1939,
Farrel Schnering, an ex-Communist who had edited Wisconsin Communist Party's *Voice of Labor* and served as correspondent for the *Daily
Worker*, testified that in the spring of 1935, Christoffel "had become a
member of the Communist Party." In 1947, Schnering told the HELC
subcommittee that in the mid-1930s Eugene Dennis, then the Wisconsin Communist Party leader, recruited Christoffel after an Allis-
Chalmers craft union organizational drive had stalled. The young
union leader, the ex-Communist said, was "despondent" about "the
future of [Allis-Chalmers] trade unionism."[16]

Finally, in 1941, Kenneth Goff, another former Wisconsin Communist, told a Wisconsin Senate committee that Christoffel attended a
1936 meeting with Dennis and other Wisconsin Communist leaders to
make plans for "when war and strike situations arose" and for Wisconsin political activities. Allegedly, Christoffel "was sitting in as a representative of the party, working in the Allis-Chalmers Union."[17]

These three ex–Communist Party members testified to state and
federal investigative committees that Harold Christoffel was indeed a
party member. But all three were classic "God-that-failed" Communists. Their recent conversions from Communism to Christianity
surely shaped the character of their political convictions and made
questionable the veracity of their testimony. As the Cold War developed after World War II, Budenz, who had recently returned to the
Catholic fold, was an almost "professional" anti-Communist witness.
After his reconversion to Catholicism, he taught economics at two
prominent Jesuit universities, first at Notre Dame and then at Ford-
ham. Historian Robert Ozanne even doubted Budenz's charge that
Christoffel called the 1941 strike for "Communist foreign policy
aims."[18]

Schnering too shifted from Communism to Catholicism. Sigmund

Eisenscher, a young Wisconsin Communist leader, roomed with Schnering in the mid-1930s. He described him as "an alcoholic and a woman chaser." The Wisconsin Communist Party expelled the "dissolute character" for his alcoholism. After his expulsion, Schnering became a member of the lecture bureau of the Holy Name Society, an organization for Catholic men. He also worked as an investigator for the Dies Committee on Un-American Activities. And Goff moved from the Wisconsin Communist Party to the Church of Christ, where he served as pastor in the small town of Delevan, Wisconsin. He was a decidedly odd personality. Walter Uphoff, a Wisconsin Democrat and labor educator, recalled a bizarre tale about Goff: He allegedly had an intentional trolley accident in which he lost part of his foot and then donated $3,000 of the subsequent $5,000 out-of-court settlement to a Communist front organization. According to Uphoff, Goff demonstrated "the intense emotion that was related to his political commitment, left and right extremism."[19]

The testimony of these three God-that-failed Communists formed the only direct basis for charges that Christoffel was a Communist Party member. Still, a considerable amount of other evidence suggests some close relationship between the Communist Party and Local 248 officials and shop representatives. As part of a massive research project on labor and Communism, Allis-Chalmers officials assembled a voluminous file on Communism. According to Hugh Swofford, a *Milwaukee Sentinel* labor reporter, Ellis Jensen, an Allis-Chalmers researcher and Story's speech writer, compiled an "A–C Communism file" that occupied "12 to 14 steel file drawers." The Allis-Chalmers research included information gleaned from governmental, UAW, CIO, Communist, Catholic trade union, Milwaukee, and West Allis publications and newspapers from the 1920s through the 1940s.[20]

This massive research project served as the foundation for Harold Story's 1947 testimony before Taft's Senate and Hartley's House committees that produced the conservative revisions of the Wagner Act to weaken the militant CIO unions. Much more important, in the fall of 1946, the Allis-Chalmers Communism file formed the basis for a series of ghostwritten articles that Allis-Chalmers officials secretly passed on to the *Milwaukee Sentinel* for publication as the John Sentinel series. Ellis Jensen, a former Protestant minister and son of a Janesville quarry owner, actually wrote the Hearst exposé of Communist labor activities in West Allis, Milwaukee, and Wisconsin generally. The anti-Communist series undermined Allis-Chalmers worker morale and contributed to UAW Local 248's defeat in the long 1946–1947 strike. Moreover, the Allis-Chalmers research resulted in two internal corporate histories on the "Destructive Effect of Communist Control of a Labor Organization."[21]

The substantial Allis-Chalmers material established an extremely damning circumstantial case against the Communist activities of Christoffel and other leaders of UAW Local 248. In their testimony, Story and other officials told the HELC that Local 248's officers, bargaining committee members, and shop floor representatives were "either communists or consistent Party liners." They charged: "The Local has operated consistently for the past ten years as a highly-prized adjunct to the Party apparatus, in order (a) to propagandize the workers and the entire community with the Communist Party line dictated by the Kremlin, and (b) to advance definite communist objectives." The Allis-Chalmers officials also offered evidence that UAW Local 248 crushed rank-and-file opposition, reprinted material from and sponsored subscription drives for Communist publications, promoted attendance at Communist labor schools, had Communist speakers for union meetings, maintained close relations with and supported local Communist front organizations, participated in public Communist Party activities, "consistently adhered to the Communist Party line on all political issues," fraudulently called the 1941 defense strike, and supported Communist candidates for public office.[22]

Except for the questionable testimony of Budenz, Schnering, and Goff, most of the Allis-Chalmers charges about the Communist Party membership of specific union leaders involved either circumstantial evidence or guilt by association with Communists. Still, the Allis-Chalmers union leaders were neither innocent victims nor innocent bystanders. Some Communists who remained in the Communist Party and some who abandoned it but retained their leftist convictions reported working closely with the Allis-Chalmers union leaders. Years later, even Christoffel and Buse admitted their connections to and associations with Wisconsin Communists.

In the mid-1930s, the Wisconsin presence of Eugene Dennis certainly shaped Wisconsin and Milwaukee industrial unionism. From 1935 to 1937, the future American Communist leader was secretary of the Wisconsin Communist Party. According to Wisconsin Communist Eisenscher, Dennis succeeded in "building a mass movement" in a complicated setting where the reigning labor leaders were Socialists. At the time, in Milwaukee, the AFL leaders worked closely with the Socialist Party. In Wisconsin, the Socialist Party began its decline and the New Deal Democratic Party began its rise. And, in the nation, industrial unionism captured the imagination of millions of American workers. As Wisconsin Communist Party leader, Dennis experimented with and developed new Popular Front alliances and strategies that broke down Communist Party isolation and later propelled him to the Communist Party's top leadership.[23]

Under Dennis's tutelage, the Wisconsin Communist Party was

deeply involved in the formation of the Wisconsin CIO. Much later, Peggy Dennis remembered her husband's organizational work among the new generation of industrial unionists. Her account of Dennis's union activities sounded remarkably similar to the actual organization of the Allis-Chalmers plant: "In the kitchen of a C.I.O. organizer he helped committees map a two-prong campaign to organize the factory and to wrest a charter from the AFL." She recalled their work among the "new union activists" at Falk, Harnischfeger, and Allis-Chalmers. On the formation of the Wisconsin CIO Council, she wrote: "Emil Costello became its chairman and Harold Christoffel, the young president of the new industrial union at the giant Allis-Chalmers machine building complex, became its secretary." John Blair, a Communist unionist who lived near and worked at the West Allis plant, recalled, "Gene [Dennis] was in touch with some people in the [Allis-Chalmers] plant and I helped maintain laison [*sic*] between them and Gene as far as possible." He also remembered, "Gene was called on for advice by some of the leading people of the A-C workers."[24]

Moreover, Eisenscher also recalled his organizational activities in the huge West Allis plant. Working there after a six-month stint at a New York Communist training school, he recalled, "I got acquainted with people like Christoffel and others who became a part of the newly born labor movement in Wisconsin." Eisenscher estimated that the combined "YCL [Young Communist League] and Party forces" amounted to about a hundred Allis-Chalmers workers. Since both Christoffel and the Communist Party desired industrial unionism, Eisenscher remembered "a great deal of cooperation" with the young CIO leader. He added, "We mobilized our own people to give support."[25]

For many, the acid test of Communism was the failure to sign Taft-Hartley non-Communist affidavits. In late 1947, after the UAW convention voted that locals who wished to use the NLRB should comply with the signing of non-Communist affidavits, all but one of the Local 248 officers resigned from their union positions. These included President Robert Buse, Vice President Joseph Dombek, Recording Secretary Fred McStroul, and Treasurer Linus Lindberg. Christoffel, then head of the Allis-Chalmers shop bargaining committee and not covered by the Taft-Hartley law, remained in his union position. At the time, Robert Buse told the UAW Executive Board, "We felt that even if we would remain as officers of the Union . . . , the Allis-Chalmers Company would try to delay bargaining in order to get a contract for workers using as an excuse the lies and slander they have heaped upon the officers." Despite Buse's rationalization, almost all of the Local 248 leaders failed to pass the test.[26]

During the 1947 HELC hearings, Harold Christoffel and Robert Buse categorically denied Communist Party membership, although they did acknowledge some associations with Communists and some support of Communist Party front organizations. With frequent lapses of memory, Christoffel was much more cautious and circumspect in his testimony than Buse. Thirty-five years later, Christoffel remembered, "Yes, I met Dennis. I met everybody who was active in labor and so-called progressive movements." He recalled his disaffection with the Socialists, who controlled the Milwaukee AFL. They, Christoffel remembered, "were not active in the CIO organizing. They were tied with the AF of L and the AF of L sat on their hands. . . . We certainly were disillusioned with the Socialists." When asked what he appreciated about his association with Dennis, the former union leader responded, "Well, [there was] nothing to appreciate. I mean I met him a few times and talked to him, but that was it."[27]

When asked if he knew Fred Blair, the Milwaukee Communist leader, and Eisenscher, the earthy Buse, who came from a farm family, responded: "Oh sure, I got acquainted with them. Sig Eisenscher worked at Allis-Chalmers. . . . Almost everybody knew Fred Blair. He was around like horseshit." He added: "But as far as the Communist Party having anything to say, they didn't have nothing to say as to what we were going to do or did." The Communists, Buse also recalled, "were no factor at all. I knew those guys and they weren't effective in the shop." Moreover, he remembered "no more than half a dozen" Communist Party members at Allis-Chalmers. Buse also denied that he ever met Eugene Dennis.[28]

Christoffel also remembered the meaning of the "Red" and radical labels in the tempestuous 1930s and 1940s. "In those days," he said, "you didn't put your head under a bushel because somebody said he was a Communist or he was 'Red.' " He added, "Well, the only ones who aren't called Red aren't doing anything." Christoffel readily acknowledged his political radicalism. "Oh, we were all radicals. There's no question about that. God almighty, there's no question that we were all radicals."[29]

To be sure, some relationship existed between the Local 248 leaders and the Wisconsin Communist Party leaders. However, the available evidence hardly justified Story's bold and hyperbolic proclamation to a Senate committee that

> Local 248 was not formed for a legitimate trade union purpose.
> It was formed for a communist purpose. It was conceived, born, and midwifed in the Milwaukee downtown office of the Communist Party.
> Its sire was Eugene Dennis, at that time secretary of the Party in Wisconsin. Today Mr. Dennis is Earl Browder's successor as secretary of the Communist Party, U.S.A.

To blame Dennis and the Communist Party absolved the Allis-Chalmers firm from any responsibility for a genuinely turbulent labor relations history in the West Allis plant.[30]

In his investigation of the influence of Communists on trade unions, Robert Ozanne used the Allis-Chalmers local as an important case study of a Red-dominated union. Researching and writing at the height of the domestic Cold War against American labor, Ozanne held little sympathy for the left Allis-Chalmers union leadership. In fact, he simply assumed that Christoffel and other Local 248 leaders were Communists. Nonetheless, Ozanne drew an ambiguous sketch of the militant industrial union. On the one hand, it was a Communist union; on the other, it sought legitimate trade union goals.[31]

His ambiguity frequently resulted in sometimes stunning verbal gymnastics. In his comparison of Communist and conventional trade union objectives, he wrote, "Actually it would be very difficult to differentiate this type of Communist activity from simple aggressive union leadership." Moving specifically to UAW Local 248, Ozanne observed: "Since the Communist leaders of Local 248 couched all of their bargaining demands in conventional trade union language, it is not possible to differentiate their bargaining behavior from normally alert aggressive unionism. The line between aggressive unionism and disguised Communist incitement tactics is too thin to draw." Ultimately, he concluded: "The evidence will not, however, substantiate a clear verdict." In other words, the Local 248 leaders may or may not have been Communists.[32]

For Ozanne, two main features distinguished Communism from conventional trade unionism. First, Communists supported Party foreign policy aims and "time and again jeopardized and sacrificed the bread-and-butter interests of the union members in favor of advancing the Soviet foreign policy." In the 1930s and 1940s, the Local 248 leaders certainly passed resolutions at union meetings and published articles in the union newspaper that followed the Communist Party line. The union also made small donations to various Communist front organizations. But the historical record does not reveal a disregard for the economic interests of Allis-Chalmers workers. Second, Communist unions were "characterized by undemocratic methods and minority control." Admittedly, Local 248 leaders engaged in some questionable practices. But they also confronted an implacable anti-union management that fostered several small "independent" unions and encouraged AFL organizational campaigns in the Allis-Chalmers shops.[33]

In his overall assessment of Christoffel, even Ozanne concluded that the Local 248 leader "was engaged in such a bitter struggle with

Allis-Chalmers management that he was probably unwilling to be sidetracked merely to comply with Communist policies. Harold Christoffel was a trade unionist many years before he became a Communist. He probably became a Communist in the belief that the party would help him build his union." Ironically, if Christoffel ever actually joined the Communist Party, he did so because he saw it as an aid in his fight with management to further his trade union goals.[34]

Finally, Ozanne grudgingly acknowledged Christoffel's genuine popularity among rank-and-file Allis-Chalmers workers. Harold Christoffel, he observed, "was probably genuinely popular" and "was a bonafide local Allis-Chalmers worker." In its struggle to create "successful trade unionism," Ozanne concluded, "the Christoffel regime brought tremendous strides in working conditions, job security and wages."[35]

Ultimately, proof of actual Communist Party membership or non-membership is impossible. Certainly, the Local 248 leaders were militant industrial unionists. In Cold War America, this often characterized non-Communist leftists as Communists. Some of the local's leaders may well have been Communists, that is, Communist Party members. Others may well have been, to use the Cold War phrase, "fellow travelers." One historian has suggested the term "non-red baiters" for those who accepted a broad left and liberal coalition and who tolerated Communists as one component of a larger group of labor radicals. Within the context of the 1930s and 1940s, many of the principal social actors would most likely have worn the labels of "leftist," "radical," or possibly even "Red."[36]

But their activities and beliefs did not necessarily mean that they blindly supported the foreign policy interests of the Soviet Union or endorsed what Cold Warriors labeled the "crimes of Stalin." The Achilles heel of American left unionists was the absence of a viable and independent Socialist or even Marxist tradition. For a brief moment in the 1930s, the Communist Party's Popular Front policies both sustained a youthful protest against the apparent failure of capitalism and fitted the popular insurgency of the tempestuous times. In the postwar realignment of the balance of world power, the American Communists' subordination to the Soviet Union's interests transformed an American left tradition into a national security threat.

Essentially, this study examines this very basic issue of rank-and-file support for militant, industrial unionism. Covering the period from the early 1900s through the 1940s, it enters into the hidden and contested terrain of the workplace to discover and uncover the social and technical dimensions of this worker militancy. First, it analyzes the industrial background and the Allis-Chalmers traditions of technical innovation and open shop labor policies from 1900 to 1930. Then, it examines the making of a militant industrial union as a response to new industrial technologies, antiunionism, and economic upheaval in the Great Depression. Next, it explores the consolidation of union power on the shop floor through two increasingly bitter strikes in 1939 and 1941 and against the opposition of conservative AFL and independent unionists. Then, through a discussion of the shop steward structure and grievance procedure, it analyzes the workplace strength of the militant UAW local in the 1930s and 1940s. It also examines the wartime social transformation of the workplace and the resulting struggles with management. Finally, it investigates the 1946–1947 strike and the unmaking of the militant union in the context of the evolving international and domestic Cold War.

This study focuses on several important themes. First, it views the 1930s and the 1940s as a continuous stage in American labor history. As did other CIO unionists, rank-and-file Allis-Chalmers workers built a unique and powerful industrial organization that effectively challenged management on the shop floor. In the postwar period, corporate, governmental, and some union officials tamed the militant unionism. Second, in their shop floor militancy, the CIO unionists created powerful workplace structures that successfully challenged and curtailed managerial control. Eventually, the militant union attempted to transform the economic power of the workplace into the political power of the ballot box. Third, the experiences of Allis-Chalmers workers illuminate the bitter, fratricidal war between the AFL and CIO. This in turn offers some important insights into the social bases of labor radicalism and labor conservatism. Most important, this case study illustrates the unique character of the CIO as militant, industrial unionism.

The verdict of history is often unkind to losers. The militant CIO unionists certainly lost their struggle with a powerful management. Nonetheless, unless we examine the experiences of the defeated, we forgo insights about the character of American society and into alternative visions for American society. To this end, we must keep in mind Elizabeth Fox-Genovese and Eugene D. Genovese's reminder about the important political dimension of social history: "history, when it transcends chronicle, romance, and ideology . . . is primarily the story of who rides whom and how."[37]

# 2

## THE MAKING OF MILITANT UNIONISM I: MECHANIZATION AND DEUNIONIZATION, 1900–1930

For the first third of the twentieth century, mechanization and anti-unionism shaped and reshaped the social and economic experience of Allis-Chalmers workers. During the eras of Progressive and Wilsonian idealism and the more conservative New Era, U.S. industrial leaders appropriated the reigning ideology of technological progress and the seemingly benign rhetoric of the open shop and American plan to support their single-minded efforts to dictate wages, hours, and working conditions.

In the United States' machine age, industrial leaders believed that mechanization clearly represented the only road to social and economic progress. The United States moved to dominate the global economy, and technological progress was its reigning ideology. Perhaps Henry Ford, the reputed technological genius of the machine age, best captured the mood of the times with his proclamation that "machinery" was "the new Messiah." The machine age meant the mechanization and internal reorganization of U.S. industry. Few Americans could challenge the new god of technological progress. Only the rare social critic even considered the negative influence of the machine on workers and their work.

Related to this was the perception by U.S. industrial elites of trade unionism as a brake on social and economic progress. Through their monopoly of the labor market and their protective work practices and work rules, AFL craft unions, managers agreed, inhibited the development of industrial technology. They couched their antiunionism in a seemingly benign rhetoric. In the 1900s, if craft unions demanded the restrictive closed shop to control access to jobs, management simply wanted the open shop that allowed workers the freedom to choose whether they desired unionism. Open shop industrialists often proclaimed that they had no interest in whether workers were union members. They simply would not bargain with unions. Without collective bargaining rights, craft unions lost their control over labor markets and the reason for their existence. In the 1920s, antiunion corporate leaders again assumed the rhetorical high ground with the American Plan, the antiunion open shop resurrected under the banner of Americanism. The new managerial rhetoric implied that unionism was un-American.

The labor history of the Allis-Chalmers Manufacturing Company typifies the evolving pattern of technical change and antiunionism. The firm participated in what historian Philip Scranton has labeled "the more treacherous entrepreneurship of specialty production." Dependent on special orders for single or small batches of similar products, the large Wisconsin firm pursued a strategy of product diversification in order to remain competitive and to ensure continuous production and corporate profits. Especially after the 1910s, this diversification strategy involved a shift toward large batch, or even mass, production. Increasingly, the manufacture of smaller products—blades for turbines, switchgear, multiple pulleys, small electric motors, and tractors—dominated the Allis-Chalmers product line. The company continuously expanded through corporate mergers and new plant construction, thus exhibiting technical dynamism in the manufacture of new and different products.[1]

Such corporate strategies continuously reshaped and re-formed the social and technical world of Allis-Chalmers workers. Initially, the social matrix of production followed the standard pattern of craft production. The workplace was dominated by skilled white male craftsmen from the metalworking and, later, electrical trades. Within the classic social dichotomy of craft production, skilled metal and electrical craftsmen directed the shop activities of unskilled laborers. The most highly skilled workers came from predominantly native-born American and German backgrounds; the unskilled were largely of Polish, and later Slavic, extraction. Except during the two world wars, few women worked in the Allis-Chalmers plant. And there were virtually no black workers there until World War II.[2]

The Allis-Chalmers Manufacturing Company originated in 1861 when Edward P. Allis, a Milwaukee tannery owner, purchased Decker and Seville's Reliance Works. Renamed the E. P. Allis Company, the new enterprise employed about 150 workers who manufactured flour and sawmill equipment and cast-iron products. In the 1860s, Allis purchased another Milwaukee firm, the Bay State Iron Works, which produced steam engines, boilers, portable sawmills, and gearing. Continuously expanding through the late nineteenth century, the company employed around 1,800 workers in 1900. At the time, E. P. Allis produced three principal lines of industrial products—flour mill equipment for large grain-processing firms in Michigan and Minnesota, sawmill equipment for the North Wisconsin timber industry, and steam engines and other capital goods for the rapidly expanding midwestern metal-making and metalworking industries. The E. P. Allis workers manufactured the "big stuff" for America's expanding urban and industrial markets.[3]

In 1900, the old Reliance Works was unable to satisfy the growing demand for Allis products. Edwin Reynolds, who had succeeded to company leadership after Allis's death in the 1890s, developed plans for a massive new plant in North Greenfield, soon to be renamed West Allis, a new Milwaukee industrial suburb. He also inaugurated plans for corporate merger and consolidation to acquire other industrial facilities. The Reynolds program for plant expansion and merger ultimately changed the name and nature of the E. P. Allis enterprise.

In November 1900, the E. P. Allis firm purchased a 100-acre West Allis site with access to three major railway lines. In May 1901, the company merged with the Fraser-Chalmers Company, a Chicago mining machinery firm; the Gates Iron Works, a producer of mining and cement-making machinery; and the Dickson Manufacturing Company, a manufacturer of coal-mining and sugar-milling machinery. The merger formed the new Allis-Chalmers Company, which expanded the original product line of capital goods. Several months later, the new Allis-Chalmers firm began the construction of the West Allis Works, a modern plant eventually to employ over 10,000 workers. In the future, other mergers and new additions to the West Allis Works further expanded the product line and physical facilities.[4]

First opened in September 1902, the new Allis-Chalmers West Allis Works was a thoroughly modern plant for the batch production of large machinery. For historian Daniel Nelson, the new West Allis facility was a prime example of the "new factory system." Along with the Westinghouse, National Cash Register, U.S. Steel Gary, and Detroit automobile plants, the West Allis plant was one of the "model" new factories. Compared to their predecessors, these new factories were "immense" and freed from "technical restraints" in their use of work space. Because of considerable planning, Nelson observed: "the flow of work between departments became an important factor in building design." A prominent mechanical engineer, Reynolds designed the new facility on a "unit" plan that took into account the sequential flow for manufacturing the "big stuff" and allowed for future expansion with the construction of additional units.[5]

The new West Allis plant reflected the firm's traditional products and its need for highly skilled workers. It followed the classic pattern for increasing batch production through the extension of traditional production units rather than the redesign of small elements of the labor process. To use Alfred Chandler's term, the manufacturing principle was to achieve more "throughput," that is, faster movement through the sequence of productive operations. In other words, Reynolds designed the new plant around traditional craft skills. But the sequential operations also pushed skilled craftsmen to work harder through the reduction of downtime between operations. Moreover, the new plant offered opportunities for the adoption of the latest machinery in various shops and departments. The new machinery in turn eroded traditional craft skills.[6]

The immense scale of the new buildings testified to the dimensions of the Allis-Chalmers products. The pattern shop and pattern storage area occupied almost 68,000 square feet. The new foundry of 124,000 square feet contained three fully equipped modern cupolas and three separate bays with a higher center bay for large work. A third area, three times the size of the second, contained two machine shops, a blacksmith shop, and an erecting shop. In all, the West Allis plant encompassed 585,000 square feet of factory floor space.[7]

Shortly after the completion of the new West Allis Works, management officials decided to enter the electrical equipment field in direct competition with General Electric and Westinghouse. In 1904, Allis-Chalmers purchased the Bullock Electric and Manufacturing Company of Ohio, which produced electric motors, generators, and transformers, and acquired the engineering and technical skills for making electrical products. In 1905, officials decided to expand the West Allis plant for electrical production with the addition of another unit for additional pattern shop, foundry, erecting, and machine shop space. They also added a shop for the manufacture of electrical products. Upon completion in 1907, the seven new shops followed the original dimensions of Reynolds's original plan, expanding the West Allis Works to over 1.4 million square feet of floor space.[8]

In the West Allis plant, massive machine tools finished huge castings from the various Allis-Chalmers foundries. In these early years, the firm's products included large steam engines, steam and water turbines, electrical generators, pumps, ore crushers, and cement, flour, and lumber mill machinery. In the 1930s, Allis-Chalmers officials proudly proclaimed: "Castings of any size up to 120 tons are made here [in the West Allis plant]. To date the foundry has produced 160 castings weighing over 100 tons each." The large and unique industrial and electrical products demanded very complex industrial machinery and highly refined skills from workers in the metal and electrical trades.[9]

Around World War I, Allis-Chalmers officials initiated a different form of mechanization, a move that would gradually shift important parts of the West Allis plant from batch to mass production. Until then, mass production techniques were simply adjuncts to specialty or batch production. For example, water and steam turbines required thousands of small parts for their blading. Other Allis-Chalmers products also needed many duplicate parts for their manufacture. All of these required specialized machinists for large production runs of similar parts. But these specialized workers never outnumbered the more skilled craftsmen needed for specialty or batch production.

War production and tractor production, however, transformed the technical and social contours of the West Allis plant. The high profits from military goods pushed specialty and batch manufacturers to adopt mass-production techniques that reshaped work processes and worker skills. At the same time, the introduction of a new Allis-Chalmers product line, tractors in the 1910s and agricultural equipment in the 1920s, prompted Allis-Chalmers officials, engineers, and managers to shift from batch to mass-production methods. These created a dual industrial structure, containing elements of both batch production and mass production.

For the Allis-Chalmers corporation, military production began in the summer of 1915. On the one hand, the old line shops manufactured traditional products, such as engines and turbines for naval vessels. On the other hand, a retooled machine shop produced artillery shell casings, which required mass-production methods. For the latter, the initial war order was a subcontract for machine work on 2 million shell casings. With an initial investment of $230,000 in machinery and equipment, the firm received a $3.7 million subcontract for the high-volume production of shell casings. Wartime mechanization transformed the social dimensions of work and skill in the West Allis plant. It also expanded the work force from about 3,200 to 5,500 workers.[10]

At about the same time, the corporate decision to manufacture tractors proved a very successful market strategy in product diversification. In contrast to the boom-and-bust feature of specialty production, tractor production offered the advantage of steady revenues in an era of mechanized American agriculture. This second experience with mass-production techniques also significantly transformed manufacturing operations in the West Allis plant, gradually altering the social contours of work and skill in the specialty production plant. Along with the manufacture of smaller standardized products, such as electrical switchgear, texrope drives (multi-belted pulleys) to power machine tools, and smaller electrical transformers and relays, tractor production embedded the more modern production methods more solidly in the large Allis-Chalmers plant.[11]

Allis-Chalmers entered the tractor field in 1914 with the introduction of the Model 6–12, a small, one-plow tractor. The diversification plan apparently met with some success, for in 1917 the company formally established its tractor division. Initially, the move into tractors hardly transformed work routines and work processes in the West Allis plant. Early photographs revealed the most conventional tractor assembly methods. Tractor production facilities were not separate; the various parts and components were allocated to already existing foundries and machine shops. Then skilled workers actually built tractors from scratch at stationary locations. The innovative production methods of Detroit had not reached West Allis.[12]

Nonetheless, the expanding market for Allis-Chalmers tractors began another process of plant expansion and technical innovation. In 1919, officials created the No. 1 Tractor Shop from the remodeled pattern storage building, equipping it with machinery for tractor production. This shop eventually produced about thirty tractors a day. In 1920, officials also decided to add a new foundry on the West Allis industrial site near the new tractor shop. Since tractors required different production methods than heavy industrial equipment, the new foundry was devoted solely to the manufacture of tractor castings and parts, mainly for engines and transmissions.[13]

By the late 1920s, Allis-Chalmers was the third-largest producer of agricultural equipment in the United States. In order to compete more effectively with the larger firms, officials decided to purchase the Monarch Tractor Company in 1928 and the La Crosse Plow Company in 1929. They also completed the construction of second tractor shop in 1929 and of a third in 1938. Even through the economically difficult 1930s, the successful tractor division yielded from 25 to 60 percent of Allis-Chalmers profits.[14]

In the new shops, Allis-Chalmers production engineers paid considerable attention to plant layout, integration of manufacturing operations, modern machinery, and simplified work tasks. In the No. 2 Tractor Shop, William Watson, the plant superintendent, related: "About 160 machine tools were bought and installed in the new tractor building, which also includes assembly and some storage space." For the most part, this equipment consisted of special-purpose machines that produced large numbers of duplicate parts. The tractor shop foundry had "mechanical molding equipment" to produce castings for transmission cases and rear axle housings. "Hence," Watson reiterated, "from start to finish, new equipment is used throughout."[15]

In the No. 3 Tractor Shop, Joseph Geschelin described facilities and equipment that approached prevailing automotive practices. According to the Detroit automotive journalist, the new tractor shop and foundry "embod[ied] the very latest principles of modern plant layout." It "feature[d] one of the most interesting mechanized final assembly lines to be found in the tractor industry." Finally, its production machines "compare[d] both in modernity and practice with the best we have seen in the leading plants of the automobile industry."[16]

Although the West Allis plant started as a batch production facility for the manufacture of the big stuff, two decades of product diversification and mechanization transformed a large part of it into a mass-production one. Over time, semiskilled production workers gradually replaced skilled tradesmen and became an increasingly important group in the shops. Moreover, the American Federation of Labor's craft unionism became increasingly irrelevant to the work force.

In the late nineteenth century, American labor experimented with the inclusive, reform unionism of the Knights of Labor and the exclusive craft unionism of the American Federation of Labor. So too did the Allis workers. From the beginning, the early Allis works served as a small center of a growing Milwaukee trade union movement. In 1886, when the eight-hour movement captured the imagination of Milwaukee workers, the Knights of Labor established a separate Reliance Assembly for Allis workers. In the midst of the enthusiasm for the eight-hour day, the Reliance Assembly enrolled over six hundred Polish workers in a single day. Its membership now numbered a total of 1,600, including all the iron molders. During the May Day walkouts for the shorter workday, observers attributed the riotous conduct to undisciplined Polish workers. Although the Allis workers did not figure prominently in the Bay View massacre (the tragic Milwaukee episode that followed the Chicago Haymarket affair and resulted in the death of five and the wounding of another six persons), the Wisconsin National Guard occupation of the Reliance works surely dampened their ardor for action. Moreover, Allis's conceding the eight-hour day also had its intended effect. With the subsequent demise of the Knights, the AFL gradually grew and picked up skilled Allis workers. The International Molders Union (IMU) and the International Association of Machinists (IAM) were especially successful in the Allis shops. By 1900, the machinists' and the molders' unions were firmly rooted in the E. P. Allis plants.[17]

From the 1890s through the 1920s, Allis-Chalmers metal trades workers experienced the social and economic aftershocks of work reorganization, occupational specialization, and mechanization. Essential to the late nineteenth-century American industrial transformation, the metal trades grew and matured with the rise and consolidation of American industrial capitalism. From mid-century, skilled metalworkers developed a craft ethic, or shop culture, that protected and defended their rights and privileges in the workplace. The craft culture derived from the metal craftsmen's monopoly of skill and knowledge about manufacturing processes. Initially, the craft ethic evolved from informal work groups that created informal customs and rules and governed day-to-day shop behavior. Later, with the growth and consolidation of craft unions, the metal trade unions translated the informal customs and rules into a more formal system of union practices and work rules. The AFL craft unions, David Montgomery observed, "codified craftsmen's norms," which "represented new collective efforts to defend the autonomy and dignity of the craftsmen" against increased corporate power.[18]

Perhaps the nineteenth-century labor slogan, "A fair day's work for a fair day's pay," best encapsulated core values beneath the work culture and work conflicts of these highly skilled craftsmen. Centering on the fundamental elements of the wage-effort bargain, the phrase captured the deep-rooted working-class sense of fairness and equity in the relations between labor and capital. One side of the slogan, "a fair day's pay," emphasized the conventional and well-examined economic or monetary gains of American workers. The other side, "a fair day's work," however, revealed a central concern with a more hidden, less understood terrain of working conditions and work effort, especially work pace. The worker's financial compensation was equitable only when work effort balanced wages. Craft culture and traditions attempted to force an equitable balance of the two sides of the work equation. In the industrial age, labor and management struggled bitterly over working conditions and work effort. Indeed, the rise of systematic, and later scientific, management constituted a corporate assault on the work culture of craft unionism.

For skilled metal tradesmen, workers' control of production was a major line of defense against the nineteenth century management assault on craft work traditions and work customs. Through their craft skills and detailed knowledge of production processes, that is, the "art or mystery of the trade," these independent skilled workers over time invented and established informal and formal traditions, customs, and practices that asserted worker rights and prerogatives at the workplace. For Montgomery, the concept of workers' control of production captured the essence of the craft defense against modern management strategies. "The functional autonomy of craftsmen," he related, "rested both on their superior knowledge, which made them self-directing at their tasks, and the supervision which they gave to one or more helpers." Through a "disciplined ethical code," the autonomous craftsmen controlled almost all dimensions of the work process. The craft ethic included the "stint," or a worker-determined output quota that controlled the pace of production, a " 'manly' bearing toward the boss," and "manliness toward one's fellow workers."[19]

This aggressive "manly" posture toward the boss, Montgomery noted, "celebrated individual self-assertion, but for the collective good." It also contained "connotations of dignity, respectability, defiant egalitarianism, and patriarchal male supremacy." In order to exhibit manliness, a skilled metal trades worker was "expected to refuse to obey any objectionable orders from bosses, even if he had to quit." After this male workplace culture was linked to an equally male AFL craft unionism, the amalgamation of shop and union traditions of the autonomous craftsmen, union work rules, and mutual support posed a formidable threat to managerial control of the workplace.[20]

In his similar examination of British and American machinists from the 1890s to the 1920s, sociologist Jeffrey Haydu emphasized the concept of craft control. "Trade customs and the craftsman's own judgment," he claimed, "sharply circumscribe employers' roles in training apprentices, assigning workers to machines, choosing manufacturing techniques, setting the workpace, and supervising workers." Craft control involved training of young apprentices, important decisions about work and production, informal and formal work rules, and freedom from supervisory authority. It sustained a "craft ethic" in the form of "a shared commitment to the standards and dignity of the trade." For example, young apprentices learned not only the different machines and techniques but also the culture of the craft. The apprentice participated in a social and cultural learning process, "an initiation into the 'traditions, customs, and usages' of the particular workshop and entire trade." These included "loyalty" to fellow workers and the trade, "manly pride" in work, a "skeptical attitude" about the bosses' abilities, and an "outright contempt" for unapprenticed workers.[21]

The metal shop craft culture was neither an egalitarian nor an inclusive workers' culture. The profound contempt for unapprenticed workers targeted those who "stole" a trade, specialized green hands, immigrant handymen, and unskilled women. These unskilled or less skilled workers undermined craft work standards and wage levels. Shop culture was an exclusive culture that rested on special skill and knowledge. It contained an almost unbridgeable social divide—brain with its discrete tactile skills and brawn with its ponderous strength. In American machine shops, Haydu noted: "work was generally split between the relatively high skilled craftsmen, responsible for most productive tasks, and unskilled laborers and helpers, who fetched materials, helped lift heavy pieces, and cleaned up." Moreover, these social divisions bore obvious cultural or ethnic dimensions. Often, the brains were the native-born Americans or northern Europeans and the brawn was southern and eastern European or African American. In 1888, the Order of United Machinists and Mechanical Engineers of America, which became the International Association of Machinists, described a qualified craft union member—"a white, free born male citizen of some civilized country." In iron molding, a similar ethnic exclusiveness prevailed. Originally the domain of a labor aristocracy, its rapid expansion brought in large numbers of formerly despised Irish workers. Soon the Irish molders looked down on the Poles, Slavs, and African Americans who performed the hardest and dirtiest foundry chores.[22]

From the 1890s on, management strategies increasingly challenged workers' or craft control of production at the workplace. The rise of systematic and scientific management eroded metal trade skills through the specialization of work tasks, the division and subdivision of labor, and mechanization. The managers also threatened the craft work culture. According to Haydu, modern managers "emphatically asserted" their right to control the workplace in modern industrial establishments. The managerial challenge included deskilling, piecework, and a "more exacting and detailed management supervision of workers." In response to skill dilution, metalworkers felt economic concerns over the erosion of "wages and jobs" and moral concerns about "craft control" and the "standards of the trade." Skilled worker "resentment of managerial initiatives" emphasized the themes of "economic insecurity and moral outrage." In both small and large firms, the metal trade workers, Montgomery noted, engaged in "the most bitter and protracted struggles" over changed "work practices."[23]

In these factory struggles, craft customs and work practices clearly restricted the implementation of modern and innovative technologies. For example, IAM members pledged never to operate two machines, never to work for less than the standard wage, and never to do piecework. In May 1900, the editor of *Engineering Magazine* decried the existence of inefficient union practices. From his perspective, the restrictive work practices included "a limitation on the number of apprentices; prohibition of piece work; refusal to run more than one machine, to work with non-union men, or to give instruction to a handy man; dictation of minimum wages; and even limitation of product and of speed of working." In an era of rapid technological innovation, craft union rules limited or retarded both management control of the workplace and the introduction of the most modern industrial equipment. Some work practices were outright restrictions of production; others increased the cost, and hence reduced the profit, of the new technologies.[24]

From the 1890s through the 1930s, Allis-Chalmers workers experienced nearly four decades of almost continuous work reorganization and mechanization. Successive waves of technical innovation transformed the deliberate pace of their skilled work and reshaped their relations with other workers and with managers in the Allis and West Allis shops. Over the decades, they witnessed the erosion of their crafts and customs through the division of labor, the fragmentation of crafts, and mechanization.

For the managers, the very existence of craft unionism inhibited the modern advance of technological progress. For specialty, batch, or mass production, industrial modernization presented real opportunities to remain profitable in extremely competitive product markets. Whether the new machines required skilled or semiskilled workers, craft unions severely circumscribed their introduction and application. Consequently, Allis-Chalmers workers and managers collided over fundamental concerns about technology and work. In the first decades of the new century, metal trades craftsmen three times struck the Reliance and West Allis works. From management's perspective, unions impeded technical development, so unions had to be destroyed. Mechanization logically resulted in antiunionism and open shop policies that effectively destroyed AFL unionism in the West Allis plant.

Since machinists always constituted the most numerous skilled trade in the Reliance and West Allis works, they were the first craft to confront the issue of mechanization and the related problem of skill dilution. Members of a prototypical skilled trade, the machinists suffered constant work reorganization and mechanization from the 1880s. For machinists, the 1890s, when American industry moved toward mature industrial capitalism, meant the most dramatic changes in technology, work, skill, and control.

Harold Groves, a Wisconsin economist who worked closely with the machinists' union, characterized the machinist as a "carpenter who worked in metal." The "metamorphosis of the machinists' craft," he related, started with the trade's origins and evolved through several phases that diluted or removed skill from different aspects of the metalworking craft. First, the decline of the traditional "all-around skilled mechanic" began with "the specialization of the machinist." Through work specialization, the metal trades employers reorganized the job so that the machinist performed only one of the craft's many specialized tasks, such as drilling, turning, milling, or fitting. Although the machinist remained a "comparatively skilled workman," it took "less knowledge and education to master one machine than many." In other words, work specialization narrowed or diminished the range of craft skills. Second, an "overlapping" phase saw "the dilution of the machinists' skill." In this instance, the transformation came "not from changes in the machinists' work but rather in the machines he operates." With the introduction of single-purpose machines, a skilled mechanic "set up" the work while a semiskilled specialist actually did it. Sometimes, a less-skilled "handyman," or "rougher," performed the initial machine operations and a skilled machinist finished the task to finer tolerances.[25]

According to Groves, the "final and crowning step" of the mechanic's decline "was (and is) the introduction of semi-automatic and fully automatic machine." This total mechanization of the machinist's craft involved the creation of "a complicated device upon which hours of skilled labor have been expended by a designer . . . and emobod-[ied] the skill necessary to do fine work." The craft's elite status, with its apprenticeship and all-around knowledge, was threatened by the specialized machine, and the automatic machine undermined the trade's most sacred work traditions, the trade's "manliness." For with the new automatic devices, numerous unskilled "unapprenticed boys, girls, and women" could easily and readily replace male craftsmen in the shops. As the new century dawned, American machinists faced considerable social and psychic unease about continuing technical innovation.[26]

After 1888, the formation and rapid growth of the International Association of Machinists were a workers' response to the first two phases of the transformation of the machinists' craft. By the end of the 1890s, the machinists' union and the metal trades employers were on a collision course. In January 1900, the Chicago IAM District 8 spearheaded an IAM national drive against the technical and social erosion of the machinists' trade. The IAM district proposed an agreement that included demands for the nine-hour day, closed shop, recognition of shop committees, minimum wages, and seniority for layoffs. On March 1, after the employers balked, over five thousand machinists struck the Chicago metal trades shops and plants. As some employers broke ranks and settled with the union, the National Metal Trades Association (NMTA), a recently formed employers' group, negotiated a national agreement, the Murray Hill Agreement, that limited management concessions and ended the Chicago machinists' strike. Although the Allis workers did not go out, Edwin Reynolds, who headed the Allis firm, was one of three NMTA negotiators. In early May, an intense round of negotiations in New York resulted in the Murray Hill Agreement, which, over the course of a year, phased in a nine-hour day. Although the agreement contained a statement of non-discrimination against union members, it avoided any commitment to the closed shop. Moreover, a board of arbitration would decide the several other crucial issues, such as the definition of a machinist, wages, apprenticeship rules, and seniority. Finally, the IAM leaders pledged not to restrict production and not to strike.[27]

The Murray Hill Agreement ended the machinists' strike and offered only minimal concessions to the IAM. The metal trades employers' organization had outmaneuvered the machinists' union. For shop machinists, the agreement never really addressed the fundamental issues of craft control and trade standards. Moreover, when the metal trade employers planned to reduce hours without the expected increase in wage rates, the Murray Hill Agreement fell apart, and the IAM decided to fight the NMTA employers. On May 20, 1901, 58,000 IAM machinists joined in a national strike to defend against the technical and organizational erosion of the machinists' craft.[28]

Only two weeks after the merger that formed the Allis-Chalmers Manufacturing Company, Milwaukee machinists joined their union brothers in the national strike for craft standards, union rights, shorter hours, and higher wages. A shop committee of Allis Chalmers machinists demanded a 12½ percent wage increase and a reduction of the working day to nine hours. The other important matter was deep opposition to the new and hated piece-rate and premium wage payment systems.[29]

Allis-Chalmers took the lead in combating the Milwaukee machinists' locals. The IAM strike gave it the opportunity to eliminate union recognition, to break the union hold on the workplace, and to establish the open shop. When Allis-Chalmers machinists walked out, Reynolds proclaimed: "The men have taken the bit into their mouths, and I guess we shall have to let them chew it for a while."[30]

When the Milwaukee strike began, eight hundred Allis-Chalmers machinists marched out of the Reliance Works. A few days later, fifty Reliance patternmakers also struck. In the strike's first weeks, 83 percent of the machinists and 63 percent of the patternmakers left the Allis-Chalmers plant. The thorniest strike issues involved worker concerns about technical change in their shops. The skilled workers wanted their fair share of the fruits of the new production methods and technologies. In their demand for shorter hours with the same pay, the machinists intended to capture the economic benefits of new machinery. In their demand for the abolition of piece and premium payment systems, they intended to resist and to oppose management intentions to increase work effort.[31]

Confronted with the growing AFL strength and its threat to management control of production, Allis-Chalmers officials and other Milwaukee industrialists firmly opposed the machinist's strike demands. Two weeks into the dispute, Reynolds issued a statement that mirrored the NMTA declaration of principles. "Since we as employers," the Allis-Chalmers engineer declared, "are responsible for the work turned out by our workmen, we must therefore have full discretion to designate the men we consider competent to perform the work and to determine the conditions under which that work will be performed." Reynolds clearly stressed management's right to control production.[32]

In June, company officials threatened strikers with the loss of their jobs, announcing that workers who failed to return would be "no longer considered in our employ." They also secured court injunctions that proscribed all manner of strike activities and weakened union efforts to maintain morale. Gradually, the Allis-Chalmers and Milwaukee machinists returned to work. In late July, the machinists' walkout ended in a total defeat for the workers.[33]

As with the machinists, the Allis-Chalmers molders also witnessed extensive work reorganization and mechanization in the 1890s. For the more repetitive large batch production runs, the initial process of mechanization began with the invention of hand, and later pneumatic, hydraulic, and steam, ramming devices to shape the sand around patterns for the mold. Then, mechanical engineers devised pattern-drawing machines to remove the pattern from the mold. In the 1890s, the Tabor and other molding machines fully mechanized the molders' ancient craft. Mary Loomis Strecker, a labor economist, reported, "The brains which formerly had vested in the molder were transferred entirely, through the efforts of engineer and pattern-maker, to the machine." Although these machines had the greatest effect on molders who manufactured large runs of similar products, they sometimes affected those who produced the "big stuff" in specialty plants.[34]

The mechanization of molding also brought the specialized molder into the foundry. Trained in only a few weeks, an unskilled laborer became a "handyman" molder who could easily produce large runs of similar products. "The value of the machines to manufacturer," Strecker noted, "is largely determined by the amount of labor and skill they eliminated from the molding process." Often referred to as a "Castle-Garden man," a term alluding to their recent immigrant origins, the handyman molders changed the social contours of the foundry, previously dominated by American-born, or at least northern European, workers. Furthermore, without a formal molder's apprenticeship, the specialized molder did not bear the molder's shop tradition of the "set," or stint, the informal output quota that the molders and later their union attached to a particular pattern. In addition to eliminating the skilled molder, the new machines also raised productivity and improved quality. One foundryman claimed that the modern machines raised productivity from 100 to 500 percent.[35]

At first, the International Molders' Union (IMU), one of the stronger national craft unions, was indifferent to the introduction of technical improvements into foundries. Their venerable craft, these skilled craftsmen believed, required human intelligence to fashion the castings for the machine shop. After the rapid diffusion of the new molding machines in the 1890s, however, union molders started to resist the encroachment of the new machinery that brought unskilled workers, less skilled work, or lower wages. For the IMU, the central issues were the regulation of apprenticeship and the use of machinery. In their defense of craft standards, they attempted to limit work on these machines to skilled molders. They also attempted to organize the handymen into the IMU. Like the machinists' union, the IMU intended to defend craft control and trade standards.[36]

For the brief period from 1898 through 1901, the IMU and the National Founders Association (NFA), the employers' organization, maintained an uneasy truce over the recognition of the molders' union and the application of the new foundry technologies. Nonetheless, the foundry owners resented union efforts to limit and control the application of new technologies. At the 1902 NFA convention, however, "strong sentiment was expressed, not only in favor of the machine as a paying device, but also the use of laborers as operatives." Moreover, the employers' organization pledged full support for any member who fought union opposition to molding machines. For the founders, the numerous advantages of the molding machines included the "freedom from dependence on skilled labor" and "from negotiations with the Union," improvements in patterns, molds, and castings, "increased output varying from double to forty times the production of the hand system," and significant decrease in production costs.[37]

Once again, a metal trades union and a metal trades employers' organization were on a collision course. In 1903, the founders started to introduce the new machines on their own terms without union interference. The result was a bitter industrial war between the IMU and the NFA, where the founders refused to allow any union limitations on managerial control of foundry work practices. They also ended prior recognition of the union. A series of strikes in 1903 and 1904 culminated nationwide in the "great molders' strike", which started on May 1, 1906. Besides mechanization, the critical strike issue was the shorter, nine-hour day. The IMU's symbolic choice of May 1 evoked the tragic Great Upheaval of 1886.[38]

Although the Milwaukee founders offered a 10 percent wage increase and the nine-hour day for skilled molders, the IMU molders "enthusiastically" voted for the May Day strike for increased pay, restored IMU recognition, and the inclusion of coremakers into IMU agreements. With the exception of Allis-Chalmers, the Milwaukee founders had ceased their formal recognition of the molders' union in 1904. And Allis-Chalmers officials announced that they would stop recognizing it when the existing IMU contract expired. In their wage offer, the Milwaukee founders attempted to play on the divisions of skill among molders, offering higher wages to the floor molders but lower wages to the bench molders. The less skilled bench molders' work on small castings was most susceptible to the new mechanized foundry processes.[39]

According to differing accounts, from nine hundred to twelve hundred molders, including 400 from Allis-Chalmers, struck the Milwaukee foundries. In the first days, worker solidarity appeared to prevail and to overcome the limits of craft identity. Some machinists even suggested a general citywide metal trades strike. But the machinists resented the molders who had crossed IAM picket lines in 1901, and they soon crossed the IMU picket lines. After the first week, over fourteen hundred molders had walked out of Milwaukee's principal foundries. In response, the Milwaukee Metal Trades and Foundrymen's Association (MMTFA) made an "emphatic declaration for the open shop and a decision to fight the molders' union."[40]

From this point on, the struggle between the molders and the founders grew into a bitter contest of wills over the union shop and the open shop. In mid May, MMTFA secretary W. J. Fairbain threatened the strikers with the loss of their jobs. "Many strikers," he stated, "will be unable to get their jobs back, as non-union men are filling their places." Moreover, Fairbain emphasized the central issue of management control of production. The metal trades employers, he added, "are not waging war upon labor, but simply insisting upon the right to run their own shops as they see fit." As labor and management positions stiffened through the strike, the founders hurried to introduce the new molding machinery. In June 1906, the NFA announced that almost a thousand new molding machines had been introduced since the strike began.[41]

Throughout the molders' strike, MMTFA members and Allis-Chalmers officials followed the pattern of the national founders organization. In late May, one Milwaukee newspaper reported a number of college students working in the West Allis plant. With the new machinery, inexperienced temporary workers could perform the tasks of the skilled strikers. "Members of the Foundrymen's Association," Fairbain told a reporter, "are putting on all the so-called 'handymen' they can get, and there are a great many of them." About twenty-five Ohio college students reportedly were working in the Allis-Chalmers plant; about seventy-five more were expected in the next few days. Still retaining their craft pride, the Allis-Chalmers strikers claimed that the students would not be of much use in the West Allis foundries. Nonetheless, management, one observer reported, used "unskilled men from the streets and boys from high schools." The mechanized foundry technology provided the technological means to break the skilled molders' strike.[42]

For almost two years, Allis-Chalmers officials savagely fought union molders in the West Allis plant. Scabs and strikebreakers maintained foundry operations, and Burr-Herr detectives policed the plant. One Burr-Herr agent claimed that he was offered ten dollars for each striker he beat up. The NMTA also supplied the Milwaukee founders with seventy-five nonunion strikebreakers. Court injunctions were major instruments for breaking the Milwaukee molders' strike. Broad injunctions prevented picketing and persuading workers to join the strikes. The union appealed and won the right for peaceful picketing and persuasion—but to no avail because legal appeals took two years.[43]

In court testimony, John P. Frey, an IMU leader and later head of the AFL Metal Trades Department, castigated the lawlessness of NFA, MMTFA, and Allis-Chalmers officials. The foundry employers, he charged, directed a "wide spread conspiracy" of "the National Founders' Association, the Allis-Chalmers Company and other foundrymen in Milwaukee." They "engaged in a series of lawless acts" for more than a year, including "beating up of striking molders," intimidating "those friendly to the strikers' interests," and creating "disturbances which could be used as grounds for the granting of injunctions against the strikers." Frey also denounced the Allis-Chalmers' effort "to break the strike through the employment of professional sluggers and gun men, and the services of thugs, many of them with criminal records, to work in the struck shops as strike-breakers."[44]

During World War I, American machinists again engaged in a series of national strikes that ultimately touched Milwaukee and reached into the West Allis shops. At the time, the IAM called a number of "munitions strikes" in the metalworking shops and plants. According to Montgomery, these strikes were a part of a "control strike wave" that lasted from 1916 to 1920. They resulted in the IAM's phenomenal wartime growth from 54,000 to 331,000 members. The expansion of arms production created a tight labor market for machinists, skilled craftsmen, and semiskilled machine operators to fill huge war orders. Around the nation and in Milwaukee, IAM organizers directed another organizational campaign among the principal open shop metal firms.[45]

As the European war expanded, Allis-Chalmers managers and engineers tooled up in 1915 to reap the enormous profits of expanded war production. After receiving large government contracts for artillery shell production, they purchased "40 new lathes of great size designed especially to produce shrapnel shell cases." Over the next year, the firm hired five hundred specialized machinists on the piecework system for military production. One skilled machinist lamented the chaotic shop and the repetitive work for shell production. The West Allis machine shops were "a continuous circus." The labor shortage attracted all sorts of workers. "Lathes," he said, "are being run by tailors, carpenters, and shoemakers." The amount of spoiled work was a "shame" even though Allis-Chalmers "forfeit[ed] $2 for every shell scrapped." Under such conditions, many quit, "but more are being taken on. Some that are mechanics will do all right, but others will not make their salt." While the less skilled machine operatives made good money on military work, the craft-proud machinists decried the speedup and lower quality.[46]

Following the introduction of a piece-rate system, Allis-Chalmers machinists threatened still another skilled worker strike. One skilled machinist complained about the system's effect on workers' wages and work quality. "The company," he stated, "will not get real results until it puts machinists on the work at 35 cents an hour. It will then be able to bank on the product, while it can not do so now, with the low wages it is paying." The reorganized work processes and new machinery challenged craft traditions and drove the workers toward another organization and confrontation with management.[47]

In early 1916, the Milwaukee Federated Trades Council (FTC), the AFL craft union council, inaugurated the "Labor Forward Movement," a special committee to organize Milwaukee's open shop firms. Jacob Friedrich, a Milwaukee IAM organizer, later recalled that "large numbers" of Allis-Chalmers workers enrolled in the machinists' union and "immediately started agitation for a strike, figuring that it was the prudent time because of the European war work coming in." On July 17, 1916, twelve hundred workers struck the huge West Allis plant for the eight-hour day with no reduction in pay.[48]

On the first day, hundreds of Allis-Chalmers workers ritualistically marched out of the West Allis and old Reliance plants. One observer described the scene at the West Allis Works: "Promptly at 10 a.m. the men began to stream out of the Allis-Chalmers Co. They carried their tools in boxes, on their shoulders, in tool bags and suitcases, together with their working clothes and overalls. They were lighthearted and orderly." The streetcar company had twenty extra trolley cars waiting for the strikers. Many workers left in their own automobiles. The account showed the elite status of the striking Allis-Chalmers machinists. The tools testified to their skill, their dress to their pride, and automobile ownership to their affluence.[49]

After the strike started in the West Allis and Reliance plants, the Milwaukee IAM leaders conducted shop votes in other metal trades firms. They pursued a strike strategy of steadily increasing pressure on the open shop employers. By July 21, a total of 3,000 machinists from nine plants walked the streets and over 10,000 more threatened to strike the other Milwaukee machine shops. Although the IAM wanted state arbitrators to negotiate the eight-hour strike, the MMTFA refused to arbitrate and chose to wait it out. As in the earlier work stoppages, the other metal tradesmen continued to work. Gradually, the machinists' strike fever wore off. After about eight weeks, Milwaukee and Allis-Chalmers machinists drifted back to their shops, having suffered still another major defeat. In mid September, the MMTFA leader proclaimed that the Milwaukee metal shops maintained the prestrike work week and retained the "open shop principle."[50]

After World War I and through the 1920s, the "American" Plan supplanted the open shop as the principal employer campaign against craft unionism. An extension of the open shop, the new employer strategy appropriated the rhetoric of Americanism and identified even the most conservative craft unions with the taint of Bolshevism. In essence, the American Plan combined the older notion of the open shop with the corporate paternalism of welfare capitalism. Although mechanization made unskilled and semiskilled workers expendable, the more modern firms needed the skills of a solid core of craftsmen. If the skilled workers did not get the benefits of union representation, they at least received the largess of munificent employers. The postwar labor plan also attempted to inculcate worker loyalty to the non-union firm.[51]

The Allis-Chalmers labor program incorporated the main elements of the American Plan. In a talk to University of Wisconsin students, Harold Story, the Allis-Chalmers attorney, emphasized the benign and peaceful character of the nonunion era. From 1919 to 1931, the labor-management climate contained a "FRIENDLY relationship" "company picnics," "FREE legal aid," and "FREEDOM from labor disputes." Harold Christoffel, the Allis-Chalmers union leader, remembered things quite differently, "Talk of unionism was not permitted and the employees heard even discussing the possibility of a union were immediately discharged."[52]

In the mid-1930s, Story revealed the profound depth of the Allis-Chalmers paternalistic philosophy toward workers. Under "sound" employer-employee relations, the Allis-Chalmers labor strategist told a Wisconsin legislative committee, "The company organization has many of the characteristics of the family unit. Management stands in the position of parent." In its paternal authority, officials and managers were assured the right and responsibility to control the workplace. Especially since his firm employed a large number of young workers, he added: "management has a real parental responsibility in providing the discipline necessary to make members of the group pull together."[53]

Moreover, the special parental relation, Story argued, required protection from any outside interference, namely, trade unions. "Thus," Story continued, "I think it is just as unfair for a labor union . . . to interfere with the relations of that employer's industrial family group as it is for a total stranger to mix into the affairs of an actual family unit." Although the Allis-Chalmers attorney conceded the union right to solicit membership, he denied it the right to interfere with management control. He concluded, "The moral being that it's okeh [sic] to woo the children, but leave the old man alone."[54]

In the large Milwaukee firm, welfare capitalism took several forms. Since the 1880s, the Allis Mutual Aid Society cared for permanent workers and their families in the event of sickness, accident, or death. Voluntary worker contributions financed the health and insurance program. For the most part, only the skilled elite of mostly native-born American and northern European workers could afford to participate in the plan. In 1905, the company constructed a clubhouse for the recreational and educational activities of its managers, foremen, and skilled workers. In the 1910s, it established a commissary department that sold shoes, overalls, and snacks to workers at cost. In 1916, it paid a 10 percent bonus to workers with the company for more than one year. Most often, it was the most skilled and reliable workers who avoided the transiency and poverty of casual employment and received these benefits. The firm also participated in Milwaukee and West Allis high school apprenticeship programs to train the sons of skilled workers. These public programs removed craft unions from the education and socialization of young workers. In the 1920s, the company also offered a two-week vacation to workers continuously employed more than one year. In 1925, it opened a new West Allis shop hospital with physicians, nurses, and a dentist to attend to worker injuries and illnesses. Through the depression years, its relief committee provided Christmas food, fuel, clothing, and toys for needy Allis-Chalmers families.[55]

For the most part, these programs catered to the skilled craft elite of the West Allis shops. In many instances, the Polish, Slavic, or Italian workers remained in the volatile unskilled labor market of frequent layoffs or high labor turnover. Job-tenured corporate benefits attached skilled workmen and their families to the Allis-Chalmers firm.

By the 1930s, three decades of mechanization had transformed the sprawling West Allis industrial complex. *Fortune* magazine labeled the large, diversified Allis-Chalmers firm "America's Krupp." Like the huge German industrial conglomerate, the Milwaukee firm manufactured a full line of industrial and electrical products. "These spacious areas and ponderous shapes," the reporter wrote, "are admirable symbols of the work in progress behind the stone walls of the West Allis Works, for the Allis-Chalmers Manufacturing Co. is engaged in the heaviest of heavy industry. Its enterprises are so numerous that it believes only one other company in the world[—]Krupp of Essen—is capable of producing a greater assortment of those primary tools from which man wrests goods and power from the earth." The specialized manufacture of these primary tools rested on the most refined skills of Allis-Chalmers metal and electrical tradesmen. "The manufacture of these goods," the reporter noted, "which the Allis men call 'the big stuff,' is not manufacturing at all, but engineering."[56]

Specially engineered large products, however, did not present the entire picture of the massive industrial complex. For the Allis-Chalmers plant also manufactured tractors, agricultural implements, and other mass-produced goods. The *Fortune* correspondent described it as "an industrial hybrid with an assembly line full of bright orange tractors moving animatedly against a backdrop of looming pumps, turbines, crushers, and other made-to-order heavy machinery." Although it originally specialized in specialty and batch production of "the big stuff," the West Allis plant now also mass-produced small products. These included "a certain number of more or less standardized industrial items like motors and controls, small pumps, V-belt drives, and the like" and the products of the tractor division, "whose assembly line is the least spectacular part of the West Allis Works but whose product is the biggest money maker."[57]

According to *Fortune*, the tractor division was "a magnificent hedge against depression in the industrial lines." The mass-production work in the tractor shops sharply contrasted with the craft production of massive capital goods. "In contrast to the deliberate putting together of the 'big stuff,' " he noted, "the tractors move down an assembly line that has the clatter and tempo of its Detroit prototypes." The tractor division's success through the difficult depression years allowed the Wisconsin firm to weather the economic catastrophe without severe losses in the profit column. In the 1930s, he concluded, "the once wispy tractor tail has come to wag the dog."[58]

Through the 1910s and 1920s, Allis-Chalmers Manufacturing Company shifted into different areas and forms of production that restructured work skills and social relations in the various shops and departments. In the mid-1930s, Harold Story described the products of the West Allis Works: "roughly 50 per cent are special machinery and 50 per cent are mass production machinery." No longer solely concentrating on the "big stuff," the West Allis shops developed a bifurcated structure of production and a corresponding set of social relations for production. Both highly skilled craftsmen and less skilled production workers inhabited the same industrial facility.[59]

The Allis-Chalmers vice president also testified about the general character of work and skill levels in the West Allis plant. Harold Story told federal officials: "I think we have all degrees of skill from the very highest to what is normally classed as unskilled labor." Questioned about "trade classifications," he replied: "there is a varying degree of skill in all departments." He could identify only the drafting department as having "a homogeneous situation" in skill levels. It was often impossible to sort out the skilled from the less skilled shops. Even in the electrical department, he noted, "you will probably find some unskilled with the skilled."[60]

Another Allis-Chalmers official concurred. In response to one question, William Watson, the vice president for manufacturing, agreed that the plant divisions followed the product lines. Asked specifically about the skills of machinists in the West Allis tractor shops, he replied, "Well, we really term them specialists and machinists. A specialist is a man that learned one operation, might be [a] machine, might be assembly. That is what we call mass production." He also believed that these workers were "at best semi-skilled workers." Plant management classified an overwhelming majority, or 64 percent, of the Allis-Chalmers workers as machinists. These included 1,851 in the machine shops, 781 assemblers, and 68 punch press operators. The vast majority of these were probably semiskilled production workers.[61]

Allis-Chalmers workers also testified about the specialized character of their tasks. Harold Christoffel, for example, recalled that he had served a formal apprenticeship in the Allis-Chalmers plant to learn the electrician's trade. However, he identified himself as "an electrical worker" and not an electrician. When asked whether his line of work was associated with this "skilled craft," he replied, "The work which I perform is highly specialized and would not necessarily constitute craft work."[62]

In contrast to the early years of specialty and batch production, the West Allis plant was primarily a mass-production plant and was ready for a new form of unionism. "Throughout the plant," the NLRB panel ruled, "there is this continuous production process. This is also in the various departments where the work is highly specialized." Although many skilled workers still labored in the West Allis shops, they had had a problem with the AFL's divisive craft unionism. George Geiger, a veteran Allis-Chalmers iron molder since 1886, told the NLRB: "I really believe in industrial union[s]. I do not believe in craft unions because I seen that one craft union would go out on strike and the other would laugh at them." Combined with the corporate open shop tradition and the gradual increase in the number of semiskilled production workers, this attitude led to the inexorable drift toward militant industrial unionism in the 1930s.[63]

# 3

**THE MAKING OF MILITANT UNIONISM II: FROM COMPANY UNION TO UAW LOCAL, 1930–1937**

The history of labor-management relations, the social and economic convulsions of the Great Depression, and the supportive labor legislation of the New Deal shaped union formation in the 1930s. Three decades of technical change and antiunionism combined with the Great Depression's economic deprivation to instill a restiveness and a new militancy in Allis-Chalmers workers. Gradually, almost inexorably, Allis-Chalmers workers ended the open shop era and experimented with various organizational forms from a paternalistic works council to AFL craft unions and finally to a left CIO union. Until the eventual domination of CIO unionism, the various forms of worker representation often coexisted and competed with each other.

Union building involved an amalgam of mixed and overlapping groups of social and institutional actors. On the eve of the Great Depression, over seven thousand Allis-Chalmers workers were almost equally divided between industrial craftsmen and semiskilled production workers. For the most part, they were white men. Only a few women and no African Americans worked in the sprawling West Allis plant. A decade of corporate growth meant a diverse age structure of young, middle-aged, and old workers. Ethnically, the Allis-Chalmers workers were a varied lot, reflecting Milwaukee's diverse social amalgam of native-born and immigrant workers. Native-born Americans and Germans most often were the skilled craftsmen; Poles and Slavs most frequently toiled as unskilled laborers and semiskilled machine operators. Politically, too, they reflected Milwaukee's eclectic traditions. Some were conservatives; some moderates; others Socialists in the Milwaukee German tradition. Still others were Communists in a southern or eastern European tradition.

For millions of ordinary Americans, the Great Depression was a formative and transcendent experience that scarred their memories and psyches. Nationally, unemployment averaged 25 percent in 1932. In major industrial areas, the average was much higher. In Milwaukee, the number of employed wage earners fell from 117,758 in 1929 to 66,010 in 1933, a staggering 57 percent. In the West Allis plant, the work force plunged from a normal contingent of over seven thousand to fewer than three thousand workers. For Allis-Chalmers workers, the economic devastation and dislocation meant unemployment, underemployment, job transfers, and wage cuts.[1]

Although the massive layoffs of the depression years mainly affected the ordinary production workers, they also meant numerous job transfers and temporary layoffs for the younger skilled craftsmen throughout the West Allis plant. The firm, as a batch producer of the big stuff, needed to retain its most skilled workers. Consequently, the unskilled, the semiskilled, and the young bore the brunt of the depression layoffs. In 1932, two future Allis-Chalmers union presidents, Harold Christoffel and Robert Buse, took long layoffs. The young Christoffel went bumming out West with Fred McStroul, a high school friend and future union officer. Buse, a self-taught and semiskilled machinist, attempted to operate a machine repair shop. For the older men, highly prized craftsmen, the major trauma was the transfer to less skilled, less meaningful, and less prestigious work in the mass-production shops. They also faced underemployment with short days, short weeks, and short pay envelopes. On top of this, Allis-Chalmers announced two general 10 percent wage cuts, in 1930 and 1932. Even workers who avoided the psychic pain and economic deprivation of layoffs suffered difficult times.[2]

Organized into the Federated Trades Council (FTC), the Milwaukee AFL leaders were ill-prepared to meet the social and economic convulsions of the early 1930s. The widespread mechanization of American industry made the craft form of union organization obsolete. For Milwaukee's craft unionists, the Roaring Twenties were the open shop Lean Years. Milwaukee's antiunion decade seriously eroded AFL membership. One Milwaukee FTC leader, Jacob F. Friedrick, recalled a failed effort to reorganize the metal trades. In the spring of 1929, he remembered, the FTC Metal Trades Council funded an organizing drive for the "various metal groups, the molders, the boiler makers, the blacksmiths, machinists and so on." The AFL organizational campaign included the large and coveted Allis-Chalmers plant. Despite the economic collapse, the AFL drive continued into 1930, when the metal trades craft leaders abandoned it. The Milwaukee AFL was unique. It a had a strong connection to the Socialist political tradition of the city's German community. But in the 1930s, American craft union conservatism, and later the Democratic New Deal, loosened the political bond. "The Socialist Party of Milwaukee," said one Milwaukee labor historian, "was dying." And, with its demise, the Milwaukee AFL was severely weakened.[3]

By the early 1930s, craft organization had flagged, the Great Depression had deepened, unemployment had risen, and worker dissatisfaction had mounted. At the time, only the Communist Party voiced a strategy of resistance and urged Allis-Chalmers workers to fight the layoffs, short hours, and wage cuts. In the 1920s, a small and isolated group of Slavic Communists tried unsuccessfully to organize the West Allis plant. They managed to publish sporadically an "inflammatory" shop paper, the mimeographed *Allis-Chalmers Worker*. As the economic crisis deepened, this Communist nucleus grew and began to influence and mobilize the discontent of increasingly angry Milwaukee workers. When company officials announced a second round of wage cuts in 1932, the *Allis-Chalmers Worker* agitated against the reductions with the slogan "Fight the Wage Cut! Build the Union!" The Communist Party shop paper, reflecting Third Period tactics, urged the formation of Metal Workers Industrial Union (MWIU) shop "committees" and "grievance committees in every department." Several months later, the Communist Party Unemployed Councils and MWIU sponsored a September "Hunger March to Allis-Chalmers." In an appeal directed to Allis-Chalmers workers, the marchers demanded either "work or cash relief" for the unemployed, a $20 per week minimum wage for the employed, the payment of insurance benefits for employed and unemployed alike, an end to favoritism in job assignments and to unpaid idle or waiting time in the shops, and to abolish the "spy and blacklist system." These demands reflected working-class strivings for economic security and human dignity and opposition to arbitrary management authority.[4]

Although such efforts stirred up some worker discontent and generated some worker activism, a genuine, though unintended, surge of labor organization arrived only with the Roosevelt revolution. During Franklin D. Roosevelt's famous "Hundred Days," Congress passed the most important economic component of the early New Deal—the National Industrial Recovery Act (NIRA) of 1933. Although its provisions were weak and sometimes unenforceable, national legislation for the first time endorsed and encouraged worker self-organization and collective bargaining. The new legislation soon had a direct effect on the labor-management relationship in the West Allis shops. Almost immediately, the moribund AFL came to life and attempted to organize skilled Allis-Chalmers workers. The Communist Party campaigned to bring industrial unionism to mass-production workers in the West Allis plant.

In the spring of 1933, the AFL resumed organizational activities at the West Allis plant. When FTC leaders realized that favorable legislation would pass Congress and signed into law, they intensified their efforts to organize the craftsmen. "As a matter of fact," Jacob Friedrick later recalled, "I, myself, in the spring of 1933 addressed a noon day meeting at the Allis-Chalmers plant." Through the summer, the AFL Metal Trades Council sponsored a series of mass meetings for Milwaukee blacksmiths, machinists, boilermakers, molders, patternmakers, and other metal craftsmen. At the time, the *Milwaukee Journal* reported, "Union meetings are being held here nightly and labor is invading industries which always have been closed to unions, with considerable success, the leaders say."[5]

Although Communist Party activists denounced the Roosevelt NIRA as a tool for company unionism, they too stepped up their organizational activities. One West Allis Communist leader wrote to the *Party Organizer*: "We are holding shop gate meetings every day and the various sections as well as the T.U.U.L. [Trade Union Unity League] have issued and are issuing leaflets linking up concrete issues in the shop with the Act." The huge West Allis plant was the main focus of the Communist Party organizational activity. The same leader wrote that "shop gate meetings and leaflets" mobilized "comrades and sympathizers inside the shop" in order "to build a union under our leadership."[6]

During the AFL and Communist Party campaigns, Allis-Chalmers managers quickly recognized the obvious threat of worker restiveness and developed a strategy of containment. Harold Story, their chief labor strategist, nervously noted: "Every depression creates a spirit of restlessness in labor." Because of widespread unemployment and wage reductions, he added, labor felt "entitled to retrieve its economic position as soon as possible, (or as a matter of fact before it is economically possible from the management viewpoint of cash position)." The new labor legislation's emphasis on "the right of collective bargaining," Story reasoned, "would aggravate the spirit of restlessness and would incite labor to find an emotional outlet for their feelings by way of collective bargaining either through outside unions or some other form of organization." In response to the new federal legal framework and to widespread worker unease, company officials created the West Allis Works Council (WAWC), a tamer "emotional outlet," to forestall genuine trade unionism.[7]

The idea of the WAWC followed the standard corporate program for worker representation in American industry after World War I. In the 1920s, the large electrical and agricultural implement firms, such as General Electric and International Harvester, two major Allis-Chalmers competitors, established works councils as a mechanism for the plantwide representation of their workers. Story later testified that the idea for the Allis-Chalmers plan came from a Metropolitan Life Insurance Company pamphlet that suggested different forms of workplace representation. The corporate works council movement was a managerial response to the transformation of the internal order that accompanied the modernization of plants and factories. In a sense, corporate officials and managers struggled with the same issues as the labor proponents of industrial unionism. The mechanization of production, diminution of skill levels, and reformulation of management practices—all transformed the internal character of the American workplace. As skilled craftsmen increasingly gave way to production workers, modern managers recognized that craft unionism no longer adequately represented the interests of all the workers in large industrial establishments. Moreover, the management science of human relations revealed the importance of grievance resolution to worker satisfaction and efficient production. The formal systems of workplace representation seemed to provide the technical solution to the organizational problems of modern American industry.[8]

In 1923, Carroll E. French, an early analyst of the corporate works council or shop committee movement, described the changed conditions of production and the emergence of this new form of worker representation. "The shop committee," he noted, "rests upon the assumption that the normal economic relationship of labor and capital is the individual factory . . . . It has grown up outside of trade unionism and has flourished especially in unorganized industries." Generally, the plant-based works council constituted a means of worker representation for the new production workers. For the managers of modern plants, the works councils afforded a means for collective negotiations with workers on narrowly circumscribed subject areas of grievances, productivity, and shop conditions. In other words, management would institutionalize new works councils for plantwide negotiations, often sidestepping traditional craft union structures.[9]

Since the disastrous molders' and machinists' strikes, Allis-Chalmers workers had had no form of representation. Management alone determined wages, hours, and working conditions. Workers who even mentioned unions often faced immediate discharge. Factory spies assiduously reported minor and major worker indiscretions. Indeed, Robert LaFollette's Senate committee, which investigated corporate abuses of worker freedoms, reported that the Allis-Chalmers corporation spent over $7,300 on private detective agencies from 1933 to 1936. The firm's membership in the National Metal Trades Association provided access to additional antiunion services.[10]

After the passage of the National Industrial Recovery Act (NIRA) in 1933, Allis-Chalmers managers formally inaugurated the WAWC, following a plantwide election for works council representatives. The WAWC statement of objectives emphasized the principal goal—"the development of spirit of cooperation and mutual understanding." The new plan established "an orderly method" for workers to "present to the management their views and recommendations on all questions of company policy relating to working conditions, health, safety, hours of labor, wages, economy, waste preventions, recreation, education, and other matters of mutual interest." The newly elected WAWC representatives considered workplace issues within the domain of traditional trade unionism. Of course, they only made "recommendations"— which Allis-Chalmers managers did not have to follow.[11]

In order to ensure conservative representation, the works council initially included five management and twenty worker spokesmen. At the outset, these five managers held the representative body's principal offices and guided its official proceedings. In the first year, management members served as the WAWC's chairman and secretary, who were also members of the important Fact Finding Committee. The twenty worker representatives came from sixteen different divisions of the large industrial complex. The larger West Allis shops had more than one worker representative.[12]

After a year, the federal NIRA guidelines for collective negotiations forced the management representatives to quit the WAWC. Once they left in 1934, William Watson, an Allis-Chalmers vice president, pronounced: "When the Works Council was started it was the intention of the Company and it is still their intention, that the workmen should control it." Furthermore, he concluded, the WAWC "was an effective agency and generally credited with a good record of employe representation."[13]

Still, Allis-Chalmers officials carefully designed and structured the worker organization to ensure a conservative orientation. According to Harold Christoffel, the works council constitution contained selective requirements for worker representatives. These included the election of a council member "whose name appears on the company's pay roll continuously for the 12 months immediately preceding the nomination, who is 21 years of age or more, and who is an American citizen." Management intended these requirements to guarantee more cautious and conservative worker representatives. "The Works Council," Harold Story recalled, "contained our outstanding, mature, skilled men. They were men whom we knew, who on account of their closeness to management, could bargain effectively [and could] effectively attain all that the Company could afford to offer at that time." Allis-Chalmers managers wanted long-term workers who had a commitment to the firm, older workers who did not display hotheaded immaturity, and American citizens untainted with radical alien ideologies.[14]

Allis-Chalmers managers cautiously guided the WAWC's direction and activities in other ways. Initially, shop supervisors could serve as worker representatives. But this too was changed to comply with National Recovery Administration (NRA) guidelines. "The company," Christoffel claimed, "paid all the expenses of the council, but paid no attention to even its mildest recommendations." Its principal committee, the Fact Finding Committee, which studied, investigated, and reported on wages and hours, could make only recommendations to management. "The findings and report of such committee," its constitution noted, "shall be advisory only and shall not in any manner bind the Works Council." Management even distributed Works Council literature to workers through the shop foremen.[15]

Despite management efforts to direct and control the West Allis Works Council, the representative institution marked a formative phase of worker empowerment. The workers for the first time possessed a plantwide instrument to express their views on wages, hours, and working conditions. This was a significant departure from the long-standing open shop tradition. The passage of the NIRA and the creation of the works council, Story said, "was the commencement of the era . . . of collective bargaining." And the plantwide elections of worker representatives engaged the attention and participation of thousands of Allis-Chalmers workers in their departments and shops. For example, in June 1934, fully 93 percent of the 2,990 shop employees participated in balloting for WAWC representatives.[16]

The WAWC and its Fact Finding Committee discussed numerous issues that affected the rank-and-file workers. The WAWC minutes indicated much worker discussion and debate about a diverse range of shop questions. Some revealed depression-induced fears about economic and job security. These included discussions about married women working in the shops, company sale of coal, and seniority. Others reflected worker desires to be treated with dignity and respect—such seemingly minor issues as the allotment of parking spaces, delivery of paychecks, use of plant gates, and matters of shop safety. Still other issues demonstrated a gradual drift toward more conventional trade union concerns. For example, the Tank and Plate Shop workers almost unanimously voted for a 15 percent wage increase. Within a year, the question of trade unionism became the most contentious, divisive issue in the council's deliberations.[17]

Of course, the managers and workers had different evaluations of the West Allis Works Council. To managers, the new institution came perilously close to trade unionism. Harold Story fearfully described how workers' individual complaints came to their works councilmen, who in turn raised the problem with management through the WAWC meetings: "That was a somewhat of an . . . unorganized kind of collective bargaining." After its first year, the WAWC even negotiated a 12 percent general wage increase, which boosted wage rates to pre-depression levels. To trade unionists, the WAWC was a company union that did little more than retard genuine trade unionism. To be sure, some union activists used works council seats to secure mobility within the shop and to facilitate union organization. On putative works council business, an activist could covertly talk with and organize shopmates into a union. Nonetheless, Harold Christoffel facetiously claimed that after "many meetings and long arguments," the Works Council's main accomplishments were the installation of wooden toilet seats and vending machines. "This employee representation plan," the future Allis-Chalmers union leader concluded, "was intended only as a pacifist measure and was shorn of any power with which the employees could bargain."[18]

Almost immediately after the WAWC's creation, Christoffel and other electrical workers formed an International Brotherhood of Electrical Workers' (IBEW) craft union. The rebirth of Allis-Chalmers craft unions apparently began with an IBEW organizational drive in fall 1933, most likely a part of the FTC's metal trades campaign. Initially, Milwaukee IBEW Local 494, a citywide craft local, tried to enlist Allis-Chalmers workers with the New Deal appeal that "the President wants you to join a union." From fall through summer 1934, the *ACWU News* reported, "meetings were held among the Allis-Chalmers employes at which the attendance varied from three to 30." The original IBEW unionists were highly skilled workers in the electrical maintenance department. Two IBEW leaders, Edward Brown, an international representative, and Charles Thurber, a Milwaukee business agent, directed the Allis-Chalmers organizational drive. Because of their sour experiences with Milwaukee craft locals and the great size of the West Allis plant, Allis-Chalmers workers demanded and received their own autonomous craft local. In August 1934, a group of eighteen Allis-Chalmers electrical workers received a charter for IBEW Local 663, which slowly increased to about thirty-six members.[19]

Despite this, the history of craft union division and failure proved a barrier to union growth in the West Allis plant. Veterans of past struggles with the open shop management opposed the AFL form of skilled worker organization. Julius Blunk, an older worker and an early Allis-Chalmers union activist, claimed that Allis-Chalmers workers had clamored for a single industrial union since 1916. "The attitude of the men," he asserted, "is that they want one union at Allis-Chalmers; they don't care which it is, but they want one union." In addition, the financial burdens of the Great Depression made it difficult for workers to pay the inordinately high AFL initiation fees, which could be as much as $250, and the equally stiff monthly dues. The new Allis-Chalmers IBEW Local 663 had much lower initiation fees. The reduced fees were intended to attract semiskilled and unskilled production workers. But they were still too high: after a year, in August 1935, the Allis-Chalmers local had only fifty workers.[20]

After a full year of activity, the IBEW unionists had reached a serious block to craft organization. At this point, Harold Christoffel and Julius Blunk, the two most committed and active union organizers, devised a new plan to organize the electrical workers in the West Allis plant. Through a special arrangement with the international union, they "registered" electrical workers into the IBEW at a nominal dues rate of $1 per month. Effectively, Allis-Chalmers IBEW Local 663 had two groups of members— Class A members with full voting and benefit rights in the international union; and Class B members, who identified themselves as unionists in the struggle with management. The Class B members were assigned to IBEW Local 663-B, sometimes disparagingly referred to as a "Peanut" local by Allis-Chalmers workers.[21]

The novel organizational strategy proved an immediate success. "Under this plan [of registrants]," the union reported, "the local took in 'everyone from the sweeper to the foreman in the electrical department.' " In the West Allis electrical shops, both skilled and production workers flocked into IBEW Local 663-B, which effectively became an industrial union among electrical workers. The AFL electrical workers' union membership swiftly grew from about twenty members to around four hundred fifty members. As the most organized group of Allis-Chalmers workers, they soon inspired and encouraged other AFL unions in the West Allis plant. In fact, the Allis-Chalmers IBEW local grew so strong that in 1935 it forced management to recognize informally its steward structure. Still, the traditional AFL leaders continued their practice of cutting separate deals. After the initial IBEW success, International Representative MacLogan "suggested that the electrical workers seek to obtain a contract and not concern themselves about organizing the rest of the plant." But the electrical workers stressed solidarity with their other shopmates, recalling the weakness of partial organization. "The men in the electrical union decided," the *ACWU News* related, "that it was imperative that the other employes at Allis-Chalmers be unionized."[22]

The IAM manifested the much less successful and more typical organizational pattern for other craft unions in the West Allis plant. Frank Bolka, a young machinist and leftist, played a central role in the effort to organize the machinists. Like Christoffel, he had a strong commitment to expand worker rights in the Allis-Chalmers shops. He had begun work with Allis-Chalmers as a general machinist in 1929. But like so many other American workers in the 1930s, he was laid off in May 1931, returning only in March 1934. Although a skilled machinist, he worked a drill press in a tractor shop on his return, later transferring to more skilled work in a machine shop. Embittered by his depression layoff, Bolka had his "first experience with union activity" in 1934. He attended Milwaukee Metal Trades Council mass meetings in April and May, paid his full IAM initiation fee and dues, and served as an IAM organizer in the Allis-Chalmers tractor shop. Initially, Bolka worked with Jacob Friedrich and Otto Jirikowic, the two Milwaukee IAM and AFL leaders, and attempted to enroll Allis-Chalmers workers into the citywide IAM Local 66. As was the case for the Allis-Chalmers electrical workers, the high craft union dues impeded IAM organization. In October 1934, Jirikowic made a special appeal to the national IAM for lower dues for Milwaukee production machinists. Noting their precarious financial situation, the IAM business agent pleaded, "due to the small wages paid these workers it is impossible for them to pay the high rate of dues for the journeyman and specialist." Although struggling to build a strong union in his shops, Bolka and another Allis-Chalmers union recruit managed to elicit only thirty to forty applications in the tractor shop. Only twenty of these applicants were later admitted to the machinists' craft organization.[23]

The young unionist confronted the thankless and almost impossible task of enrolling new IAM members. The tractor shops employed nearly 1,500 workers of the 3,500 potential IAM members in the plant. At most, only 250 machinists were organized into the citywide IAM Local 66 from 1934 through 1936. According to Bolka, the highly specialized tractor shop workers opposed the IAM because of the high initiation fees and dues and the anticraft tradition that dated back to the failed 1916 machinists' strike. Still, firm in his union convictions and protected by federal legislation, Bolka pushed the union cause. After his transfer to a more skilled job in the general machine shop in 1935, he enrolled about one hundred fifty of the four hundred workers eligible for IAM membership. His relentless organizing created a nucleus of committed union members and union activists in the Allis-Chalmers machine and tractor shops. By 1936, "the men," Bolka later proclaimed, "were crying for one union, especially the machinists . . . if we wouldn't do something about it wouldn't be no time at all before we wouldn't have no members out there at all." Yet, at its enrollment peak, the IAM enlisted only 250 members of the 3,500 machinists and machine operators in the West Allis plant. In July 1936, this number fell to 225. In the absence of collective bargaining, even the organized workers began to lose interest in craft unionism.[24]

Allis-Chalmers foundry workers were the third group that saw tentative organizational efforts. The IMU Local 125 campaign achieved only slight success. With a separate charter as IMU Local 58, John Rucich, Fred McStroul—Christoffel's high school friend—and Michael Boblin, organized only 120 of a possible 1,000 foundry workers. Once again, the business agent opted for craft self-interest and suggested negotiating a separate molders' contract. The foundry workers rebelled and returned their charter to the IMU.[25]

Other skilled tradesmen also attempted to form craft unions in the West Allis plant but were even less successful. These included the Milwaukee locals of the patternmakers, foundry workers, boilermakers and shipbuilders, and blacksmiths, drop forgers, and helpers. For the most part, the AFL business agents accomplished little. They simply met with management, hoping to negotiate separate contracts for their respective craft union members.[26]

Nonetheless, the Milwaukee craft unions did establish an important tradition of collective negotiations for Allis-Chalmers workers. Under the guidance of the larger and stronger trade unions, Allis-Chalmers craft union leaders made two serious efforts to obtain a collective agreement. Although they never received an actual contract from the intractable corporation, the they did obtain informal agreements for the resolution of shop-floor problems. They also went through an important apprenticeship in learning negotiating skills for future union leadership.

In the earliest negotiations, the AFL business agents, especially the IAM's Jirikowic and the IBEW's Brown, were the dominant figures on labor's side. Nonetheless, through sheer force of personality, the young, talented Christoffel made his presence felt. Harold Story later recalled that at first the two AFL business agents were "the dominating factors" in negotiating sessions. "Mr. Christoffel," he added, "was an ambitious personality in those conferences, but at that time Mr. Jirikowic was running the meetings. Now, after that time, Mr. Christoffel assumed leadership, full and complete." Story observed that the future union leader "was a quite dominant personality, even at that time, but at that time, he was not the controlling factor in the conferences."[27]

Soon after Allis-Chalmers unionists exerted their presence in the 1934 works council elections, company officials informally recognized and negotiated with the several craft unions. In September 1934, for example, the six leading AFL unions jointly submitted a set of proposals for union recognition and collective bargaining rights. They also demanded an AFL closed shop. A week after the AFL began negotiations, the works council also issued its proposal for exclusive bargaining rights for all Allis-Chalmers workers, invoking a recent shop election in which an overwhelming majority of workers participated. Fearful of the growing strength of the craft unions, management quickly refused exclusive recognition to the WAWC.[28]

Despite their weakness, the AFL business agents attempted to negotiate with the company's officials through the fall of 1934. At one point, IBEW agent Brown presented Harold Story with a list of AFL demands. On behalf of the electrical workers, machinists, molders, foundry workers, blacksmiths, patternmakers, and boilermakers, Brown demanded: "1. A closed shop. 2. A 7-hour day and 35-hour week. 3. Establishment of high guaranteed minimum rates plus a general wage increase of 10c/per hour. 4. Abolition of all piece work." In addition, the AFL proposal called for a shop committee and a grievance procedure to ensure enforcement of the contract. Union members also wanted of a ten-minute lunch or snack period after the start of each shift and the use of shop bulletin boards. According to Story, the union demands "created a considerable stir" among workers, who feared a possible strike. Story ignored the union demands and proposed contract after determining that only 5 percent of the West Allis workers actually paid dues to the AFL craft unions.[29]

In mid December 1934, Max Babb, the new Allis-Chalmers president, made a formal "Statement of Policy" as the company response to the passage of the NIRA and to the AFL collective bargaining efforts. The statement opened with a clear reiteration of the long-standing Allis-Chalmers open shop position. Nonetheless, in conformity with NIRA guidelines, Babb proclaimed that management was "at all times ready and willing to meet with its employes, for the purpose of collective bargaining as provided in Section 7(a) of the National Industrial Recovery Act." He then listed representatives of the works council, representatives of "any lawful labor organization" such as the AFL, and "any other representative selected by one or more of its employes" as the appropriate agents for possible negotiations. In other words, the new Allis-Chalmers labor policy simultaneously endorsed both collective and individual bargaining. The company president also promised no discrimination "because of membership or non-membership in any lawful organization." The new policy, Harold Story claimed, was "clearly a *true open-shop* policy."[30]

The president's statement detailed new corporate policies on wages, hours, and working conditions. In a clear formulation of fundamental management prerogatives, Babb asserted "the right to discharge or lay off any employee" but promised to provide the reason for such action and to offer full discussion with workers or their representatives. He announced a plan for reducing hours before layoff "but consistent with efficient operation of the plant from a competitive standpoint." In the event of layoff and rehiring, Allis-Chalmers would consider a worker's seniority and his or her "individual skill and efficient service." Similarly, a worker's promotion would rely on "length of service, ability, and efficiency." In other words, company officials asserted management's "unqualified" right to hire, fire, lay off, or promote its workers.[31]

The new policy left the question of hours to the establishment of the National Recovery Administration codes for the electrical equipment industry. However, Babb did offer time-and-a-half for all Saturday work and for all work above hours determined by the NRA electrical code. He also provided double time for work on Sundays and on seven legal holidays. On the contentious shop floor issue of piece rates, Babb said that the time study department would establish prices for jobs, but workers could obtain "full information as to the price set on the job." Finally, the Allis-Chalmers president conditionally promised wage increases in the future. "The policy of the Company as to wage increases," Babb noted, "is to share with employes any future prosperity—when it comes—by granting fair general wage increases and, in the meantime, to continue to make rate adjustments where an unfair condition exists."[32]

In a sense, the initial craft union campaigns were modestly successful if only because company officials responded to worker initiatives and demands. Under Babb's policy statement, Allis-Chalmers officials devised a strategy of divide and conquer that continued to rest on the foundation of the open shop. Although he agreed to meet with AFL and other workers, Babb agreed neither to bargain collectively nor to offer exclusive representation to any organized group of workers. Despite these limitations, the *ACWU News* characterized the craft union negotiations and subsequent labor policy as "the first genuine union negotiations . . . which recognized AFL unions as part of the representation machinery in the plant." While Babb reaffirmed the open shop and fundamental management rights and prerogatives, he publicly announced and clearly defined for the first time Allis-Chalmers labor policies and workplace rules. For the unionists, these formed a starting point for future collective bargaining and contract negotiations. As genuine unionism became a reality, shop floor leaders could negotiate the expansion of the circumscribed area of worker rights.[33]

The next, more successful, phase of unionization was the organization of Allis-Chalmers workers into one large industrial union. This time, the organizational drive derived from labor's Left. In 1934, three violent strikes (autoworkers in Toledo, longshoremen in San Francisco, and teamsters in Minneapolis) revealed the firm commitment of leftist leaders and rank-and-file workers to a new form of inclusive industrial unionism. In early 1935 the AFL split, as John L. Lewis led a group of national AFL unions that also pushed for industrial union organizational drives.

From 1935 on, the Communist Party took a more direct, active role in Allis-Chalmers union formation. At this time, the Communist Party developed its Popular Front strategy of cooperating with "bourgeois" institutions in the struggle against fascism. Until the Popular Front, the Communist Party labor strategy had involved the organization of workers into separate Communist labor organizations. In Milwaukee, this meant the organization of Allis-Chalmers workers into the Communist Metal Workers Industrial Union. The Popular Front, however, meant greater cooperation with the emergent Committee on Industrial Organizations and later the Congress of Industrial Organizations (CIO).

In early 1935, the Communist Party increased its activity in Wisconsin, Milwaukee, and West Allis. In February, Eugene Dennis moved to Wisconsin and assumed leadership of the Wisconsin Communist Party. A keen strategist, he developed an innovative Popular Front program that involved Wisconsin industrial unionists. At the time, Christoffel and other unionists recognized the limitations of craft organization and feared the possible failure of Allis-Chalmers unionization. Peggy Dennis, also active in Wisconsin, recalled that the Wisconsin Communist Party was "a small but cohesive" group of six hundred members. It "had more than one hundred union officials, nearly three hundred of its members active in the C.I.O. and A.F.L., and a popularity and influence beyond its numerical status." Moreover, the Wisconsin Communist Party had a plan for organizing the Allis-Chalmers plant.[34]

Before the CIO's creation, the Milwaukee Communist Party tactic was to transform the Allis-Chalmers Works Council into an industrial union. The Communist Party encouraged union activists to seek WAWC seats and raise union demands. One Allis-Chalmers Communist, John Blair, remembered the 1935 works council elections: "Allis-Chalmers had established a company union. The progressive people in the plant ran for the posts of representatives on the company union. When elected, they exposed the set-up by making real demands in behalf of the workers." In one appeal to Allis-Chalmers workers, West Allis Communists called for a "fight to choose real representatives" and rhetorically asked "WHAT HAS IT DONE FOR THE WORKERS?" Their response: "The answer is that it has done nothing *for*—us but everything to stall off our every attempt to secure higher wages and better conditions." In fact, they planned to transform the company union into a real union. "The only way we can carry on the fight for higher wages and better conditions," they argued, "is to kick the Company Union out of our way and to build a powerful REAL union to permanently protect our interests. This means we must elect the best fighting workers of our departments to the 'Works Council' and make a Shop Committee fighting in our interests." This was close to the technique actually adopted by the union leaders in the West Allis plant.[35]

In the works council elections, AFL activists managed to elect nine union representatives. While the nonunion workers had a slim majority of WAWC representatives, the general tenor of the works council meetings surely had a more combative atmosphere as unionists attempted to push this representative institution toward a more confrontational position. Furthermore, the craft unions, especially those of the electrical workers and machinists, established committees to handle worker grievances in their shops and departments. Essentially, these shop committees evolved into informal steward structures for the resolution of disputes between workers and their supervisors.[36]

Shortly after the WAWC elections, Harold Story first expressed anxiety about militant, left unionism at the West Allis plant. In July 1935, he recounted to a class of University of Wisconsin law students the "fable" of a mouse ("organized labor") and an elephant ("industrial management"). In his talk, he conveyed his fears about the growing strength of labor Communists. "Through the mouse of unionization," he warned, "the elephant of industry has made important concessions to labor as a whole which it would not have otherwise have done without the activities of the mouse. But if the mouse grows to elephantine size, it can exert a force, which, instead of being beneficial, will likely be destructive." Story preferred labor as "a lesser constructive force" and feared it as "major destructive force." In other words, he preferred AFL unionism to a growing radical call for industrial unionism.[37]

Clearly, the recent works council elections were influencing Story when he asked: "In just what manner will outside unions become a destructive force?" He responded: "The answer is found in the fact that the communistic element is gradually burrowing into A.F. of L. unions." He then cited several examples of AFL charges against the Communists, including a recent "warning" from the Wisconsin State Federation of Labor Convention. Moreover, as "concrete evidence" of the Communist influence, he described "two circulars disseminated in our West Allis plant by the so[-]called Allis-Chalmers Communist Party." One criticized the Allis-Chalmers "Roosevelt-LaFollette Works Plan" and the other castigated the AFL leadership. With the steady growth of AFL unionism at Allis-Chalmers in mind, Story commented, "I am not worried about the leadership of such men as Jacob

Friedricks [*sic*], Jack Hanley, and Henry Ohls [*sic*] of the state Federation of Labor, but I am concerned about the ability of such men to control the members of affiliated unions and thus direct the policy of local unions which have local autonomy." Obviously, he feared the emerging Left-dominated craft unions in the West Allis plant.[38]

Meanwhile, in 1935, the U.S. government once again spurred Allis-Chalmers workers to renewed organizational efforts. Although the Supreme Court had recently invalidated the NIRA, Senator Robert Wagner sponsored new federal legislation to put teeth into and to strengthen the enforcement of U.S. labor policies. Passed in July 1935, the National Labor Relations Act (NLRA) forcefully ensured the right of American workers to organize autonomous unions and to bargain collectively with employers. The act created a strong National Labor Relations Board (NLRB) to enforce the new law's provisions. With the full backing of federal law, Allis-Chalmers workers moved more steadily in the union direction.[39]

For the company officials, the federal legislation threatened to undermine management control over the workplace. During congressional debates on the Wagner Act, Otto Falk, chairman of the Allis-Chalmers board, labeled the proposed law as "the most potent weapon yet devised to provoke discord and jeopardize the future of industry." The legislation was "dangerous on three grounds." First, Falk noted, it rested on "the exploded theory that the interests of employers and employees are antagonistic, not mutual." Second, it permitted workers "to indulge unrestrained in every practice which is specifically forbidden to employers." And, third, it provided a "political" labor board "powers which it has not considered safe to entrust to any court in the land." Under the Wagner Act, Falk believed, the control of Allis-Chalmers and other firms would devolve on workers, their organizations, or a politically appointed labor board.[40]

In December 1935, the Allis-Chalmers union leaders secured a charter for Federal Labor Union (FLU) Local 20136, for the organization of production workers who did not fit into one of the AFL craft groups. In the summer of 1936, disheartened with the stalled growth of AFL craft unions, Christoffel and others decided to build an industrial union out of the shell of the FLU. If Christoffel and other left unionists worked with Dennis and other Wisconsin Communist labor leaders, they most likely cooperated in planning to use the small FLU as a vehicle for industrial unionism. Allis-Chalmers officials later charged that Harold Christoffel devised a "clever plan . . . to destroy the Works Council and to undermine the AFL craft unions in the plant." They claimed that Christoffel and Dennis secretly met in the spring of 1936, "when it was decided a drive was to be made to organize an industrial union at Allis-Chalmers." The apparent tactic was to amalgamate the skilled craft unions into one large industrial union. On April 20, the union works council delegates proposed a resolution urging "all employes to attend an AFL mass meeting for Allis-Chalmers employes." Two days later, a special works council meeting "vigorously debated" and "narrowly defeated" the unionists' proposal. Gradually, a "rift" developed between the more militant trade unionists and the more conservative workers on the plantwide representational body. The Allis-Chalmers unionists initiated a more concerted effort to organize along industrial lines. By the late summer and fall of 1936, the small federal local began serving as the mechanism for the eventual emergence of industrial unionism.[41]

In late July 1936, two Milwaukee AFL leaders, the FTC's Jacob Friedrick and the IAM's Otto Jirikowic, fearing Communist-inspired industrial unionism, inaugurated another round of craft union negotiations for an AFL contract. Although Allis-Chalmers president Babb cautiously avoided any genuine concessions, the independent Allis-Chalmers unionists deeply resented the outside AFL negotiators. A few weeks later, they devised their own plan to amalgamate and to coordinate the various Allis-Chalmers AFL union activities. If unionism was to survive, they believed, union interest had to be revived among all Allis-Chalmers workers.[42]

On August 18, two Allis-Chalmers IBEW leaders, Christoffel and Blunk, called a mass membership meeting of the "Allis-Chalmers A. F. of L." The purpose of the meeting, Christoffel said, was "to enable all Allis-Chalmers A. F. of L. members and interested employees to get together and discuss their common problems." At the meeting, the plant bargaining committee reported on shop grievances and negotiations with management. Although no formal contract existed, the union committees negotiated with their foremen, supervisors, and managers. Moreover, union shop stewards for the electrical, foundry, machine shop, and maintenance workers reported on the status of grievances in their shops and departments. Finally, Christoffel announced that Allis-Chalmers AFL leaders had discussed the form of union organization. "As an outgrowth of this meeting," he continued, "it was recommended that steps be taken to organize the unorganized workers into the Federal Union on an industrial basis and that the organized A. F. of L. men at Allis-Chalmers simply register with the Federal Union so that it can act as one body." In effect, Christoffel publicly urged all Allis-Chalmers workers and also AFL members to join the FLU.[43]

Similar to the IBEW strategy of union "registrants," this amalgamation of craft and production workers facilitated the reorganization of Allis-Chalmers craft unions and allowed the effective coordination of all union activities in the West Allis shops. It was the first concrete step toward industrial organization. In language that recalled the old IWW, Christoffel said, "many men were not interested in the A. F. of L. on a craft basis [and] have long been interested in the 'one big industrial union' idea, and as the plan suggested takes care of craft unions, whole hearted support was expected." The AFL members and others "unanimously" endorsed the Christoffel recommendation. Christoffel chaired the subsequent FLU meetings, where the Allis-Chalmers workers moved more decisively toward industrial unionism and confrontation with the venerable Milwaukee AFL. At one meeting, Otto Jirikowic, the Milwaukee IAM business agent, even spoke on "the need for workers to organize into unions." Then, apparently to affront the AFL speaker, the industrial unionists announced an October "Open Federal Union Mass Meeting" at the large South Side Armory.[44]

At the FLU meeting, the Allis-Chalmers AFL members abandoned their craft unions and enrolled en masse in FLU 20136. The meeting's minutes reported: "all those signed up and those transferring are to be initiated, and the Federal Union [was] established on an Industrial basis." Instead of an AFL stalwart such as Jirikowic, the guest speaker was Emil Costello, a Left leader of the Wisconsin Provisional CIO Committee. The rebellious workers had finally established an industrial union for all Allis-Chalmers workers. Also, the meeting's minutes dropped the heading Allis-Chalmers AFL and added instead Allis-Chalmers Federal Union. After shop steward reports, the Federal Union conducted a mass initiation for new FLU members and for former Allis-Chalmers craft union members. "From the spirit shown," the minutes reported, "it was evident that all of the organized as well as the unorganized men were ready to back the Federal Union and thereby form a solid Industrial Union." From this point on, the politics of Milwaukee and Allis-Chalmers labor became increasingly byzantine as AFL leaders, CIO leaders, and Allis-Chalmers workers all vied for control of the largest industrial plant in Wisconsin.[45]

According to the *ACWU News*, "From October, 1936, until January, 1937, the Federal union grew until it had over 2,000 members." To AFL leaders, who had invested so much time, energy, and resources in the organization of the West Allis plant, the Allis-Chalmers union leaders and rank-and-file workers had betrayed AFL assistance and traditions. After the IMU protested to AFL president William Green about the FLU enrolling skilled molders, other national AFL leaders added their voices against FLU enrollment of skilled workers. At the October FLU meeting, Christoffel challenged the AFL and told FLU members: "the Federal Union does not in any sense force men to join its ranks. The Union is simply an organization of men for the purpose of collective bargaining. Through constructive organization men can better their position which in turn betters society. The men in the Federal Union simply urge their fellow workers to join with them in their struggle to make the world a better place for people to live." Despite AFL objections, Christoffel strongly defended the organization of Allis-Chalmers workers into one big industrial union. For a time, the rebel FLU leader deferred making a formal response to AFL secretary Frank Morrison. In November, Jirikowic sent another protest about Christoffel's actions to the IAM president. "If this outfit," the Milwaukee IAM leader wrote, "is to continue under a federal labor union, I feel it is not much for us to do in the line of organizing and I believe that some pressure could be put on this group to have these people cease organizing craftsmen under a federal labor union charter."[46]

Allis-Chalmers officials, as well as conservative unionists, apparently had good reason to fear the emergent FLU. A union button campaign saw Allis-Chalmers workers boldly and publicly display their prounion sympathies. At a membership meeting, Christoffel emphasized the importance of wearing union buttons: "workers in the shop are measuring the Union's strength by the number of men and women they see with Union buttons. Buttons should be worn in plain sight, and if lost should be replaced at once." Antiunion rumors began to circulate through Allis-Chalmers shops and departments so, by displaying their union badges, the industrial unionists publicly asserted union identity. As the FLU membership grew, the stakes became higher, and the struggle for Allis-Chalmers became more intense.[47]

In December, Milwaukee AFL leaders more clearly recognized the significant loss of the plant. In a letter to the IAM president, Jirikowic criticized the 2,200-member FLU that paid FTC per capita dues only for the original seventeen members. He decried the "rampant" rumors about the FLU's possible CIO affiliation and alluded to the Communist domination of the Allis-Chalmers workers' organization. Referring to the FLU letter about Allis-Chalmers's union reorganization to President Babb, Jirikowic directed the IAM president to "the term used 'have in a sense been reorganized' and also . . . 'internal organizational change.' " These phrases, the Milwaukee IAM leader wrote, were obvious indications of the Communist orientation of the FLU leaders. "Such language," Jirikowic concluded, "is very familiar in communist circles."[48]

In January 1937, FLU 20136 held its first election of union officers. The elected leaders would continue to guide the Allis-Chalmers campaign for industrial unionism: Harold Christoffel, president; Frank Bolka, vice president; Julius Blunk, financial secretary; Fred McStroul, recording secretary; and Clarence Charbonneau, treasurer. They represented a cross section of the principal Allis-Chalmers union groups and departments, the electrical workers, machinists, and foundry workers. They were also a mix of shop veterans and young workers, both skilled and unskilled. The new FLU Executive Board more broadly represented workers from the different shops and departments in the West Allis plant. At this time, the FLU members voted that "the Executive Board take steps for the complete organization of the Allis-Chalmers Co."[49]

On consolidating his leadership position, Christoffel finally and aggressively responded to the AFL secretary-treasurer regarding the AFL's complaints about the FLU recruitment of skilled molders. In his letter, Christoffel frankly admitted that the FLU took them in and that FLU also enrolled former members of the electrical workers, machinists, boilermakers, patternmakers, and other crafts. "We feel fortunate," he told the AFL leader, "that these men who have seen fit to sever their connection with these unions have been kept in the A. F. of L. through the medium of the Federal Union." In his defense of industrial unionism, Christoffel directly challenged the AFL's venerated craft principles.[50]

Furthermore, Christoffel offered an extensive justification for accepting members from the craft unions. "The workers of Allis-Chalmers," he wrote, "have had a sad history." In 1906 and in 1916, the molders and machinists suffered disastrous defeats. With the passage of NIRA, they "tried to overcome this by organizing all the various craft groups in their respective unions. This activity of the past few years has been very ineffective and as time went on the little that was accomplished was threatened with failure." In addition, Christoffel stressed the current success of industrial organization and the recent failure of the Milwaukee craft organization: "Their experience has taught the Allis-Chalmers workers that the only way to organize the plant of some seven thousand workers including a dozen or more crafts, was by forming one union in the plant. To carry out this work with the assistance of the Milwaukee Federated Trades Council and the Wisconsin Federation of Labor was sought but was not received." Then, he concluded, "The men are determined to build a union at Allis-Chalmers. They have tried the crafts and failed. Now they will either build a solid union at Allis-Chalmers or give up all." Since numbers and money talked, he enclosed a copy of the FLU financial secretary's report and a check to cover the AFL's per capita tax and initiation fees.[51]

Finally, Christoffel registered a formal complaint with the AFL and asserted the autonomy and independence of the Allis-Chalmers local union. He reported hearing that AFL organizer Paul Smith had approached Allis-Chalmers officials as a representative of FLU 20136. "We hope that this is not true," Christoffel wrote, "for we are strongly opposed to have any official contact management without first contacting our organization." In other words, Christoffel informed the AFL that no one would represent Allis-Chalmers workers except their own union and leaders. The AFL tradition of outside business agent representation would no longer hold in the West Allis plant. From the beginning, then, the fledgling industrial union maintained its independence from AFL leadership.[52]

In February, the struggle between the federal union and the local and national AFL organizations reached a climax. At the time, the FLU attempted to gain its full representation on the Milwaukee FTC. Against the backdrop of continued Milwaukee worker organization, mainly into industrial unions, of growing hostility to industrial unions within the AFL, and of tensions between the Allis-Chalmers industrial and craft unionists, the delegates for over 2,000 Allis-Chalmers FLU members would have drastically upset the balance of union power on the Milwaukee AFL council. In fact, AFL attorney Joseph Padway claimed that the Allis-Chalmers FLU leaders planned "to oust the existing [FTC] officers on the night of the election by an overwhelming influx of delegates from the organization." In the wake of vigorous Milwaukee CIO campaigns, his observations made sense: The Allis-Chalmers delegates along with others in or sympathetic to the CIO would have the numerical strength to control the AFL trades council.[53]

Shortly after FLU 20136 sent its per capita tax to the Milwaukee FTC, its leaders appointed ten delegates to the Milwaukee AFL council on the basis of its claim of 2,006 members. When the Allis-Chalmers union members petitioned for their representation on the Milwaukee labor council, IMU and IBEW leaders protested the seating of those who came from a union that raided their craft members. Consequently, the FTC seated only three Allis-Chalmers delegates, based on thirty-nine FLU members "as representatives of unskilled labor," then referred the matter to the AFL for further investigation. At the subsequent FTC meeting, a stormy discussion pitted Milwaukee industrial unionists against craft unionists on the question of seating the full Allis-Chalmers delegation. According to Allis-Chalmers union leaders, "AFL leaders threw cold water on the Allis-Chalmers union." The FTC voted not to seat the Allis-Chalmers delegates until an AFL investigation. A bitter power struggle was under way, and both sides began to shore up their positions.[54]

Just before the contentious FTC meeting, the Allis-Chalmers unionists had prepared for a decisive break with the AFL. They seemed committed to the AFL until late February, notwithstanding persistent rumors about their joining the CIO. At this time, FLU leaders recommended that the shop "stewards take up the sentiment of the workers in regard to C.I.O. affiliation and to be brought up at the mass [membership] meeting." The shop stewards also selected a committee of five to study the possibility of such affiliation. Both the shop stewards and this committee ultimately recommended CIO affiliation. Then, the FLU membership referred the question to its executive board. The whole matter required extreme caution. The rebellion of a relatively small local union against the formidable AFL demanded time, energy, and legal preparation.[55]

As the important FTC meeting approached, the FLU leaders obviously expected major problems. In late February, the executive board started a series of complicated legal maneuvers to save and retain the FLU's financial and other resources. It passed a resolution which gave $5,000 in trust to three FLU members—Edward Collins, Joseph Lewis, and William Schmelling. The money was (1) to disseminate information on the principles of unionism and labor history; (2) to assist or encourage the formation of unions among Allis-Chalmers workers; and (3) to establish a school for teaching labor problems. If these were impossible, the three persons were "given the money as individuals" in order to accomplish anything "lawfully necessary for the purpose of elevating the moral, intellectual, social, and economic conditions of workers of the Allis-Chalmers Manufacturing Company" and "to spread the doctrine of unionism among said employees." A second board resolution transferred "any and all property, records, equipment, claims of any nature, kind or description now in the possession of Federal Labor Union No. 20136" to the three FLU trustees. Two days later, the FLU membership unanimously endorsed the executive board's action.[56]

While the Milwaukee AFL leaders tried to negotiate an Allis-Chalmers craft union contract, the industrial union leaders began to work out plans for CIO affiliation. Throughout the nation, the UAW's monumental sit-down struggle with General Motors had inspired the admiration and respect of American labor in the winter of 1936–1937. In February, two dramatic events very likely influenced the attitudes of Milwaukee and Allis-Chalmers workers toward the UAW. New Wisconsin UAW locals won major victories against hostile, antiunion corporations in the nearby cities of Janesville and Racine. In Janesville, General Motors workers, who had participated in the national UAW sit-down strikes, had recently won their strike for union recognition and returned to their jobs. In Racine, after a bitter 106-day strike, J. I. Case workers obtained the first Wisconsin UAW agreement with the large agricultural equipment firm. The Racine UAW local became the exclusive bargaining agent for all Case workers. Clearly, the UAW was on a roll: it had taken on two of the larger Wisconsin firms and won.[57]

Such a new, robust union was the kind that Allis-Chalmers workers desired. At an early March executive board meeting, FLU leaders decided to contact Homer Martin, the UAW president, to address the membership meeting, prepare a leaflet for his speech, and obtain the services of an attorney for the final break with the AFL. Five days later, Christoffel directed the shop stewards "to inform the workers in their sections [of] the procedure of the business to be taken up at the Membership Meeting to be held on Sunday March 14th at the Paradise Theatre." The executive board minutes noted: "quite a discussion on the C.I.O. question." At the next executive board meeting, the union leaders acted to protect the remaining union funds. The FLU officers each received $1,000 and signed an agreement to perform "services for the purpose of spreading and teaching the principles of unionism, and generally perform services in the elevation and improvement of the moral, intellectual, social, and economic condition of the Workers." The executive board also recommended a resolution for membership adoption, which stated that the formation of an Allis-Chalmers UAW local met the FLU's moral, intellectual, social, and economic criteria and which empowered the officers to transfer FLU funds and property to the UAW.[58]

Then Christoffel wrote to thank UAW president Homer Martin for accepting the invitation to speak at the next membership meeting. In this letter, he also briefly outlined the events leading to the Allis-Chalmers drift toward CIO unionism and his rationale for switching to the UAW. "While our Federal Union has been chartered for over a year," Christoffel wrote, and really active "only during the last three to four months," it became a major "factor in the plant." The "men in the various craft unions," he added "decided, almost to a man, that they would get nowhere unless they organized on an industrial basis." The General Motors sit-down strikes obviously inspired "the general 'C.I.O.' feeling" among Allis-Chalmers workers. "There is little doubt," Christoffel optimistically noted, "that the membership will indorse [sic] this recommendation unanimously." Concluding on the same bullish note, he requested that Martin bring "at least a few thousand application blanks, dues receipts, shop buttons, and whatever else you think we will need for an immediate start."[59]

The March 14 FLU membership meeting attracted from fifteen hundred to two thousand of the then approximately three thousand union members to the West Allis Paradise Theatre. Homer Martin was unable to attend, and Ed Hall, a UAW vice president from the Milwaukee Seaman Body plant, substituted as the main speaker. Before the meeting, Hall, Leo Kryczki, a Milwaukee CIO leader, Emil Costello, a state CIO leader and assemblyman, and George Kiebler, a UAW regional leader, advised the Allis-Chalmers FLU executive board on procedures for affiliation with the UAW and for contract negotiations with management. The assembled federal union members unanimously endorsed resolutions to affiliate with the UAW-CIO and to nominate and elect the FLU officers and committeemen to similar posts in the new UAW local. A new UAW bargaining committee presented and the membership accepted a resolution to "take steps to demand a closed shop, wage increase, better shop conditions, etc." Ed Hall gave a speech "on the activities of the Auto unions and told the membership that they should never sit back until they had been given sole bargaining for the Allis-Chalmers workers." Finally, Costello welcomed the new UAW members on their vote to join the CIO. A few weeks later, the Allis-Chalmers workers received their charter as UAW Local 248. As testimony to the independence of the local union and its leaders, they called themselves the Allis-Chalmers Workers Union, UAW Local 248.[60]

Although Milwaukee AFL leaders continued to hope for a craft union contract, Allis-Chalmers officials prudently opted for recognition of the powerful new Allis-Chalmers UAW local. In their view, several factors favored the firm's recognition of the militant UAW rather than the more cautious and conservative AFL. Most important was the power of numbers. If union membership had grown rapidly with the formation of the federal industrial union, it positively soared with the shift to the UAW-CIO. In May 1937, Julius Blunk, the beleaguered Local 248 financial secretary, apologized to George Addes about the delayed payment of the UAW per capita tax. Rapid union growth and fifty days of collective bargaining with Allis-Chalmers officials wore down the veteran electrical worker. Blunk, who kept the union's records, reported that the FLU had 2,090 Allis-Chalmers workers at the time of UAW affiliation and that the UAW local had 7,414 Allis-Chalmers workers by four months later. This constituted an overwhelming majority of the West Allis workers.[61]

Equally important was the threatened militancy of the now-united Allis-Chalmers workers. At a July NLRB hearing on union representation for the plant, AFL attorneys claimed that during contract negotiations the new UAW local threatened departmental sit-downs in the West Allis plant. In the middle of contract negotiations, Harold Story gave a speech to a group of young economics students. His topic, "Sit-Down Strike—a Symptom," indicated a pressing matter that his firm confronted. He began with a complaint against the drive for worker organization and the worker militancy expressed in " 'unpeaceful' [sic] picketing" in recent years. He then condemned the sit-down strike. This new union tactic was "the symptom of a fatal disease—the cancer of anarchy which without the proper use of the x-ray of reason, will inevitably cause the death of democracy and the decomposing growth of a governmental 'ism.' " Story blamed the union disease both on employers who failed to recognize the right of collective bargaining and on unions that sought the "political and financial power of larger memberships." These two things, he concluded, resulted in "an abnormal and unhealthy growth of unionism—induced almost by governmental fiat."[62]

On April 12, the sit-down contagion spread to Milwaukee with a UAW strike at the recently organized Seaman Body plant. On the same day, "governmental fiat" gained greater force when the Supreme Court upheld the constitutionality of the Wagner Act, a decision that dashed the hopes of open shop employers who had expected "labor's Magna Carta" to follow the fate of the NIRA. Two days later, the Wisconsin governor signed a state labor relations law, Wisconsin's "Little Wagner act," which added state support to the organization of workers and strictly regulated corporate representation plans. Allis-Chalmers officials soon disbanded the West Allis Works Council and moved to negotiate with UAW Local 248.[63]

The creation of UAW Local 248 ended a bitter four-year union struggle in the West Allis plant. During this struggle, different groups—workers and managers, unionists and nonunionists, and industrial unionists and craft unionists—all had fought to win the hearts and minds of a majority of Allis-Chalmers workers. Ultimately, the proponents of industrial unionism won, because workers took stock of the altered character of their working conditions, the antiunion policies of the large open shop employer, and the futility of divisive craft organization. The industrial unionists won because the CIO was a qualitatively different form of unionism. The AFL was accommodating toward management; the CIO was combative. The AFL recommended negotiation; the CIO threatened strike. And the AFL appointed business agents to represent workers; the CIO elected shop stewards. But although the CIO unionists won the initial battle, more struggles awaited their industrial union campaign to establish social and economic democracy at the workplace.

# 4

## CONSOLIDATING THE UNION: MANAGEMENT OPPOSITION AND LABOR'S CIVIL WAR, 1937–1941

Once established, the new Allis-Chalmers UAW local faced two formidable obstacles—continuing management opposition to unions and civil war between industrial and craft unionists. First, although Allis-Chalmers officials recognized the new realities of political and economic power, they never completely abandoned their original open shop policies. The New Deal and the almost total union organization forced management to recognize and to negotiate with the robust young UAW local. The production-minded managers in the shop wanted some accommodation with the unionized workers; but the profit-minded officials in the front office wanted to push back the advance of aggressive industrial unionism. In the mid-1930s, Harold Story, who represented the latter, assumed the leading role in the development of Allis-Chalmers labor policy. He developed a variety of techniques to weaken CIO strength at the workplace.

Second, the Milwaukee AFL old guard resented the young Turks' betrayal of craft principles. A social matrix of skill and ethnicity divided craft from industrial unionists in the West Allis shops. The more skilled workers were often older American-born or Americanized German workers who produced the big stuff. Robert Buse, a self-taught machinist who led Local 248 in the 1940s, recalled the attitude of the "higher crust of workers" toward the less skilled. He remembered, "They thought that they were better than the rest of the guys and a notch above them. . . . They held the other guys out [of the machinists' union]." The haughty and prideful social conservatives looked down on the younger and less skilled production workers, who often had southern and eastern European roots. The skilled workers formed the social basis for opposition to the more militant and confrontational CIO unionism. They supported Homer Martin in the UAW, the several "independent" unions, or the AFL in the West Allis shops.[1]

In the 1930s, national and state labor legislation dramatically recast the legal framework for American unionism. In 1933, the National Industrial Recovery Act first attempted to define labor's right to organize; in 1935, the National Labor Relations Act—the famous Wagner Act—actually defined and protected it. The national mood for labor reform prompted states around the nation to supplement federal protection with state legislation. In Wisconsin, Harold Story, the counsel for the state's largest firm, played an increasingly prominent role on the state legislative stage.

In early 1935, while Robert F. Wagner's labor relations bill made its way through Congress, the Wisconsin State Federation of Labor (WSFL) sponsored a similar bill in the Wisconsin Assembly. When the assembly conducted hearings in June 1935, Story led the corporate opposition, emphasizing his concerns about the growing Communist menace in American unions. "There is," the Allis-Chalmers attorney said, "a radical fringe in unionism that is comparable to the chiseling fringe in industry. We fear that this would make unionism a dominating force and would be playing into the hands of Communists." In a sophisticated effort to weaken the proposed law, Story and other industrial leaders supported it, but with reservations, while recommending an unfair union practices section to undermine union power. In the end, the bill passed in the assembly but was narrowly rejected in the senate.[2]

Two years later, the WSFL sponsored labor legislation to apply the basic principles of the Wagner Act to Wisconsin. Lloyd Garrison, a University of Wisconsin law professor, drafted the bill. In the winter and spring of 1937, a joint committee of the state legislature conducted hearings on the proposed legislation. Once again, Harold Story led the employer offensive against it. In the midst of Milwaukee labor's turmoil over industrial unionism, his legislative testimony compared the current "labor disturbances" to a recent flood, the "unleashed, uncontrollable forces of . . . the raging Ohio River." Although he again endorsed the basic principle of labor legislation, Story foresaw the "definite probability that the union movement will create results even more destructive than the Ohio River in its present rampancy unless labor leaders guide the forces of unionism constructively and peaceably."[3]

As leader of employer opposition, Story desired to limit labor's power, to "remodel" the bill "here and add to it there" with specific amendments. He proposed a definition of "collective bargaining" that included the phrase, "a genuinely mutual effort to reach an agreement"—a weakening of the concept of "majority rule" to protect the rights of skilled workers—and a list of "unfair" labor practices, including such activities as coercion or intimidation, and sit-down strikes. He also asked for representation only for "bona fide," or financially audited, labor organizations. Story's defense of minority union groups was in blatant support of Allis-Chalmers interests. For this same reason, he catered to the AFL desire to protect the "rights of skilled workers." In safeguarding a minority voice for skilled workers, Story's clever strategy was further to weaken a socially divided Allis-Chalmers work force.[4]

Nonetheless, despite the employer reservations and minor amendments to the original bill, Wisconsin legislators could not ignore the resurgent state labor movement. Both the assembly and senate passed and Governor Philip LaFollette signed Wisconsin's Little Wagner act in April 1937. At the time, LaFollette proclaimed that the new labor law was "the Declaration of Independence of Labor." While Wisconsin legislation applied the main features of national measures to intrastate disputes, it also contained tougher provisions against management, especially an outright ban on company unions and a more stringent list of employers' unfair labor practices. The new law also created a three-member Wisconsin Labor Relations Board (WLRB) that determined the bargaining agent, listed labor unions, offered mediation services, and investigated unfair practices. The basic thrust of the new Wisconsin law was to protect and defend worker rights and organizations. Story lost the legislative fight, but he would return.[5]

With a legal framework of federal and state protection for unionism and collective bargaining, UAW Local 248 swiftly moved from plant organization to collective negotiations. Immediately after the March 1937 vote for UAW affiliation, Local 248 members passed an ambitious motion for the bargaining committee to "take steps to demand a closed shop, wage increase, better shop conditions, etc." A national UAW leader cautioned the new UAW members "that they should never rest until they have been given collective bargaining rights for the Allis-Chalmers workers." On the same day, the Local 248 executive board met to work out plans for the forthcoming negotiations. It was a brainstorming session with several state and local UAW and CIO leaders. UAW vice president Hall suggested a special meeting of officers, executive board members, bargaining committee members, and shop stewards to develop contract proposals on wages, hours, seniority rights, and other plant issues. The inclusion of shop stewards guaranteed union sensitivity to rank-and-file concerns. Through the negotiations, the shop stewards actively participated in the collective bargaining process. When negotiations stalled, they threatened sit-down strikes in the tractor shops.[6]

At Allis-Chalmers, formal collective bargaining began on April 3, when union attorneys first presented the list of union demands to management officials. During the negotiations, a WLRB mediator reported that the principal union demands were minimum wage rates and exclusive bargaining rights. In addition, the local demanded the "right to say who shall and shall not join the Union." Plant officials were reluctant to accept this last demand, which could have led to the unionization of shop supervisors. "The company," the mediator wrote, "interprets the demand for the inclusion of foremen as an attempt on the part of the Union to take over the management of the company." To further complicate matters, the AFL craft unions refused to allow the UAW-CIO to bargain for their members. "All AFL unions," the mediator noted, "are in conflict with the United Automobile Workers, who are asking that the company recognize them as sole bargaining agents." But he reported that, despite the AFL protest, the CIO union was the major organized force in the plant. "The C.I.O.," he observed, "now has a clear majority of all employes."[7]

At a large May union meeting that attracted 7,500 Allis-Chalmers workers, Harold Christoffel appealed for rank-and-file unity and support in the contract negotiations: "the Bargaining Committee is helpless without the full strength of the organization in back of them." A unanimous resolution empowered the bargaining committee to accept an amended agreement, to sign a contract if its final provisions proved satisfactory, "to call departmental stoppages if the proposals were not satisfactorily met," and "to call a strike vote to be conducted by an impartial governmental agency."[8]

The demonstration of union solidarity and the threats of economic force prompted real negotiations and worked to the union's advantage. On May 28, Harold Christoffel and Max Babb signed the first agreement between UAW Local 248 and the Allis-Chalmers Manufacturing Company. According to the union president, the "power of organization" forced management to accept a union contract. When asked about the effect of the large union meeting, Story replied that it had "some psychological significance. We were in a period of collective bargaining where the element of psychology, and poker playing, all the rest of it entered the picture." He also described the crucial elements of the negotiating sessions: One is "what your prospects are from the profit side. Another is the temper of the people, and not in your plant, but in the country; a restiveness, the strike fever if you will." This was an obvious reference to the nationwide outbreak of UAW's sit-down strikes at the General Motors and Chrysler plants.[9]

The first collective agreement was modest. It codified some of the arrangements in the earlier Allis-Chalmers statements of policy. The union accepted the existing practices for the length of the work day and the work week and for overtime. Management agreed to furnish each employee with information on the piecework or standard time rates. For the first time, however, the union gained a formal procedure for layoff, rehiring, and transfer of workers. A seniority committee would make a comprehensive plant survey of the seniority of hourly workers, would develop departmental seniority lists, and would establish plant rules for layoff, dismissal, and transfer. The agreement contained provisions against strikes and lockouts. The union offered to aid "in the enforcement of the reasonable discipline" of its membership. The latter hinted at the possibility of an accommodative labor-management relationship.[10]

The most intractable issue was union security. Allis-Chalmers officials refused to budge on the union demand for a closed or union shop. They made only modest concessions on union security and remained firm in their open shop position. "The Company," the agreement noted, "recognizes and will not interfere with the right of its employes to become members of the Union." It would "not aid, promote, or finance any labor group or organization . . . for the purpose of undermining the union." Neither the union nor its members would "intimidate or coerce employes, or solicit membership on Company premises, or conduct on Company premises any activity other than that of collective bargaining and handling of grievances." The question of exclusive bargaining rights was left to the decision of the National Labor Relations Board (NLRB), whose decision would be incorporated into the agreement. Although the union did not obtain the desired closed or union shop, management now provided it with a modest assurance of union security.[11]

In July 1937, an NLRB panel visited Milwaukee for hearings on Allis-Chalmers. It was a major case, establishing a national precedent on minority union rights in an organized plant. At these hearings, the AFL forcefully argued for the representation of craft unions at Allis-Chalmers. Eventually, the NLRB ruled on the structure of the plant and the nature of the Allis-Chalmers bargaining unit. It decided to conduct separate elections among four groups of workers—three small craft groups (the technical engineers and draftsmen, the maintenance electricians, and the firemen and oilers), and a large industrial group, the production workers. The AFL unsuccessfully protested the NLRB decision to include both skilled and semiskilled workers with the production workers. In January 1938, the NLRB conducted representation elections for the West Allis plant. The UAW local and AFL craft unions appeared on the ballot for all groups. UAW Local 248 won a huge majority among the production workers, although the three small craft groups voted for independent or AFL unions.[12]

Although the AFL maintained the principle of the integrity of crafts, the UAW controlled the West Allis shops with its decisive victory among the more than 8,400 production workers. In the NLRB election, the young CIO union received 72.3 percent of the total eligible voters and 78.4 percent of the actual ballots cast. Still, the victorious UAW local had cause for some concern, since 1,645 workers voted against it. The total of 1,675 void, blank, and anti-UAW ballots, not to mention the 653 (7.8 percent) workers who were indifferent to the election, represented sizable opposition. Some were conservative skilled craftsmen who opposed the more militant, confrontational stance of the CIO union. Others were antiunion, who opposed even the conservative AFL. In the future, these dissident and dissatisfied workers would form a the nucleus of a disruptive element in Local 248 internal politics and in the plant.[13]

Nonetheless, the CIO union rightfully claimed a "decided victory" for Allis-Chalmers workers. The NLRB had validated its existence, and the election results demonstrated a strong desire for industrial unionism. "The significance of Local 248's victory is nationwide," the *ACWU News* proclaimed, "but to our local it means that no other organization, whatever it may be, can legally bargain for the 8,400 production workers. We have achieved sole bargaining rights." Given the long Allis-Chalmers open shop tradition, the young and militant industrial union could boast a substantial achievement.[14]

However, the militant minority needed to widen the base of CIO activists and to nourish a worker commitment to CIO unionism. An important feature of their industrial unionism became the creation of social, cultural, and other institutions for expressing and maintaining union and CIO solidarity. Initially, these included educational classes for shop leaders and rank-and-file workers, union dances and divisional parties, a union flying squadron, and a women's auxiliary. Later, the union added a sports program to compete with the management program, a legislative committee to lobby state government officials, and a fair employment practices committee to address the concerns of African American workers. The objectives of these programs and activities were to instruct workers in the principles of CIO unionism, strengthen worker commitment to it, and defend it against more conservative opponents.

Compared to similar union activities today, the extent of membership participation was staggering. For example, after UAW Local 248 won the 1938 NLRB election, Harold Christoffel announced a "victory dance." The union celebration was a dramatic expression of worker consciousness and union solidarity. The UAW local rented the large Milwaukee auditorium for its "victory celebration, dance, and floor show." Admission was free for paid-up union members and their spouses or girlfriends, who all received tickets from shop stewards or committeemen. This ensured the payment of union dues and connected rank-and-file workers to their shop leaders. A prominent Milwaukee orchestra, Heinie and his Grenadiers, and "several good floor shows" provided entertainment, and the union sold beer at five cents a glass. Approximately 15,000 persons attended what the *CIO News* called "one of the largest parties ever in Milwaukee."[15]

Several months later, UAW Local 248 held a similar social affair to celebrate its second contract with Allis-Chalmers. Held in early June, the Local 248 Victory Dance attracted thousands of rank-and-file union members. Once again, the stewards and committeemen passed out free tickets for all union members in good standing. As the *CIO News* reported: "12,000 strutted their stuff" at the grand affair in the Milwaukee auditorium. This time three prominent orchestras, Jackie Heller, Russ Roland, and Seppl Keilhoefer, entertained the unionists and their guests. The union struggle, then, centered not only on pure and simple economic gains but also involved alternative social and cultural activities that would cultivate the loyalty of its members.[16]

The Local 248 flying squadron was another institutional expression of worker consciousness and union solidarity. It was the militant union vanguard in the bitter campaign against management and against other area antiunion employers. Originally, UAW locals established flying squadrons to supply foot soldiers for picket lines and other strike support in the massive wave of UAW sit-down strikes. Large and burly activists, they usually served as picket captains during Allis-Chalmers strikes or augmented the number of pickets during other CIO strikes. In February 1938, the local's executive board approved a resolution "to recommend to Local 248 that the local organize and maintain a 'Flying Squadron' and further that Local 248 purchase appropriately marked hats to be worn by members of the 'Flying Squadron.' " The membership approved.[17]

Finally, UAW Local 248 established the Women's Auxiliary for the wives and girlfriends of unionists. At an April 1938 shop stewards meeting, Harold Christoffel spoke about the need to organize the union members' spouses and to strengthen the Local 248 Ladies Auxiliary, "especially, at this time, with negotiations going on, so that the wives will stand by their men in whatever action they may take." The union leadership perceived these women, like the flying squadron, as an important weapon in a possible Allis-Chalmers strike. Without their active support, a strike could end in defeat and demoralization.[18]

The formation of the Committee for Industrial Organization in 1935 and later the Congress of Industrial Organizations (CIO) in 1938 resulted in a war between industrial and craft unionists. After half-hearted efforts at breaching the gap between the AFL and CIO failed, the deep divisions that so rocked America's labor movement resumed as a bitter struggle between the two contrasting visions of American unionism. People who had formerly worked closely in the effort to build unions soon became enemies in a war for union membership. All in all, the intense competition aided the labor movement since both the AFL and CIO grew, and union membership more than doubled in the 1930s.[19]

Conservative-radical factionalism broke out within the UAW in 1937 as a contest between UAW president Homer Martin and members of the UAW Executive Board. The UAW at that time, Walter Galenson observed, "resembled nothing so much as a feudal kingdom. Martin, the principal leader sat on an uneasy throne, surrounded by semi–independent and self-sufficient lords whose allegiance to him was minimal and whose efforts to unseat him were tempered only by the fear of splitting the organization and leaving it at the mercy of outside foes." A former Baptist preacher, Martin rose to the UAW presidency through his oratorical skills. The rank-and-file militancy of the GM sit-down strikes appalled him, for he had an essentially conservative social outlook.[20]

Often impetuous, lacking administrative skills, Martin ruled over a divided union kingdom that split into the Progressive and the Unity caucuses. The Progressive caucus included Martin and his forces; the Unity group his opponents, a majority of the UAW officers and executive board members. After months of factional squabbling, Martin presented a twenty-point program that offered a short-lived truce. However, when the UAW executive board criticized his one-sided proposal, Martin became angry, and factional differences increased. His suspension of four UAW vice presidents and the secretary-treasurer widened the rift. Protesting the suspensions, six executive board members, including future UAW president Walter Reuther, "walked out of the board [meeting] and refused to attend any further meetings." Martin eventually expelled three executive board members. The national CIO tried unsuccessfully to bridge the gap between the two factions.[21]

The UAW civil war reached the UAW locals through 1938 and 1939, as Martin supporters and executive board supporters battled each other for control of the numerous UAW locals around the nation. Only after UAW members learned of Martin's attempt to negotiate a "sweetheart" deal with Ford's notorious Harry Bennett did membership support swing to the Unity caucus. In 1939, the two UAW factions formalized the breach and called separate conventions, in Detroit and in Cleveland. At the Detroit convention, the Martin group rejoined the AFL. Now two autoworker unions—the UAW-CIO and the UAW-AFL—competed for members in the nation's auto plants.[22]

Several fundamental issues were the basis of the UAW split—the degree of autonomy of the local unions from the international organization, the nature of authority within the labor organization (top-down vs. rank-and-file authority), the character of unionism (cautious vs. militant unionism), and the tolerance for political groups, especially the Communist Party, within the UAW. Martin and his followers favored more power for the international union, top-down authority, and conservative unionism. In addition, they were staunchly anti-Communist.

The UAW factional struggles reverberated in local unions throughout the nation. In its early years, the non-Detroit locals were a powerful force within the UAW, and UAW Local 248 was one of the larger of these. Moreover, its left leaders opposed Martin's social and economic conservatism and financially supported the suspended executive board members and the anti-Martin Unity Caucus. Consequently, the Wisconsin Martin supporters worked to move the militant UAW local into the conservative camp.

George Kiebler, the former president of Seaman Body UAW Local 75, was a flamboyant and controversial UAW organizer and the principal Martin supporter in the Milwaukee area. In mid July 1938, Kiebler and several other conservative UAW and CIO unionists raided UAW Local 248 headquarters. Local 248 supporters charged: "a group of thugs and burglars calling themselves members of the CIO broke into the local office of Local 248 . . . and robbed the office grabbing all they could seize in their panic." During the raid, Kiebler quickly produced a letter from Martin appointing him administrator of the militant UAW local. Although twenty Martin "henchmen" participated in the raid, Local 248 leaders anticipated the attack and lost only unimportant files and $300 in cash. According to union supporters, the Martin raiders "manhandled the office girls and prevented them from calling help." Fred McStroul, the union recording secretary, claimed, "The girls' bodies bore black and blue bruises days after the robbery occurred." He also charged, "Kiebler's associates in the crime are men who have already been discredited in the labor movement."[23]

If Kiebler had the backing of the UAW international president,

Local 248 officers had the solid support of the rank-and-file Allis-Chalmers workers. Shortly after the raid, union members endorsed resolutions to protest the action and to protect the local union. Ed Hall, a suspended UAW vice president from Wisconsin, told local union members that he was "certain the membership has the utmost confidence in Harold Christoffel." The union rank and file expressed its "unanimous support" for the Local 248 officers, bargaining committee members, stewards, and committeemen. It warned Allis-Chalmers officials against recognizing anyone except the "duly elected" officers of the union. The union members then called on CIO president John L. Lewis to resolve the UAW factional dispute.[24]

Most important, the Local 248 members acted to protect the union's financial resources from the Milwaukee Martin supporters. They established an Allis-Chalmers Workers Trust Fund to control union financial assets during the factional dispute. They also empowered the trustees to donate up to $250 per week to the five suspended UAW officers "to assist them in their efforts to keep the International in the hands of their membership under democratic control."[25]

Nonetheless, Kiebler acted as Martin's administrator for UAW Local 248, installed a new set of Local 248 officers, and dismissed the executive board members. But since Christoffel and the other officers had rank-and-file support, Allis-Chalmers officials wisely refused to recognize Kiebler's authority over their workers. President Max Babb claimed that Allis-Chalmers workers themselves elected the Local 248 officers and chose UAW Local 248 as their bargaining agency.[26]

The embattled UAW local also took the offensive against Kiebler and other Martin supporters. Union lawyers applied for an injunction to restrain Kiebler from "interfering with the union." Eventually, a Milwaukee court issued an order restraining Kiebler from interfering with the local or representing Allis-Chalmers workers. Union and women's auxiliary members also picketed Kiebler's offices to disrupt dues collection and to discourage financial support for Martin. The Local 248 stewards and committeemen formally requested Allis-Chalmers officials to keep the five Kiebler-appointed union officers out of the West Allis plant. The Milwaukee UAW local members suspended the Kiebler-appointed officers and tried three for "disloyalty, disruption, and undermining the union." The UAW local's trial committee revealed that one "sabotaged" dues collection in 1936 and disrupted the state CIO convention in 1937. Two other Kiebler officers participated in anti-union activities since the AFL's first organization in 1935. They also conducted secret meetings, engaged in plots, and agitated against the union. The trial committee recommended the expulsion of the three from the UAW local.[27]

In late August 1938, Homer Martin attended a meeting at the Milwaukee Eagles Club to garner support from, and to explain the UAW split to, Minnesota, Illinois, and Wisconsin UAW members. He appealed to his supporters to purge the Communist leaders from UAW locals. Christoffel, leading a group of 350 anti-Martin UAW members, conducted "a siege of the hall and forced [the Martin] officials attending to run a gauntlet." Disparaging Kiebler's rank-and-file support, Christoffel told reporters: "In Wisconsin, Martin's agents have built a machine comprised of tanneries, tavern owners, beauty shop operators, building trades, cookie factories, and other plants with no connection to the auto industry."[28]

After months of factional strife, in early September CIO president John L. Lewis forced a peaceful settlement. The Lewis plan called for the reinstatement of the expelled executive board members and for CIO arbitration of the internal UAW dispute. Although Martin Red-baited his opponents, many of the larger UAW locals had refused to send their dues to Martin's office. Cut off from funds, Martin soon entered negotiations with CIO leaders. After nine days of talks, the two sides agreed to submit the issue of reinstatement of expelled officers to the CIO, establish a joint committee on UAW and CIO cooperation and dispute resolution, recognize the full autonomy of the UAW, and support disciplinary actions against violators of UAW policies and constitution. In Milwaukee, a majority of the UAW locals, including the large Allis-Chalmers and Seaman Body locals, backed the Lewis peace plan. They represented 65 percent of the Milwaukee UAW membership.[29]

In the middle of this UAW factional dispute, the Milwaukee Workers Industrial Organization (MWIO), an independent Allis-Chalmers union, emerged from the West Allis shops to complicate the internal politics of UAW Local 248. Organized in early August 1938, the independent group petitioned the WLRB for listing as a labor union in the West Allis plant. According to Thomas J. Bergen, the MWIO attorney, an "anonymous 'Workers' Committee,' composed of Local 248 members" announced the formation of the independent union that "had been secretly organized and represented a majority of the Allis-Chalmers employes opposed to both factions in the UAW." The MWIO grossly exaggerated its claim to represent 3,000 members. The reason for the new union, Bergen said, "was the widespread disgust at the plant with Communist sympathies of the present leaders of the UAWA." David Brann, a Milwaukee Martin representative, conferred with the MWIO leaders and agreed to fight the Communists and their sympathizers within Wisconsin UAW locals. Although some workers expressed their dissatisfaction with militant industrial unionism, the MWIO's characterization as an "industrial" union also indicated a deep dissatisfaction with AFL craft unionism even among conservative workers.[30]

The social backgrounds of the MWIO leaders were quite different from the CIO militants. They all had middle- or lower-middle-class social backgrounds and apparently suffered downward social mobility in the depression years. The president was an Allis-Chalmers electrician who had formerly been a salesman. The secretary, who had managed a fuel and ice company, worked as a coil winder. And Ralph Rehberg, a UAW Local 248 executive board member who organized for the MWIO in the tractor shop, also was a former salesman. He was a Catholic and sympathized with Father Charles Coughlin, the demagogic Detroit radio priest. Thomas Bergen, the MWIO attorney, added another Catholic dimension to the dissident union organization. In the early 1930s, he had worked as a clerk for the Knights of Columbus. With the Spanish Civil War and the charges of Communist persecution of Spain's Catholic church, American Catholic workers represented a growing force opposed to Communist unionists.[31]

In the UAW factional dispute, the MWIO rejected the militant Local 248 leaders and supported their suspension by Martin. Specifically, the dissident faction endorsed the suspensions because the union officers were "in sympathy with the Communist movement." The MWIO charged that they operated an undemocratic union machine, did not use secret ballots in union elections, and selectively distributed ballots to supporters. The MWIO opposed the suspended Local 248 leaders for "their sympathies, their incompetence, their minority leadership, and their control of the ballot." One MWIO member even circulated false charges that Christoffel received an exorbitant salary as union president and owned an expensive speedboat and a lakefront summer home. The MWIO also found kindred spirits in the Martin faction. After a meeting with MWIO leaders, the Martin administrator announced that the Martin group and the independent union "were both fighting the same thing—'the control of the UAW local by persons with Communist sympathies.' "[32]

After the Local 248 trial and expulsions of the independent union leaders, the MWIO proved a paper organization without substantial support among Allis-Chalmers workers. At the end of September, it voted to disband as a formal organization. Only eleven members attended the final meeting of the independent union that had claimed to represent over 3,000 Allis-Chalmers workers. After the remaining MWIO and Local 248 leaders met, the *CIO News* reported that the dissident workers "would continue to carry on their opposition to Local 248 within its ranks." With Martin still looking over his shoulder, Christoffel chose to follow a policy of union harmony. "All members in good standing," he said, "shall in the future as in the past have full rights on the union local floor." However, he warned, the union "will hold responsible for their acts all who attempt disruption."[33]

With UAW Executive Board consent, Martin appointed a second administrator, John Murphy, to oversee UAW Local 248. Murphy, who ran the local from October 1938 through March 1939, continued to rely on Brann, a Martin stalwart, for assistance. Christoffel remained under suspension as the Local 248 president. Nonetheless, in a conciliatory spirit, the Local 248 Executive Board endorsed Murphy's appointment. At a late October membership meeting, the Executive Board recommended the recognition of "the authority of the International," but it also called for a new election of officers in the "immediate future." The Local 248 members passed resolutions that expressed their complete confidence in the CIO and urged the administrator to retain the local's bargaining committee and steward structure.[34]

In November, Murphy called his first membership meeting for Allis-Chalmers unionists. The agenda included one very contentious issue—the report of the Local 248 trial board on the Rehberg case. Since Rehberg supported the MWIO, the trial board recommended that he be "expelled from the union" and "branded as an undesirable." It even advised that "the local do all in its power to keep him from future employment in the plant." Pandemonium broke out at the fractious union meeting. The union conservatives and Rehberg supporters vigorously objected to the harsh punishment. One dissident publicly challenged the trial board's decision, and a scuffle ensued. "At this time with the approval of the attending membership," the union minutes noted, "Rehberg and his group were escorted from the hall." Actually, the minutes failed to describe the scene accurately: they were unceremoniously carried out. In a backhanded criticism of Murphy, the minutes concluded: "It was the opinion of the Local that the disorder at the meeting resulted because the Chair did not immediately rule on a point of procedure."[35]

Following the disorderly meeting, Murphy refused to call any membership meetings for several months. The UAW Local did not meet again until the March election of delegates for the anti-Martin Cleveland convention. Nonetheless, the local continued to function with the publication of the Local 248 edition of the *CIO News*, the development of its extensive worker education program for shop leaders, and the processing of shop grievances. In a December statement to local members, Christoffel urged union members "to maintain Local 248 solid, militant and with the membership all in good standing." In early 1939, the UAW Executive Board members and CIO leaders recommended the continuation of Murphy's stewardship. In mid March, the Executive Board ruled that the forthcoming 1939 UAW-CIO Cleveland convention would decide on the restoration of autonomy to UAW Local 248.[36]

During the mid March membership meeting, Leo Kryczki, a prominent Milwaukee CIO leader, presided over the selection of delegates to the UAW-CIO Cleveland convention. The Christoffel slate won an overwhelming victory in the balloting for the anti-Martin convention. Nonetheless, UAW factionalism took its toll. Murphy reported a decline in the dues-paying membership from 7,000 to 2,700. Amid the intraunion squabbles, worker indifference undermined commitment to the UAW local. Moreover, union enthusiasm surely waned under the conservative administrator. Shortly before the Cleveland convention, the UAW Executive Board voted to withdraw Murphy as Local 248 administrator. Most likely, R. J. Thomas, who wanted the UAW presidency, did not wish to alienate a large and influential pro-Communist bloc of UAW delegates. At the Cleveland convention, Thomas became the new president of the UAW.[37]

In mid April, UAW Local 248 conducted its first independent meeting since fall. Christoffel "expressed the appreciation of the officers to the Stewards, the Committeemen, Flying Squadron, Women's Auxiliary and the rank and file for their magnificent support for the cause they and the officers felt were right." Robert Buse, a bargaining committee member, called for "a rousing vote of thanks to the officers for their courage and devotion to our Local and to the CIO in the face of the most trying of circumstances." Julius Blunk, the secretary-treasurer, commented on the new UAW constitution. It would, he said, "prevent reoccurrence of the International President having authority to establish administratorships over innocent locals." Although the split into the UAW-AFL and UAW-CIO had ended internal factionalism on the national level, the war continued on the Allis-Chalmers shop floor. The agreement would soon expire. And Harold Story would soon succeed in obtaining more conservative state labor legislation.[38]

In late 1930s, Wisconsin public opinion quickly turned against the labor movement. The public, especially large farmers, wearied by sit-down and other strikes and by the AFL-CIO feuds, supported more conservative labor legislation. Also, the 1938 collapse of the Farmer Labor Progressive Federation severed the fragile political bond between workers and farmers. Moreover, two incidents, the CIO organization of a cooperative creamery in Richland Center and the Franksville cannery strike where farmers lost a spinach crop, turned Wisconsin farmers against unions. In the late 1930s, Edwin Witte, a WLRB member, noted that the farmers, small-town businessmen, large antiunion employers, and the "neutral" public strongly opposed labor's forward march. The last group, he added, "was disgusted with union tactics and their aggressiveness." In the 1938 governor's election, Wisconsin voters ousted Philip LaFollette, the Progressive incumbent, and elected Julius Heil, a more conservative Republican and Milwaukee industrialist.[39]

Against this background, Harold Story operated to lead the employer offensive against labor in the Wisconsin legislature. The Allis-Chalmers attorney actually wrote the Wisconsin Employment Relations Act (WERA) of 1939, which repealed the 1937 Little Wagner act and could best be labeled the "Little Taft-Hartley act." In early 1939, Story worked with a coalition of industrial and agricultural interests to develop new labor legislation designed to readjust the legal balance of power in favor of employers. Introduced in January 1939, the WERA, also called the Wisconsin Employment Peace Act, substantially revised the 1937 labor code. When it finally passed the legislature and received Heil's signature in April 1939, the omnibus antiunion law had provisions that curtailed many of militant labor's aggressive tactics. Edwin Witte labeled the new law "a radical anti-union measure."[40]

Both CIO and AFL leaders vigorously denounced the proposed revision of Wisconsin labor law. Gunnar Michelson, a Wisconsin CIO leader, called it "a semi-fascist measure to destroy union labor." Even Joseph Padway, a respected and normally cautious AFL attorney, declared, "This bill is founded in Fascist doctrine." The new legislation defined a legal labor dispute as one "between an employer and a *majority* of employees." In other words, a legal strike required a majority of a firm's collective bargaining unit, not a majority of voters or union members. The measure also created a Wisconsin Employment Relations Board (WERB), but it was weaker than the old WLRB. Moreover, the WERA contained a detailed list of unfair labor practices for unions as well as employers. The proscribed union activities included coercion and intimidation, violation of the terms of a collective agreement, secondary boycotts, sit-down strikes, and failure to provide ten-day notice for strikes involving perishable farm or dairy products. One proscription forbade picketing or boycotting unless a majority of the collective bargaining unit voted for the strike on a secret ballot; another effectively prohibited mass picketing, an often successful union tactic.[41]

The WERA also listed employer practices that restricted or weakened union activities. It forbade employers to grant a union shop unless three-fourths of the bargaining unit voted for it in a secret ballot—a measure that took advantage of a divided and weakened labor movement. It even prohibited employers from entering negotiations with less than a majority of the bargaining unit. Furthermore, the restrictive law denied dues checkoff unless a worker made a written request for the deduction. It even permitted company unions, which the earlier law specifically banned, and gave strikebreakers rights as employees and union voters, another previously forbidden practice.[42]

In other words, the WERA was an employers' law that incorporated many of Story's earlier proposals and mirrored his direct experience with militant CIO unionism. In a highly factionalized plant such as West Allis, several provisions strengthened management's position and weakened the union's. For example, UAW Local 248 had a militant minority and a much larger group of less active supporters, and it faced strong conservative opposition. Within this context, many ordinary workers were frequently indifferent to either faction. They simply followed the flow of events, supporting the union faction that seemed to prevail at a given moment. Often, they only reluctantly participated in the major union activities such as strike votes. Strikes broke out only when the militant minority forced the indifferent and uncommitted workers to act and to support the struggle against management abuses. If such action were to require an affirmative majority for a legal strike and its support activities (such as boycotting or picketing), the militants would face the formidable problem of gaining the support of indifferent workers who only hesitatingly engaged in militant action.[43]

Furthermore, in the factionalized Allis-Chalmers situation, UAW Local 248 faced the nearly impossible task of obtaining a three-fourths majority for a legal union shop. Edwin Witte also feared the legislation's effect on the right to strike. "The restrictions on the right to strike," he wrote, "for the first time introduce the concept that only majority strikes are legal and render impossible all 'quickee' [sic] strikes." For a highly contested industrial terrain, Story had cleverly crafted legislation that would aid management's future struggles with UAW Local 248.[44]

In 1939, Allis-Chalmers workers conducted their first strike since the abortive 1916 machinist's walkout. This twenty-six-day strike was the first of three sharp contests that grew in intensity and duration between 1939 and 1946. In all three, union security was the fundamental issue. Although Allis-Chalmers officials recognized and negotiated with UAW Local 248, they firmly held to their open shop principle and refused to grant the CIO union exclusive recognition. They consistently maintained that no worker would be forced to join a union and that no worker's job would be dependent on union membership. Despite three long and bitter strikes, they refused to concede the closed or even the union shop. Within the divisive context of UAW factionalism and AFL aggression, Local 248 leaders demanded means to defend their union from both internal and external threats. Shortly after the UAW had removed the administrator, union leaders started to reassert control over the divided work force and shore up their membership. Soon after contract negotiations began, management and labor deadlocked on several principal issues—a closed shop, a joint CIO agreement for the three (Boston, Pittsburgh, and West Allis) plants, wage adjustments, and an improved vacation policy.[45]

Throughout the negotiations, union meetings revealed shop floor tensions simmering beneath the surface. Early in the negotiations, union leaders reported problems with "anti-union people in the shop who spread intentional, malicious rumors about our organization." In early May, Julius Blunk told a stewards and committeemen meeting that Allis-Chalmers managers were "trying to drive a wedge between the young and old" workers, an indication of a growing division between younger production workers and older craftsmen. At a subsequent union meeting, the bargaining committee reported that two anti-CIO workers were "again actively engaged in attempting to set up an Independent Union [IU] at Allis-Chalmers." As each faction tried to enlist members for its respective conservative or militant union causes, the divisive tensions finally reached breaking point in the West Allis shops.[46]

In late May, the strike broke out with a shop floor demonstration of union power that led to the declaration of a union "work holiday." This May strike occurred because management encouraged the organizational activities of UAW opponents. Ed Hall, who aided the Allis-Chalmers negotiations, described to the federal conciliator how IU organizers precipitated the walkout. A UAW regional officer "had hatched a plan to have a group take out . . . an independent unionist, from the plant and beat him up." But the Local 248 group became so enthusiastic about the proposed confrontation that the regional director "got fearful that real injury might come to this man" and warned management about the impending crisis. Story then removed the Local 248 opponent from the plant. After this, several bargaining committee members marched a group of three hundred union members to the foundry to confront the IU member. After they discovered his absence, in a "state of feverish excitement, they pulled several thousand claiming that the company was in league with those who were trying to break the union." The walkout was a visible and dramatic ritual of union power. It also illustrated the unstable character of Allis-Chalmers shop floor relations. After the walkout, union leaders declared an "indefinite work holiday"; management declared a lockout and announced that the plant "would be closed until further notice."[47]

Once Allis-Chalmers workers hit the streets, the AFL craft unions complicated matters by entering the fray. In early June, Otto A.

Jirikowic, the IAM business agent, wrote to William Watson, the vice president for production. The Milwaukee AFL leader noted that "the C.I.O. had cancelled their 1938 contract," which left IAM members "without a bargaining agency." He then offered to have IAM District 10 "represent such employees who are members of our union, or who are eligible to become members." Jirikowic had some strong IAM supporters in the West Allis plant, among them George Humphrey, Gilbert Schimmel, and George Sprague.[48]

These three skilled craftsmen attempted to establish an independent union and to inaugurate a back-to-work movement. In a violent confrontation, sixty Local 248 flying squadron members stormed an independent union meeting and physically assaulted several participants, seriously injuring the three opposition leaders. Sprague suffered a broken leg, rib fractures, concussion, and lung injury. Another received cuts on his head and shoulders; the third a head injury.[49]

Still later, the bitter labor strife again spilled over into the streets of West Allis. On June 12, UAW strikers massed at the plant gates. Earlier, Allis-Chalmers had arranged for the governor to invoke the Wisconsin Labor Peace Act limiting mass picketing and to call out the state militia to break the strike. According to a federal conciliator, Local 248 leaders "staged" a "riot" in order to "determine whether the militia would be called." When union members blocked and fought with office workers arriving for work, 1,000 CIO sympathizers stood across the street and watched. The Milwaukee newspaper noted the "partially successful attempts" of union strikers "to keep about 1,000 office workers from entering the plant." In one incident, the strikers disarmed a policeman who drew his club during one of the scuffles. Before the outbreak of mass picketing and violence, the state CIO leadership warned that if the militia were called out, they would initiate "a general strike, or holiday, . . . in Milwaukee."[50]

The next morning, picket line violence returned. The *Milwaukee Journal* recounted: "stones, eggs and fists greeted nonstriking office workers attempting to enter the factory." This time, police officials used tear gas to battle "a crowd of about 5,000." The Allis-Chalmers strikers injured thirteen people, including ten policemen. Most of the fighting, the newspaper reported, "centered about the streetcars, which provide the most feasible method for workers to enter the plant" and which ran right up to the West Allis plant gates. "Groups of workers," the *Milwaukee Journal* added, "would board the streetcars a few blocks from the plant, presenting passes to the motorman. They would then go to the back of the car and cut or snarl the trolley ropes. Police countered by having peace officers board the cars along with the strike sympathizers, but they were unable to prevent all damage."

At one point, after a motorman repaired damaged trolley lines, a group of strike sympathizers "sat down on the tracks in front of the car."[51]

The Local 248 challenge to different independent union groups and to the Wisconsin Labor Peace Act became a serious challenge to public authority. Local law enforcement officials asked for the state militia to control the violence. Governor Heil called a conference of Milwaukee county law enforcement authorities to assess options for handling the social turmoil. After it adjourned, he proclaimed: "Without law and order there is anarchy. There will be no anarchy in Wisconsin while I am governor." But he did not call out the state militia. Since the union threatened a citywide general strike, Heil, who owned a large metal firm, never called up the Wisconsin militia. He urged both union and corporate officials to begin real negotiations and even publicly joked with the strikers. Shortly thereafter, Allis-Chalmers officials seriously began to negotiate with the militant UAW local.[52]

Union security remained the crucial issue in the renewed negotiations. It was an indirect manifestation of the question of the relative power and authority of management and of the union at Allis-Chalmers. In his reports, the federal conciliator alluded to this intractable problem: "Some of the [union] bargaining committee want further embarrassment of the company and [the] company is equally insistent that the authority of that [bargaining] committee be clipped." Having enrolled about 90 percent of the work force, the union demanded a closed or union shop to protect its membership from the AFL and independent unionists. Then it could shift its attention and energies to other shop floor problems. The company adamantly refused to recognize this demand for "the closed shop or any modification of the same," even though the union leaders suggested "the advantage of disciplining the men" with a union shop. Firm in their open shop principles, Allis-Chalmers officials continued to resist the union demands for membership security and for a closed or even more limited union shop. In the hands of a militant and aggressive union, they reasoned, such security would provide an effective shop floor challenge to management control. They firmly maintained that "discipline within the plant is its function which they are quite able to take care of and they feel that this would be stifled under [the] union shop."[53]

In the end, although each side claimed victory, the final contract was a typical compromise for both. Allis-Chalmers officials resisted the demands for a union shop and joint agreement, but they could not restrict the grievance procedure. In an announcement of union gains, Christoffel claimed: "In lieu of its union shop, the union has received the full protection it desired." This protection rested on contract provisions that included greater union authority in the grievance procedure, signing of a final agreement after completion of negotiations at the other plants, and retention of the right to strike during the contract. Other union gains included more vacation days, future negotiations on wages, detailed company information on piecework rates, limited seniority for foremen who returned to the shop, union consultation on layoffs, call-in pay provisions, and seniority for six months after layoffs. Allis-Chalmers officials also agreed to a five-day suspension for five independent union leaders. Although UAW Local 248 never gained its main objective of some form of security, it had survived a major test of strength against a hostile, antiunion employer.[54]

Once the strike ended, labor factionalism resumed in the West Allis shops. Local 248 leaders now attempted to eliminate the IU members. Since they had failed to achieve a union security provision, union leaders devised two different strategies against the shop floor dissidents: first, formal protests and grievances to management officials; second, informal shop floor demonstrations of union power. The union filed grievances against the organizational activities of the four MWIO organizers. The union bargaining committee also insisted on a Labor Advisory Committee meeting to discuss the dismissal of the five most active independent unionists. At one point, Allis-Chalmers managers even suggested that the union pay the IU members to keep them from the plant. In response, Christoffel replied: "the only thing the Union would give these men was a free ride to the graveyard and a special dispensation, five dollars worth of roses for each." Management, however, did agree to lay off the two for unauthorized union activity.[55]

In the second strategy, union shop leaders led sometimes peaceful and sometimes violent shop floor demonstrations against antiunion workers. In these important rituals of power, the militant minority showed hesitant workers the social and political costs of indifference. In one case, twelve union men ejected Shellie Jenkins, a black worker, from the plant. They "escorted a colored employe to the gate," Allis-Chalmers officials reported, "and told him 'don't come back' after repeated threats for refusal to join the Union." The same day, they also noted, "departmental work stoppages occurred in the tractor shops to protest the fact that George Vandenberg, who it was claimed belonged to the Independent Union, was working, and [the] refusal of Casper Rogers to join Local 248." When the two IU members returned from their layoff, management faced still another union protest. "[T]he Company," they noted, "was immediately confronted with a departmental shutdown, unquestionably engineered by the Union, when the men refused to work because of their presence." The union members eventually forced both dissidents to reapply for union membership.[56]

For management, such shop floor demonstrations were intolerable challenges to their control and workplace discipline. William Watson and Harold Story held special supervisory meetings to discuss "the breakdown of shop discipline, the rights of employes and the Company's desire for fair and impartial treatment in matters of union affiliation." Nonetheless, in the absence of a closed or union shop, Christoffel and other union leaders vowed "to exert pressure for [the] discipline or discharge of all dissidents." The UAW local persisted with grievances to "pressure" all Allis-Chalmers workers to acquire membership in the union.[57]

Through the late summer and fall of 1939, the Independent Union continued its organizational efforts. At this time, two skilled craftsmen, George Sprague and George Humphrey, were respectively president and secretary of the dissident organization. Eventually, they allied with AFL unionists in the Allis-Chalmers shops. In August, the anti-UAW group claimed almost 2,000 members. At a fall meeting of 500 members, the oppositional group announced plans to file an NLRB petition for a new certification election. The new Allis-Chalmers union, Sprague claimed, was "not fighting the CIO at Allis-Chalmers but rather the leadership of the CIO Local there." It continued its organizational campaign through the winter and spring of 1939–1940.[58]

At the same time, the Milwaukee AFL also inaugurated a more aggressive campaign to organize Allis-Chalmers workers into craft unions. In January 1940, Jacob Friedrick, the FTC's general organizer, wrote to John Frey, the head of AFL Metal Trades Department, about his plan to regain the West Allis plant for the Milwaukee AFL. The IU group, Friedrick wrote, claimed almost 2,600 members and wanted to affiliate with the AFL. The main problem, he added, was a "satisfactory set-up," for they wanted "one single organization regardless of any craft lines." Although the Milwaukee AFL leader advised the Independent Union leaders about the AFL wisdom of "proper trade organizations" and of the later development of "a method of joint action," shop traditions ran so deep that Friedrick could not convert the conservative unionists to the AFL cause. Even these potential AFL unionists retained bitter memories of craft factionalism.[59]

Through Friedrick's AFL-tinted glasses, these union novices simply could not comprehend the years of AFL wisdom and experience. The IU leaders, he wrote, "seem unable to understand the reasons why we are not ready and willing to take them in upon the basis that they suggest, . . . which is the result of years of experience, simply because some new group seems to feel that some other set-up is preferable, does not quite seem to register with them." Nor could the AFL stalwart resist the temptation to avenge Christoffel's CIO treachery of the more recent past. Friedrick suggested the possibility of forming separate Allis-Chalmers craft locals, united under the aegis of an Allis-Chalmers Metal Trades Council. If the Independent Union could be brought into the AFL, he reminded Frey, "it, of course, would result in a tremendous advantage to us and a corresponding set-back to the C.I.O."[60]

Several months later, Otto Jirikowic, the IAM District 10 leader, wrote to Joseph Padway, an AFL attorney, and announced his intention to organize the West Allis plant. "I believe," Jirikowic wrote, "that the CIO can be licked, if the Independent Union will play ball with the Machinist's Union."[61]

This AFL-CIO war in the West Allis shops complicated the Allis-Chalmers collective bargaining relationship. In late March 1940, Local 248 and Allis-Chalmers officials resumed another round of contract negotiations. Although union members articulated demands for more paid holidays, double time for Saturday work, payment of the average earned rate for untimed jobs, worker initiative in retiming jobs, and information on job prices, the union leaders and members also insisted on union security. Avoiding reference to the closed or union shop, they put forward a demand of "seniority for union members only" to open the door for the all important issue of union security. If only union members had seniority, it would encourage union holdouts to join UAW Local 248. Otherwise, the nonmembers could jeopardize their jobs in the event of an economic downturn.[62]

In April, Local 248 leaders resumed workplace confrontations with independent union leaders. In one instance, a group of CIO militants forcefully removed George Humphrey, the Independent Union secretary, from the plant. Fred McStroul, a Local 248 officer, and a "large number" of union members carried him "from the plant during the noon hour and warned him 'not to come back to work.' " The IU activist, Allis-Chalmers officials reported, "was carried out face down with a man on each arm and leg and another grasping his belt. This incident created great excitement and unrest in the shops." The company promptly disciplined McStroul and four other CIO shop leaders. In another incident, a large union group "invaded" an independent unionist's "department and pushed, pulled and poked him around." In order to maintain shop peace, management officials requested the resignation of two independent leaders and offered them a $900 dismissal settlement. But the two workers threatened to file unfair labor practice charges against the company, and the union also forcefully protested the proposed settlement. In late April, forty union members gathered at the plant gates to prevent three Independent Union members from entering.[63]

Through the negotiations, Local 248 leaders insisted on the discharge of two opposition leaders and demanded probation for others.

The union maintained that "the six employees are a disturbing influence in the plant and are mostly responsible for the present dispute." Nonetheless, despite important differences, both the company and the union were in a more cooperative mood than in 1939. As a consequence of the disruptive 1939 strike, the federal conciliator reported: "There seems to be a tendency on the part of both parties to settle this matter by themselves." Furthermore, Max Babb, the Allis-Chalmers president, directed the negotiations and did not display Story's deep anti-CIO sentiment.[64]

In succeeding conferences, the federal conciliator reported that union and company negotiators solved "many shop grievances." These seemingly minor grievances mirrored the basic concerns of the workers in the Allis-Chalmers shops. The company agreed to issue new pay stubs with notations for all deductions, to eliminate deductions for scrap in the foundry, and to provide job classification lists to the union. In addition, management also settled the problem of layoff and hiring at the departmental level, agreed to maintain a list of laid-off workers for three years, and stopped forcing workers to punch out on time clocks for the twenty-minute lunch. All in all, the contract negotiations became a forum to air some 134 shop grievances that had been "unsettled or settled unsatisfactorily" in the recent past. The final contract included a fund for the adjustment of wage inequalities, the establishment of a mechanism to negotiate other wage brackets, the reinstatement of the five discharged CIO workers, the discharge of the two AFL unionists and the probation of the four others, and an additional vacation day.[65]

Most important, Allis-Chalmers officials offered a modest union security proposal. "Management," the federal conciliator reported, "in [a] signed statement to [the] Union [indicated] that [the] corporation . . . will not tolerate any disturbances in the plant because of anti-union activity. This statement hits at the independent union, which, it seems, was the main issue." In effect, the conciliator couched the union security question in the language of management discipline. Although the federal conciliator promised to forward a copy of the agreement to Washington, the union officers never signed the contract because they wanted to test the company's commitment to a more permanent relationship with the union. Specifically, they wanted to see how Allis-Chalmers would handle the AFL or independent unionists in the plant. As it turned out, the Local 248 leaders would continue to skirmish with these non-UAW dissidents after the settlement.[66]

In the late summer of 1940, the AFL returned to organize the Allis-Chalmers plant. David Sigman, a special representative to AFL president William Green, initiated and directed organizational efforts against the CIO in Wisconsin. For several months, the campaign to bring Allis-Chalmers workers into the AFL commanded a considerable amount of his time and attention. In late August, Sigman met with Jacob Friedrick, the FTC leader, Charles Heymanns, a Wisconsin state AFL organizer, and a delegation of Allis-Chalmers workers. Most likely, the Allis-Chalmers workers were members of the feeble Independent Union who were now ready to make some arrangement with the Milwaukee AFL. After several meetings with FTC and WSFL leaders, Sigman discussed an organizational plan with Friedrick and Sprague. According to Sigman, "Mr. Sprague was advised that organization work would be carried on by the Milwaukee Federated Trades Council and they would have to abide by the policies set down by the Milwaukee Federated Trades Council and American Federation of Labor."[67]

By mid October, the Milwaukee, the state, and the national AFL organizations had made considerable progress in their plans to regain the Allis-Chalmers plant. Apparently, Story and other company officials viewed the AFL campaign with the hopeful expectation of more amenable labor relations. Sigman reported: "Met with Harold Story, Vice-President of the Allis-Chalmers Manufacturing Company, regarding organization of the Allis-Chalmers' employes into the American Federation of Labor." Story, chagrined at Christoffel's successful and militant industrial unionism, conceived a company plan for accommodation with a more conservative craft unionism, but only if the AFL challenge succeeded. The next day, after a meeting with Friedrick and some Allis-Chalmers workers, Sigman noted: "Organization work has been started to organize the employees of the Allis-Chalmers Manufacturing Company into the American Federation of Labor." Subsequently, he began to attend regular Saturday morning meetings with workers who were disaffected with the CIO in the West Allis plant.[68]

The next week, Sigman and Friedrick took up the case of "two discharged employees . . . who refused to join the C.I.O." The Milwaukee FTC, Sigman reported, intended to file a charge of unfair labor practices with the NLRB. At the same time, they sent the first of several letters to all disaffected Allis-Chalmers workers. In it, they decried the "arbitrary, undemocratic, and high-handed manner" of the CIO local's "radical leadership." And, while they rejected a federal or any other industrial approach to the organization of the West Allis plant, they offered a proposal for "a joint council or committee representing all of the trades or groups [to] formulate a joint agreement taking care of the interests of all." Friedrick and Sigman noted that the various Milwaukee AFL unions—patternmakers, machinists, molders, electrical workers, and others—had agreed to this joint organizational campaign under the direction of the FTC and the national AFL.[69]

Shortly thereafter, Christoffel reported to Local 248 members about "the grave activities of the A. F. of L. and some of the ridiculous letters which were being sent to some of the membership." This competition for members certainly exacerbated shop floor problems. The small but solid nucleus of conservative AFL and independent unionists presented a genuine threat to the stability and security of UAW Local 248, especially when they had the full support of the Milwaukee and international AFL organizations.[70]

Between May and December 1940, UAW Local 248 vigorously conducted nineteen work stoppages to protest AFL or nonunion workers in the West Allis plant. These stoppages varied in size from one by a single CIO worker who for several hours refused to work with a nonunion worker to large demonstrations against the AFL members and company policies. In fourteen work stoppages, an entire department shut down for anywhere from five minutes to a whole day. The overwhelming majority were departmental stoppages in the tool room, tractor shops, foundries, pattern shop, and No. 6 erection shop. In four incidents, large groups of union workers marched from one department to another in order to demonstrate against nonunion members. As the workplace incidents grew more disruptive, Allis-Chalmers managers or supervisors disciplined the protesting workers—a half-hour foundry stoppage ended when managers threatened to shut it down for the day, a union demonstration in the erection shop resulted in three-tenths of an hour docked pay for participants, and two other departments were shut down for the entire day. Thus, the struggle between the CIO and AFL resulted in considerable turmoil at Allis-Chalmers.[71]

The case of Charles Straessle, an AFL machinist in No. 6 erection shop, illustrated the contentious shop floor animosities. In the fall of 1940, Straessle was the object of five different work stoppages in the Allis-Chalmers shops. He was most vocal in his antagonism toward the UAW local and its leaders. At one point, according to a company investigation, he commented that "he would not wear a CIO button even to the toilet." Because of his vocal and public hostility, he became a target of the UAW's aggressive campaign against nonunion "hitchhikers." If the union enrolled the most outspoken holdouts, such as Straessle, then the remainder of the workers would readily follow. On October 16, CIO union militants halted production in the erection shop for one and one-half hours and demanded the dismissal of Straessle. They maintained that his anti-UAW comments violated the sections of the contract that forbade negative and disruptive statements against the UAW local in the plant. In the course of the stoppage, some fifty UAW members threatened and coerced Straessle, extracting a signed union pledge card from him. Jirikowic, the IAM leader, reported that Straessle signed the pledge card only after threats of "bodily harm" and "under duress." Subsequently, Straessle renounced his CIO membership.[72]

Unchastened, Straessle continued to antagonize UAW unionists. Eight days after the initial stoppage, "a large CIO group" again halted production in the erection shop and demanded "that Straessle be removed from the department." This time, the shop superintendent advised the recalcitrant AFL unionist to reconsider his anti-CIO position. According to Jirikowic, the superintendent stated "that he couldn't shut down the department on account of one man, meaning Charles Straessle." The foreman told the AFL worker "not to come to work Friday night or any other night until he notified him," and imposed a three-day disciplinary layoff. On November 1, when the AFL unionist returned to the shop, CIO workers conducted a third "demonstration." The company docked the pay of the UAW workers who participated. Still, three days later, the company reported: "One hundred men gathered in the plant to demand that the company 'do something about Straessle.' " On November 15, seventy-five union workers conducted a final demonstration against the AFL worker during shift change and held up work on the night shift for about ten minutes. The Straessle affair then moved to the grievance machinery. In one grievance, the union charged him with "undermining Local 248." In another, they simply demanded the "discharge of Charles Straessle." Never formally resolved, the Straessle case faded into the background as labor and management moved toward a more decisive confrontation.[73]

The fratricidal struggle between conservative and militant unionists continued through fall 1940; then it exploded into the controversial Allis-Chalmers "defense" strike of 1941. Ultimately, a mid December confrontation at the plant gates between CIO and AFL workers escalated in January into the seventy-six-day defense strike. The midnight incident resulted from a Local 248 campaign to force two other AFL members, Michael Bohacheff and Nicholas Imp, to join the CIO union. IAM loyalists and vocal opponents of CIO unionism, they worked together in one of the tractor shops. Their all-out AFL organizational efforts aroused the ire of UAW co-workers.[74]

Bohacheff, the more irascible of the two, clearly had problems with his fellow tractor shop workers. An Allis-Chalmers arbitrator later characterized Bohacheff as "a cantankerous, excitable, and peculiar individual." According to the CIO News, Bohacheff fell behind in his UAW dues and attempted to arrange a deal to return to his membership status of good standing in the UAW. "When he couldn't chisel on

Local 248," the CIO newspaper reported, "he joined the AFL for a cheap way out." The arbitrator also noted "a background of friction between Bohacheff and members of the C.I.O. in the plant." In addition to joining the AFL, Bohacheff further annoyed his union shopmates and violated their shop norms with his public posture as "rate buster." As a rate buster, Bohacheff violated deep and long-standing shop traditions to preserve work standards and prevent cuts in their piece rates.[75]

Consequently, CIO unionists repeatedly harassed him in the shop and insisted that he pay the delinquent dues. Bohacheff detailed the CIO harassment to Milwaukee IAM leaders. Through the fall of 1940, these leaders reported, Bohacheff "has been bothered, pushed around, and molested, both outside the plant and in the plant by members of the C.I.O." They charged that Local 248 members hid or stole his tools and tampered with his machine, and "[v]arious employees, members of the C.I.O have moved about his machine in such a manner that wrenches are thrown off with the evident intent of injuring him. He has been called dirty names in the presence of his foreman, and in the presence of other employees, but no disciplinary measures have been taken." In a futile attempt to calm the situation, Allis-Chalmers officials transferred Bohacheff from the tractor shop to the No. 4 Machine Shop. In the eyes of UAW supporters, however, the transfer seemed an outrageous promotion for a union disrupter.[76]

The CIO harassment continued in the machine shop. After midnight on December 18, at the end of the second shift, a shop dispute spilled over to the plant gates. Groups of Local 248 members waited at all the plant gates to talk with Bohacheff about his UAW membership status. According to Otto Jirikowic, "a group of rowdies . . . some seventy in number . . . attempted to do bodily harm" to Bohacheff and Imp who left the plant together, "because these two men were members of the Machinist's Union . . . and not members of the C.I.O." When the CIO group accosted the two AFL members, they fled to their car and locked its doors. An arbitrator later noted, "some of them tried to open the door, and there may have been some rocking of the car." As the two frightened AFL workers tried to drive away, Frank Korb, a UAW member, either jumped on the front bumper or was hit and grabbed onto the vehicle and held on while it sped away. Korb was not seriously injured, but the incident infuriated the other UAW members, who chased and hurled stones at the escaping automobile. A CIO car cut it off. Korb jumped or fell off. The two AFL workers immediately raced off to the West Allis police station, followed there by Local 248 members. Bohacheff and Imp charged the union with mob action; Korb wanted warrants issued against them for attempted murder.[77]

A few days after the incident, the federal conciliator recounted it to the director of the U.S. Conciliation Service. In his mind, the Allis-Chalmers dispute had deep roots in the bitter AFL-CIO conflict. James P. Holmes wrote: "Efforts are being made by the AFL, who formerly were in the Milwaukee plant, to regain it." Milwaukee IAM leader Jirikowic claimed that "the AFL is determinedly behind this effort." The conciliator believed that two important factors complicated the uneasy situation in the West Allis plant: first, the company's unsettled and indecisive labor policies, and, second, the UAW's radical leadership.[78]

According to Holmes, Allis-Chalmers officials were uncertain and divided about "the PROPER method of handling labor relations." On the one hand, Harold Story was "very definitely committed to a policy of more definite resistance to the demands of the CIO, especially . . . those which are unreasonable and high-handed." On the other hand, Max Babb, the Allis-Chalmers president, and William Watson, a vice president for production, he added, "have followed a policy of appeasement." Always conniving and manipulating, Story, a master labor strategist, created the contentiousness that encouraged AFL activities. Since the Wisconsin labor law favored management, and the strong AFL presence divided labor, Story's resistance faction now took on a much more combative and aggressive posture toward the CIO union.[79]

Although the federal conciliator sketched a grim outline, he expressed optimism about a favorable outcome and erroneously concluded that "there was no present stoppage imminent." To support this contention, he noted that "the great majority" of Local 248 members were "conservative" and that Christoffel would risk neither his leadership nor the CIO majority by an untimely strike.[80]

Over the next several weeks, the union and company positions solidified around the Imp and Bohacheff incident. Although the Christmas holiday intervened, tensions escalated quite rapidly. For Local 248 leaders, the incident symbolized management's rigid opposition to CIO unionism, and of the pressing need for union security in the West Allis shops. In late December, UAW Local 248 posted a notice on the Allis-Chalmers bulletin board calling for an emergency membership meeting on the "hit-and-run case." After the district attorney refused to issue arrest warrants for the two AFL workers, Christoffel sent Wisconsin governor Julius Heil an open letter that demanded that "these two men be arrested for their criminal acts." If the two returned to their jobs, he threatened to shut down the whole plant. Clearly, the union was raising the stakes and moving aggressively toward confrontation.[81]

A few days later, the Local 248 executive board informed Allis-Chalmers president Babb that the union now rejected the "tentatively accepted" April 1940 agreement and still had "strike sanction from [the] International [Union]." A master strategist, Christoffel had cleverly revised the union acceptance of the 1940 agreement. At the executive board meeting, "Much discussion was held and it was decided that the activities of the Company shielding anti-unionists be settled once and for all." For UAW Local 248, the AFL organizational drive clearly diverted attention from more pressing union matters, such as collecting union dues, maintaining members, and processing worker grievances. The union leaders wanted a definite settlement of the union security question.[82]

On January 2, Frank Bolka, the Local 248 vice president, described the tense situation to shop stewards and shop committeemen. The bargaining committee, Bolka said, informed the company "that Bohacheff and Imp will have to be kept out if the plant is to run." The Allis-Chalmers firm, he added, "has not kept its word in regard to anti-union activities." In an allusion to Story's strategy of CIO resistance, Bolka ominously informed the stewards and committeemen that "a section of the management appears to give aid and comfort to these disrupters." Julius Blunk, the usually cautious secretary-treasurer, stated, "if the company wants a fight now is the time to give it to them. . . . we must have a union shop in order to prevent future troubles." Then, the assembled stewards and committeemen passed a resolution to "serve notice on the Company and conciliation department that we will accept nothing less than a union shop." The shop floor leaders also went on record "to instruct every Steward and Committeeman to contact every man in the shop, as yet not in the union, saying that he must either be in the union or could not work in the plant." In effect, the rank-and-file leaders unilaterally declared the plant a union shop.[83]

On January 9, thousands of Local 248 members assembled at the State Fair Park Coliseum, and Christoffel reported on the negotiations. "Story," he said, "was again the Company spokesman and from all indications he or whoever he represents is going to attempt to smash our organization." The battle lines were drawn. The union members authorized a formal strike vote. They also rejected the management proposal for a resolution of the dispute, an impartial referee to adjudicate the Imp and Bohacheff incident. Christoffel told the Milwaukee press that Allis-Chalmers officials offered "nothing in pay increase demands, no bargaining on job security and rehiring almost 1,000 employees now laid off, unsatisfactory seniority provision and nothing on union shop demands." After a strike vote, Christoffel,

UAW regional director George Nordstrom and UAW vice president Ed Hall reported that 90.3 percent of the union workers voted to hit the streets.[84]

But UAW Local 248 needed to complete one more formality for a legal Wisconsin strike vote. Unlike federal labor legislation, which required the affirmative vote of a majority of the bargaining unit, Wisconsin labor law required a majority of those who worked in the plant to vote for a strike. This meant a majority of both union and nonunion workers. Unable to prove that a majority of the Allis-Chalmers workers voted at the State Fair Park meeting, UAW leaders conducted second ballot two days later, and then reported that Allis-Chalmers workers voted 5,958 to 758 for a strike.[85]

Thus began the controversial seventy-six-day Allis-Chalmers "defense" strike. It was a truly classic labor-management confrontation. At 10 A.M. Wednesday, January 22, the *Milwaukee Journal* reported that the workers "forced a shutdown of all production." From the beginning, Allis-Chalmers officials highlighted the issue of defense production. The strike, the Milwaukee newspaper reported, halted "work on national defense and quasi-defense orders." Allis-Chalmers estimated the value of defense orders at $25 million, with an additional $14 million planned.[86]

On the strike's first day, the workers demonstrated an impressive display of union solidarity. UAW Local 248 totally shut down the huge plant without a picket line. Since Wisconsin labor law outlawed mass picketing, the union posted gate watchers, and then motion picture cameramen, for the identification of strikebreakers. The union president told reporters, "present plans are to conduct a strike without picketlines, but to keep small groups of 'watchers' at the plant gates." The absence of pickets, he added, demonstrated that "the workers are solidly in favor of the walkout."[87]

In the first weeks, Allis-Chalmers, UAW, and AFL leaders skirmished for the most advantageous public position. Management officials repeatedly criticized the CIO interruption of defense production. In one instance, Allis-Chalmers officials insisted and UAW leaders acceded to the removal of already completed defense work from the plant. Corporate officials added complications when they submitted a list of nonunion members to pack and ship the military work. The UAW leaders resolutely demanded a solution of the union security problem. In an effort to ensure worker support for this complex strike issue, they escalated their demands—a fifteen-cent-per-hour raise with a seventy-five-cent minimum hourly wage, a stronger seniority provision, the rehiring of one thousand laid-off workers, and the payment of "union members" for lost time during the strike. Christoffel told the press, "Only Union men will go back into the shop after this strike." He added, "What we want in the Allis-Chalmers Company is an American union shop and substantial wage increases." In contrast, AFL leaders, who continued their organizational drive, emphasized AFL conservatism, the "reasonable, fair, and patriotic position" of AFL unionism.[88]

The Allis-Chalmers strike quickly attracted national attention, and Red unionism emerged as a public issue. In a speech on the floor of the House of Representatives, conservative Michigan Republican Clare Hoffman charged that Communism was the basic issue of the strike. "Christoffel," Hoffman declared, "is more interested in 'red' activities—in holding up defense orders—than he is in the welfare of the nation." The CIO union, specifically "Christoffel and the Communists," Hoffman declared, wanted "control of this factory. Having control, they would be in a position to prevent operation. An ideal position of a 'fifth column.' " In response to Hoffman charges, Christoffel told reporters that there "is no need to deny again that I am a communist." Two weeks later, AFL president William Green also charged that Communists influenced CIO policies. In addition to other CIO strikes, the Allis-Chalmers strike was "wholeheartedly in line with Communist Party policy toward defense."[89]

The intractable Allis-Chalmers situation obviously needed something to move the parties from dead center to compromise. The national defense issue attracted the attention of federal officials. At this time, Conciliator Francis G. Haas related: "W[illiam]. D[avis]. thinks [that we] will have to bring all parties to Washington." Soon other government mediators reached a similar conclusion. William Knudsen and Sidney Hillman, directors of the Office of Production management, decided to invite both sides to Washington.[90]

In mid February, management and labor representatives flew to Washington to meet with Knudsen and Hillman. The Allis-Chalmers strike attracted the attention of the highest levels of government. Sidney Hillman, the OPM labor representative, even discussed it with President Franklin D. Roosevelt. After meeting Roosevelt, Hillman expressed optimism about a strike settlement. They "hoped to settle" the difficult dispute "within a day or two." He added that they believed "the situation was 'not disturbing in relation to the size of the country.' " At the OPM meeting, the principal corporate representatives included Allis-Chalmers president Babb, Story, and Leo Mann, a notorious Milwaukee antilabor attorney. The union delegation included international UAW leaders R. J. Thomas and Ed Hall, Regional Director George Nordstrom, Christoffel, and three other local union officers. Deeply divided, the reluctant representatives went to Washington with totally different agendas. The UAW leaders wanted a union shop or some other form of union security.

The corporate officials maintained their open shop position and articulated a philosophy of management control.[91]

Government officials considered arbitration as a possible solution to this difficult strike. Hillman was an innovator of arbitration systems for the Amalgamated Clothing Workers Union. Along with other New Deal labor officials, who viewed the federal government as a mediator in the public interest, he favored arbitration as a means for industrial peace. Although a union shop was not possible, Hillman believed, the UAW representatives "might accept a lesser provision 'which would serve to protect the union's security in the plant.' "[92]

For several days, management and labor wrangled with government officials, and all struggled with each other over proposals for a strike settlement. At the first session, Mann opened with a reading of the Allis-Chalmers open shop position. Although company negotiators accepted arbitration, they initially refused to allow shop discipline as a subject for the decision of an outside arbitrator. After two days, however, they made an important concession that stated that "the failure of the Company to discipline an employee for interference with the status of the Union" would violate a contract provision on "shop discipline." For management, the "stumbling block" was the arbitrator's jurisdiction, which touched on the extremely sensitive question of management rights. They refused to allow a referee to decide on the union shop or to "touch on matters which it contends are private affairs."[93]

After several days, the Hillman arbitration proposal became the means for the tentative resolution of the union security issue. According to the conciliator, Hillman urged both sides to "get together on the impartial referee proposal as an alternative to the union's demand for an all-union shop [to] guarantee the union's security in the plant." Nonetheless, he added, "wrangling over the extent of the jurisdiction" of an arbitrator occupied much of the Allis-Chalmers discussions. The contentious talks involved fundamental disagreements over the principles of union security and management rights.[94]

After four long days, labor, management, and government officials crafted a tentative settlement, the Washington Agreement, for the long defense strike. In it, the two sides agreed that Allis-Chalmers management would "maintain discipline on company premises" and would "strictly enforce its rules and regulations." For a disciplined worker, this policy would be "applied without discrimination with respect to his membership or status in any union." The union had the right to appeal to an "impartial referee," if (1) the worker was not guilty of the infraction, (2) the worker did not interfere with shop discipline, or (3) the discipline discriminated against the union or the worker relative to membership or status in the union. The agreement empowered the referee to set aside the discipline and compensate for lost time. Moreover, the union could appeal management's failure to discipline a worker if (1) the employee was guilty, (2) the worker interfered with shop discipline, *and* (3) the failure to discipline the worker discriminated against the union or the worker relative to membership or status in the union. If the referee made all three findings, "the company shall discipline the employee." In all appeals, a worker's union membership status would not "constitute interference with shop discipline." Future negotiations would deal with the appointment of the referee, the functions of the referee, and the appeal procedure.[95]

At the final OPM session, all parties refined the numerous details. The conciliator recalled: "Hillman read a short statement to the effect that this settlement . . . is not a closed shop agreement and is not to be interpreted as such. He then read the settlement and both sides agreed to it." Christoffel raised some questions about future negotiations, the nature of shop rules, and the selection of an arbitrator. After this, the union and management agreed to negotiate the unsettled items in Milwaukee. The union promised a union ratification meeting in two days and a return to work in three days.[96]

But the Washington Agreement quickly came apart over the difficult union security problem. The union leaders understood that the new arbitration system would include a provision ruling on maintaining membership. After a Milwaukee negotiating session, the conciliator reported that union leaders "insisted that the Knudsen-Hillman settlement of Saturday night meant 'maintenance of membership.' " Although the conciliator disagreed, union leaders told him that one federal negotiator "told them in Washington that the Union was to have its membership 'maintained.' " Allis-Chalmers officials were "infuriated by" the new union interpretation. When they refused to consider an arbitrator's authority to rule on maintenance of membership, UAW vice president Ed Hall threatened: "If company wants to fight, we will give it a real fight, and will pull the [other Allis-Chalmers] plants at LaPorte, Boston, Pittsburgh, etc." The strike negotiations, the conciliator concluded, were again hopelessly "deadlocked." Another agreed: "the parties are actually FARTHER apart . . . than at any time during the negotiations."[97]

At their February 24 meeting, Local 248 members voted for a union proposal that included the Washington Agreement and "an added clause to the effect that the Company would discharge any employee who is not a union member." In effect, the rank-and-file workers again voted for a union shop. Despite the membership vote, Max Babb refused to believe that his workers supported a union or closed shop. In an open letter to all Allis-Chalmers workers, he reaffirmed the management open shop position. The Washington Agreement, he wrote, broke down, because the union interpreted it as meaning a "closed or all-union shop." Only when all Allis-Chalmers workers *"of their own free will"* chose "100% [union] membership in our plant" would management concede on the union shop issue. "But," Babb continued, "we will not grant any union the right to *force* our employes into joining its organization." He then alluded to a more confrontational end to the long strike: "Talk among workers of a 'back-to-work' movement has been growing."[98]

As the government settlement disintegrated, Allis-Chalmers officials developed other means to end the bitter strike—a legal challenge of the union strike vote combined with a back-to-work movement. When Hillman asked Knudsen to obtain management approval for another proposed compromise, Allis-Chalmers officials had already made other plans to end the strike. After contacting them, a "highly indignant" Knudsen informed Hillman that Allis-Chalmers "was 'going to court' in about ten days." They now intended to petition the WERB for a new election to decide whether to continue the strike. The conciliator reported that they claimed that "the original strike vote was 'ambiguous.' "[99]

Allis-Chalmers officials inaugurated a public campaign to discredit the local union leadership. The larger strategy was the creation of a back-to-work movement among conservative and strike-weary workers. In early March, they charged that the UAW leaders had conducted an illegal strike vote. While federal officials explored the possibility of a federal takeover of the West Allis plant and a special Department of Labor board to investigate the walkout, Allis-Chalmers officials developed their Wisconsin solution to the strike.[100]

One Allis-Chalmers board member told a federal conciliator "to let us alone and give us three weeks and we will take care of this situation." At a meeting with Knudsen, three top officials confidently predicted a quick end to the strike: "Knudsen asked Mann how long the strike would run. Mann said he guessed about three weeks, because the Wisconsin Labor Board will probably order a strike vote and if a majority of the strikers vote to return to work, the strike will be over." Harold Story's 1939 Wisconsin Employment Relations Act would serve corporate ends.[101]

At the corporation's request, the WERB conducted hearings on the Local 248 strike vote. At the hearings, Max Babb claimed that he had received "hundreds of letters" from workers "who wished to return to the job but are afraid of the union." The workers, he said, "were afraid of physical violence, insults to themselves and their families and union threats that they will have no jobs when the strike is over if they go back to work now." He firmly believed 95 percent of the workers were against the union and about half of the union members signed their union cards only after threats and intimidation.[102]

In response to the Allis-Chalmers president, Harold Christoffel testified about the firm's "considerable union opposition" and its refusal to accept a union security clause. In addition, the union president blamed the labor troubles on the activities of "disrupters" in the West Allis plant. He also threatened to call 6,000 Allis-Chalmers workers to the hearings to testify about how they voted on the strike. In fact, the union actually began a "parade of witnesses"—about eighty-one strikers every twenty-five seconds—to testify about their strike votes.[103]

Allis-Chalmers officials then charged that UAW Local 248 stuffed the ballot boxes to obtain the required majority of the bargaining unit for strike approval. On the day of balloting, Leo Mann contended, Allis-Chalmers representatives counted only 4,547 workers who entered the union hall to vote on the strike, a figure far lower than the union's announced 6,700 voters. After an inspection of the company observer site, the *Milwaukee Journal* reported, "The investigation showed that the passing streetcars and trucks interfered with the view of the union office entrance." Allis-Chalmers officials also produced two handwriting experts who examined the strike ballots and contended that 40 percent of the ballots, about 2,400 of the 6,759 ballots cast, were "found to be fraudulent." In a "surprise statement," Local 248 leaders agreed with these findings but claimed that the AFL and IAM were responsible for the forged ballots. Still, the union's public image suffered.[104]

Following the WERB announcement of ballot fraud, a coordinated back-to-work movement coalesced around the AFL and other conservative workers. Through the strike, the AFL had continued its organizational drive and conducted meetings among Allis-Chalmers workers. An anonymous worker attributed the major source of the UAW opposition to the skilled craftsmen. "I, like about 40 percent more of the union," he wrote, "am absolutely against demanding the dismissal of these two fellows [Imp and Bohacheff]—who happen to belong to the A.F. of L.—these 40 percent are all skilled men, while the other 60 percent are the weaklings, such as young single men, sweepers, hitchers, cranemen, and other unskilled workers." Obviously, the resentment against militant unionism rested on a deep antagonism between the skilled craft workers and the less skilled production workers. For many conservative craft workers, the press accounts of union strike fraud discredited and undermined the authority and integrity of the UAW leaders.[105]

Allis-Chalmers officials modeled their anti-CIO strategy for the defeat of militant unionism after the previous week's Chicago International Harvester strike, which had a much stronger AFL presence.

Shortly after a court injunction to limit CIO picketers, the AFL marched three thousand workers into the Chicago agricultural equipment firm and broke the CIO strike. In the Milwaukee press, the front-page headlines on the Chicago strike presented Allis-Chalmers officials with a more forceful means for the resolution of their strike. Momentum for an back-to-work movement quickly grew.[106]

At the end of March, Allis-Chalmers and AFL officials implemented their well-orchestrated back-to-work movement. Since the beginning of the strike, some AFL unionists and some strike-weary workers had already returned to their jobs. As the strike progressed, the AFL and independent unionists also raised the national defense issue with the formation of American Workers for Defense, and its auxiliary, All-American Women, as patriotic, anti-CIO organizations of Allis-Chalmers workers. On March 24, the day after the reopening of International Harvester plant and two days after the WERB announcement of voting irregularities, an "anonymous" letter called for a back-to-work parade into the Allis-Chalmers plant. Although about eight hundred persons gathered the next day for the march, the union reported only fifteen actual "strikebreakers." Soon the crowd dispersed and left.[107]

The next day, on March 26, a delegation of top Allis-Chalmers officials arrived in Washington to meet with OPM director William Knudsen and Secretary of the Navy Frank Knox. They presented a transcript of the WERB hearings and the ballot fraud evidence to the federal officials. Immediately after the meeting, Knudsen and Knox dispatched a telegram to Allis-Chalmers officials asking them "to resume operations without delay." Two days later, the officials used the Knudsen and Knox telegram to inaugurate a massive back-to-work movement. "In compliance with the U.S. government's wires to us and the union," Max Babb wired all Allis-Chalmers workers, "we are notifying you to report for your regular shift Friday so the plant can be in full operation as soon as possible." The government, Babb continued, was "relying on the patriotic spirit of our workers to return to work on vitally needed defense orders without delay." Individual telegrams went to each Allis-Chalmers worker. Informing John R. Steelman about this, Story also expressed his readiness "to negotiate as soon as the union indicates a willingness to break the deadlock which has existed so long."[108]

The Milwaukee AFL unions also took advantage of the charges of a strike ballot fraud. Initially, the AFL leaders simply stepped up their organizational efforts. In one flyer, they wrote: "The admissions by the officers of the C.I.O.-U.A.W #248 of fraud in the strike referendum ballot should conclusively prove to you that your interests lie with an organization responsible to its members." In another, they charged that the UAW local "forfeited any claim on their loyalty and respect" and urged Allis-Chalmers workers "to repudiate such leadership." They noted that, although some "urged" AFL participation in "back to work movements," the AFL could "not honestly act unless and until a majority of the Allis-Chalmers employees come into our organization, as hundreds have already done." After the Knudsen-Knox and Allis-Chalmers telegrams, events moved rapidly, and the AFL actively joined the strikebreaking campaign. "A.F. of L. members," Jirikowic wrote the IAM president, "are returning to work as fast as possible, and the membership drive will still be carried on." To Jirikowic, the prospects for AFL unionism looked good.[109]

On March 27, the WERB publicly blamed Local 248 officials for ballot fraud. It ruled that the Allis-Chalmers strike was "not authorized by a majority of plant workers as required by state law." The union officers, it added, "caused at least 2,200 votes to be marked as favoring the strike and caused such other ballots to be counted and reported as votes of individual employees of the Allis-Chalmers Manufacturing Co. in favor of a strike." Union officers were responsible, the WERB reasoned, since they and the election committee were "in charge" of the strike election. The Wisconsin labor board planned to schedule a new election within fifteen days.[110]

In the afternoon, around fifty of the three hundred workers who had initially received telegrams reported for work at the West Allis plant. Babb announced that seventy-eight hundred workers received telegrams, that three hundred had immediately been recalled, and that the remaining would be called to work on Friday. At the plant gates, Local 248 members carried "Show Your Pass" signs and photographed returning workers with motion picture cameras. CIO pickets taunted and jeered at the strikebreakers.[111]

With thousands of workers scheduled to return to work, tensions mounted in West Allis. On Friday, Allis-Chalmers officials informed the navy department and the OPM that "about 2,000 production workers had entered the plant through a throng of strikers and sympathizers." In a telegram to Steelman, Babb criticized the UAW leaders' "defiance" of the government call for an "immediate return to work" as the UAW local's "mass picketing . . . blocked" the plant's main gate. He praised state and local authorities who had "cooperated fully to protect our employees' right to work and [had] preserved peace and order." Press accounts indicated that "about 300 production workers exclusive of foremen and management forces" returned to work. Union president Christoffel claimed that only forty-six of the four thousand recalled production workers reported for the first shift. The *Milwaukee Journal* reported that workers returned in a "slow trickle Friday morning which increased in volume as the day went on." A "crush of strikers and sympathizers" prevented over twelve hundred workers from entering the main gate of the plant.[112]

On Sunday, 6,300 workers attended a union meeting at the State Fair Park coliseum. Some union members and Allis-Chalmers officials claimed that the meeting was "packed" with members of other CIO unions. With a "sprinkling" of dissenters, the union members voted to continue the strike until the government forced acceptance of the OPM proposal. The plant reopening, the union leaders charged, was "a menace to the rights of all labor" and a "precedent" for "governmental strikebreaking." After the meeting, thousands of union members paraded around the Allis-Chalmers plant. The *Milwaukee Journal* reported that the back-to-work movement "was more noticeable on Saturday morning than it was on Friday." In the afternoon, seventy deputy sheriffs held back a crowd of two thousand union supporters. "The crowd," the newspaper added, "was in a kidding mood. It berated departing and arriving workers with cries of 'scabs,' 'skunks' and 'rats' and many boos."[113]

On Monday, the inevitable finally happened. Government authorities prepared for a tense new week. Five hundred police and special deputies were on hand. The Milwaukee police even stationed an armored vehicle nearby. Sheriff B. J. Shinners established a limit of three union "watchers" for each gate. Allis-Chalmers officials claimed that 58 percent of the first-shift work force returned to work. A morning crowd of two hundred swelled to twenty-five hundred for the afternoon shift change. As police stood guard, the crowd booed and jeered the returning workers. At an open-air rally in front of union headquarters, Christoffel called, "let the scabs go in and make love to the bosses." He ridiculed the Milwaukee police department's "armored fortress." Robert Buse told strikers and sympathizers: "Those who go in will be branded 'scabs' for life no matter where they go." Later in the day, the sheriff's deputies stopped a two-hour strike demonstration with "four barrages of tear gas."[114]

The street violence escalated the next day. In the morning, union workers interrupted streetcars bringing workers to the West Allis plant, pulling the trolleys from their power source and cutting the cables. The union passed out leaflets that claimed that Sheriff Shinners provoked the violence, and the crowd chanted "Down with 'Baseball Bat' Shinners." Numerous fights broke out between strikers and nonstrikers. "Sharp clashes," the *Milwaukee Journal* reported, "also occurred between police details and strikers." By nightfall, the conciliator reported that a "serious situation has developed." State and local authorities were unable to handle the prounion crowds: "Local #248 UAWA stormed the plant this PM. Police ran out of tear gas. Governor [Heil] was there in Cadillac car which was banged up and splashed with red paint." Strikebreakers could not leave the plant, and six hundred second-shift workers "fought their way into the plant."[115]

In reports to President Roosevelt, J. Edgar Hoover described the situation as "virtually insurrection." The FBI director wildly claimed, "a mob of some twenty thousand men has been attempting to storm the plant since 2:30 this afternoon." He also noted, "The mob appeared intent upon breaking into the plant and assaulting the workers therein and destroying the plant." Those inside, he added, were "arming themselves for defense against the strikers."[116]

Shortly after midnight on April 2, Governor Heil wired the president. "This afternoon," he reported, "a mob created a condition of riot and civil commotion in this community and created disorder which is beyond the control of all peace officers which can be assembled by the combined forces of the State, county, and local communities. The situation is absolutely out of control of all peace officers available." He concluded, "In the meantime in order to prevent bloodshed, I am requesting the company to cease all production operations."[117]

The widespread community violence quickly sobered both sides in the rancorous confrontation. The plant closing removed the provocative sight of strikebreakers forcing their way through the gates. After the plant had closed, the newly created National Defense Mediation Board (NDMB) called the two contending parties to Washington to renegotiate a settlement. The NDMB's objective was to reduce labor-management conflict in the interest of increased military production for the European war. For two intense days of negotiations, William H. Davis, the NDMB chair, and other board members presided over hearings, trying to resolve the seemingly insoluble Allis-Chalmers dispute. Unlike the OPM, the NDMB had full presidential authority to impose a settlement on labor and management.[118]

During the April 5 and 6 hearings, the original issue of union security remained the most contentious. Allis-Chalmers officials perceived two interrelated problems blocking a settlement. First, they refused to surrender their long-standing open shop position, continuing to insist that no worker's job should be dependent on membership in a labor organization. Second, they feared union, or other outside, incursions into the sensitive realm of management rights. Neither the union nor an arbitrator should be allowed to determine corporate policies.

The NDMB panelists repeatedly advised Allis-Chalmers officials that union recognition would solve their labor troubles. At one point, the NDMB chair admonished Allis-Chalmers attorney Leo Mann, "Here is a situation where a great majority of the men do belong to the Union and the Company would have a more peaceful time if the 100 percent would join the Union." With a union shop, Mann argued, Allis-Chalmers officials feared that the union would expel workers in order to have them discharged from the plant. In response, Davis suggested leaving the question of discharge to an arbitrator. Mann's position, the NDMB chair reasoned, was a "shadow" of the real issue, since "the referee would have the power to decide it."[119]

Still, the Allis-Chalmers attorney held fast to the company's open shop principle. "On our position," Mann told Davis, "union membership has nothing to do with whether a man works or not." Denying any corporate role in anti-CIO activities in the West Allis shops, the attorney disingenuously claimed: "We don't support an employee for the purpose of undermining. He merely works for us; we pay him for his work." Mann, Davis argued, was splitting hairs. The company position, he said, was that they would not support undermining the union, but "they nevertheless reserved the right to approve backhandedly the undermining of the Union." An arbitrator, Davis reasoned, would solve the firm's problems with the union. "If you have got any wisdom at all in this situation," he told Mann, "you will leave" this issue "to an arbitrator and get an arbitrator who is man enough and has the courage and knowledge of the subject to decide these questions."[120]

Through many long hours of argument and discussion about management prerogatives and rights and its fears of union power, Davis continued to insist on arbitration as the best basis for strike settlement. At one point, in complete exasperation, Davis declared: "Mr. Mann, you have been in a war with this Union. We are trying to establish peace with this Union. You have got to live with them. It is like your wife."[121]

After two days of intense disagreement over fundamental principles, the NDMB finally achieved a settlement of the Allis-Chalmers strike. It was a one-year agreement that combined the basic provisions of the 1940 contract and the referee provision of the initial Washington Agreement. The settlement placed limitations on union activity in the West Allis plant and ensured management's right to maintain discipline there. In an effort to resolve the difficult union security issue, the NDMB proposal utilized the earlier OPM formula for an impartial referee "to decide questions of activity which constituted 'undermining the union' and resulted in disrupting shop discipline." The new agreement also provided for specific procedures for the referee, permitted the union to appeal the application or nonapplication of discipline, and incorporated the West Allis shop rules into the new contract. In addition, the settlement included clauses on nondiscrimination against strikers, on the prohibition of strikes, lockouts, or interruption of production, and on renewed wage negotiations with a blanket wage increase retroactive to the date that the plant reopened. The impartial referee provided the important wedge that eventually ensured union security against AFL and company provocations. On April 6, both

Allis-Chalmers and UAW officials approved the NDMB settlement and ended the controversial defense strike. The next day, Local 248 members also ratified the settlement with a voice vote.[122]

In the meantime, Allis-Chalmers managers prepared the plant for full operations on April 8. But the resumption of production did not come easily. Two days after the reopening of the plant, Story wired Secretary of Labor Frances Perkins, "Mr. Christoffel and his bargaining committee are again causing trouble." Apparently, the union members ratified the settlement with a voice vote. "Mr. Christoffel," Story charged, "now says that an oral ratification is not binding on the union because its constitution requires a strike settlement be ratified by secret ballot vote." After the recent charges of ballot fraud, the union leader was now a stickler for procedural detail.[123]

After seventy-six days on the West Allis streets, the union still took a hard line on the union security issue. According to the Allis-Chalmers attorney, the union leaders told the federal conciliator "unless we conduct ourselves in accordance of their construction of the contract, . . . they will wage guerilla warfare in the plant, interrupting production, pulling switches, dropping wrenches on workmen, etc." They also threatened to "promote strikes" at the three other Allis-Chalmers plants where the CIO represented the workers.[124]

In a second telegram to the secretary of labor, Story decried Christoffel's continued obstruction. The Local 248 leader was still claiming that the union was not legally bound to the NDMB settlement since there had been no secret ballot. According to the attorney, Christoffel declared that "any ratification" of the NDMB settlement "would depend upon whether the company, in the union's opinion, is living up to the union's interpretation of the Washington agreement." Story also noted: "Definite signs of deliberate insubordination in the plant today by union representatives." The union repudiation of the NDMB agreement, he again charged, "is to be followed by guerilla warfare in the plant as recently announced by the union."[125]

The controversial defense strike certainly interfered with the production of important materials for Britain's defense against Germany. But its direct causes were the intransigent management opposition to CIO unionism and the fratricidal AFL-CIO civil war. Despite the later assertions of Louis Budenz, union security, not Communism, was the fundamental reason for the long and bitter defense strike. Informed observers said so at the time. Before the strike broke out, one federal conciliator reported, "Mr. Christoffel indicated that they were not contending for a closed shop, but that they were contending for 'peace and security.' " Another believed that AFL "disrupters" were behind the dispute, and that only twelve of the some two hundred nonunion members were real "trouble makers." And Thomas F.

Burns, an OPM labor representative, recalled a conversation with Harold Story, who expressed his dissatisfaction with the 1939 contract. The principal management objective, Burns informed Hillman, was "to get rid of the leadership of the local union, especially that of Mr. Harold Christoffel."[126]

The Allis-Chalmers UAW local had survived the management anti-union campaign and the AFL raids. And the NDMB settlement provided UAW Local 248 the means for eventual union security. With a provision for relatively unrestricted arbitration, the future Allis-Chalmers referees or arbitrators decided issues that gave UAW Local 248 some membership security. Through the late 1930s and into the World War II years, the aggressive shop steward structure, the thoughtful and strategic selection of grievances, and the decisions of the impartial arbitrator permitted UAW Local 248 to obtain security and to challenge management at the workplace. In effect, the militant CIO union continuously expanded the boundaries of union and worker rights and continuously redefined the "workplace rule of law."

# 5

---

# CHALLENGING MANAGEMENT RIGHTS:
## WORKERS, SHOP STEWARDS,
## AND GRIEVANCES,
## 1935–1945

During the formation of UAW Local 248 and the rancorous conflict with AFL unions, union leaders began to create an institutional structure to defend workers and to challenge management at the workplace. They created an aggressive, dense shop steward and committeeman system that constituted the essence of militant CIO unionism. This was a qualitatively different form of unionism from AFL "pure and simple" unionism. At first, Local 248 leaders used this shop floor system of worker representation to explore the boundaries of union and management power. Over time, they developed a strategic sense of using grievances to challenge management's perceived prerogatives and rights. Through the forceful use of shop floor grievance, they asserted worker rights, undermined supervisory authority, and questioned the character of technical innovation.

Moreover, the Second World War fundamentally transformed the social character of the shop floor and the nature of the American system of labor relations. After 1940, the growing demand for military products resulted in a severe labor shortage. The need for industrial workers drew large numbers of new workers—women, young people, and blacks—into the West Allis shops. Often ignorant about the formative years of unionism, these workers presented problems for both the corporation and the union. Nonetheless, the flexible and democratic union structure also managed to represent the varied interests of these new workers. Furthermore, the new wartime labor relations system under the National Defense Mediation Board (NDMB) and the National War Labor Board (NWLB) finally provided union security through the maintenance of membership and dues checkoff.

With assured membership stability, the union leaders continued and expanded their aggressive challenge to management control of the workplace. In the end, the militant UAW local transformed the labor-management relationship and presented an intolerable challenge to Allis-Chalmers officials.

Through the late nineteenth and early twentieth centuries, shop floor representation was a fundamental concern of organized and unorganized American workers. Since the workplace was an inherently authoritarian institution, three forms of worker representation evolved to assert and defend worker rights, to bring "industrial democracy" to American shops and factories. First, AFL unions created external business agents and sometimes in-plant shop committees to represent and defend skilled craftsmen. Second, during World War I, American industrial firms developed corporate representation plans, or company unions, in response to labor appeals for democracy in the workplace. Third, during the union drives of the 1930s, CIO unions blended the AFL tradition of union representation and the corporate tradition of plantwide representation to create aggressive shop steward and committeemen systems of worker representation. These systems evolved into CIO union locals where the rank-and-file workers built their own organizations from the bottom up. During the era of union building, all three forms coexisted in the West Allis plant.[1]

Although AFL shop committees sometimes relied on shop stewards, CIO unions rested on much denser networks of shop representatives to maintain direct contact with their large memberships in huge industrial plants. Much like the employer shop committees, the CIO shop stewards provided plantwide systems of representation for rank-and-file workers. "The Shop Stewards," a UAW pamphlet emphasized, "are the most important officers of the union. Through the Shop Steward the organized workers get away from individual and into the realm of collective bargaining." The shop stewards presented worker grievances and other demands to management, dealt with foremen and superintendents, functioned as "the direct representatives of the organized workers in the plant," and often served on the plant bargaining committee.[2]

The AFL and the CIO had quite different visions of the functions and activities of their shop stewards. In a 1935 pamphlet, one AFL union emphasized "the benefits and advantages of practical cooperation," which would promote "efficiency" and would "abolish industrial strife, with all of its attendant evils." In sharp contrast, the CIO image of the shop steward's role was far more aggressive and combative. One early UAW pamphlet noted that the CIO shop steward carefully monitored shop conditions by maintaining seniority rules, handling union discrimination cases, controlling speedup, safe-guarding sanitary conditions, and weeding out "all stool pigeons and suckers."[3]

The CIO emphasis on the resolution of shop grievances evolved into a new institutional form of workers' control. For example, a UAW pamphlet advised shop stewards that they could monitor the speedup of work in their shops and departments: "*Control speed-up* by seeing that the foreman doesn't pit one worker against another, by working with time study in timing the job, and by taking up grievances of speed-up with the foreman." In addition, it suggested a strategic plan to uncover grievances that avoided individual shop problems and es-tablished broad precedents for large numbers of workers. "Try and find some grievance," the pamphlet urged, "which will effect [*sic*] the whole department."[4]

Furthermore, unlike AFL business agents who represented local or international craft unions, CIO shop stewards clearly had a much more representative and democratic character. They represented workers in their particular shops or departments. CIO pamphlets stressed that the shop steward should know the particular shop or depart-ment and should be elected by its members. The "most practical" method of steward selection, one pamphlet advised, "is to elect the most capable man or woman in the department." They derived their power from neither a distant AFL office nor from management but rather from the rank and file, the ordinary workers in the shops. The UAW literature repeatedly emphasized the democratic nature of union power: "Where the foreman's power is handed down to him from the corporation owner at top, the steward's power comes from the workers below."[5]

A strong CIO shop steward system emerged from the looser system of AFL shop committees in the West Allis plant. It was a most effec-tive organizational tool in the explosive period of FLU and UAW growth. The early Allis-Chalmers AFL and FLU meetings often high-lighted the reports of departmental shop stewards. In August 1936, at the first Allis-Chalmers AFL membership meeting, shop representa-tives from several departments and shops reported about successful, although informal, negotiations on wages and working conditions. In October, the FLU Executive Board recommended the election of shop stewards from all West Allis departments. Slowly, these union repre-sentatives gained the respect and allegiance of their fellow workers.[6]

In the first stages of rapid membership growth, the informal FLU steward structure soon adapted to the new shop conditions. In Janu-ary 1937, the Executive Board established a committee of five "to organize and direct departmental membership drives in conjunction with the shop stewards." It later recommended a study of the steward systems of other Milwaukee unions. In February, FLU shop stewards convened for the first time as a body in a basement hall of the South Side Armory to create a committee to study the question of joining the CIO. In March 1937, a few days prior to UAW affiliation, the shop stewards discussed the makeup of the grievance structure. They decided that each Allis-Chalmers division would have a steward chairman and a steward secretary. This organizational structure copied the WAWC representation system, but it possessed a denser network of shop representatives. Subsequently, the union leaders divided these parts into smaller shop units, represented by shop committeemen.[7]

In 1937, Julius Blunk, the Local 248 recording secretary, described the union's shop steward and committeeman system to a NLRB panel. As in many smaller firms, such as Chrysler, Nash, and Packard, the UAW at Allis-Chalmers had a very large number of union representatives. "Local 248," Blunk said, "has a system of stewards and committeemen. . . . A division is headed by a steward and secretary who are in charge of that particular division." Beneath the two divisional stewards, he added, "we have a system of committeemen who may function over a number of men, anywhere between twenty-five and fifty. The number varies as it applies to the unit." The shop representatives processed "their own grievances as far as possible." He estimated that approximately two hundred and twenty-five committeemen monitored conditions in the West Allis plant. In all, around 265 union representatives uncovered and processed Allis-Chalmers grievances.[8]

The union steward structure often confronted management's authority structure. According to Blunk, the union hierarchy of representation replicated the management hierarchy of authority. "We have a system," he testified, "where the stewards structure parallels the set up of management. The committeeman equals the foreman; the steward of the division equals the superintendent, or, rather, parallels the superintendent." Moreover, Blunk's use of the term "equals" revealed the extent of the union challenge to the management perception of the factory order.[9]

The Allis-Chalmers grievance procedure developed two parallel tracks for the resolution of disputes. First included in the 1937 contract, the grievance process started with shop committeemen and then moved up to the divisional shop stewards, the bargaining committee, and the union officers. For the company, it began with the shop foremen or assistant foremen, the department head or divisional superintendent, the Labor Advisory Committee (LAC), the Shop Management Committee, and the Official Committee of the Board of Directors. In other words, at the first step, the worker or shop committeeman took the grievance to the foreman or assistant foreman. If the dispute was not resolved within twenty-four hours, other worker representatives took the grievance to progressively higher levels of management. Although minor details changed with each contract, this remained the basic procedure until the NDMB capped the grievance process with an impartial referee or arbitrator.[10]

The combination of this grievance procedure with a dense system of shop representatives challenged the traditional distribution of workplace authority and power. An early UAW pamphlet commented on the difficulties of "educating foremen to collective bargaining." Before unionization, these shop supervisors "were little tin gods in their own departments. They were accustomed to having orders accepted with no questions asked. They expected workers to enter into servile competition for their favors." After the formation of a UAW local, "the foreman finds the whole world turned upside down. His small-time dictatorship has been overthrown, and he must be adjusted to a democratic system of shop government."[11]

For Harold Christoffel, these shop stewards and committeemen were the core of CIO industrial unionism. They addressed "general working conditions, the things which are closest to the workers' hearts." They also brought genuine worker representation to the West Allis shops. In contrast to the AFL representation, Christoffel noted: "Any grievance in the shop is taken care of by the steward structure. In other words, the real union work is done in the shop by the stewards. That is one of the differences between industrial and craft unions. Industrial unionism depends upon the democratic set-up of the stewards to represent the workers and the craft unions are represented by the business agents." At one steward meeting, Christoffel reiterated the democratic theme of rank-and-file participation in union affairs. He cautioned the shop leaders "not to let their representation think that they were better than the men they represent as they are only servants of the men."[12]

Many Allis-Chalmers workers echoed their union leader on the importance of shop stewards in the union grievance procedure. Michael Boblin, a foundry worker and shop steward, voiced the common view of his shopmates. With the organization of the UAW-CIO, he told a NLRB panel, "The changes are so great that it is astounding." Asked about the changes, he replied: "In the betterment of the conditions, the treatment by the foremen, superintendents, the increase in wages, and so forth." Harold Schuelke, a boilermaker's helper, described how the steward structure altered the distribution of power in the shop. "The committeemen," Schuelke said, "work in the capacity of taking up grievances to the foreman, with the complaint men, and if it cannot be settled satisfactorily, the committeeman goes to the steward, or the steward takes it up further." For these and other workers, the shop representatives completely transformed their working lives and represented an important connection to their union.[13]

Despite their important assistance to fellow workers, these new rank-and-file leaders often faced a difficult and thankless task. One steward, Walter Miller, claimed that he represented from 160 to 165 workers from several different crafts. The company paid him for only one hour per day for his steward activities. Consequently, Miller wrote up worker grievances at home. Often verbally articulate, the stewards possessed a shop floor charisma that made them leaders in their division. They had the "guts" to stand up to and talk back to the shop foremen and superintendents. But the shop stewards often had had little formal training in writing and must have struggled to draft the written presentations of grievances.[14]

The shop stewards possessed a deep commitment both to unionism and to their fellow workers. When queried about the "special rights and privileges accorded to stewards and committeemen," Blunk responded, "He has no particular rights or privileges; it doesn't entitle him to better work; he doesn't get any more work; he is not exempt from union dues; he has the privilege of going to three or four more meetings a month than what the average member has to; those are the privileges he has." Besides collecting and bringing union dues to the office, he added, the shop stewards "must devote anywhere from five to six hours a week on their own time and they must pay their dues as well as any members." Their satisfaction derived from their commitment to their union, their fellow workers, and a more democratic workplace.[15]

For UAW Local 248, the education of shop floor leaders was an important union activity. In September 1937, the Local 248 Educational Committee discussed the union's proposed educational program for all levels of union leaders—the officers, the shop stewards, and the committeemen. "We must accept the fact," the union committee concluded, "that the backbone of American democracy must be a strong and enlightened labor movement. In other words, the heart of American Democracy must be trade union democracy." The educational program, it decided, should include courses in American labor history, trade union tactics, and public speaking. The educational committee also recommended involving the entire class in the discussions, purchasing UAW educational materials, developing cooperative programs with other unions, making up a weekly schedule of classes, and including spouses, girl friends, and families in the union programs. To this end, the Allis-Chalmers union hired Herman Schendel, a former Milwaukee teacher, to develop and to coordinate the comprehensive program.[16]

Besides the formal classes, the frequent meetings of the stewards and committeemen also served an educational purpose. The union representative, Blunk noted, "must be acclimated; it takes time to learn to be a steward." The shop steward meeting, he observed, "is called primarily to set up a basis for handling grievances." Once they got together, the more experienced stewards aided the novices. "Some stewards," Blunk continued, "are more efficient in handling grievances than others. In this gathering we come together for the purpose of exchanging ideas on how we may obtain the best results in settling our grievances as they arise in the shop." The steward meetings, he concluded, "are in the nature of a school."[17]

For UAW Local 248, the steward structure and grievance procedure were much more than an institutional form of worker representation in the plant. The union leaders used them to register worker discontent with working conditions and to test the limits of worker authority and power in the shops. Most often, the union grievances turned on disputes over interpretation of the contract and touched on questions of wages, hours, and working conditions. In a sense, these grievances penetrated to the core of "pure and simple unionism." A careful examination of the more fundamental and basic questions revealed that worker disputes went far beyond the bounds of conservative trade unionism. Beneath the surface, the issues involved worker dignity, authority relations, and technical innovation. Gradually, Local 248 leaders used the grievance procedure to rationalize workplace relations within the framework of what has been labeled a "workplace rule of law." Later, after the rationalization of Allis-Chalmers labor relations, they expanded the boundaries of union control and directly contested management's shop floor power.[18]

As windows into the workplace, the Allis-Chalmers worker grievances disclosed a broad range of concerns about working conditions and management policies. The union contract, while it often mirrored some shop floor issues, really represented the institutional concerns of the international and local union leaders. In contrast, grievances came from below, from the rank-and-file workers. To be sure, union leaders pressed hardest on those grievances that would establish union precedents for the whole plant. Nonetheless, they also needed to attend to the individual interests of workers in order to ensure their attachment to the union.

In the West Allis plant, the first union grievances were cautious, tentative explorations of the nature of the grievance procedure and the boundaries of management authority. From 1937 through early 1939, one hundred and ninety-four grievances went to the Labor Advisory Committee, the third step of the grievance procedure. They represented the tip of an iceberg of contention. Clearly, myriad others were resolved informally at the lower-level stages of the grievance procedure, often with the foreman or superintendent. In fact, an Allis-Chalmers subject index of grievances indicated that some 2,500 grievances from 1937 to 1940 encompassed an extremely wide range of issues—procedures for grievances and collective bargaining, seniority, transfers, layoffs, discrimination, antiunion statements, discourtesy toward or intimidation of union representatives, management discipline of workers, hiring and firing, working conditions, wage rates, paychecks, and numerous other matters.[19]

The first sixteen Labor Advisory Committee responses to worker grievances illustrated the initial union exploration of the limits of management control on the shop floor. They went to the management committee shortly after the signing of the first agreement and after a union shop stewards' meeting on departmental grievances. Seven of these grievances involved individual rate adjustments under the 1937 agreement. Others involved inclusion of bonuses with vacation checks, checks for wage adjustments, wage adjustments for heat treaters and spray painters, and seniority and transfer policies. Neither adventurous nor innovative, these first grievances simply tested the methods and procedures for the resolution of worker problems.[20]

As the union gained experience, it developed a strategic and tactical sense of the use of the grievance procedure. The initial grievances for women and for No. 2 Tractor Shop workers illustrated this evolving pattern. Other grievances appealed earnings of all workers in the heat treat department, hourly rates in the fuel pump department, and record keeping for incentive rates in the switchboard department. Many grievances stressed basic questions of human dignity and worth. Often these grievances dealt with working conditions and job safety. For example, workers in the electrical department called for electric fans in the lavatory because the temperature was too high and "the air stuffy and stagnant." Also, the women workers of the electrical department demanded their own rest room, since the one that they used in a nearby shop "was overcrowded." Allis-Chalmers officials refused to install fans and promised a new women's rest room if they expanded the electrical shop. In another instance, the No. 2 Foundry workers wanted the "regulation of the heat and temperatures in the basement." The company installed new heating equipment. But management rejected these calls for improved working conditions: for example, solderers who requested gloves to protect hands from "burrs" and "chemicals" and yardmen who asked for "rubber boots and hats" for protection in their outside work.[21]

Still other grievances presented a significant challenge to the shop floor authority of straw bosses, foremen, and supervisors. In one instance, a shop steward protested the "general lack of cooperation between Harvey Tischak, Inspector, and the employees of the No. 2 Foundry Cleaning Room." The inspector, the union charged, undermined "harmony" in the department and gave "the impression that he is superior and uses this as a weapon." The union wanted the man "transferred" or "cautioned as to his general attitude to his fellow workers." In its response, the LAC declined to transfer the inspector. Nonetheless, Allis-Chalmers officials did caution him "to use fair judgment which always has been the policy of the Company."[22]

Such a grievance had important implications for the tenor and mood of workers in the department. Obviously, Allis-Chalmers officials supported their low-level inspector. They did not remove him from his position. Still, the inspector knew that the foundry workers and the union kept a close eye on him. And if he did not receive a transfer or a reprimand, the company did caution him about the use of fair judgment. As a result, his authority declined.

Another important category of grievances touched on the complicated question of new production technologies. An Allis-Chalmers subject index of grievances listed almost twelve hundred, or about 48 percent of the total, involving wages. Many of these protested the unfair setting of wage and piece rates, requested the presence of union representatives for time studies, or demanded access to management time study records. Often, the reasons for adjustments in wage rates were technical changes in production methods. Since the early twentieth century, Frederick Taylor's notions, and especially those of Frank Gilbreth, informed reorganization of the work processes and improved forms of plant layout. When the company changed its production methods, it attempted to change the day or piece rates for a job classification. Time and motion studies were a managerial means to ensure the gains that came from technical improvements on the shop floor.[23]

At Allis-Chalmers, many grievances involved the problems of rate cutting, setup prices, engineering changes, requests for new time studies, and pressures for increased efficiency and higher output. Clearly, these reflected more than a simple worker concern for more money. They often directly or indirectly mirrored worker concerns, fears, and anxieties about new technologies and new work routines. For workers, wage grievances frequently constituted a means for resisting new technologies and new production methods. For union activists, such grievances often channeled and mobilized the workers' customary sense of equity and fairness, a mood captured in the labor slogan of "a fair day's work for a fair day's pay." In many ways, the union institutionalized informal forward-looking values about worker rights in the process of technical advance.

Because the Allis-Chalmers plant underwent considerable technical change through the 1920s and 1930s, the installation of new production systems in the West Allis shops frequently raised tensions between managers and workers and resulted in many grievances from union workers. For example, with the construction of the mechanized No. 3 Tractor Shop in 1937, managers and engineers installed new mechanized molding units in the No. 2 Foundry. Early in 1938, Julius Blunk wrote to two neighboring UAW locals with a similar "conveyor system" in their plants. "We would like to have some man in your organization, who is thoroughly familiar with your foundry problems," Blunk requested, "come before our foundry people to enlighten them on the worker's problems." His letter concluded: "The situation is new to us and we need all possible advice."[24]

After this initial inquiry to other UAW locals, the foundry shop steward began to file a number of grievances on behalf of the workers in the No. 2 Foundry. According to one grievance report, wage rates were the surface issue. Although workers in the older No. 1 Foundry received piece rates for their work, those in the new "32 man unit" received hourly rates. Under more traditional production methods, they preferred piece rates because they could control their output and their level of wages. But since a conveyor system regulated the pace of production, management no longer needed piece rates as incentives for greater output and shifted to an hourly pay system. In the new mechanized foundry, workers received less pay than their fellow workers in the older foundry. Within a short period of time, all classes of foundry workers—iron molders, pourers, shake-out men, sand mixers, casting separators, and sand separators—filed grievances requesting substantial raises in their hourly rates to equalize pay scales in the old and new units. The molders felt that their wage rate "is not enough money for the type of work they are doing and being in a foundry." The pourers argued that "they have to pour all day long and keep the same pace as the line." The sand separators believed it unfair that they receive the same rate as ordinary laborers. The steward noted, "These men must work harder than laborers and they feel they should receive more pay." The foundry workers evidently believed that the labor-saving machines did not save their labor. If they worked harder at the pace of the conveyor, they should receive greater compensation for their efforts. The LAC denied the requests for wage increases. Although the surface issue was foundry wages, the underlying one was the mechanization of the foundry, which altered work routines, increased effort, and changed the structure of work relations.[25]

Grievances flowed from the recently mechanized No. 2 Foundry for several months. After engineers installed a newer sixteen-man unit, foundry workers again protested the introduction of an improved technical system. The less skilled workers—pourers, casting sorters, and shake-out men—contested their low hourly rates. The more skilled molders, who were now on piece rates, insisted that technical difficulties contributed to lost time and reduced pay. "While waiting for iron and the line is full," the foundry steward wrote, "they cannot put molds on the line, also breakdowns due to the cause of the machinery." Sometimes, the skilled molders outpaced and outperformed the mechanized conveyors in their quest for higher wage rates. At other times, the machinery broke down, increased their idle time, and reduced their pay. Apparently, the molders earned more pay under the older and more traditional production methods. Since they could control the pace of their production in the older shop, they could produce at a more consistent rate than in the new shop and thus could increase their earnings. Although the LAC refused to increase the hourly rates of the less skilled workers, it did offer the skilled molders regular day rates for their lost time. Management strategy was to satisfy the grievances of the more skilled, more valuable, and hence potentially most threatening workers and to ignore the needs of the less skilled workers.[26]

Nonetheless, the mechanized foundry remained a hotbed of contention and a source of many grievances from Allis-Chalmers workers. In the summer of 1938, the molders voiced a common complaint about cutting piece rates. "When you bring a job down from the No. 1 Foundry to the No. 2 Foundry," the two foundry stewards wrote, "you are cutting the price by more than half, and we have the same amount of work." In other words, the mechanized foundry workers received half the pay for the same amount of work or effort. The molders believed that physical effort should determine the amount of their wages. Management labeled this view the quantum theory of work. In line with the contract provision that permitted rate cuts for "new production methods," the LAC ruled that the reason for reduced prices was "different working conditions" and "different equipment" in the two foundries. However, these differences mattered little to workers who saw themselves produce more of the same product and exert more physical effort for lower wage rates.[27]

In the winter of 1938–1939, Harold Christoffel, the union president, presented still another grievance on the mechanized No. 2 Foundry units. In a letter to Allis-Chalmers officials, he noted the continuous "problems" since the installation of the mechanized units. Expressing the sentiments of the shop workers, he called for an increase in the base rates of pay, retiming of the piece-rate jobs with allowance for "various operations and disturbances," and more equitable resolution of earlier grievances on workers' rates. Finally, Christoffel observed, "When these units were installed, the men were repeatedly told that they would make at least as much as they made before." The foundry workers, he argued, now suffered from "greater fatigue for the same time worked for which less monies received." To be sure, mechanization may have eased some physical burdens, but it also increased the pace and intensity of the work. The union president argued that since the men actually worked harder in the mechanized foundry, they should receive greater compensation. Christoffel believed that foundry workers should benefit from improvements in industrial technology. Once again, the LAC refused to adjust the foundry wage rates.[28]

The loss of such an important grievance certainly angered union leaders and rank-and-file workers and added fuel to the fire of shop floor dissension. Over time, these and other losses strengthened labor's resolve to seek a more equitable mechanism for the resolution of workplace disputes. Moreover, taken together, these foundry grievances demonstrated that mechanization was truly a complicated problem for those employed in the West Allis shops. Wages represented the form of the grievances, but the details touched on the nature and character of work, the structure of relations between managers and workers and between skilled pieceworkers and less skilled hourly workers, mechanical problems of new industrial systems, and questions of worker or union control of technical innovation in the shop.

In 1937–1938, a similar situation developed in the new No. 3 Tractor Shop when managers and engineers improved production methods for machining and assembling tractors. Union grievances in this newly mechanized shop concerned taking production workers off the line to repair flawed work, maintaining seniority for workers transferred to the tractor lines, and lunching between jobs on the production lines. The repeated breakdowns also caused numerous grievances about abusive foremen who pressured workers to maintain output quotas. Despite the considerable technical sophistication of line production methods in this period, the worker grievances revealed that the Allis-Chalmers assembly lines continued to fall far short of the state of the art of modern production technology.[29]

The tractor shop difficulties also involved technical problems with "new systems of manufacture," the tune-up of new equipment, and the development of new work skills. Once again, a technical question manifested itself as a wage question. "It is estimated," wrote William Watson, the plant production manager, "that the tuning up of new systems of tractor production in the foundries, tractor and general machine shops will require from thirty to ninety days more." Clearly, it took considerable amounts of time, energy and thought to coordinate the men, machines, and materials for new methods of tractor production. Therefore, Allis-Chalmers officials established "temporary" hourly rates and piece-rate prices for the production workers.[30]

The newly mechanized tractor shops required many major and minor adjustments for a whole range of men and machines throughout the plant. Foundry and tractor shop grievances detailed how it affected the foundry and tractor shop and influenced different aspects of work on the shop floor. Since the new production methods and practices did not operate at maximum efficiency, Allis-Chalmers workers often demanded a more equitable solution to their problem of reduced income. They also resented the changes in their working conditions, particularly those that eliminated their craft customs and traditions and undermined their perceptions of their dignity and worth. In pursuit of these early grievances, workers tried to control the introduction of new industrial methods and techniques and to alleviate their effect on the shop floor. Interestingly, they never seemed to challenge directly the necessity for improved technologies. Instead, they attempted to contain their influence on their terrain and reap a fair share of its benefits.

By the late 1930s, the steward structure and grievance procedure institutionalized the militant defense of worker rights on the shop floor. In 1940, a Local 248 pamphlet cited grievance resolution as a major advantage for unionized workers. In a comparison of 1929 and 1940 shop conditions, the union pamphlet proclaimed: "Grievances!! Sure, we had plenty of them—but we didn't dare tell the Company about them. We went *home* and kicked about what went on at work. The Company transferred and demoted just as it saw fit. Whatever the question was, the Company ran the show." When the Great Depression came, it continued, Allis-Chalmers workers worked harder to forestall the inevitable layoffs. "We got panicky," the union pamphlet noted, "and competed against each other to keep our jobs. And the harder we worked the worse it was for all of us." After the layoffs, two general wage cuts compounded the workers' severe economic difficulties. "We were like sawdust," the union pamphlet concluded, "just unorganized wood. All the Company had to do was keep us good and scattered and they could tramp on us just as they pleased."[31]

After the formation of the UAW local, the union pamphlet noted, Allis-Chalmers workers experienced no wage cuts during the 1937–1938 recession. The union contract and grievance procedure established orderly practices for layoff and rehiring. "Instead of being sawdust under the Company's feet," the union noted, "we are a club now, that we can use to protect ourselves when we are attacked." Things had changed considerably since the onslaught of the Great

Depression. "But the biggest thing we have is a voice—democracy on the job—the right to speak up when we don't like something. Anyone of us can protest now—and not get fired, because all the other workers are in back of us."[32]

In the Allis-Chalmers grievance process, the union contract established a system of rules for the operation of the plant, a workplace rule of law. If management wanted to fire a worker, it needed to show a "just cause." If it wanted to hire, it did so "according to a rule, a rule that protects all of us." The new rule of law touched various aspects of shop floor life. The union pamphlet concluded: "Wage adjustments, promotions and demotions, transfers, piece-rate adjustments, petty straw bosses—all can be handled through the union without anyone losing his neck for it. . . . All of this is quite a bit different from the earlier days when we took what the Company did—and did our squawking at home." To be sure, Allis-Chalmers officials still had the final say in the resolution of worker grievances; but workers now had a collective voice in important workplace issues.[33]

In 1940, Don D. Lescohier, an Allis-Chalmers consultant and former John R. Commons associate, surveyed the labor relations situation. Despite the absence of formal and official union recognition, he found an aggressive challenge to management control of the workplace. One section of his report on "The Closed Shop and Seniority" described the Allis-Chalmers grievance procedure as "a menace to the successful operation of the business." His thorough analysis of recent union grievances revealed a complex strategy in "the character of the grievances it has been bringing in, its attacks upon the disciplinary controls of the foremen and superintendents, and its repeated defiances of company authority in the shop." Moreover, Lescohier observed, "Union violations of the contract have consisted principally of invasions of management's control of the shop and grievance tactics designed to stretch the meaning and widen the interpretation of the Agreement."[34]

The 1941 strike settlement fundamentally shifted the balance of power between management and labor and resulted in a stronger union presence in the West Allis plant. With the addition of an impartial referee, the new grievance procedure removed management's unilateral authority in the resolution of grievances. Since management no longer arbitrarily defined the workplace rule of law, the aggressive union gained in authority and power. From this point on, the Local 248 leaders redefined the workplace system of industrial jurisprudence into an even more confrontational challenge to management control.

With increased war production in the summer of 1941, management faced a major labor problem—a deeply factionalized labor force of militant unionists, conservative unionists, and antiunion workers. The recent "defense" strike clearly exacerbated these tensions. After the government endorsed the back-to-work movement, almost half the Allis-Chalmers work force returned to their jobs. Some supported the AFL, some opposed CIO leaders, and many patriotically deferred to federal authority. Apparently, the long strike had also weakened the morale of many union supporters, so when workers returned to the plant in early April 1941, deep divisions arose between those who had stayed out and those who returned. It was an explosive mixture of CIO members, AFL members, and American Workers for Defense (AWD) supporters. Each faction taunted and reviled the others for their behavior during the strike.

In the first days after the strike, these different worker factions aggravated the normal shop floor tensions and problems. For example, the AWD contained only strikebreakers and scabs. The AFL had supported the back-to-work movement, advised its members to cross CIO picket lines, and used appeals to worker patriotism in its efforts to enroll Allis-Chalmers workers in the AFL cause. On the other hand, the UAW local ensured its membership loyalty with a requirement that CIO union members turn in their old membership cards and, before receiving new ones, sign a witnessed pledge card as proof that they had not broken the strike. Workers from each side displayed their CIO, AFL, and AWD buttons to demonstrate their respective positions on the controversial strike. These and numerous other problems soon went to the new refereed grievance procedure.[35]

In his first grievance rulings, Lloyd Garrison, the Allis-Chalmers referee, decided cases that reflected these social and political strains. One case involved an independent unionist who allegedly threw paint on the Local 248 offices. Another ruled on the antiunion activities of Imp and Bohacheff, who had precipitated the 1941 strike. In both cases, Garrison ruled that much time had passed since the original incidents, that the facts could not be proved, and that discipline was not warranted.[36]

A third decision was an important general grievance on the wearing of buttons in the West Allis shops. It went to the heart of the union concern about peace and security. It examined the disruptive factionalism of CIO, AFL, and AWD supporters in the shops. For Garrison, the AWD button presented problems because it was patently disruptive of shop discipline. Unlike the CIO button, "a traditional and customary incident of membership in a bona fide labor organization," the AWD button, Garrison observed, had "a dynamic and aggressive quality." Therefore, he concluded: "The wearing of the A.W.D. button is, in short, a method of spreading and perpetuating dissention [sic] among the men and of attacking the C.I.O., and as such constitutes a prohibited 'activity' under the Agreement." He directed company officials to tell all employees to stop wearing the AWD buttons in the West Allis shops and departments.[37]

The AFL buttons presented a much more complicated problem. According to Garrison, some Allis-Chalmers workers received and wore AFL buttons "without even signing an application blank." Others wore them with a sincere and thorough commitment to AFL unionism. Accordingly, Garrison decided that some AFL buttons had as their "only object" the advertisement of "opposition to the C.I.O. in order to weaken their position." Because of the AFL-CIO factionalism, he ruled: "under the peculiar circumstances existing in the Allis-Chalmers plant, all A.F.of L. buttons tend to have an unsettling and provocative effect and that therefore only those men who can show a clear title to the buttons by virtue of membership should be entitled to retain them." He directed management to verify such entitlement with a request that the worker present his AFL dues book. The company should ensure that "a man who wears an A.F.of L. button in the plant has some color of title to it as evidenced by a dues book." While this limited UAW interference with the minority status of legitimate AFL workers, Garrison noted that other provisions in the contract prevented AFL members from direct and indirect union activities such as the solicitation of members, the posting of notices, or the distribution of leaflets in the plant. These decisions legitimated the CIO in the West Allis plant.[38]

The deeply factionalized work force was but one problem that demanded the attention of management. As Nelson Lichtenstein has noted, an "enormous demographic transformation" of the American industrial work force occurred during World War II. As the United States became more involved in defense and war production, the traditional work force, the "older white male workers," who had been "union conscious in the prewar years, were moving to new jobs, taking supervisory positions, or enlisting or being drafted into the armed forces." To fill the social void, he observed, "came a flood of new recruits: women, blacks, teenagers, . . . many from low-wage unorganized industries or first-time entrants into the factory workforce." For some new workers, "unions seemed irrelevant" since they received "relatively high, steady war industry wages." As the West Allis work force grew from about eight thousand to eighteen thousand through the war years, it replicated the national pattern of social transformation and introduced three new groups, women, African Americans, and youth to the wartime work force.[39]

With the expansion of Allis-Chalmers industrial facilities and the departure of draft-age male workers for European and Pacific battle-fields, women war workers entered the West Allis plant in ever-increasing numbers. In July 1937, women numbered only 144 in a total production work force of 4,727, or 3.0 percent of the total. They performed relatively light work in traditional women's jobs as core-makers and coil winders. In December 1941, the expansion of defense production increased the number of women workers to 750 of the 11,250 Allis-Chalmers workers, or 6.7 percent of the total. By late 1942, approximately twenty-five hundred men were on military leave of absence from the West Allis plant. The 385 female workers in January 1942 increased to 2,770 in August 1944. At its peak, the wartime employment of women amounted to 25 percent of the West Allis works. These women worked in sixty-one different shop classifica-tions, which included traditional women's jobs and many nontradi-tional ones, such as "crane operation, riveting, soldering, brazing, and gear cutting."[40]

But this was only at the main West Allis plant. Allis-Chalmers opened two other Milwaukee-area industrial plants for the produc-tion of war materials. These were the Supercharger plant and the interconnected Hawley plant (which manufactured equipment for the Manhattan Project) and the Electrical Control plant (which manufac-tured electric control panels for navy ships). Both the Supercharger plant and the Electric Control plant employed large numbers of women. For example, the Supercharger plant, which manufactured turbo superchargers for the Army Air Force's "flying fortresses," first opened in early 1942. It expanded quite rapidly. In 1943, Christoffel reported: "This is the largest aviation plant in the area. It employs well over 80% women." In September 1944, the Supercharger plant employed 5,600 workers, of whom 3,000, or 53.6 percent, were women.[41]

At the Supercharger works, plant managers and engineers simpli-fied and redesigned tasks for the new, female work force. Tradition-ally, the electrical and metalworking shops were male-dominated. A craft tradition guided skilled male journeymen through their varied tasks and routines. But Supercharger work, the plant superintendent claimed, had to be "tailored" for women. He cited the example of gauges that "showed quite a swing of the needle to register a thou-sandth of an inch." Unfamiliar and unschooled in the use of shop equipment, women workers may have missed important "dimensional variations" without the redesigned gauges. In 1942, the Supercharger plant employed seventeen men to redesign the tools and to solve the "special problems" of women's tasks. Moreover, foremen were "espe-cially trained by management to instruct women in the operation of big machines." For plant managers, the special job simplification and job redesign program so greatly improved worker productivity and product quality that one researcher reported that this plant "achieved the lowest unit cost among supercharger manufacturers."[42]

In addition, Allis-Chalmers officials offered a full range of training programs, social activities, and welfare services for women and other workers. For training women workers, management "offered shop math, blueprint reading and precision measuring." In an effort to win worker loyalty, the firm sponsored welfare and recreational activities—bowling and softball teams, a rifle club, parties and picnics for shop groups, United Service Organization campaigns to donate cookies, cakes, pies, and money for servicemen, and campaigns for War Loan, Red Cross, and Community Chest drives. The Foremen's Club brought in guest speakers. The Welfare Department handled 7,773 cases of absenteeism and illness. In 1944, an employee counseling program conducted over one thousand interviews on myriad problems from evictions to citizenship papers. Sometimes, these Allis-Chalmers activities reflected gender-based stereotypes on women's roles and interests. For example, in a pun on the corporate name, Allis-Chalmers officials adopted "Allie Charmer" as the firm's female image. Allie Charmer was a female cartoon figure and mascot for the firm's literature and activities for women workers. A gendered and weakened image, it replaced the more powerful and conventional wartime icon, Rosie the Riveter.[43]

In 1942, the Allis-Chalmers Industrial Relations Department published a pamphlet, *Women: Safe at Work at Allis-Chalmers*, to acclimate women to the new world of the workplace. In its opening lines, the brochure praised the new role of women in industry:

> Every day, women's war efforts open up new and exciting fields. Working shoulder to shoulder with men in factories, women are being called to master the various crafts of the machine age . . . and master them quickly.
>
> In this and in every other critical period of our history, women are making a real job of it. Just as the pioneer women took up the musket to defend the home, so today women are taking up the wrench, the riveting gun, the micrometer.

On the surface, the pamphlet appeared to present a stirring appeal about the new role of women in American industry.[44]

However, the pamphlet emphasized the traditional and gender-stereotyped work skills of dexterous, fine handwork. In a section that described "fingers" as "fighters" in the war effort, the pamphlet advised: "Skillful, quick-moving fingers and keen eyes uniquely qualify you and millions of other women for home, shop and office work today. Precision work is at once your pride, your breadwinner, and your bit for victory." The patriotic rhetoric praised skill, but the reality stressed repetitive precision work.[45]

The Allis-Chalmers pamphlet contained other gender-based stereotypes about its female work force. It paternalistically cautioned women workers to avoid frantic or frenzied behavior. "Try to develop a calm and quiet way of working to promote safety." At the same time, it advised women to avoid feminine dress: "Experience, often tragic, brings quick agreement on WHAT NOT TO WEAR. Frills are out! Skirts, jewelry, cuffs, ties, loose belts, metal fastenings, long sleeves, outside jackets, outside pockets, flowing sleeves and thin-soled, high-heeled, narrow-toed shoes are hazards in any job, especially around *moving* machinery." Instead of "glamorizing the jobs" with "tricky work outfits," the Allis-Chalmers approach emphasized a more serious attitude to the traditionally male world of the shop floor. "The girls," a corporate researcher related, "wore a rather unattractive, though practical, one-piece work outfit made of heavy grey and white striped denim." The "idea" was "to 'de-sex' the women's appearance."[46]

A patriotic tone also saturated the Allis-Chalmers characterization of women war workers. The women were a "national strength" and "Uncle Sam's girls," working for "freedom's cause." Allis-Chalmers officials connected health to good citizenship and patriotism. "You, as a woman worker," the pamphlet observed, "will want to know best how you can best preserve your health as you serve in new capacities." In fact, illness was near treason. "These are days," the pamphlet warned, "in which lost minutes may mean a lost cause. Every sniffle of a cold is sabotage! Preventable aches and pains as well as accidents are definitely unpatriotic."[47]

If Allis-Chalmers officials stereotyped, undervalued, and demeaned women's role and contribution to the war effort, Local 248 leaders recognized the need to represent women workers, frequently voicing ideals and principles of the equality of men and women. Although some lapses existed, the Allis-Chalmers electrical and metal tradesmen asserted the principle of "equal pay for equal work." The union position stemmed from several considerations. Unionists may have simply taken the purely pragmatic position that lower wages for female workers undermined males' wages. They may have feared that avoiding women's issues could exacerbate the persistent factional struggles at West Allis. Or they may have actually taken their democratic rhetoric seriously. At any rate, they frequently defended female grievants and recruited women into the Allis-Chalmers union.

For example, shortly after the Supercharger plant opened, the union newspaper featured a story on seven of Local 248's leaders in the new factory. "They are women and each is a leader," the *CIO News* reported, "taking their place along the side of the men to build a better union, raise wages and improve the conditions in the shop." Since the UAW local began, Mary Roeder had served the local as a "committeewoman." Esther Zarling was an executive board member. "I'm not the veteran unionist that Mary is," she said, "but I've been here long enough to know that the union is the solution for both men and women. My dad and I are both a part of 248." Five others were either shop stewards or committeewomen. Another newspaper issue featured three black women, two filers and a drill press operator. All three expressed a hope for more skilled work and a chance to earn piece rates.[48]

Black workers were also a new element in the volatile social mix in the West Allis plant. Compared to the massive migration of women into the Allis-Chalmers shops, the entry of African American workers occurred on a much more limited scale. They represented a very small proportion of the Milwaukee and Allis-Chalmers work force, because the wartime black migration to Milwaukee came in a rivulet rather than a flood. In 1940, they numbered 8,821, or 1.5 percent of the total Milwaukee population. In 1945, they increased slightly to 10,200, or 1.6 percent of the urban population.[49]

Moreover, Milwaukee's ethnic composition most likely made the West Allis plant an inhospitable world for black workers, as the largest ethnic groups—Germans, Poles, and Slavs—in Allis-Chalmers labor were known to be openly hostile to blacks. At the West Allis plant, for example, the foundries, which were a traditional stronghold of black workers in other firms, employed large numbers of Slavic workers. AFL craft unions, furthermore, systematically excluded black workers.

Consequently, few African Americans ever saw the inside of the large Allis plant. Only 110 African Americans worked there in 1941 and only 693 in 1945. As with women workers, Allis-Chalmers employed the few blacks in racially stereotyped occupations. According to the historian Joe Trotter, they "refused to hire Afro-Americans in capacities other than porters, janitors, and common laborers." Moreover, only 306 of the black workers were Americans; Allis-Chalmers managers imported 387 Jamaican contract workers for the foundries.[50]

In the later war years, Jamaican workers labored in the iron foundries of the West Allis plant. According to Alberta Price Johnson, Allis-Chalmers officials housed these workers in army barracks at Mitchell Field, the Milwaukee airport. In contrast to such segregation, the UAW local welcomed the black Jamaicans to union social and cultural activities. More important, it also praised them as models for American workers. The *CIO News* specifically pointed to their involvement in socialist Jamaican labor politics.[51]

Given the hostile ethnic traditions at Allis-Chalmers and the small numbers of black workers, Local 248 leaders conducted an amazing struggle to achieve social and economic equality for these Allis-Chalmers workers. As early as 1937, Julius Blunk, the Local 248 financial secretary, criticized the arrangements for a Milwaukee UAW convention ball as "non-union, unethical racial discrimination." In response to a request to sell tickets for the convention ball, Blunk wrote to the chair of the convention committee: "We wish to say that among our membership there are many colored members who are 'strong' union men and active in labor's 'big drive' and the membership cannot cooperate with your plan under the color discrimination conditions." In a 1940 *CIO News* article, Luther McBride, a black Local 248 shop steward, observed that white union members needed to "break down old prejudices which permit situations to occur where white workers are placed in competition with Negro workers and dangerous hostilities arise." In a critique of Allis-Chalmers racially divisive policies, the African American unionist stated: "I have actually seen situations where a member of management will play upon these prejudices to keep workers in turmoil."[52]

In 1941, two symbolic acts revealed Local 248's public position on the controversial issue of racial equality. First, the union membership endorsed a resolution that supported A. Philip Randolph's proposed march on Washington for equal employment of African Americans in defense production. Second, the Local 248 executive board sent "an official protest to the Navy Department of the United States against a regulation requiring Negroes to wear an insignia with the letter 'N' to designate their race." Moreover, two union letters also revealed a commitment to racial justice. In one, the Local 248 membership endorsed R. J. Thomas's threatened dismissal of Detroit UAW members who struck against the upgrading of black workers. "At its last membership meeting," Harold Christoffel wrote Thomas, "the Local voted unanimously to support your courageous action in breaking up the attempts of the Fascists to introduce their racial hatred tactics into the Packard Local." One month later, the Local 248 president criticized an Allis-Chalmers employee newsletter that announced "A well known 13 piece 'darkie' band" at a USO party. "We cannot," he protested, "at any time tolerate any expression such as 'darkie' or similar discriminatory words, particularly at a time when our Negro brothers and sisters are giving their lives on the battle fronts or all their energies and effort in production for Victory."[53]

Although Allis-Chalmers officials claimed to employ black workers in proportion to the Milwaukee-area population, they consistently hired them into unskilled and semiskilled occupations: moreover, they firmly refused to upgrade black workers into more skilled and more highly paid ones. Local 248 leaders forcefully pursued a CIO policy of equal employment opportunities for all workers. After Roosevelt established the Fair Employment Practices Commission, the Milwaukee CIO unions used the new federal agency to improve conditions for black workers. "UAW Local 248," Trotter noted, "established its own FEPC committee" with a black foundry worker as chair. It "vigorously worked for the employment and upgrading of black workers at the Allis-Chalmers Corporation. The union sent representatives to the Chicago hearings and endorsed written affidavits of racial discrimination at the plant."[54]

Young workers were a third problem group for Allis-Chalmers officials. Until the war, the firm proudly employed older skilled craftsmen. With twenty-one as the draft age, youths between sixteen and twenty-one constituted another substantial pool for potential unskilled workers. If young men were untrained in industrial skills, they were also unskilled in the discipline of regular work. Many immature, undisciplined, and sometimes irresponsible workers filled vacant unskilled positions in the West Allis plant in wartime.

For union leaders, the young and inexperienced workers presented difficult shop floor problems. During World War II, Christoffel remembered that "some were less committed" to the union cause. Too young to remember the bitter struggles against management and too inexperienced to attain the oppositional culture of the workplace, the young workers often expressed indifference to the union cause and union traditions. Without family responsibilities, they were also an extremely volatile social group. They had a high rate of labor turnover, especially those who worked in the Allis-Chalmers foundry. In 1945, Fred McStroul, the recording secretary, recalled that at the "No. 1 Foundry, I believe there has been almost 100 percent turnover." In the extremely tight wartime labor market, senior workers moved on to the more desirable Allis-Chalmers shops. Or the more talented moved on to better-paying jobs in other Milwaukee-area factories. As a result, many young and green foundry workers were taught little of shop or union traditions.[55]

In 1942, Allis-Chalmers officials established a Discipline Control Board (DCB) to enhance management control over the fragmented work force and to alleviate discipline problems, especially among the young industrial recruits. The DCB was the creation of Lee H. Hill, an Allis-Chalmers manager promoted to vice president for industrial relations in 1941. A most unusual labor manager, Hill combined practical shop experience with a theoretical outlook on American industrial relations. An electrical engineer, he had worked for Westinghouse and the American Brown Boveri companies before coming to Allis-

Chalmers, where he managed the transformer division from 1931 to 1941.

During his tenure as head of Allis-Chalmers's industrial relations department from 1941 to 1945, Hill also served as an industry member of the National War Labor Board (NWLB), the wartime agency to mediate labor-management disputes, an industry member of the Sixth Region of the War Manpower Commission, and an industry delegate to the president's Labor Management Conference. During and after the war, he wrote several books on management issues of the war and postwar years.[56]

In August 1942, Lee Hill created the DCB to reassert management authority over a unionized and changing workplace. His ideas and activities were closely related to Harold Story's legal thinking on labor and management relations. The DCB reflected Hill's important distinction between workers as employees and workers as union members. In addition, it handled the difficult discipline problems associated with large numbers of new workers. First, it sought to bring order to the new and different groups of new workers. Second, it attempted to distinguish management's disciplinary functions from its functions in union relations and to reassert management control over matters of discipline. Through their aggressive use of the grievance procedure, union leaders had managed to enhance labor's power and threaten management's authority on the shop floor. For this reason, the DCB program intended to circumvent union participation in the discipline of workers.[57]

According to Hill, the DCB was "not a creature of the collective bargaining agreement at all." In other words, it attempted to remove discipline from the grievance process. The union could not appeal a management decision to discipline a worker until after punishment had been administered. And then it could appeal the administered discipline to the impartial referee only if the referee found that the employee had not interfered with shop discipline, if the act had not interfered with shop discipline, or if the administered discipline had constituted discrimination against the union or the union member.[58]

Many disputes between workers and foremen resulted in heated exchanges and bitter shop floor confrontations between workers and supervisors. Under the new disciplinary system, the foreman declared an offender "under discipline" and simply sent the worker home. Then the DCB conducted a hearing, exercised its judgment, and administered its discipline. At the DCB hearing, the unrepresented worker faced interrogation by two industrial relations staff members, his shop supervisor and the shop foreman who had originally sent the worker home. After the formal hearing and imposition of punishment, management notified union officials, who then had to decide whether to pursue the case in the costly arbitration process. Moreover, the new procedure removed the union from involvement in these important workplace disputes, demonstrating to other workers the union's apparent weakness.[59]

The DCB reimposed imperious managerial authority in the West Allis plant. It established a corporate "workplace rule of law" that used legal mechanisms for the management control of worker actions. "Determination of penalties for infractions of shop discipline," the DCB chair wrote, "free from inequalities and just as the courts of law, is one of the latest important personnel problems to be attacked by modern industrial relations techniques." In other words, the DCB dispensed corporate justice for infractions of corporate rules. The centralized system of corporate justice permitted the evolution of a common body of judicial procedures and precedents. "A careful record of penalties," he added, "is kept and is consulted during each hearing. It becomes, in effect, a common body of law." Moreover, the formal hearing bore the social trappings of authority and deference due a courtroom. "Even when a severe penalty has been imposed," the DCB chair related, "the employee has accepted it with far better grace then [sic] he would accept an arbitrary decision handed down by his immediate supervisor." In other words, a formalized and ritualized authority was contrived to intimidate the accused worker.[60]

Allis-Chalmers officials stressed that prevention, not punishment, was the chief object of its new disciplinary institution. The DCB's penalties, a pamphlet asserted, "have never been for *punishment* purpose, but for the much more important object of preventing further violations by the same employee or by others." The Allis-Chalmers worker who made a "mistake" received "a fair, impartial hearing of his side of the story." The DCB offered "all parties a chance to 'cool off' and get together under circumstances where the truth can be arrived at and where difficulties can be more easily settled." In addition, the disciplinary hearings allowed "a more thorough explanation of the employe's responsibilities and obligations than is possible in the busy shops."[61]

From the worker's perspective, the DCB was not such a benevolent institution. Using wartime rhetoric, some workers even called it the "Gestapo Board." Whenever a dispute or disagreement arose in the shop, the foreman quickly placed the worker "under discipline." Depending on the hour of day, the worker either went directly to the DCB or went home and reported to the DCB the next morning. At the board hearing, he or she faced only management representatives. For the ordinary worker, a DCB appearance was an intimidating social ritual of subordination and submission. A photograph of a DCB hearing reveals a blue-collared worker, seated at a round table and facing four stern management representatives wearing suits and ties. At the table, a microphone is pointed toward the worker's face formally to record his statements. The DCB members hold notes, papers, and employment records relating to the worker's case. No shop steward defends the worker. Only after the managerial imposition of discipline did union officials become involved in the dispute or disagreement. Moreover, the private procedure avoided the public posturing connected to shop floor rituals of power.[62]

An Allis-Chalmers pamphlet offered public reasons for the creation of the wartime disciplinary board. The shop floor problems it described stemmed from industrial inexperience. "Everyone in the plant," it noted, "has the right to expect an orderly, well run shop in which he can do his work without interference from anyone else." To be sure, the vast majority of the war employees worked hard and did not cause problems for others. "But," it continued, "there are always a few people who just naturally seem to get out of step with everybody else. They don't do their own jobs and they interfere with other people in their work. Discipline means preventing this sort of thing." Often volatile and hot-tempered, young workers seemed to attract the DCB's special attention. A 1942 management brief for the WLB revealed the management attitude toward young workers: "Youths lack the toughening that comes from years of work. . . . Neither have they developed stabilized work habits." The young, inexperienced workers had not acquired the appropriate industrial habits of hard and disciplined work.[63]

The DCB's most common problem was "habitual absenteeism." And some, Allis-Chalmers reported, "were young people on their first real job. Their paychecks simply burned their pockets until they took time off to spend the money." Although absenteeism was "comparatively low," the firm warned workers that "*any* unnecessary absenteeism now during wartime is serious and should be reduced to the absolute minimum." In the West Allis plant, the greatest problem was with "repeaters" who accounted for the most absenteeism. The DCB handled 143 such cases in its first year.[64]

The DCB also investigated eighty-four cases for the youthful offenses of horseplay and fighting. To be sure, many workers played to relieve the tedium of hard work, but hotheaded new recruits often transgressed over the behavioral boundary into physical violence. One shop rule forbade "Fighting or attempting bodily injury to another employe on Company property." Another forbade "Engaging in horseplay or disorderly or immoral conduct on Company property." Horseplay and fighting were "extremely serious" because of "safety hazards involved." In fact, horseplay often resulted in fighting. "Most of the fighting cases (except a few involving habitually quarrelsome people)," Allis-Chalmers warned workers, "resulted from sudden loss of temper over a practical joke." The DCB dismissed twelve workers for such offenses.[65]

The DCB also handled cases of insubordination, loafing, theft, and other improper conduct. These, too, violated shop rules. Fourteen disciplined workers who reported to work drunk were mostly "young men whose chief trouble was lack of a few more years in which to develop better common sense." Except for three, they returned "with a new realization of their responsibility to their shop and their fellow workers."[66]

The transformed social composition of the plant created a disruptive mixture of new male youth and new female workers. Not surprisingly, young workers were also responsible for much of the abusive treatment of women workers on the shop floor. These incidents frequently involved "namecalling, threats, improper remarks to girl workers and other forms of juvenile behavior by persons who hadn't quite grown up." The male shop world required considerable constraints on the many new war workers. "Considering that some thousands of young women," the firm related, "have been brought into what was formerly largely a man's shop, where man's language was freely used, the number of cases of improper language in a girl's presence is practically zero."[67]

If the Discipline Control Board reflected the Allis-Chalmers vision of industrial law, then the grievance process mirrored the Local 248 one. Although unintended, the federal system of wartime labor regulation allowed militant union leaders to extend their shop floor strategy of challenging management rights. In the late 1930s and early 1940s, the New Deal labor technocrats developed the concept of "industrial jurisprudence" to guide and to reshape labor relations in order to defuse industrial conflict. The major federal labor agencies, the NLRB, NDMB, and NWLB, employed industrial relations experts, such as William Leiserson, William Davis, George Taylor, and Lloyd Garrison, to implement a broad plan for containing worker militancy and creating industrial harmony. Using a juridical model, they pushed for the development of formal grievance and arbitration systems to codify workplace rules. With a formal system of collective bargaining, a workplace rule of law would ensure worker rights, worker-management cooperation, and industrial efficiency.[68]

In his classic 1941 study of the influence of union policies on management, Sumner Slichter first articulated this notion of "industrial jurisprudence." The collective bargaining process, he argued, was "a method of introducing civil rights into industry, that is, of requiring that management be conducted by rule rather than arbitrary decision."

As with more formal legislative and legal procedures, collective bargaining allowed "men [to] devise schemes of positive law, construct administrative procedures for carrying them out, and complement both statute law and administrative rule with a system of judicial review." In a like manner, Slichter reported, workers, "through unions, formulate policies to which they give expression in the form of shop rules and practices which are embodied in agreements with employers or accorded less formal recognition and assent by management; shop committees, grievance procedures, and other means are evolved for applying these rules and policies; and rights and duties are acclaimed and recognized." For Slichter, this workplace system of law involved the mutual recognition of "rights and duties." It was a consensual system of industrial governance that assured mutual recognition of labor and management's respective roles and statuses. In fact, Slichter feared insufficient management attention to the important problem of "[p]rotecting the status of management and preserving its essential prerogatives."[69]

This top-down vision of the evolving labor relations system, however, did not account for all of the social actors of the industrial relations process. In addition to the New Deal labor bureaucrats, managers and workers were also part of the labor relations process. They did not necessarily agree with the novel wartime labor policies. If a large corporate liberal firm such as General Motors energetically tried systematically to define a new workplace juridical regime, a smaller and more competitive firm such as Allis-Chalmers resisted with equal vigor the outside imposition of workplace rules. If Sidney Hillman was a strong proponent of labor-management cooperation through arbitration systems, Harold Christoffel was a proponent of controlled conflict within the context of aggressive shop steward and grievance systems.

Within this context, militant union leaders established an adversarial regime of shop floor relations that continued challenging management rights. The alternative system involved militant leadership, dense shop steward structure, and the arbitration system. Under the 1941 NDMB strike settlement, the impartial referee made the final decision on worker grievances. Especially after 1943, when the NWLB granted union security through the maintenance of membership and dues checkoff, UAW Local 248 followed a strategy of relentlessly pursuing shop floor grievances to alleviate management abuses of authority and to expand the boundaries of worker rights. Through the war, the UAW local sought a new variety of worker or union control of the shop floor.

In effect, the NDMB and the NWLB policies fundamentally restructured the relationship between labor and management at Allis-Chalmers. Shortly after Pearl Harbor and America's entry into World

War II, Franklin D. Roosevelt transformed the NDMB into the more powerful NWLB. Created by executive order under the president's war powers in January 1942, the twelve-member NWLB was another tripartite federal agency for the wartime resolution of labor-management disputes. Containing four representatives each from the public, the labor, and the industrial sectors, it had authority to adjust "labor disputes which might interrupt work which contributes to the effective prosecution of the war." In time, the NWLB developed a three-stage process of labor dispute resolution: first, collective negotiations between labor and management; second, mediation by the U.S. conciliation service; and, third, formal NWLB resolution of the labor-management conflict.[70]

The NDMB and the NWLB, observed Nelson Lichtenstein, "were as important as the Wagner Act in shaping the American system of industrial relations." The NWLB established "for the first time industry-wide wage patterns," fixed "a system of industrial jurisprudence on the shop floor," and shaped "the internal structures of new industrial unions." This powerful force tried to tame the militant CIO unions and to create a "responsible unionism" in American industry. But Allis-Chalmers union leaders had an alternative vision of the role of the state in labor relations. Rather than as a creator of a workplace rule of law, they saw the federal government as a guarantor of the rights of workers.[71]

In the spring of 1942, UAW Local 248 initiated contract negotiations that eventually moved through the federal dispute resolution process. The Allis-Chalmers case took a full year of contentious negotiations to realize a wartime labor agreement. After the collapse of local negotiations, the NLRB combined the West Allis case with the cases of three other CIO locals and certified the new case for an NWLB hearing. A regional NWLB panel heard two weeks of testimony and sent its recommendations to the full NWLB. Through all levels of negotiation and mediation, the fundamental issue involved union versus management control of the workplace. Once again, union leaders demanded union security and hoped to relieve shop stewards of the burdensome chores of maintaining members and collecting dues. Management negotiators wanted to restrict labor's shop floor power and again refused to concede on union security. In addition, they desired to curtail the workplace power of shop stewards and committeemen through a restricted definition of grievances and shop floor activities.[72]

For the most part, the Allis-Chalmers brief criticized the CIO invasion of management terrain. "The proposed changes," officials charged, "fall naturally into four categories, namely: 1. Disruption of discipline; 2. Undermining of management control; 3. Union usurpation of management functions; [and] 4. Unfair and arbitrary changes."

After several years' experience with militant CIO unionism, they publicly expressed a fully articulated philosophy of management prerogatives and rights.[73]

The elusive concept of management control involved the authority to determine the working conditions in the Allis-Chalmers plant. According to the Allis-Chalmers brief, the CIO unions attempted to undermine management control by demanding labor-management conferences during working hours, disallowing company interpretations of the collective bargaining agreement, denying workers the right to discuss grievances first with foremen, forbidding company representatives to question employees, desiring union input in the selection of company representatives, consolidating union offices, granting full employee rights to union officials, and eliminating management superseniority. Essentially, Allis-Chalmers officials deeply resented any union interference in the operation of the West Allis or other plants.[74]

The regional board's management and public members accepted the Allis-Chalmers arguments about union irresponsibility during the 1941 strike. Consequently, the majority recommended the denial of membership maintenance and dues checkoff. Nonetheless, after the national board conducted a second round of hearings in February 1943, the NWLB issued a divided decision on March 30. Most important, the NWLB reluctantly granted union security through maintenance of membership and dues checkoff to all of the Allis-Chalmers CIO locals, including UAW Local 248. The NWLB tailored the union security provision to the strict requirements of Wisconsin law. Nonetheless, despite these modest limitations, the maintenance of membership clause was a significant victory for the union.[75]

In his opinion, Taylor chastised both the UAW local and the Allis-Chalmers firm for attitudes and behavior that had created the bad labor relations climate. In the past, UAW Local 248, Taylor asserted, "engaged in tactics and policies which were highly irresponsible." He added, "the company cannot be absolved of all responsibility for the unsatisfactory labor relations which prevailed in those years." Despite deep differences, he now believed that the two sides had made "very real progress" in the recent past. The referee procedure taught the two sides "how to deal with each other on a more reasonable basis." UAW Local 248, he also observed, "must be credited with the absence of interruption to production in wartime." Hence, the NWLB chairman reasoned, "the institution of this [membership] clause will materially assist the parties in their efforts to improve the labor relations situation at Allis-Chalmers and thus contribute to the successful prosecution of the war."[76]

A governmental decree had once again granted what years of

protracted collective bargaining and bitter shop floor struggle had failed to yield—a degree of union security. Despite the NWLB's intention to contain the shop floor activities of militant unions, Local 248 leaders greatly benefited from the provisions for membership and financial security. Relieved of the burdensome task of constantly recruiting and maintaining members and collecting monthly dues, the UAW local's rank-and-file leaders soon shifted to a direct challenge to management prerogatives and rights in the West Allis shops. As in the past, the Local 248 officers channeled shop floor dissatisfaction and militancy through the grievance procedure. Then the union officials carefully examined these grievances at the first steps to uncover those that could be applied to large numbers of workers in the shops. They then appealed these selected grievance cases to the referee.

The tactical and strategic processing of grievances was a central feature of the local's shop floor power. During the NLRB hearings, one panelist questioned Christoffel about "the reasons why so many petty grievances" were processed; the union president replied, "they were test cases, aimed to determine the limitations of the agreement and/or to demonstrate the shortcomings of the agreement." Later, one Allis-Chalmers referee observed: "the Union seldom brings a case which has not collective significance."[77]

The shop stewards were the mainstay of the Local 248 industrial relations strategy. During the war years, the *CIO News* featured profiles of several Local 248 shop leaders. These often illustrated their important attributes. For example, one idealized shop steward, "Big Bill" Zastrow, the union newspaper reported, worked in the West Allis brass foundry. A popular shop leader, he "is more than big. He's a 100% Union guy and a real example for every steward in the Union." Zastrow's shop was completely organized. After the 1941 strike, he and his fellow brass foundry workers had earned several kegs of beer from the union, because not one of them scabbed or crossed the picket line during a government sponsored back-to-work movement. The brass foundry workers readily followed Big Bill's leadership. Although "a rough and tough guy," Zastrow was "the big favorite of the men in the foundry hot spot."[78]

For fifteen years, Zastrow worked in the West Allis brass foundry. "Bill never forgot," the *CIO News* reported, "what it was to work there without a union. And he never let any of the other guys forget it either." Brass foundry organization obviously depended upon Zastrow's brawn and rough demeanor. When a new worker entered his shop or when a union member got "weak" and tried to "search for some excuse for not paying his dues and doing his share," the big, burly molder "walks up to him, and with his gruff voice and a manner that leaves no mistaking, says: 'Look it; we got a 100 per cent department here. Every guy is in the union. We made a lot of changes around here and we intend to keep them. We got a lot more work to do. You better join up with the rest of us. We don't like no hitchhikers in this place.' "[79]

However, the UAW shop leader did much more than threaten his shopmates. As an active shop steward, the union newspaper noted, he used the grievance structure to protect the shop floor rights of the brass foundry workers. "Wage adjustments, working conditions, a tough foreman—no matter what it may be—Bill wades in, with his 100 per cent department in back of him and the whole union in back of that department." The resolution of shop floor problems attached the brass foundry workers to Zastrow and to the union. "They see the union, through Bill, really doing a job, protecting them every day, and fighting for their rights." And, the union newspaper concluded: "He's a solid oak, the kind of guy who knows his rights and has the guts to fight for them."[80]

Another ideal shop leader was Virgil Steele, a black shop steward for the No. 1 Foundry. Over the years, he kept the foundry on "an even keel" and won "the respect of the overwhelming majority of the men." His success rested on "his patience and his understanding." The UAW shop leader, the *CIO News* related, "sympathizes with every man who has to toil in such a place as a foundry; and this sympathy enables him to understand how the men feel and how to solve their grievances." Although years of foundry work had undermined his health, "he does keep plugging away and he says he will continue to do so, as long as the men want him to." Education was important for him. "[A]lways a serious student of the union movement which he is fighting to defend and build," he liked to read and study union problems and attended union labor classes at day's end.[81]

In their pursuit of worker grievances, such shop floor leaders demonstrated their commitment to the twin causes of CIO unionism and their fellow workers. At the NLRB hearings, Allis-Chalmers officials strongly protested Local 248's use of the grievance system to serve union ends. Between April 1941 and May 1942, they surveyed 682 grievances that required the firm's written response, that is, grievances appealed to the third step. The grievance study, the Allis-Chalmers NWLB brief noted, "clearly indicates the use of the grievance procedure as a tactical device by the Union, rather than its use as a device for the clearing of actual employe complaints." Herein were two quite different visions of the workplace rule of law. For union leaders, the grievance procedure assured the affirmation and extension of worker rights in the West Allis shops. For corporate officials, it simply "cleared" or resolved worker complaints.[82]

What galled Allis-Chalmers managers was the dramatic increase in the number of appealed grievances. In 1937, the monthly average was only 6.5 appealed grievances; in 1938, it was only 9.5. Especially after the bitter defense strike, the number of appealed grievances rose to a staggering monthly average of 53.1 in 1941 and 86.6 in 1942. Moreover, the peak months for grievances usually coincided with contract negotiations.

Even more galling to Allis-Chalmers managers was the source of the appealed grievances. In management eyes, workers alone should be the origin of shop complaints. Between April 1941 and May 1942, however, the Allis-Chalmers survey indicated that fourteen individuals, all "officers or other representatives of the Union," initiated around 50 percent of the appealed grievances. One person, the Local 248 sergeant at arms, initiated 75 appealed grievances, accounting for 11 percent of the total. Four bargaining committee members filed 87 appealed grievances. Eight shop stewards filed 176 grievances. And one shop committeeman filed 15 appealed grievances. Allis-Chalmers managers conveniently ignored the psychology of shop floor authority relations. Often, a timid, recently unionized worker was reluctant to confront a shop supervisor. The union, aggressively pursuing shop floor problems, sought to overcome such worker timidity.[83]

In the Allis-Chalmers brass foundry, a series of arbitration decisions and a short work stoppage revealed how much the referee restricted management rights. During the 1941 strike, the brass foundry was a solid union stronghold. For this solidarity, the brass foundry workers also earned the enmity of corporate industrial relations officials. After Lee H. Hill took charge of the Industrial Relations Department in the fall of 1942, he attempted to break the unity of the militant Allis-Chalmers shop and to install a piece-rate system in the brass foundry. This shop, Harold Christoffel said, was "[o]ne of the best organized units in the union; so [the] company directed its fire against it."[84]

In the brass foundry, workers struggled with supervisors over management's unilateral imposition of piece rates. For factory workers, incentive systems, such as piece rates, were hotly contested shop floor issues. Frequently, a worker's skill level and the form of work reflected where a worker stood on the contentious question of piece rates. On batch production jobs, a highly skilled worker would tend to favor piece rates. On high-volume, mass-production jobs, a less skilled worker preferred hourly or day rates. Since batch production often took more time, skilled craftsmen might nurse a good job and hasten a poor one. In mass-production shops, workers often struggled with managers over fractions of a second. Management here used piece rates to spur production workers on to greater output. In the Allis-Chalmers brass foundry, which produced small parts for electrical equipment, the work was skilled but had the repetitive character of mass-production work. Hence, the brass foundry workers tended to favor hourly or day rates over piece rates.

When managers attempted to impose piece rates in the West Allis brass foundry, workers appealed the new piece-rate system in several grievances to the Industrial Relations Review Board (IRRB) and conducted the only wartime work stoppage at West Allis. In one grievance, John Kaslow, the brass foundry steward, chastised a shop supervisor for timing a job and interfering with the brass molders' work. In the process, he ridiculed management ineptitude. Basing his protest on the brass molders' craft skills and craft pride, he argued that the brass molders "feel capable to perform the mechanics of their trade, [and] object to have Mr. Bacon attempt to show them how to perform the work." He ridiculed the hapless supervisor's mistake: "After putting on a show, as to how the job was to be done, he then rolled the job over and it fell apart." The shop steward concluded: "We request that management inform Mr. [B]acon to stick to his job of holding the watch and his mouth and let the mechanics do the work."[85]

In another grievance, the brass foundry steward protested management's forcing workers to accept piece rates. Kaslow charged that management was "bribing" workers to accept the piecework system. One brass foundry worker received additional money in his pay envelope. When he questioned it, the superintendent told him, "well you earned it, it's yours, you are working piecework." Despite the tantalizing prospect of higher wages through piece rates, however, the brass foundry worker insisted on an increase in hourly wages, not in piece rates. Several other brass foundry workers had similar experiences. At a meeting, they told the superintendent: "No piece work—more money by the hour."[86]

Through the year, the brass foundry remained the source of still other contentious grievances over piece rates. In December, union officials appealed several brass foundry grievances to the IRRB. When union officials attempted to call Zastrow to the hearing, the IRRB chairman "refused to call him." Then: "As Mr. Christoffel arose to call Mr. Zastrow," a management official "yelled out, 'If Zastrow comes up he'll be fired.' " Consequently, Christoffel filed another grievance that charged management with "illegally threatening to lock out workers under the guise of discipline." He demanded a "reasonable hearing" on the brass foundry grievances, severe discipline for management representatives, especially the shop superintendent for "obstructing the grievance procedure," and company payment of "the full expense of the Brass Foundry hearing." Management refused the union leader's demands.[87]

In January 1943, the intractable piece-rate question prompted the only Allis-Chalmers wartime work stoppage. Although short in duration, the brass foundry job action indicated the depths of worker resentment against the unilateral imposition of a new wage system. The stoppage originated when management hired a new worker who broke shop solidarity and accepted the Allis-Chalmers piece-rate plan. Because of the shop's solid anti–incentive stance, however, he faced extreme social pressure from the other brass foundry workers. After a few days, they forced him to quit Allis-Chalmers. The union grievance noted that he "did not like the antagonism of others in the foundry."[88]

Two days later, when the molder reappeared "ready for work," the brass foundry workers refused to begin their day's work. "Mr. Zastrow and other members of the Union," the referee related, "assuming that" the worker "had quit, greatly resented his re-employment, especially because hours had recently been reduced in the foundry and also because . . . a molder of less experience . . . had been put at laborer's work." The work stoppage only lasted one-half hour, from 8:00 to 8:30 A.M. According to the referee, the testimony conflicted over shop committeeman Zastrow's role in the refusal to work. Management witnesses claimed that the militant steward led the walkout; union witnesses denied management's charges.[89]

Despite the shop floor tension and anger, union bargaining committeeman Robert Buse arrived in the shop around 8:15. He and "other Union Committeemen, including Mr. Zastrow, got the workers back to work by eight-thirty." In order to maintain war production, the brass foundry workers even volunteered to "to work for an additional half hour at the end of the day, without pay, in an attempt to make up the production that was lost." Despite his efforts to convince the brass foundry workers to return to their jobs, Allis-Chalmers officials "sent Zastrow home, supposedly fired, for inspiring a stoppage."[90]

The DCB decided to discharge the popular shop floor leader. An appeal to the IRRB resulted in lighter discipline—a six-week layoff because of his age and long years of service. "Right after the company laid me off," Zastrow told the *CIO News*, "I told all our people to stay on the job and win the fight there. Our people know what the company is aiming at and they won't get their goat so they lose their heads. It's hard to do when the company is doing everything to get a guy mad. But the only way to lick this outfit is to stay on the job." Another shop committeeman received only a one-week layoff. Christoffel charged that Allis-Chalmers officials laid off the brass foundry leader "to break morale of workers because Zastrow is acknowledged leader of department."[91]

In mid January, Walter Fisher, a Chicago lawyer who had replaced

Garrison in 1942, issued several decisions on the brass foundry grievance cases. Ruling first on four consolidated piece-rate grievances, the arbitrator noted: "The question is whether the Company has by the Agreement contracted itself out of the right to install piece work rates in the brass foundry." He then cited a contract provision that stated that various rates of pay "shall remain in effect during the term of this agreement." With this contract language, he concluded: "a piece work or incentive system cannot be installed in the brass foundry without the consent of the Union." In effect, the union had won a major victory.[92]

A little over a week later, in his decision on the refusal to call Zastrow to the IRRB meeting, Fisher decided that nothing improper happened at the meeting and that nothing called for action by the referee. Nonetheless, Fisher's ruling contained an ominous warning to Allis-Chalmers officials. After noting that management requested a decision on the referee's authority to discipline company representatives, he added: "it seems to me wiser not to decide the question in advance of an actual, specific case." In other words, the Allis-Chalmers referee left open the possibility that, at some point in the future, he might issue a ruling that would permit the discipline of a company official.[93]

Finally, Fisher ruled on brass foundry stoppage. He concluded that Zastrow "did not conduct himself in a proper manner on that Friday morning." Although he conceded that the work stoppage could have been "a spontaneous reaction" to the reappearance of the disliked molder, "there is also considerable evidence that Mr. Zastrow made himself the spokesman of those who determined not to work" with the molder. The brass foundry committeeman "made strong statements in opposition to Bingham's going to work under circumstances that were likely to lead to a stoppage."[94]

As a union representative, even a low-level one, the arbitrator maintained, Zastrow "should have made every effort to prevent the matter from being handled in any other way than through the grievance procedure." Before the beginning of the shift, "Mr Zastrow's conduct . . . encouraged the stoppage and justifies discipline." Allis-Chalmers officials, Fisher believed, did not impose the appropriate discipline. "I do not believe," he reasoned, "the Industrial Relations Review Board gave any or at least adequate weight, to the prompt and effective action of the Union officers and Committeemen, including Zastrow, in correcting the error that had been made." Consequently, Fisher recommended a reduction of Zastrow's disciplinary layoff to three weeks from six weeks.[95]

Though tactfully and cautiously phrased, Fisher's three brass foundry decisions clearly tended to favor and to enhance the union's power. First, he would not allow Allis-Chalmers officials to impose piece rates unilaterally in the brass foundry or in any other shop. Second, he left open the possibility that other situations might require discipline of management. Third, while agreeing that the shop committeeman merited discipline, he significantly reduced the punishment. Obviously, the prospect of similar decisions in the future gave Allis-Chalmers managers cause for great concern.

With more than a little overstatement, UAW Local 248 heralded the Fisher rulings as major victories for union members. The brass foundry decisions, the *CIO News* reported, were "one of the greatest victories the local has gained since it puts an end to the whole program of company disruption which the latter has been waging in the brass foundry in recent months under the guise of seeking an increase in production." The referee brought some justice to the workplace. The *CIO News* added, "Without this arbitrator set-up and the right to challenge company actions before such an impartial man, Local 248 would have had to suffer no end to injustice."[96]

Allis-Chalmers officials made two attempts to overturn of the brass foundry grievances. After the Zastrow decision, the union claimed: "the Company brazenly questioned the whole right of the Referee to alter its sovereign judgment and launched an attack on his statements praising the Union as 'strong' and its leadership as 'responsible.' " The *CIO News* reported: "This is the first time that the company has openly disputed a Referee's decision." When the company requested a rehearing, Fisher responded, "There must be an end to disputes at some point and a time at which decisions are final." He concluded, "I believe that this point has been reached in this case," and denied a rehearing. When management again requested a rehearing, Fisher again denied it. Robert Buse told union stewards that the Allis-Chalmers brief for these appeals intended "to blacken the name of the Union and its leadership" for a future appeal to the War Labor Board.[97]

In these and other referee decisions, Walter Fisher undermined the authority and reputation of management in the West Allis plant. Consequently, Allis-Chalmers officials precipitated a crisis by demanding Fisher's resignation in July 1943. In a union brief arguing against the demand, Harold Christoffel charged that "they are asking his resignation because he did not go along with the company all of the time." Before the arbitration system, the Allis-Chalmers managers made the final determination in all grievance cases. Now, the referee made more than a few of the decisions favoring the union. The specific incident that precipitated the crisis was Fisher's decision to reinstate an improperly discharged union official. In other words, Fisher asserted an important principle—the right of the referee to oversee and to overturn corporate decisions about discipline. Notwithstanding the union argument, Allis-Chalmers officials managed to force Fisher's resignation, but allowed him to complete work on already argued cases.[98]

In November 1943, the NWLB assigned William H. Spohn, a Madison attorney, as the new referee for the Allis-Chalmers arbitration cases. Like Fisher, Spohn was a regional figure without a large, national vision of labor relations. Spohn too emphasized the rights of workers over the containment of militancy. The surviving records of Spohn's decisions revealed the nature of Allis-Chalmers's shop floor antagonisms, the complexities of the basic issues in union-management relations within the plant, and the means by which the union extended its control at the workplace.[99]

One decision dealt with cuts in the piece rates for several drilling operations in a machine shop. Angered at the wage cut, union machine operators charged that the change was an unauthorized reduction in piece rates. Citing the agreement with Local 248, management maintained that "the decreases were occasioned by new or changed production methods." The agreement permitted cuts in piece rates when the methods of production changed. The dispute centered on the history of the design of a fixture, a device that held work to the drilling machine. The company claimed that production engineers discovered "latent defects" in the fixture and had it "reconstructed" in the tool room. But Spohn ruled against management's contention that it had reconstructed the fixture and in favor of the union's view that the union repaired it. He also overturned the IRRB decision and awarded back pay to the affected workers. This seemingly petty squabble reached to the heart of the day-to-day needs and concerns of workers in the Allis-Chalmers shops. It touched on the important issues of equity and justice, arbitrary managerial authority, and basic notions on the nature of wages and profits.[100]

In another decision, Spohn ruled on a case involving a group of tractor shop assemblers who lost about twenty hours of pay because of a shortage of crankshafts in their department. The workers complained that they did not receive their average hourly pay for their idle time while on duty in their shop. The company claimed that the workers were not paid because they did not perform alternative tasks such as the subassembly of engine components. In response, the assemblers stated that no one directed them to perform the alternative tasks. In his ruling, Spohn turned the notion of managerial prerogatives on its head and favored the tractor shop assemblers. He insisted that management function properly and manage its workers in the plant, and he awarded the tractor shop workers twenty hours of back pay.[101]

In a machine operator's grievance, Spohn reasserted the referee's authority to reduce a punishment that management had imposed. In this instance, the machine operator argued with his foreman over the timing of the job. In the course of the argument, the foreman ordered the worker "to go to work or go home." At some point, he pushed the machine operator. "Thereafter," Spohn related, the worker "became angry, swore, and called the Foreman names and invited him out of the plant to engage in combat." The DCB gave the worker a seven-day layoff, and the IRRB upheld the punishment. However, because the foreman had laid hands on the worker, Spohn overruled the IRRB, reduced the amount of discipline, and ordered back pay. Company officials maintained that "the amount of discipline lies in the discretion of management." Moreover, they added that the referee "has only the authority to review the action of the Company and not to substitute his judgment for it." Clearly, this was in line with the Allis-Chalmers vision of management rights. Nonetheless, Spohn decided that the referee had "the duty to determine what discipline shall [be] impose[d]."[102]

In addition to defending the general interests of Allis-Chalmers workers, UAW Local 248 also represented the specific interests of African American and women workers. In a workplace best characterized as a traditional stronghold of white, male dominance, the defense of black and female workers demonstrated the progressive social character of CIO industrial unionism. With such a small number of black workers, mostly temporary Jamaican migrants, the union leaders could readily have ignored their shop floor problems and avoided risking the ire of its overwhelmingly white male membership.

Nonetheless, union leaders attempted to use the grievance procedure to ensure social and economic justice at the workplace for African American workers in the West Allis plant. For example, in early 1942, the UAW local filed two grievances to protest the Allis-Chalmers hiring and transfer policies for black workers. In one grievance, Lee Kimmons, the Local 248 FEPC chair, "testified, that in hiring employees the Company severely discriminates against Negroes and, with insignificant exceptions, limits Negroes as are employed to work in the foundries." In another, Kimmons questioned the failure of African Americans to obtain better job assignments. He "asked to be a molder, a coremaker, a crane operator, and an assemblyman in the Tractor Shops; and he cited unsuccessful efforts on the part of several other Negro employees to get transferred from the foundry to other jobs." In these grievances, the union leaders made the novel argument that contractual clauses on "working conditions" and "breach[es] of shop discipline" clauses granted the referee authority to decide these cases. In the end, Lloyd Garrison supported the management position that the clauses did not apply to the case. "The whole problem raised by this case," he argued, "is a social one, which . . . I do not think comes within the purview of this Agreement."[103]

During the 1946 contract negotiations, Local 248 leaders strongly argued for a nondiscrimination clause in the new contract. When management negotiators balked, Joseph Dombek, the Local 248 vice president, said: "I recall that I raised a specific instance where a superintendent bluntly stated he had no use for the God-damned niggers." The union, he protested, "had no right to raise it as a grievance because it wasn't covered by the contract." Another incident involved the discharge of a black woman. After a management negotiator wanted more real evidence for the "C" cases—that is, the "colored" ones—Dombek recalled the case of a black female worker who "had no time card to punch." After an inquiry at the front office, Dombek discovered that they were writing her a "payoff" check. When Dombek asked the superintendent about the discharge, he replied that "She was incompetent." Upon further questioning, Dombek said: "[T]hen, it came out, after discussion and . . . better than three hours of argument, that this girl was being discharged because the assistant foreman and the superintendent had no use for negroes." Only after receiving threats of the union's going to the Milwaukee Urban League, publishing an account in the *CIO News*, and sending a letter to President Truman did Allis-Chalmers officials reinstate the woman. Such shop floor struggles earned the respect and loyalty of African American workers for the cause of militant CIO unionism.[104]

Grievances also mirrored the shop problems of women entering the male workplace and the union concern for female interests, even though women, like blacks, were employed only for the war's duration. For example, one decision demonstrated how the entry of women into a predominantly male shop world raised the question of gendered social roles at the workplace and created new and sensitive issues for supervision. It concerned a confrontation between Tractor Shop worker Harriet Bopp and Assistant Foreman Charles Yankel. As the Tractor Shop workers lined up to punch out on the time clock, Bopp went to the front of the line at the invitation of a fellow worker. According to Bopp, the assistant foreman "without a word spoken grabbed her arms, shoved her backwards and pressing his body against hers trapped her in a corner, from whence she could not escape; whereupon she slapped him with the fingers of her open hand." Other witnesses disagreed about the details. In the end, the female worker received a six-day layoff for striking her supervisor.[105]

Although Spohn decided that Yankel "issued a reasonable order" that the woman worker "refused to obey," he concluded, "The irrefragable fact here is that a foreman of his own motion came into bodily contact with a woman worker." Since DCB did not take this into account, Spohn reduced the firm's punishment from a six-day to a two-day layoff and ordered the payment of four days' back pay.[106]

Moreover, the union repeatedly attempted to adjust inequitable wage practices. In the 1942 NWLB negotiations for a new contract, Local 248 leaders called for "equal pay for equal work" and for substantial wage increases for female and young workers. The union proposal requested a raise in the starting wage rates, from fifty-three to eighty-five cents an hour, a 70 percent increase, which would have the greatest effect on women. In an effort to divide male and female workers, corporate officials argued that adult men had "a right to expect a wage differential based upon their experience." Moreover, they added, the union proposal "would equalize starting pay for persons whom everyone knows are unequal in ability."[107]

Company officials then compared female to male workers and developed a management notion of a woman's work and worth. "Women workers, whether adults or minors," they bluntly put it, "are ordinarily not worth as much as men at the time they start with the Company." Their reasons included less "physical strength," "work experience," "adaptability," as well as larger "indirect costs," and "more expensive facilities" for their "personal welfare and comfort." In management's view, biological, social, and cultural differences between men and women made women less productive and more expensive to employ.[108]

But Local 248 leaders disagreed with management's views. In an important grievance, the union leaders attempted to correct the situation by challenging the inequities of the separate *J*, or journeyman, for men's and *F*, or female, for women's rates. As part of a separate contract agreement that protected men's wage rates, Allis-Chalmers officials had agreed that "when a woman *replaces* a man, and does any job he ever did, she gets the rate of the man." But they also claimed the right to apply an *F* rate to jobs that had "never been performed by men." Through a narrow interpretation of work performed by men, they assigned women *F* rates for numerous "new" jobs. According to the union, Referee Spohn wrote: "All men are said to receive Journeymen's rates while a woman near any one of them and doing *substantially* the same job might be paid a Female rate."[109]

On the basis of his authority to interpret contractual provisions, the agreement's language, and previous decisions, Spohn issued a divided decision that both favored and opposed the principle of wage equality for men and women. For long-standing piece-rate jobs performed by both men and women, such as the filing stator job, Spohn pointed to the absurdity of the management position. "I cannot believe"" he ruled, "because a woman's hand manipulates the file, she is doing 'women's' work, while the same operation, if performed by a male, would be a 'man's' job." As a result he held that women were entitled to the same rate as men for similar piece-rate tasks, operations, or jobs. For other piece-rate jobs, women, who replace men, would receive the male rate, and new jobs, which were the same men's jobs, would be paid the male rate. However, the referee believed that the contract provisions definitely excluded wage equality in two specific instances. First, if a job, such as coil winding, had always been performed by women, it would continue at the female rate. Second, a lower female rate would continue to apply to women's day-rate jobs. Although not a complete victory for the union, the appealed arbitration case did move in the direction of wage equality for men and women in the West Allis plant.[110]

Clearly, the Local 248 leaders had a conflictual notion of the workplace rule of law. The grievance procedure presented a major union challenge to the authority and activities of Allis-Chalmers managers, supervisors, and foremen. Management officials frequently complained about the unreasonable number of union grievances filed at the early steps and appealed to the IRRB. In 1941, 682 grievances went to the IRRB; in 1944, 1,853. In 1946, over 8,000 grievances were stalled at the IRRB. In 1939, management spent 220.5 hours processing grievances; in 1944, 3,172.6 hours. According to company and union testimony, the IRRB favored the union in only 1 percent of the appealed cases, whereas the referee favored the union in 25 percent of his decisions. And, although the company won the overwhelming majority of the decisions, the union did attain significant victories with favorable referee decisions. In legalistic logic of the workplace rule of law, the union successes relied on innovative interpretations of contract language.[111]

Labor historians have not adequately analyzed the way that seemingly procedural "legal" rules challenged management at the workplace. But important parallels to the Allis-Chalmers situation can be found in Sidney Lens's postwar review of CIO grievance procedures. In a *Harvard Business Review* article, Lens suggested a conflictual rather than a consensual view of the CIO grievance procedures. The wartime experience of UAW Local 248 seemed to match this model of grievance resolution. In his examination of wartime grievance processes, Lens criticized the "tendency to consider the growth of formal and complex grievance machinery . . . as the expression of a desire for 'peace and stability' on the part of the contending parties, perhaps even as a step toward the ultimate resolving of conflict between them." Lens offered an opposite view resting on the uncomfortable notion of "[s]o-called 'class warfare' " at the workplace. Instead of

promoting stability and resolving conflict, Lens argued, the new grievance procedures were "used as a weapon in that [shop floor] strife or
perhaps more accurately, as a way to muster strength for it."[112]

According to Lens, the militant CIO leaders creatively protected and
expanded the rights of industrial workers. "The direct purpose of grievance machinery," he wrote, "then, is to protect the standards established by the contract, correct inequities and abuses, and establish new
practices and procedures." In effect, the grievance procedures were "a
form of constant collective bargaining." They constituted a new
method in the union struggle for worker rights. They were not "a
deterrent to class war." They were "merely an attempt to *organize* the
conflicts between unions and employers and to *contain* them within
certain specified bounds." Although Lens spoke about organization
and containment of worker protest, his most important point was the
premise of shop floor struggle and conflict.[113]

Indeed, the actual Allis-Chalmers workplace experience mirrored
Lens's view of the structure and function of the grievance machinery.
The shop steward, he observed, was "the hub of the grievance machinery." In the Lens theory and in Allis-Chalmers practice, several
levels of union activists participated in the grievance process. "The
dynamic, militant union," he wrote, "will always have a well organized grievance machinery, active stewards, top grievance committees, and a great preoccupation by the top leadership with grievance
work." Moreover, in both instances, the use of the grievance process
demonstrated a larger strategic vision. "The aim of a vigorous union
leadership in all grievance practice," Lens reasoned, "is to consolidate
its membership, to unify its ranks, to build up the enthusiasm of its
followers so that in the one big yearly emergency . . . the union can
wave the big stick, can threaten (and deliver) a complete plant shutdown in case of no agreement."[114]

This conflictual view of the workplace rule of law certainly applied
to the social and economic contest in the West Allis plant. If New
Deal labor technocrats and Allis-Chalmers officials conceived of industrial jurisprudence as a mechanism to contain and restrain industrial conflict, the militant Local 248 leaders asserted an alternative
vision of the workplace rule of law that further expanded worker
rights and restricted management rights. The militant, conflictual,
and alternative vision constrained management behavior and actions
in the West Allis plant. As soon as wartime federal authority disap-
peared, Allis-Chalmers officials consciously planned a major confrontation to weaken union control and to reassert management power
at the contested workplace.

# 6

# THE UNMAKING OF MILITANT UNIONISM I: THE INDUSTRIAL AND POLITICAL BATTLEGROUND, 1944–1946

On the surface, as the war dragged on into 1944, Allis-Chalmers labor-management relations seemed somewhat routine. The union was finally entrenched in the West Allis plant with its new union security guarantee. The National War Labor Board and the grievance system regularized a form of ritualized conflict between the union and management over contractual provisions. And production boomed, with no end of war orders in sight.

But below the surface, the changed social composition of the work force and the management's dissatisfaction with growing union power boded ill for the future. In 1944, Harold Christoffel could look back proudly, perhaps even arrogantly, on almost a decade of union growth and consolidation and could look forward to increased wages and benefits for his fellow workers. But Harold Story, perhaps smarting from Christoffel's victory in the 1941 strike, anticipated an end to the war and to union meddling in management rights at the workplace. He planned not only "reconversion" to peacetime but also a confrontation with UAW Local 248 that would tame its aggressive leaders.

The future shape of labor-management relations was barely visible in early 1944. But slowly, a few incidents—the first serious challenge to Christoffel's leadership and a rank-and-file rebellion against the union in the foundry—revealed the looming confrontation. The leadership challenge and the foundry rebellion indicated management's renewed efforts to reassert management rights and set the stage for an eleven-month strike in 1946–1947.

The Local 248 leaders relied on the solidarity of labor; the Allis-Chalmers managers, on the financial strength of capital. But this time, the union leaders would find the support of the rank and file insufficient armor against the overwhelming power of the Allis-Chalmers management and the federal government. The 1946 strike would be a classic and dramatic labor-management confrontation.

In 1944, a union leadership crisis began with the reclassification of Harold Christoffel to a 1-A draft status. As a union leader, Allis-Chalmers officials reasoned, he did not deserve a military deferment. Before Christoffel left for army service and eventual assignment in the Philippines in 1945, a new union leader needed to be groomed. Christoffel returned to the shop as an electrical worker for another year, and Robert Buse, the union vice president, succeeded him as Local 248 president. Union members endorsed a proposal to designate Christoffel an "honorary president" of the UAW local.

But Buse's election to president was not without a challenge. In the 1944 elections, an opposition slate led by Julius Blunk, a union pioneer, ran against the existing leadership. More ominously, Buse received only 62 percent of the votes cast, and turnout in the election dropped to about 30 percent of the union members. New wartime workers and long hours had eroded interest in union affairs.[1]

In May 1944, an even more difficult question arose—whether a shop supervisor could serve as a union steward in his department. Al Tarman was a low-level shop supervisor. A candidate on Blunk's opposition slate, Tarman aroused the ire of the Christoffel-Buse faction. For a shop supervisor, traditional union practice required a temporary withdrawal from the union leadership position. But when Christoffel sent Tarman a curt letter: "you are not eligible to act as Steward, as you are acting as a supervisory leader," the issue took on larger meanings.[2]

The dismissal of the popular Tarman, who was technically not a foreman, precipitated a rank-and-file rebellion of foundry workers against the Local 248 leadership. Obviously, the many unresolved or lost grievances exacerbated tensions among union members. Moreover, the shop was a place where several strands of wartime social upheaval came together. It employed large numbers of unskilled Slavic and Polish workers, African American and Jamaican workers, and unskilled and unruly youth. A week after Tarman's dismissal, Robert Buse and John Kennedy, the new vice president, conducted a divisional meeting to elect a new shop steward. About two hundred foundry workers attended. After two hours of bitter wrangling, one foundry worker received, but declined, the nomination to replace Tarman. The next day, Christoffel told Allis-Chalmers officials to remove Tarman's name from the steward list. A week later, Buse received a petition from 325 Division 4 foundry workers demanding the reinstatement of Tarman.[3]

Although Christoffel and Buse gradually softened their hard-line position against the union dissidents, the Tarman issue disrupted several subsequent union meetings. At the July membership meeting, Christoffel offered a motion to rescind the disciplinary action against Tarman and to reinstate him as a union member. Two of the motion's supporters stated that Tarman could retain his union membership, but "he should not hold the job of Union Steward, while he is a supervisor, for no man can serve two masters." But Tarman adherents insisted that "he also be reinstated as Steward." After their motion to reinstate Tarman failed, 150 foundry workers rose and would not take their seats. "The members," the minutes noted, "refused to be orderly so that [sic] Chair declared the meeting adjourned."[4]

At the August meeting, Christoffel challenged Tarman's right to attend the union meeting. Nonetheless, the popular foundry leader seated himself. "In the meantime," Tarman related, "Brother Christoffel re-appeared with about 35 sergeant-of-arms and tried to remove me. A free-for-all fight broke out in the hall involving about 75 men." After things settled down, the UAW regional representatives worked out a compromise to reinstate Tarman as a member of the union. The union members once again voted against Tarman's reinstatement.[5]

In the end, the national UAW upheld Christoffel's position on the removal of Tarman as divisional shop steward in the foundry. Although the UAW encouraged foreman unionization in the Foreman's Association of America to provide shop supervisors with a union outlook, it was another matter for a supervisor to represent workers in the UAW grievance process. In this instance, despite its vindictiveness, Christoffel's reasoning meshed with traditional union practices.

The election challenge and the foundry rebellion against the Christoffel administration manifested a severe leadership crisis for UAW Local 248. Although only in his early thirties, Christoffel had become a union establishment figure in the war years. A generational revolt continued with the new and younger war workers entering the West Allis shops. The talented young union pioneer confronted a more sophisticated Allis-Chalmers industrial relations program and led many workers who had not struggled through the UAW local's formative years.

Moreover, the relative security of federal policies and the long wartime workdays produced the classic union leader's lament of an indifferent rank and file. The election of union officers brought out only a few thousand voters. The fractious union meetings attracted only a few hundred members. Within this context, Blunk and his allies, who represented the more conservative older generation of Allis-Chalmers workers, were a serious challenge to the militant young Turks.

The third Allis-Chalmers strike originated in the union's wartime effort to gain greater control at the workplace. The aggressive and strategic pursuit of grievances altered the balance of power between labor and management. In contract bargaining, Local 248 negotiators attempted to strengthen labor's workplace power, while management negotiators tried to weaken it. From 1944 to 1946, they first bargained locally, then with the U.S. Conciliation Service, and finally under the NWLB. After Local 248 leaders reopened negotiations for a new contract, Allis-Chalmers officials refused to accede to union demands for any changes in the 1943 NWLB contract. Given the critical importance of contract language to the operation of the grievance process, each side demanded changes that would lessen the other's strength in arbitration. In late March, the two sides deadlocked and called for the mediation of the U.S. Conciliation Service. After a May contract extension, a federal conciliator aided contract negotiations. Union leaders, however, insisted on moving the case directly to an NWLB panel, where they expected a more favorable hearing.[6]

From the union perspective, the most important Allis-Chalmers demands would virtually eliminate union security, severely restrict the militant UAW local's shop floor strength, and lessen its role in the grievance process. Instead of the existing maintenance of membership provision, management negotiators demanded reregistration of all workers on dues checkoff. Then, they insisted that "all decisions on pay rates, piecework prices or standard time rates shall rest with the Industrial Relations Review Board." In other words, they refused to allow the arbitrator to decide wage questions. Third, they desired the removal of the contract clause that permitted the referee to discipline antiunion workers, a provision that provided union security. Fourth, the Allis-Chalmers negotiators wanted to designate an assistant superintendent or general foreman to act as the superintendent's representative in the grievance process. This would dilute the superintendent's authority to resolve grievances and "would complicate and lengthen the handling of grievances." Finally, they wanted to end the practice of paying the full expenses of the grievance procedure. Their demand that the union pay one-half of the lost time for grievance handling, the union claimed, "was an attempt to break the grievance structure by placing the financial burden on the union."[7]

From management's perspective, Local 248's demands would expand worker rights and augment the union challenge to management rights. For example, union negotiators wanted the protection of pieceworkers from price cuts, the inclusion of rate reviews in the grievance procedure, the participation of worker representatives in the DCB hearings, a decrease in the number of seniority groups, the granting of worker preference for job shifts, and the consent of workers for job transfers. With these changes, the union negotiators intended to re-define the issues that would successfully move through the grievance procedure to the impartial arbitrator. With the appropriate language, UAW Local 248 would win more grievance cases and enhance its control over the workplace.[8]

The two sides were far apart.

After months of fruitless negotiation and mediation, the Allis-Chalmers case again went to the NWLB. For many more months, fed-eral officials heard labor and management witnesses and read their briefs. In December 1945, a six-member NWLB panel finally issued its decision on the case. Although a typical meliorative compromise, their decision again granted UAW Local 248 major concessions. From the Allis-Chalmers perspective, the worst were the NLRB rulings that forti-fied the union position at the workplace. The NWLB eliminated the restrictive 1943 clause for union security and granted the "standard maintenance of membership and an automatic irrevocable check-off clause." This simplified the certification of union membership. The NWLB also ordered Allis-Chalmers officials to provide each worker with a job classification card, to give workers wage and job protection in transfers, and to establish pay equity for male and female workers. To prevent rate cutting, the NLWB incorporated the rate review manual into the labor-management contract. Consequently, "alleged inequities of individual day rates, piece work prices, or standard time rates" were "subject to the grievance procedure terminating in arbitration." For the first time, an impartial referee could legitimately decide wage issues.[9]

Moreover, several NWLB decisions strengthened the union in the grievance procedure. Once a foreman sent for a worker's shop stew-ard, the NWLB forbade any discussion with the worker until the union representative arrived. It also allowed union personnel to repre-sent workers in discipline cases. The disciplined worker could discuss his case with a union representative and could have union representa-tion at DCB hearings. And the improved contract language permitted more cases to go to the arbitrator.[10]

One industry panelist strongly dissented from the NWLB directive. A. E. Sinclair voiced the major Allis-Chalmers concerns about the union threat to management rights. In his objection to the " 'standard maintenance of membership' clause," he argued, "a compulsory Union in any form is unsound because it places employes at the mercy of arbitrary dictatorial domination of Union leaders." Sinclair dis-agreed with the panel on wage rates for transferred workers because, he said, "the recommendation is impractical" and "the rates are finally determinable by the referee." On the latter, he added: "The setting of rates is peculiarly a management function, the recommendation would transfer the exercise of that function to a referee. This is an unsound utilization of the impartial referee system." In objection to the wage inequity provision, he repeated this argument: "Here again, the Panel invades management[']s field of operation and places in the hands of a referee the sole power to determine matters of utmost importance to management."[11]

For the union, the NWLB decision was a Pyrrhic victory. The war ended in August 1945. The president had directed the board to phase out its activities and operations. On December 31, several days after the Allis-Chalmers decision, an executive order terminated the NWLB. Local 248 leaders argued that the NWLB panel recommendation should form the basis for an equitable contract settlement, but Allis-Chalmers officials simply ignored it, since federal authorities now lacked the power to enforce NWLB recommendations. In the midst of reconversion, the prospect of huge federal tax breaks strengthened the corporate position, while mounting unemployment weakened the union one. Once again, Allis-Chalmers prepared for a major confrontation to fight the union threat to its authority and control at the workplace.[12]

According to a 1946 UAW Research Department report on the Allis-Chalmers Manufacturing Company, high wartime profits and substantial government tax breaks provided a sound financial base to take a long strike and to break the union after the war. "Thanks to a strong shot in the arm," the UAW report claimed, "the company is today in the best position in its history." Comparing the average for the five war years with 1939, it revealed that wartime sales rose 245.5 percent, wartime profits before taxes soared 587.6 percent, wartime net profits after taxes increased 94.1 percent and wartime dividends increased 32.4 percent. Total corporate assets amounted to $179.8 million, and net working capital amounted to $72.8 million at the end of 1945. "Not only did profits skyrocket during the war period," the UAW report continued, "but the rate of profit also increased." The firm had earned 5.5 percent on its net worth in 1939; through the war years it earned "a 50.8 percent return on its 1940 net worth."[13]

But this was not the whole financial picture. Allis-Chalmers possessed additional economic advantages. If the large wartime profits ensured "financial stability," postwar tax policies gave "the guarantee of continued profits in 1946." Through the war years, Allis-Chalmers acquired a large reserve "for 'inventory, postwar adjustments, and other contingencies.' " This amounted to almost $4.3 million in December 1945. "But," the UAW report noted, "the biggest cushion of all, of course, is the one providing tax refunds in the event of losses or low earnings in 1946." Since the firm had an "excess profits tax credit base," which the UAW "estimated at roughly $9,523,800," if Allis-Chalmers broke even, it would receive a tax refund of around $4.3 million. If it lost $8.9 million, it would receive almost $12 million. And, if it lost "a really whopping" $15 million, it would get around $17.2 million. No matter what happened, Allis-Chalmers was "guaranteed a profit."[14]

Still another advantage was "the repeal of the excess profits tax." With the expected high production of the postwar economic boom, the UAW report related, "this will be a windfall." All in all, the Allis-Chalmers Manufacturing Company stood in a solid financial position for 1946. "Allis-Chalmers," the UAW report concluded, "hopes to work up a good case of pity for its 'destitute' case. But let not tears be shed. It is impossible for Allis-Chalmers to lose money this year."[15]

The union's internal problems, its contract demands that challenged management rights, and the company's solid financial prospects, all hinted at the possibility of a long strike. In late January 1946, Walter Geist, the new Allis-Chalmers president, sent a letter to prepare workers for the difficult task of reconversion to civilian production. In the first of many letters to all employees, he offered an optimistic appraisal of the postwar economic situation. He presumed that Allis-Chalmers would exceed its prewar employment peak after reconversion. In an appeal for labor-management harmony, Geist concluded: "The real purpose of this letter is to ask that you go along with us in a spirit of mutual understanding and cooperation, which will go a long way in solving our common problems. In this spirit your company will do everything possible to provide maximum employment with a minimum of hardship."[16]

Two weeks later, Allis-Chalmers officials precipitated a major crisis with their unilateral request for the resignation of referee William Spohn. They specifically cited his decisions 107 and 116 as reasons for their demand. These two rulings demonstrated just how great a threat the impartial arbitrator was to the management claim for sovereignty at the workplace.

The first decision concerned the important reconversion problem of the transfer of workers from one job to another. The union grievance involved the transfer of coremakers from the jobbing room, where they received 90 cents per hour, to the production room, where the new rate was 70 cents per hour. Although the work was nearly identical in both shops, the foundry workers claimed that the production work was harder and did not allow "control over the speed of the work." The production piece rates made it possible to earn more in the jobbing room, despite the lower hourly rate. The jobbing room, however, required a greater level of skill and control. The basic issue was where the particular wage rate was held. Did the worker hold a wage rate, or did his job classification hold it?[17]

The union did not challenge the management right to transfer the workers, only the firm's right to reduce a transferee's wage rate. "The Union," Spohn related, "contends that the reduction of an employee's rate upon a transfer for the Company's convenience is price cutting." This, the union believed, was a violation of contract. According to Spohn, Allis-Chalmers officials asserted that "a worker has a [job] classification, and that the classification, *not the worker*, has the rate." In the contract, management argued, the phrase " 'hourly rates of pay' . . . relates only to the work." The worker received "the hourly rate attached to the job [that] he is filling for the time being." This seemingly minor issue had profound implications for the operation of the West Allis plant. In the midst of reconversion, Allis-Chalmers officials could face serious limitations on the transfer of workers. If wage rates were attached to workers, this would greatly increase the expense of reassignment and transfer, so necessary for reconversion to peacetime production.[18]

In general, Allis-Chalmers officials maintained that the company retained a common law right to transfer workers to jobs with lower wage rates. Especially in the face of ambiguous contractual language, they held that the referee could not override or appropriate this right. Spohn, however, saw the situation differently. After a careful examination of the contract's language, which made repeated references to the "worker's hourly rate," he concluded: "I believe the reasonable construction of the covenant against price cutting is that where there is work for a man at the job he is performing and the Company requests him to take a job at lesser skill or effort, the contract protects him against a cut." When company officials requested a rehearing, Spohn demurred. From the Allis-Chalmers perspective, the arbitrator made a decision that rescinded two fundamental management rights—the right to transfer workers and the right to determine their wages.[19]

In his second ruling, Spohn tackled a broad range of issues about the day-to-day operation of the grievance procedure. This dispute arose when Allis-Chalmers officials unilaterally changed the form used to release shop representatives for processing grievances. In an effort to maintain tight management control on the movement of shop stewards and committeemen, they issued new procedural instructions to shop supervisors and foremen. Allis-Chalmers officials, the *CIO News* charged, attempted "to hamstring the grievance procedure by tying down the actions of the stewards, the committeemen and the bargaining committee." According to Spohn, the union grievance raised two basic issues: the right of a shop representative to "to absent himself from his work" and the type of records used for their compensation. In broader terms, what were the implied contractual rights of union representatives in the Allis-Chalmers grievance process?[20]

In his decision, Spohn considered how the collective bargaining agreement influenced and even limited management prerogatives in the West Allis plant. Any agreement, he reasoned, "removes or restricts some of the privileges and prerogatives the employer would have possessed had the agreement not been executed; it likewise grants the worker rights he would not have been entitled to in the absence of the agreement." He further noted that no agreement was "self-executing" and that any agreement required "administrative processes to truly effectuate the purpose for which it was designed." In other words, Spohn believed that the contractual agreement called for broad interpretations in order to function properly.[21]

Subsequently, Spohn ruled on several questions which dramatically extended the rights of union representatives. These rights included that of committeemen, and not only stewards, to write grievances in the shop on company time, that of bargaining committeemen to investigate grievances and to question supervisors and others in the shop, that of the union officials to call workers from the shop to attend union and management meetings for grievance discussions, that of one or more workers to present grievances to the plant superintendent, and that of stewards and committeemen to leave their work to consult with a worker on a grievance. Despite great increases in the number of Local 248 grievances, Spohn extended substantial rights and privileges to Allis-Chalmers shop floor representatives. Ultimately, he refused to permit Allis-Chalmers officials to restrict or to limit those activities necessary for the proper operation of the grievance procedure.[22]

For management, these two decisions constituted an unwarranted intrusion into management's domain. On February 8, management demanded the resignation of Spohn, who had served as referee for three years. "Referee Case[s] 116 and 107 were not the real reasons for which the Allis-Chalmers Company asked Mr. Spohn to quit," the *CIO News* reported, "but [rather] because with a grievance procedure terminating in arbitration, the Company does not have the last word when it comes to disposing of a grievance." Moreover, without the mediating hand of federal authority, Allis-Chalmers officials returned to their old antiunion policies. The *CIO News* ominously asserted, "This is Mr. Story's work. He is up to his old tricks of trying to break up the union." And it threatened, "We took him on in 1941 and we will take him on again and when this fight is over, Mr. Story may not be here any more, but the union will be stronger than ever."[23]

The grievance procedure raised central questions about the nature of the labor-management relationship. For union leaders, the important issue was the speedy resolution of grievances on the shop floor. When management negotiators argued against this, Christoffel responded: "That is what we want to avoid. We don't want to appeal the grievances upstairs. We believe that a grievance should be settled in the shop. We think this has been too much a tendency of the Company, pushing everything up to the Industrial Relations Department, and let them sit there, instead of getting into the cases and getting them settled." In another instance, Robert Buse described grievances as "a safety valve." When they were not "handled properly, generally the lid blows off with a strike or stoppage."[24]

For management officials, union grievances represented an unwarranted intrusion into management's legitimate domain. Lee H. Hill best articulated the Allis-Chalmers philosophy in his book about management rights under collective bargaining. According to Hill, the local's demand for "wide open arbitration" was one of four "union devices to attack management rights." Without the proper limitations on the arbitrator and grievance procedure, Hill maintained, "management may find that it has transferred to a third party that [which] it had reserved for itself." Clearly influenced by his Local 248 experience, he concluded, "some unions are inclined to take a good many cases to arbitration in the hope of obtaining from the referee a concession that they have been unable to wrest from management in negotiation, to secure an interpretation that might be favorable to the union position, to use the referee decision to humiliate management, or as an organizing device."[25]

Six days after the demand for Spohn's resignation, Walter Geist sent another letter to all Allis-Chalmers workers. Ominously, Geist reminded them about "unemployment due to strikes or lack of work." In a rare personal comment, he asserted, "No one wants unemployment and the hardships it brings. . . . I still recall, as if it were yesterday, the times when my father, a metal patternmaker, came home to announce that for some cause or another he was out of a job." He added, "The real burden . . . falls heaviest on the wife and mother and children."[26]

The Allis-Chalmers president then moved to the real issue—a March 4 CIO strike deadline set for several plants. After professing that he "never refused to bargain collectively," Geist criticized the excessive union wage demand. Finally, he reminded Allis-Chalmers workers of the " 'fraudulent" 1941 strike vote and the subsequent loss of $2.8 million in wages. He concluded, "We are mindful of your problems and we hope that you will understand our problems. Only as we understand each other can we hope to find a solution to our difficulties."[27]

Immediately after Spohn's dismissal, labor and management entered a hectic period of contract negotiations. For a frantic month, two federal conciliators attempted to mediate and to avert a third major strike at the West Allis plant. In the March and April mediation sessions, the basic issues were the same as in the original 1944 NWLB case. Through the two years of negotiations, the fundamental issues remained consistent—union security, the grievance procedure, and wages.[28]

In late April, Local 248 president Robert Buse sent letters to Allis-Chalmers workers and their families to announce the complete breakdown of contract negotiations. "These negotiations," he explained, "began on March 11 and continued over a period of 28 days with the Company maintaining the same position on the last day as the first." He then detailed the principal issues—a nondiscrimination clause in the contract, continuation of maintenance of membership and check-off, methods of wage payment and work standards, and grievance, disciplinary, and transfer procedures. The company, he argued, offered a 13.5-cent wage increase, "ONLY on the condition that an agreement could be reached on all other issues. Yet the company refuses to agree on any issue affecting the security of your job and your union." The union, he claimed, appealed to the secretary of labor to enter in the negotiations. "If this fails," he ominously concluded, "we will be forced to strike."[29]

At noon on April 29, 1946, around 11,000 Allis-Chalmers worker walked out of the huge West Allis industrial complex to attend a union meeting at nearby State Fair Park. A *Milwaukee Journal* reporter described the exodus:

Shortly after the plant whistles blew at noon Monday, hundreds of workers jammed sidewalks and the intersection at S. 70th st. [sic] and W. Greenfield av. [sic] It was estimated that as many as 6,000 workers packed the intersection. Traffic was impeded.

They quickly formed a parade line of march to the fairgrounds for the meetings. Two men carrying flags, one the American and the other Local 248's—marched at the head of the procession. A parade of cars brought up the rear. The marchers were four and five abreast.

The reporter also noted: "Most of the marchers carried their lunch pails as they came out of the plant." He took this as an indication that they did not intend to return to work.[30]

The departing workers, he continued, jokingly commented about their future:

"How are you going to pay alimony now, Sam?"

"Joe, do you need any hired hands on the farm?"

"I'll see you again this fall."

Such gallows humor indicated that the workers expected a strike vote and a long absence from the plant.[31]

At the State Fair Park, over eight thousand workers assembled, heard union bargaining committee reports, took a vote with raised hands, and then formally cast ballots for a strike. In early evening, the union announced that Allis-Chalmers workers voted 8,091 to 251 to walk out. Although the strike effectively started with the noon march, the union pickets would begin at 7 A.M. the next day at the start of the shift.[32]

Thus, on April 30, 1946, Allis-Chalmers workers once again hit the pavement. In the union statement on the strike, Local 248 president Robert Buse announced that "a resounding vote" demonstrated the Allis-Chalmers workers' "lack of confidence in the Company's promises to sign a new, improved contract, and that they are ready to fight for this contract on picket lines." The struggle began with the announcement that the plant was closed to all production workers except for "recognized" supervisory and maintenance workers. The union also established a pass schedule to prevent "unauthorized" workers from entering the plant. It refused to allow entry to those workers who did not show their Allis-Chalmers identification badges. On this first day, about 11,000 production workers and "several hundred" nonproduction workers failed to report to work. According to a company spokesman, "many office workers who reported without identification were turned back by the pickets."[33]

When the strike began, Allis-Chalmers officials took a hard line toward the union's aggressive picketing. After the first day, W. C. Van Cleaf, the Allis-Chalmers industrial relations head, warned the union that negotiations would resume only as long as the union engaged in "peaceful picketing." Raising the specter of the 1941 West Allis riot, the Allis-Chalmers president wired the Wisconsin governor to protest the violation of state labor laws on picketing. "Our office workers," he reported, "are being prevented from entering the plant by threats of violence. Hands are being laid upon our women. Some of our men have been assaulted." For the next day, he noted, the union threatened, "Nothing alive will walk into the plant." Geist wanted the governor's assurance that "law and order" would be restored.[34]

The next day, after pickets forced their way into the tractor shop offices and roughed up two executives, Geist again wired the governor for help: "An incipient state of anarchy has become an actuality today." Union president Buse countercharged that the company intended to "incite riot and bloodshed in an effort to browbeat its workers." Despite the Allis-Chalmers protest, the strikers were in a good mood. When they heard that the board of directors were holding their annual meeting at the West Allis plant, Buse said that "they must be properly identified before being permitted to enter." A short time later a union sound truck advised workers to permit access for those who claimed to be directors. The loudspeakers blared: "Say a few kind words to them." Picket signs read: "One Big Happy Family Without Story," referring to the Allis-Chalmers attorney, "Are You Afraid of the Workers Walter," alluding to Geist, "It's Been a Long Story, This Is the Answer," "We Want Security for Our GI's," and "Come Out and Bargain."[35]

Allis-Chalmers officials immediately filed charges at the Wisconsin Employment Relations Board against UAW Local 248. They complained about the unfair labor practice that prevented workers from entering the West Allis plant. The 1939 Wisconsin labor law guaranteed the "right to work." It also banned illegal picketing. Management charged that the union was "hindering and preventing by mass picketing, threats, intimidation, force and coercion the pursuit of lawful work and employment and [was] obstructing and interfering with entrance to or egress from the plant." For several weeks, sporadic violence broke out on the West Allis picket lines. At the end of May, the WERB ordered UAW Local 248 "to cease and desist illegal picketing at the West Allis works." The union complied.[36]

Management appealed to Republican state authorities for a strike settlement; union leaders appealed to Democratic federal authorities. By war's end, a powerful CIO lobby had gained access the highest levels of national government. In early May, federal officials called labor and management to a Chicago conference to end the strike. The federal conciliator "expected to 'review' the eight unresolved issues" with company and union representatives. Since tensions were high and tempers short, he assured both sides that he would conduct separate meetings to discuss the unsettled issues. However, the Allis-Chalmers officials balked at the resumption of negotiations. At the time, the *Milwaukee Journal* reported that a return to the bargaining table "apparently hinged on the satisfaction of the company demands for 'legal' picketing." Although the union discontinued mass picketing and assigned "observers" at West Allis plant gates for the weekend, the federal effort to mediate an end to the strike failed.[37]

In the absence of negotiations, Secretary of Labor Lewis B. Schwellenbach entered the difficult situation. On May 29, he threatened the governmental seizure of the struck plants of two agricultural equipment firms, Allis-Chalmers and J. I. Case. At a press conference, the secretary of labor announced that the postwar problems of domestic reconversion and European reconstruction created "a vital need for farm machinery." He also said that he "would recommend government seizure Monday if the respective managements failed by this weekend to 'cooperate with the conciliation service in an effort to negotiate contracts.' " In effect, he reiterated the union charge that the Allis-Chalmers company "has been negotiating through junior employees who have no authority to say 'yes' to anything." If labor and management failed to reach agreements, the *Milwaukee Journal* noted, "the government would negotiate its own contract with the unions involved in the event it took over the plants."[38]

Responding to the threatened takeover, Geist reminded Schwellenbach that management had appointed and authorized local Allis-Chalmers negotiating committees to bargain collectively "whenever requested by either the unions or the conciliation service, except where illegal picketing prevailed." He also criticized federal involvement in the Allis-Chalmers strike. "Your threat to recommend plant seizure," Geist charged, "encourages the leadership of Local 248 in their defiance of the law." After recognizing the shortage of farm equipment and criticizing the union's illegal picketing, Geist described the dire consequences of a governmental takeover: "A government which seizes a plant under such circumstances of illegal union activities not only undermines democratic laws but actually assumes powers dangerously close to dictatorial."[39]

The next day, Allis-Chalmers officials launched a coordinated corporate campaign to fend off the possible governmental takeover. First, Geist protested formally to the secretary of labor. "We have been forced to rely on the accuracy of a press release attributed to you," he proclaimed, "to learn of a threat of governmental seizure of all of our plants, many of which produce no farm machinery." Geist expressed the firm's willingness to negotiate as soon as the strikers stopped their "illegal" picketing. He also questioned the legality of a governmental seizure: "it seems clear that a governmental seizure of our plants would be an invasion of our constitutional rights and would do us irreparable injury." Within a few hours, all the other Allis-Chalmers works managers had sent telegrams to the secretary of labor. They also attacked the prospect of a federal seizure on the grounds that they were ready to negotiate.[40]

The governmental threat of plant seizure was genuine, since the secretary of labor had written to Harold D. Smith in the Executive Office of the President and to President Truman. After a brief description of the situation in the various Allis-Chalmers plants, Schwellenbach stated: "All attempts at conciliation and mediation have failed. I recommend, therefore, that in view of the vital necessity of maintaining the steady flow of products from this company, the President should exercise his powers to take possession of and operate the plant and facilities at which work interruptions have taken place." He also enclosed a copy of a proposed executive order for the recommended takeover.[41]

The threat of seizure forced Allis-Chalmers officials to return to the bargaining table. From June 3 through July 24, management and labor accepted federal mediation. Day after day, federal mediators guided union and company negotiators clause by clause through the old Allis-Chalmers contract. In the end, the two sides remained as far apart as when they began. And, once again, labor-management negotiations broke up over the grievance procedure.[42]

The threat of plant seizure always loomed in the background. In June, the *Milwaukee Sentinel*, a Hearst paper, joined the chorus of critics of government seizure. In doing so, the newspaper raised the specter of Communism. The Allis-Chalmers strike, it charged, demonstrated a Communist plan "to irritate and disrupt the orderly process of democratic society" and "to provoke and hasten the chaos of which world revolution is expected to arise." The editorial claimed that the Allis-Chalmers strike was not about union issues, such as wages, and asked: "What, then, is it all about?"

> Simply the union's intention to force government seizure of the plant, to dictate with the backing of the government, a contract which the owners will be compelled to accept in order to regain their property.
> In other words, the strike is an attempt of Communist labor agitators to use the government as a cat's paw in an act of arbitrary confiscation.

"It is," the editorial concluded, "an attempt to make American government an accomplice in that blackjacking of American industry in the name of American labor."[43]

The seizure threat was contested within the administration. In a mid June memo to President Truman, Schwellenbach described the Allis-Chalmers dispute: "Every day conferences have been held, the issues of the strike situation discussed, but not one issue has been resolved in what is now over three weeks of continued negotiations. Therefore, I cannot hold out any hope for the settlement in the near future." The secretary of labor recommended governmental seizure, but Arthur Krock, a *New York Times* correspondent, noted that the new secretary of agriculture rejected the idea of the Allis-Chalmers seizure. "If . . . the plants are seized on the grounds that the strike imperils the national economy," Krock argued, "there will be pressure for more seizures by the unions." Then he raised the specter of socialism: "That tends toward the nationalization of private industry. This is popularly supposed to be the reason why the President has resisted the Department of Labor, official advocates of planned economy[,] and many unions[,] by refusing to take over Allis-Chalmers." The proposed takeover would be "a long step" in the "general direction" favored by "the advocates of industrial nationalization" in the mining industry.[44]

In a similar vein, national columnist Frank R. Kent, criticized the CIO demands for government seizure of the Allis-Chalmers plants. In a column filled with anti-Communism, Kent charged, "Between them, the unions and the Government make a joke of collective bargaining. Between them, they are promoting the sneaking development of nationalization, which is the avowed goal of the Communists. . . . It is degrading and un-American." He concluded, "No surer way of breaking down the American system of free enterprise could be devised."[45]

Truman eventually decided not to take over the J. I. Case and Allis-Chalmers plants. In mid August, three weeks after federal mediation fell apart, the *Milwaukee Journal* reported that presidential press secretary Charles G. Ross said "that the strike was not considered a national emergency of a character to warrant seizure." An angry Robert Buse responded with frustration: "the president's action 'tells us who our friends are.' " Nonetheless, the union president claimed that the decision against plant seizure "was healthy" and "cleared the air."[46]

Chester Manly, a *Chicago Tribune* reporter, claimed that President Truman "rebuffed" his labor secretary in the "delicate" decision not to seize the plants. "The administration," he claimed, "had been under tremendous pressure to seize the plants and put the union's demands into effect by means of a government contract." Manly also mentioned UAW president Walter Reuther's threat to extend strikes "to the farm equipment industry generally in an attempt to force government seizure of the idle plants." The secretary of agriculture "deplored the loss of vitally needed farm implement production," but he did not share the Secretary of Labor's "zeal for governmental seizure and operation." Apparently John R. Steelman, now the director of reconversion and an influential labor adviser, also "strongly opposed seizure."[47]

In a long letter in early August to Allis-Chalmers workers, Walter Geist wrote a carefully crafted appeal to historical nostalgia, workers' pride of skill and craft, and postwar patriotism. After discussing the merits of "the spirit of competitive free enterprise" and the preunion era of "mutual understanding" and "peace and harmony," he chastised the union's radical leaders: "When, however, the leadership of a union, has the fundamental purpose of creating dissension between the Company and its employes it becomes quite obvious that the object is to divide and conquer, to promote class hatred, to discredit management and to make dissension and unrest a daily occurrence." Geist then vaguely raised the specter of Communism in the Allis-Chalmers workers' union. "For our future security," he concluded, "we must establish the *real cause* for these recurring strikes. Only when the real cause is removed and when union leadership makes an honest and sincere effort to do their part to bring about harmonious labor-management relations is there hope for a brighter future and real security."[48]

Through the spring and summer of 1946, the American political winds shifted in the direction of Cold War. The Allis-Chalmers strike, called shortly after Winston Churchill's famous "Iron Curtain" speech, came at the end of a national postwar strike wave to regain wage losses from wartime and postwar inflation. The failure of the proposed plant seizure reflected a national weariness with a militant and assertive labor movement. During the appeals for federal takeover, the rhetoric against nationalization mirrored the developing conservative political mood. In this changing environment, the CIO's push for an activist federal labor policy to guarantee worker rights smacked of Socialism or Communism. From the late summer on, the Milwaukee strike would symbolize the Cold War fear of the foreign domination of American labor.

From August through October 1946, the ongoing economic struggle merged with a bitter political struggle. At that time, Local 248 leaders entered the urban political arena and fielded Milwaukee CIO Political Action Committee (CIO-PAC) candidates in the August Democratic primary and in the November general election. Simultaneously, they engaged in an internal union battle against CIO and UAW conservatives who disliked the militant and leftward drift of Milwaukee unionism. From September through November, Allis-Chalmers officials and the Milwaukee press vigorously excoriated pro-Communist union leaders in the city and state labor movements. The bitterness of the economic struggle dramatically escalated. The Milwaukee strike commingled with several Cold War political battles. By November, Joseph McCarthy had become a U.S. senator from Wisconsin, and militant unionism in Milwaukee was in decline.

As the strike continued through the late spring and early summer, the politics of production meshed with urban and union politics. Milwaukee CIO leaders saw the upcoming election season as an opportunity to combat the advantage of a politically influential management. They embarked on an ambitious campaign to endorse or field pro-CIO candidates, to provide financial assistance and campaign support for them, and ultimately to remake the Milwaukee Democratic Party. Originally formed to support New Deal Democrats in 1943, the Milwaukee CIO-PAC became a vehicle for left union political involvement in 1946.[49]

In Wisconsin, a unique party structure facilitated labor's foray into politics. A much more vibrant left tradition existed in the state than on the national level. In addition to the Republican and Democratic parties, Wisconsin also had politically significant Progressive and Socialist parties that had dominated Wisconsin and Milwaukee politics since the early twentieth century. By the early 1940s, however, the national New Deal coalition had contributed to the dissolution of these two Wisconsin parties. Under Roosevelt, the Democratic Party turned to the Left and allied with both Socialists and Progressives in Wisconsin. The Republicans, still the national party for many Wisconsin Progressives, moved to the Right.[50]

In the 1946 elections, Wisconsin electoral politics became a confusing bundle of social, economic, and political contradictions. In the spring, Progressive senator Robert LaFollette personally faced the dilemma of whether to run for reelection in the Republican or Democratic primary. Faced with political extinction, his Progressive party had to re-form as a bloc in one of the two Wisconsin political parties. Although his heart was with the New Deal Democrats, he chose the Republican Party since it represented a stronger force in Wisconsin politics. As a result, he entered an electoral contest with Joseph McCarthy, the choice of a new, young generation of Republican conservatives.[51]

In Milwaukee, union activists confronted a somewhat similar decision. In line with national CIO-PAC tendencies, they decided to work with the Democratic party. Some other labor activists, particularly AFL craft unionists associated with the old Socialist urban political machine, remembered LaFollette's prounion stand and followed him into the Republican primary. Other AFL unionists supported traditional Democratic candidates. Religious and ethnic politics further complicated labor's political allegiances. By summer, Milwaukee labor and its political leaders had split into several camps, each fielding different slates of candidates for the fall elections.[52]

As the largest single CIO union, the Allis-Chalmers local dominated the Milwaukee and Wisconsin CIO councils. In Milwaukee, the CIO-PAC endorsed a full slate of candidates for the August primary election. At a July legislative conference, which met in the Local 248 union hall, 150 delegates representing Milwaukee County CIO unions selected local candidates who received CIO endorsement. The CIO slate included both representatives of the Democratic party establishment and CIO union favorites. For the fourth congressional district, the CIO delegates refused support for the incumbent, Thaddeus

Wasielewski, and endorsed a young war veteran, Edmund Bobro-wicz. They also endorsed a mixed slate of Democratic and Republican incumbents for the state senate. For the state assembly, the delegates endorsed a few traditional Democratic candidates and a large number of union candidates, including three Local 248 members and several others from UAW and CIO locals.[53]

The Republican primary pitted Joseph McCarthy, a newcomer to statewide politics, against the well-known Progressive-turned-Repub-lican, Robert LaFollette. In the August primary, McCarthy unexpect-edly defeated LaFollette, largely on the strength of a 10,000-vote majority in Milwaukee County. Milwaukee County, the *Milwaukee Journal* observed, "turned the trick for McCarthy—the same county that saved LaFollette from defeat in 1940." The next day, the Milwau-kee newspaper blamed labor for LaFollette's defeat. The AFL, the CIO, and the railroad brotherhoods, the *Milwaukee Journal* charged, "did not lift a finger for LaFollette."[54]

However, labor, particularly the CIO and the Left in the CIO, had been unable to help LaFollette because they had directed their atten-tion to the Democratic primary. In the fourth congressional district, Edmund Bobrowicz, an army veteran and former organizer for the Fur and Leather Workers Union, scored a major upset over Democratic incumbent Thaddeus Wasielewski. "The smashing primary victory," the *CIO News* proclaimed, "overcame the campaign of the present con-gressman, a campaign which was largely devoted to Red-baiting of both the CIO as a whole and its candidate." The other major Demo-cratic victors were Howard McMurray, a University of Wisconsin politi-cal scientist, for senate, Daniel Hoan, Milwaukee's former Socialist mayor, for governor, and Andrew Biemiller, a former Socialist, for fifth congressional district. In addition, many other CIO-PAC candidates won Democratic primary victories for the Wisconsin State Assembly. Emil Mattson, a founder of UAW Local 248, defeated the Democratic incumbent in the third assembly district. In all, ten union candidates won the opportunity to run for Wisconsin assembly seats. For the most part, these were rank-and-file CIO union leaders, shop stewards, and bargaining committeemen.[55]

The Bobrowicz victory was extremely unsettling for the Milwaukee establishment. An electoral novice had defeated a two-term Demo-cratic incumbent. The *Milwaukee Journal* correctly concluded that "Jimmy Higgins," the classic rank-and-file union member, provided the political "legwork" and contributed to Wasielewski's defeat. In-deed, over two hundred workers from CIO unions, Slavic organiza-tions, and the American Polish Labor Council conducted a doorbell and phone campaign in the ethnic working-class neighborhoods of the fourth ward. Wasielewski agreed with the newspaper's "Jimmy

Higgins" analysis. The defeated congressman blamed a CIO vendetta against him. He wrote his brother, "I am told they canvassed all of the wards in which I have been strong in the past from house to house and spread gossip to the effect that I was anti-labor and called the working man a loafer and a lot of other things. They followed up this personal contact with literature carrying the same message." Wasielewski mused, "[T]hat they licked me in my strong wards" was "paradoxical and ironical."[56]

The August primary activated the more conservative Milwaukee CIO leaders. Since early summer 1946, anti-Communist CIO "progressives" had held caucuses to plan a union campaign against the Milwaukee CIO's left leaders. Walter Reuther's recent winning of the UAW presidency inspired the conservative Milwaukee auto, steel, and textile union leaders. Within the UAW, "rank-and-file" caucuses emerged to fight pro-Communist union leaders. In the Milwaukee and Wisconsin CIO, Hugh Swofford, a *Milwaukee Sentinel* labor reporter, actually participated in meetings with several of these right-wing leaders. According to him, these CIO leaders "were holding secret caucuses with the purpose of ousting the alleged left wingers from power." Their hopes "rose and fell" as their fortunes waxed and waned in the struggle to oust militants from the Milwaukee CIO Council. In a pessimistic mood, one leader, Walter Cappel, told Swofford, "if the right wingers weren't successful in removing the left wingers . . . the right wing locals, some 17 in number, including auto, steel, brewery and hosiery workers, would secede from the CIO council and set up their own Milwaukee County Association of CIO Unions."[57]

Given militant labor's successful foray into Milwaukee politics and the possibility of a conservative CIO opposition, the Milwaukee newspapers expressed more than the usual interest in American labor. In their Labor Day reports, they showed a keen interest in opponents to militant CIO unionism and in Communists in the labor movement. The *Milwaukee Sentinel* featured a story on the CIO dissidents in Milwaukee—"CIO Red Purge Due Here." Swofford and Ellis Jensen, the Allis-Chalmers researcher, worked together on their long series of press exposés of labor and Communists. "On Labor Day of 1946," Swofford claimed, "I wrote the first of a series of stories on the coming right-left battle which was to get under way at a CIO council meeting to be held shortly after Labor Day."[58]

In his first article, Swofford reported on a "twin offensive" among ten steelworker and eleven autoworker locals to unseat the left incumbents on the Milwaukee County CIO Council. Moreover, electrical worker, hosiery worker, and brewery worker locals were "sympathetic" to the possible CIO purge. Over the last five months, Swofford added, "the militant locals have held 'progressive caucuses' where ways and means have been discussed of eliminating Communists from the ranks of CIO circles." Apparently, the impending struggle would revolve around CIO council resolutions that would remove Communists from the council and prevent left CIO leaders from running for office. "Reports have been rife lately," Swofford continued, "that various CIO locals in this area are dissatisfied with PAC endorsed candidates."[59]

A few days later, the *Milwaukee Journal* reported the defeat of the conservative CIO dissidents. "Opposition to the allegedly left-wing leadership of the county CIO council," the newspaper related, "got mangled Wednesday night when it tried to tangle with the incumbent administration." After votes on the two resolutions, "the score remained decidedly in favor of the incumbents."[60]

Two weeks after their defeat, the CIO dissidents returned to the Milwaukee CIO council to renew their struggle against the CIO Left. Their challenge took the form of four constitutional amendments—to ban Ku Klux Klan, Bund, and Communist Party members; to equalize participation of new locals on the council; to restrict the number of delegates from a single local to ten; and to limit the number of delegates from one local to the CIO Council Executive Board. For the most part, these changes were an effort to reduce Local 248's control over the CIO council. However, the crucial vote came on an early resolution attacking the rightist Franco government in Spain. A member of the National Maritime Union favored the disavowal of Franco. Walter Cappel, a business representative for twenty small UAW locals, argued that the council should leave international matters to the international unions. Since the large UAW Local 248 controlled 85 votes, the 101–77 vote total favored the left incumbents. Still, the ballot demonstrated a respectable showing for the right caucus. The *Milwaukee Journal* concluded that the result was "indecisive . . . for the comparative strength of the anti-left-wing bloc."[61]

The CIO-PAC political victory and the vigorous CIO right caucuses also inspired more aggressive press coverage of Communists in the Wisconsin labor movement. The two principal Milwaukee newspapers consistently pounded away at the theme of labor and Communism in the Milwaukee CIO. In late September, the *Milwaukee Journal* reported that, although the Wisconsin Communist Party was small, with only 1,200–1,300 members, its "influence is widespread and increasing." Despite its small size, the Communist Party "controls the Milwaukee county and state CIO councils through leadership and hence the destiny of 75,000 CIO workers in the state." In addition to "playing an increasing part in strikes," as among the Allis-Chalmers workers and Milwaukee public employees, it was also "increasingly active in politics." The Communist Party, the newspaper charged, "now is engaged in a membership campaign among factory workers, war veterans, and nationality groups." UAW Local 248, the "pride" of the Wisconsin Communist Party, exerted "strong influence" in labor circles. The Milwaukee newspaper then identified the principal Communists in the Milwaukee area, including Harold Christoffel, who "recently returned here a few days ago from army service."[62]

The next day, the *Milwaukee Journal* further detailed the pervasive Communist influence on the Wisconsin labor movement. "The Communists of Wisconsin," the newspaper reported, "plan unceasingly to gain control of the labor unions. Such control on a mass scale would greatly help them in their avowed aim to impose the Communist system on the United States." Citing the Allis-Chalmers UAW local as a prime example of a Communist-dominated union, it noted that Owen Lambert, a Local 248 committeeman and Communist Party member, actively recruited Party members from among the Allis-Chalmers strikers. The chief union leaders, Robert Buse, Harold Christoffel, and Joseph Dombek, it charged, were Communists. At union meetings, the Local 248 education director, "showed movies glorifying Russia and the Communist system." A subsequent article described the activities of the various Communist front groups in Wisconsin.[63]

Almost simultaneously with the *Milwaukee Journal* revelations about the Communist Party in Wisconsin, the *Milwaukee Sentinel*, with its masthead proclaiming "Dedicated to Truth, Justice, and Public Service," inaugurated its own series on the role of Communists in Milwaukee and Wisconsin. Each day from September 23 through November 21, 1946, a front-page story appeared. Written by a fictitious correspondent, "John Sentinel," the stories relied on information derived from Allis-Chalmers researchers. Hugh Swofford, the newspaper's labor reporter, identified the real John Sentinel as Allis-Chalmers researcher and speech writer Ellis Jensen. The son of a Wisconsin quarry owner and a former minister, Jensen wrote speeches for Harold Story, another son of a quarry owner, and Walter Geist, the Allis-Chalmers president. "In short daily articles," the newspaper explained, "the Sentinel will focus the light of publicity on each detail of the Communist menace here at home so that the thinking power of intelligent reader audience will be brought to bear on the situation every day." Although couched in informational and intellectual terms, the conservative newspaper clearly intended to arouse Milwaukee citizens and especially labor leaders against the "Red Fascist" menace.[64]

The initial John Sentinel article featured the political cartoon with the Stalin-headed spider and bore the title, "Stalin Over Wisconsin:

Reds Aim for Control of Our State." Elaborating on the new theme of "Red-Fascism," it denounced the "Red" leaders of UAW Local 248 and the Communist infiltration of the Milwaukee and Wisconsin labor movement. The second article featured a photograph of Joseph Stalin with quotations from speeches to American Communist leaders. After describing Wisconsin's industrial importance, John Sentinel moved to the Communist failure to capture the AFL and the subsequent Communist role in the formation of the Milwaukee and Wisconsin CIO. The key figure was Eugene Dennis, then the successor to Earl Browder as secretary of the American Communist Party, who brought together Milwaukee labor leaders "to discuss forming a big union at Allis-Chalmers, for the purpose of getting control of that plant."[65]

Subsequent articles targeted the practices and programs of UAW Local 248 and the Communist connections of its leaders. One John Sentinel article, for example, discussed the Allis-Chalmers strike: "It doesn't make sense to take 11,000 people out on a five or six months' strike at Allis-Chalmers over a few comparatively minor contract issues. We have to look for bigger causes for such a big event." The bigger cause—the "Communist policy" that opposed "American prosperity." In the analysis of the Communist plan, John Sentinel concluded: "Hence, if American reconversion is hamstrung with strikes and slowdowns, America will be unable to carry through its 'imperialist' program." In the mind of John Sentinel, the Allis-Chalmers strike obviously demonstrated that a small minority of Communist union leaders duped eleven thousand workers into a long strike for "a few relatively minor contract issues." Later articles savagely attacked Local 248 officers, bargaining committee members, and shop stewards. For the most part, they proved guilt by simple association, vague allusions, and sometimes huge leaps of logic.[66]

About the same time, Allis-Chalmers officials obtained the nomination papers for Sigmund Eisenscher, the Communist candidate for governor. They published a glossy pamphlet, *Principle Represented: Communist*, and mailed it to all Allis-Chalmers workers and to the Milwaukee press. The pamphlet contained photographically duplicated pages of the nomination papers with red lines that identified the signatures and provided the titles of Local 248 officers, bargaining committeemen, shop stewards, and shop committeemen. According to the Allis-Chalmers pamphlet, "a majority of the top-ranking officers," "[a]bout 40% of the Stewards," and many other local union members and associates signed the Eisenscher nomination papers. "And finally," it charged, "of the 227 sets of the nomination papers circulated in Milwaukee County, 84, 0r 37% were circulated by members or officials of Local 248."[67]

When congressional investigators later questioned him about the Eisenscher nomination papers, Robert Buse replied, "These petitions are circulated around in taverns and [on] picket lines. Everybody's nomination papers are." Eisenscher claimed that he needed 5,000 signatures and received "800 of these signatures from the Allis-Chalmers picket line." Although he admitted signing the Communist candidate's papers, Buse claimed that he voted for the CIO-endorsed candidate for governor, a Democrat, and also emphasized that his signature indicated "support so far as the right to run for office is concerned."[68]

The anti-Communist campaign played an extremely divisive role within the Milwaukee labor movement. In October, Joseph Mattson, the UAW regional director, wrote to Walter Reuther about the influence of the newspaper reports on the Milwaukee labor scene. In the midst of the bitter Allis-Chalmers and J. I. Case strikes, Mattson told the UAW president: "the forces of reactionary newspapers and employers are mobilizing everything that they have in an all-out drive to break our strikes, if possible, this fall."[69]

Mattson also emphasized the interconnection between the coming Milwaukee elections and internal CIO politics. "At the same time," Mattson continued, "they are using the strikes for all they are able in connection with the fall elections." For two weeks, he added, the *Milwaukee Sentinel* "carried a systematic attack that consists of the most vicious type of 'red-baiting' that we have ever witnessed in this region. They have named almost everyone, in the hope of dividing the forces within the UAW so that they may break the strike." The UAW regional director went on to suggest that the union should "consider the possibility of challenging this newspaper" or should "issue a statement to the effect that the forces within the UAW will not be divided by these kind of attacks."[70]

Milwaukee press reports on labor Communists also inspired a new opposition movement within UAW Local 248. In early October, Leon Venne, a founding member of UAW Local 248 and long-time union activist, announced the formation of the Rank and File Membership Committee (RFMC) to remove the Communist leaders from UAW Local 248. A union member since 1937, Venne had been a shop steward in the tractor shop. His experience demonstrated the process of a CIO unionist's gradual disaffection with the militant UAW local's leadership.

The UAW dissident first became disenchanted with the Local 248 leadership in the fall of 1938 amid Martin's charges about the Communist affiliations of the Local 248 leaders. He told a congressional committee, "I thought it was plain Red baiting." But he gradually became convinced that the charges were true. In his mind, the 1946 strike vote was fraudulent. At the strike vote, Venne recalled, Local 248 leaders were "agitating strike, and so forth, and the strike vote was called for." The security was loose, Venne believed, "anybody could have walked in there." At the union meeting, he remembered, Robert Buse chaired: "all in favor of holding a strike will vote aye. There was a scattering of ayes. A couple of the members rose on the floor and shook their hands trying to get the floor to speak on the issue, but Robert Buse couldn't hear any of that. 'All in favor say "Aye".' 'So ordered.' " As a result of such union methods, Venne grew more and more dissatisfied with the Local 248 leadership.[71]

In October, Venne organized the Rank and File Membership Committee, an apparent outgrowth of the right CIO caucuses, with seventy Allis-Chalmers workers on its original organizing committee. Three other Allis-Chalmers worker caucuses, which numbered around 155 workers, also offered to join with Venne's group. The new RFMC caucus issued a press release: "We of Allis-Chalmers know that we must have a union. A union to us is as important as foremen are to the management. We of Allis-Chalmers are going to have a union. We are going to have local 248." The caucus then criticized left unionism:

> We do not believe in communism or fascism. Our belief lies with Americanism. We live under a democracy, we believe in a democracy, and our union is going to be run under the democratic system.
> This is a warning to the Communists in local 248—get the hell out of our union and stay out. From now on it is open season on Communists in local 248. . . . You have taken us out on three strikes at great loss to us. You have had three strikes and you are out!

At the same time, the RFMC distanced itself from Allis-Chalmers management: "This is not an appeal for a back-to-work movement, but an appeal to a back-to-unionism movement." It appealed for conservative trade unionism that stressed "harmonious relations" among workers and with management.[72]

After the news stories about the RFMC's formation, Venne began to receive angry telephone calls from Local 248 loyalists. He recalled the threats: " 'Venne, you rat.' 'Venne, you stooge, we are coming to get you tonight.' " He also received some commendations:

> "Venne, keep up the good work. Don't let them scare you. Don't let them scare you." "Don't let them do this." "We are a hundred percent for you."
> I received hundreds of letters and postcards. Some people were so afraid that they didn't sign their names.

The anti-Communist dissident received personal threats, obscene calls to his wife, threats to his family and children, and unsolicited tradesmen and merchants who were sent to paint his house, to move his family, and to sell his house. "I was getting the 'nerve' treatment," he recalled.[73]

Shortly after he announced the formation of the new Allis-Chalmers workers organization, Venne sent telegrams to Walter Reuther and Philip Murray. "The long drawn out strike of Local 248," Venne wired Reuther, "will result in the destruction of our union at [the] Allis-Chalmers West Allis works unless you and Philip Murray give your support to the majority of the members who are sincerely interested in removing the leaders who are communistic." Venne charged that the Allis-Chalmers union was "completely under communist domination" and that the long strike was "a Communist strategic work stoppage." After claiming that many of the almost two thousand strikebreakers would hit the streets again under a new UAW leadership, Venne concluded: "There is a fast growing rank and file movement to over throw [sic] the Communist leaders of our local."[74]

In mid October, the RFMC tried to hold an evening meeting to expand its membership base. According to the *Milwaukee Sentinel*, the anti-Communist caucus attempted "a quiet little meeting at the Marine Memorial Building." Soon after the meeting began, "a squad of four appeared and cased the situation." One of the men made a phone call. About ten minutes later, John Kaslow, a Local 248 bargaining committee member, "appeared with a handful of companions." After another ten minutes, Arne Hansen, another bargaining committee member, appeared with around thirty other union members. The Local 248 "flying squad" took the floor and denounced Venne for his connections to Allis-Chalmers attorney Harold Story. A short while later, "the whole meeting filed down the stairs and into the night."[75]

After the Local 248 flying squad broke up the RFMC meeting, Venne pressed his attack on the Allis-Chalmers union's leaders at the next union membership meeting. He called for the suspension of the Local 248 bargaining committee, a UAW administratorship for Local 248, and a special committee to negotiate a strike settlement. The rank and file responded with "boos and catcalls" and the leadership charged Venne with "conduct unbecoming a union member," requested his suspension from the union, and called for a union trial to look into Venne's meetings outside the union with foremen in attendance and his public statements to the newspapers. Eventually, the UAW local tried and expelled him.

When he did return to work, he joined the ranks of Allis-Chalmers strikebreakers.[76]

Also in October, CIO conservatives, pressured by press revelations from without and the anti-Left factions from within, finally ousted the militant CIO leaders from the Milwaukee CIO Council. The anti-Left strategy centered on the admission of several new unions to the council. Especially important was the large brewery workers local, which had recently affiliated with the CIO. If this union, entitled to fifty-two delegates on the council, could be seated at a special meeting before elections were held, then the insurgents might gain control of the CIO organization. In combination with conservative steel- and autoworker delegates, the fifty-two brewery worker delegates would give the antileftists a majority on the Milwaukee CIO Council.[77]

The anti-Communists called for a special meeting for the admission of the brewery workers and other conservative locals to the CIO council. Over strong leftist opposition, the conservatives managed to schedule the special meeting for 9 A.M. Sunday, an hour which fortuitously conflicted with a Local 248 membership meeting. At the Sunday meeting, the anti-Communist group unanimously voted to seat the large brewery worker delegation and an additional twenty-five delegates from packinghouse, steel, auto, and hosiery locals. Although the brewery worker delegates were "cautious" in their statements to the Milwaukee press, one new delegate said "the brewery workers will be down there pitching to keep the labor movement American." The brewery workers' business agent facetiously lamented the "little bit of dissension," but he said the new delegates "were proud, happy, and confident of the future of your great labor organization." The following day, the CIO Right caucus sent CIO President Philip Murray an explanation of their meeting along with a copy of the meeting's minutes.[78]

At the next regular meeting, both the Left and the Right were prepared for rancorous confrontation for control of the Milwaukee CIO. In the annual election for CIO officers, the central issue, the *Milwaukee Journal* noted, was "control of the council and possibly the entire state CIO." If the incumbents attempted to "override the action of the special meeting," the rightist insurgents were already prepared with court restraining orders.[79]

The CIO Council meeting began with Left and Right struggling over the legality of the special meeting and the seating of the brewery worker delegation. The left group vigorously criticized the previous "rump meeting" that had admitted the new CIO delegates. One leftist leader charged, "This action is in concert with the Allis-Chalmers

Company to break the strike and to defeat the PAC endorsed candidates in the November election." Nonetheless, the right-wing group prevailed, and the new delegates cast their ballots in the CIO council election. In the "hotly contested election," the final tally indicated that the Right won thirteen of the fifteen CIO council elective offices. In fact, they swept the election. The Left won only two uncontested seats. Most of the Milwaukee CIO Council seats now went to members of dissident steel- and autoworker locals.[80]

Milwaukee's press cheered the results. "The defeat of the left wing group," the *Milwaukee Journal* reported, "marked the first major break in the nation in the revolt which has been smoldering against so-called Communist domination of the CIO. Milwaukee and Wisconsin represented a major stronghold for the left wingers." Milwaukee's "defeat" of the Left, the newspaper continued, "struck at the heart of the state." The Milwaukee CIO elections well might have "repercussions" in the Wisconsin state CIO organization.[81]

The right CIO leaders soon set their eyes on the forthcoming December Wausau convention of the Wisconsin State CIO. Charles Newman, the rightist secretary of the Milwaukee CIO, said that the "first order of business" would be the preparation of state CIO slates against Communists and Communist sympathizers. He also estimated that the state CIO organization would probably split evenly between the left and right factions. With inauguration ceremonies scheduled for the next regular Milwaukee CIO Council meeting, newly elected Milwaukee CIO president Arthur Conn stated, "The new administration wishes to call on the entire council affiliation to close ranks and stand solidly in this rededication of the council as a genuine American institution, devoted above all to the interests of the American working people."[82]

A *Milwaukee Journal* editorial lauded recent developments in the local labor movement. The defeat of the left leaders, it proclaimed, was "a healthy thing for the CIO movement and for organized labor in the city and the state." The Left used the unions as a "tool of the Communist party and a weapon of Russian foreign policy." Praising the hard work of conservative union leaders, the newspaper added: "The internal fight against the left wingers has been going on for months. It took courage and it took persistence." Nonetheless, more work needed to be done. An important item still remained on the *Milwaukee Journal*'s agenda—the role of the Left in the upcoming general election. "The new leaders of the CIO," the editorial advised, "will also turn their attention to the activities of the CIO-PAC in the state. The PAC, too, hereabouts, has been dominated and directed by left wingers."[83]

The fall general election campaign mirrored the growing Cold War consensus against militant CIO unionism. Despite his defeat in the

Democratic primary, Thaddeus Wasielewski did not intend to give up his Democratic congressional seat without a fight and decided to run as an independent candidate against Edmund Bobrowicz. In the South Side Milwaukee Polish and Slavic communities and the Democratic ward halls, the two congressional candidates waged an intense struggle for Milwaukee's ethnic voters. At one South Side election rally, attended by four hundred supporters, Wasielewski emphasized an anti-Communist theme: "Our fight is for God, country, home, and family. I never was anti-Russian, but I am against communism."[84]

The conservative Polish press quickly reacted to Wasielewski's charges of Communism, expressing dismay with Bobrowicz's victory. According to one Polish newspaper, Polish voters "departed from the American and Polish flag and stood under the hammer and sickle and do not even know that they committed a betrayal." In a similar vein, another declared: "The democratic candidate, even though he has a Polish name, is a man of clearly declared pro-Soviet sympathies, for whom everything that is against the politics of Moscow is 'fascistic.' "[85]

In the midst of the campaign, a *Milwaukee Journal* editorial decried the CIO's political strength. The CIO-PAC "has developed into a husky youngster." The Milwaukee newspaper feared two possible outcomes of labor's foray into politics. A labor group could capture or take control of a major political party. The result would be a labor party with "class divisions and class strife." And this "might bring an American fascism." Or a "conspiratorial minority" could gain control of the labor movement. If successful, they could "stir up strife, foment strikes, create discord." Through their control of the CIO-PAC, the Communists would "worm their members or sympathizers into positions of power." In order to survive, the CIO-PAC "must remain an American labor movement with the purpose of *improving America for Americans.*"[86]

In mid September, the *Milwaukee Journal* pulled out all of the stops in its campaign against the "Communist" Democratic candidate. In a front-page story, it proclaimed: "Deep Red is Background of Candidate Bobrowicz." The newspaper boldly stated, "Edmund V. Bobrowicz . . . is a communist." It then cited "the pattern on Bobrowicz," which included his position as international representative for the Fur and Leather Workers Union, his friendships and associations with known Communists, his engagement in Communist political activities, his "ploddingly" following the Communist Party line, and his nomination papers, which shared circulators and signers with Communist Party candidates. A classic formulation of guilt by association and innuendo, the long newspaper article detailed Bobrowicz's associations and activities in recent years. Despite the Democratic candidate's recent denials, the newspaper proclaimed: "In thought and action, he has shown himself to be a communist, spelled with a small 'c.' "[87]

The next day, the newspaper published an editorial "To the Democrats of Wisconsin." After again painting Bobrowicz with a Red brush, the editor proclaimed: "This man is an impostor in the Democratic ranks. The organized Democrats owe him neither allegiance nor support." It concluded: "The Democratic organization owes it to the people of this city and this state to repudiate this man as its candidate."[88]

Democratic leaders quickly responded. From mid September to early October, the Democratic party attempted to solve the problem of the "Red" Democrat. Initially, critics claimed that Bobrowicz did not even hold a Democratic party membership card, but he produced it as proof of his party credentials. Robert Tehan, the Wisconsin member of the National Democratic Committee, promised Democratic action against him, publicly stating that he was "violently opposed to communism and communists." At one point, Tehan even personally interviewed Bobrowicz to assess his loyalty to the Democratic party's ideals.[89]

In such a climate, the Republican candidates had a field day with charges against "Red" Democrats. At one election forum, Charles Kersten, the Republican candidate in the fifth congressional district, attacked his opponent, Andrew Biemiller, a former Milwaukee Socialist. Biemiller's "record," he charged, "stamps him as an extreme left-winger." After a reference to Bobrowicz, Kersten also quipped: "the Democratic party is in the position of 'a bear on roller skates.' "[90]

Confronted with Red charges against its candidates, the Democratic party soon decided to take action against Bobrowicz. According to the *Milwaukee Journal*, the congressional candidate was the Democrat's "No. 1 headache in the November 5 election campaign." But the CIO-PAC problem extended beyond the boundaries of Wisconsin. The National Democratic Committee, the newspaper reasoned, was "wary about repudiating Bobrowicz for fear it will offend the CIO Political Action Committee." Since the Wisconsin CIO-PAC endorsed and supported other Democratic candidates, including McMurray for senate, Hoan for governor, and Biemiller for Congress, the political situation required extreme delicacy.[91]

After intense behind-the-scenes maneuvering within the state and national Democratic parties and the national CIO-PAC, Tehan finally decided to drop Bobrowicz from the Democratic ticket and to denounce him as a Communist. He announced that he would "actively oppose Bobrowicz in the Nov. 5 election." He also urged similar action from "every loyal Democrat and every other citizen devoted to liberal principles of government." The next day, Charles P. Greene, the Wisconsin and Milwaukee Democratic chairman, added: "the entire state Democratic organization is now on record as being in favor of ditching

Bobrowicz." While McMurray, the senatorial candidate, did not immediately disavow Bobrowicz, Hoan, the gubernatorial candidate, and Biemiller and William G. Rice, two other congressional candidates, fell into line. And, after praising Tehan for his "political integrity," a *Milwaukee Journal* editorial proclaimed: "The slyly laid plan of the Communists to invade the Democratic party and to build up their power in the American congress could not go unchallenged." Eventually, McMurray also joined his fellow Democrats in the general denunciation of Bobrowicz.[92]

Once the Democratic Party regulars had repudiated the congressional candidate, they targeted other leftist CIO-PAC candidates. For example, Milwaukee Democratic leader Greene reported that his executive committee "urged Democratic voters to withdraw their support of Emil Mattson," a Local 248 member who had won a Democratic nomination for the state assembly. During a four-hour closed session, the Milwaukee Democratic leaders also investigated the charges against Bobrowicz and Mattson and interrogated three other CIO-PAC assembly candidates. The Milwaukee Democratic committee then formally "voted to revoke the membership cards of Edmund V. Bobrowicz . . . and Emil E. Mattson." The three CIO-PAC candidates "signed statements addressed to the county Democratic leadership attesting that they were not Communists." The Democratic leaders exonerated two but decided that the third needed further investigation.[93]

Two weeks before the general election, a *Milwaukee Sentinel* editorial repudiated the CIO-PAC candidates as "Moscow's Candidates." The Hearst newspaper declared: "Once again, Soviet Russia is intervening in an American election, campaigning actively on behalf of its candidates." Moscow supported the CIO-PAC in three ways—through Communist Party rallies and radio speakers, through financial assistance to states and congressional districts, and through direct appeals on Soviet radio. In an English-language broadcast, it charged, "The Russian speaker especially commended the candidates in this country WHO HAVE THE ENDORSEMENT OF THE CIO POLITICAL ACTION COMMITTEE." The long Red arm from Moscow constituted an "intolerable interference in American political affairs by a foreign government."[94]

The "average citizen," the editorial concluded, "has the right and the duty—as well as the power—to repudiate at the polls in November the CANDIDATES OF SOVIET RUSSIA for the CONGRESS OF THE UNITED STATES." And the American voter could "identify" the Communist candidates, "For, on the declaration of Moscow, the candidates of Soviet Russia are THE CANDIDATES OF PAC."[95]

Ironically, once the mainstream Democrats opened the Pandora's box of Red-baiting, the specter of Communism remained to haunt their more moderate candidates. After the Communist charges eliminated or silenced the Democratic party's Left, similar charges reappeared against the Democratic party's centrist candidates. Joseph McCarthy, the Republican candidate for the Senate, used this tactic against his liberal Democratic opponent McMurray. At a forum attended by both candidates, McCarthy "flung the charge of 'communism' at his rival." After McMurray criticized the Republican's association with American Action, Inc., a conservative political action group, McCarthy vehemently responded: "If it is organized to fight communism as they say, I welcome their help in defeating communists and those who are communistically inclined like McMurray." In his campaign literature for the fifth congressional district race, Charles Kersten successfully contrasted his Americanism with Biemiller's Communism. Thus was "McCarthyism" born, in the fire of Milwaukee labor politics.[96]

As the November general election approached, the Communist issue attracted the attention of a growing number of voters, swelling Milwaukee voter registration lists. Further, the state ballot contained a referendum on state aid for busing to private schools. Sponsored by conservative Republicans, the referendum proposed the use of public funds to transport parochial and private school children. This, too, increased voter interest in the election, especially among Catholics, who often played a conservative role in Milwaukee labor politics. By the end of October, more than 300,000 Milwaukee voters were registered to vote in the general election.[97]

Although Wisconsin Democrats later charged that Communist labor leaders were responsible for the eventual Republican victory, Milwaukee labor went in several different directions in the election campaign. The more conservative AFL leaders refused to endorse Bobrowicz and supported his Republican opponent. Thus, Frank Ranney, the Federated Trades Council leader, announced his support for John Brophy, the Republican candidate in the fourth congressional district. The Milwaukee AFL leader condemned Bobrowicz as a Communist and also repudiated Wasielewski for his support of the antilabor Smith-Connally Bill. Moreover, some conservative labor leaders even supported McCarthy, because his opponent had the CIO-PAC endorsement. However, the United Labor Committee, a new coalition of Democratic conservatives in the AFL, CIO, and Railroad Brotherhoods, although refusing to endorse Bobrowicz nevertheless endorsed Hoan, McMurray, and Biemiller, the other Democratic candidates.[98]

In late October, the struggle again shifted to the West Allis plant gates. Earlier, the recently discharged Harold Christoffel had returned from eighteen months of army service to help lead the Allis-Chalmers strikers. At a plant gate rally, around two thousand Local 248 members had welcomed their former union president. Repeating Buse's call for arbitration of the unresolved strike issues, he declared: "That is our basic answer to those who say that the company can't negotiate with this union and these Communists over here," referring to the platform group of UAW leaders. "The cheers which greeted Christoffel," the *Milwaukee Sentinel* reported, "were more enthusiastic than for the other speakers. There is apparently hope among the workers that Christoffel can do what the incumbent union leadership has failed to do—bring the costliest Allis strike in history to an early end." Despite hopes for accommodation and settlement, Christoffel and the other speakers "loosed bitter words against the Sentinel's campaign to expose the Communist dominated leadership of many CIO locals here, including Local 248." Christoffel's reappearance on the Milwaukee labor scene, however, stiffened management resistance to all union demands.[99]

One week before the general election, Allis-Chalmers officials inaugurated a back-to-work movement. In response to such corporate appeals, Local 248 president Robert Buse addressed a Sunday morning strike rally of about one thousand union members. The militant union, he announced, reached "the turning point of the strike." The Local 248 bargaining committee, he told strikers, had offered to return to work and to submit "all disputed issues to the binding decision of an impartial arbitrator." Management had refused the offer to arbitrate. He then urged strikers to return to the streets to prevent strikebreakers from entering the West Allis plant. "The only way," Buse declared, "that the company can be forced to negotiate or arbitrate is to have a show of solidarity on the picket lines." One shop steward also urged the union members to demonstrate their solidarity on the picket lines and even suggested "enlist[ing] the scabs to get on the picket lines and atone for their sins."[100]

Union attorney Dan Sobel offered advice to union pickets. He "instructed the strikers to obey the Wisconsin employment relations board rulings defining picketing at the plant." In order to avoid company charges of violating Wisconsin labor law, he recommended compliance with the earlier WERB rulings on mass picketing. "Just remember," he added, "that order does not prevent you from picketing. That is a constitutional right. Keep your hands in your pockets on the picket line and try to persuade everybody not to pass through the line." Then he reminded the workers, "But if anybody endangers your life, you have a right to protect yourself." Sobel's advice resulted in massed "belly-to-back" picketing, where striking workers formed a tight wall at Allis-Chalmers gates.[101]

The next day, five hundred to eight hundred strikers blocked the seventeen Allis-Chalmers plant gates. Three violent incidents occurred at the main gate near Greenfield Avenue and South 70th Street. The *Milwaukee Journal* reported: "Several score strikers and workers were severely mauled Monday morning in three bloody skirmishes on the Allis-Chalmers picket lines." In three instances, "the fighting started when groups of 10 to 20 non-strikers attempted to fight their way through closely massed pickets." In "each melee," the strikers and nonstrikers overpowered the two West Allis policemen on duty. "The gate," the newspaper related, "is about eight feet wide and about 35 pickets kept their tight line moving so closely that no one could shove through. A number of workers who attempted to squeeze through were bumped away and urged to go home." In the first incident, "a big worker in a white shirt," who had been denied entry, "stood back on the street, shouted to the crowd of workers outside to join him, and, then, with about 20 of them, hit the massed pickets with a flying wedge." The result was a general melee: "Strikers, nonstrikers and police were piled three deep in a furious slugging and kicking fight that lasted about five minutes." After about twenty minutes, two other incidents followed, "when other groups of workers decided to force their way through in the same manner."[102]

Over the next week, angry Allis-Chalmers strikers fiercely fought supervisors, strikebreakers, and police. For the most part, after calm mornings, violence occurred with the afternoon change of shifts. As strikebreakers exited and entered the plant, scuffles often developed into fights. Often sympathizers from the surrounding community supported the union strikers. According to one account, "From 3,000 to 5,000 spectators, including children and housewives, were gathered in the park near the plant known as Allis-Chalmers grove." The "surging mass of humanity" called the nonstriking workers "scabs," "rats," and "yellowbellies." The pickets and spectators also threw oranges, tomatoes, and paint bombs at the strikebreakers and their automobiles. Small groups of strikebreakers formed "flying squadrons" to charge through picket lines. In several instances, furious strikers damaged automobiles, overturned some, and set some on fire. Sometimes police officers escorted nonstriking workers through the picket lines. Sometimes strikers fought off police and strikebreakers. In several instances, strikers freed arrested picketers from the police.[103]

Two incidents revealed the savage intensity of the struggle to keep the West Allis plant closed. At one gate, the *Milwaukee Journal* noted, "About 80 to 100 workers massed across the street from the gate, shouted to the deputies, 'Open up a path for us; we're coming through!' " The police attempted to assist the strikebreakers. "The workers," the newspaper continued, "hit the picket line on the run, and in a moment there was a wild scuffle of workers, strikers, and officers. About 40 of the workers had gone through when pickets managed to close ranks again." At another gate, "a group of about 25 workers gathered their forces in the middle of the street and attempted to smash their way through the middle of the picket line. Fists flew briefly until the workers and pickets were disentangled by the police." At this gate, the deputies sometimes opened pathways for strikebreakers and their automobiles. The angry pickets broke the windows of two cars. "The deputies," the newspaper related, "attempted to seize one picket suspected as a window breaker but the officers were surrounded by a swarm of pickets who took the man away from them."[104]

The worst "riotous flareups" appeared on Halloween. According to the head of the Milwaukee police detail, "most of the trouble so far has occurred when large groups of thrill seeking teen-agers and spectators would shout and boo at police, egging on the pickets, and then would swarm in among the pickets whenever there was any jostling or other disturbance on the picket lines. Then a full sized fight would develop." The trouble began in the evening when an automobile drove through one of the plant gates. "At that time," the *Milwaukee Journal* reported, "there were more than 6,000 spectators milling around on S. 70th St and fewer than 1,000 pickets. Many of the spectators were youngsters." As the automobile attempted to leave, the police and deputies sought to clear a path through the pickets. "When the car reached the pavement," the newspaper continued, "some of the pickets started to close around it again. This was the signal for the crowd, and hundreds of spectators rushed in. A riotous scene developed with fists flying and rocks being thrown for around five minutes." Later, the crowd grew to around eight thousand, including about two thousand teenagers. The Halloween crowd stoned strikebreakers and police. Describing two arrested teenagers, the Milwaukee police chief said: "These youngsters deliberately threw rocks at a patrolman and a deputy sheriff."[105]

The real trouble began when "guest" pickets from other CIO unions, around two hundred fifty from the Pressed Steel Tank Company and fifty from the National Maritime Union, appeared on the scene to express solidarity with the forty Allis-Chalmers picketers. The authorities, who now had achieved a strict separation of picketers and spectators, prevented the sympathetic picketers from joining their union brothers. When the union sound truck complained about the denial of the constitutional rights of the other spectators who could want to picket, the maritime union members, the *Milwaukee Journal* noted, "broke away from the picket line for about 10 minutes and marched through the crowd that was being held back by the police. When it returned to the picket line, it had picked up about 200 additional marchers." A Milwaukee police captain decided to prevent a march to another gate and created a police line to hold back the picketers. The union supporters at the rear pushed the others into the police line. "In an instant," the newspaper continued, "what had been a shoving match became a twisting melee and, as tempers flared, fists flew and the swirling mass moved down 70th st. [*sic*] to in front of the Allis-Chalmers clubhouse." The union sound truck ordered the marchers to return to their line, and the police arrested several of the ringleaders.[106]

In the midst of the turmoil, the boundary line between pickets and spectators broke down and "several thousand spectators, including many teen age boys and girls, . . . swarmed to the west side of 70th st." The swelled ranks of the picketers started another shoving match. A final incident occurred after police arrested a spectator. As they marched away with their prisoner, "they were surrounded and pulled by about 150 to 200 other spectators who were trying to rescue the prisoner from the police." This time, however, the police held their captive. After an hour and a half, the pickets and spectators left the streets outside the West Allis plant.[107]

The breakdown of social order brought renewed calls for a return to the bargaining table, and the union again offered to have all unsettled strike issues arbitrated. Management again declined the prospect of a mediated settlement. At a Local 248 membership meeting, UAW secretary-treasurer George Addes reaffirmed the national UAW's pledge of its "unqualified" support for the embattled local. For Addes, the Allis-Chalmers and J. I. Case strikes were a part of a National Association of Manufacturers strategy for "breaking unionization in every other basic industry." The Allis-Chalmers strike, he asserted, was "a life and death struggle against one of the most arrogant, stubborn and irresponsible employers in Wisconsin." Given the strike's national significance, he promised that the UAW would continue its $25,000 strike support payments. And responding to the repeated charges of Communism, he concluded: "If fighting for a decent level of living for our families is communistic, then there are 140,000,000 Communists in America."[108]

The mood was tense on the eve of the November election. In response to a union charge that an Allis-Chalmers memorandum invited "foreman and scabs to break picket lines by force," W. C. Van Cleaf replied, "If these reports are correct, the plan has been worked out independently by employes. This is undoubtedly a protective measure against picket line violence engineered by the Communistic leadership of Local 248." At the Sunday Local 248 membership meeting, Buse appealed to one thousand union members for "a heavy picket turnout" on Monday morning. But both company and union appeals had little effect, since only 70 persons appeared for the Monday's "mass march," and the normal contingent of about 220 pickets were at the plant gates. The next day, after a full week of front-page newspaper headlines about the widespread violence on the Allis-Chalmers picket lines, Milwaukee voters went to the polls.[109]

Just before the general election, the *Milwaukee Journal* offered an analysis of Milwaukee labor's important role in the coming vote. The McCarthy-McMurray, Biemiller-Kersten, and Bobrowicz-Wasielewski contests offered exciting races between Democratic and Republican candidates. McMurray, the newspaper reasoned, "is banking on strong support from organized labor in Milwaukee, Racine, and Kenosha counties to overcome whatever lead McCarthy might pile up in rural areas." In an editorial, the influential newspaper endorsed Republican Walter Goodland for governor and Democrat Andrew Biemiller and Independent Thaddeus Wasielewski for Congress. It failed to endorse either McMurray or McCarthy in the Senate race. It also supported the school busing referendum. On Bobrowicz, the newspaper asserted, "His deceit should bring his defeat on Tuesday."[110]

The November general election was a rout for the Left, for liberals, and for the Democrats. Nationwide, the Cold War, domestic social upheaval, and labor and Communism pushed conservative Republicans into national and state offices. In Milwaukee, the long Allis-Chalmers strike, the press exposés of Communist leaders, the struggle for control of the CIO council, and strike violence produced a victory for Republicans. Although the busing referendum lost statewide, it won in Milwaukee and brought out large numbers of conservative Catholic voters who voiced their dissatisfaction with militant labor in the polling booth.

For Wisconsin and Milwaukee Democrats, the general election was a major disappointment. By a margin of over two hundred thousand votes, the *Milwaukee Journal* reported, Republican Joseph McCarthy soundly defeated Howard McMurray for the LaFollette Senate seat, "thus ending the LaFollette 'dynasty,' which had endured in the state for so many years." McCarthy won in all Wisconsin counties except Dane County, a traditional LaFollette stronghold. Moreover, the Republicans swept all major state offices. The conservative *Milwaukee Sentinel* gloated over the massive Republican victories:

"Wisconsin's administration is 100 per cent Republican.

"Wisconsin's Congressional delegation—two Senators and 10 representatives—is 100 per cent Republican."

Indeed, a fundamental shift had occurred in Milwaukee politics. "Chief surprise of the election," the Hearst newspaper continued, "was the fact that Milwaukee County, historically the home of Socialism, Dan

Hoan, New Dealism, and labor-liberalism, followed the rest of the state into the Republican column. Both Goodland and McCarthy carried the county."[111]

The *Milwaukee Journal*, the liberal voice of the Milwaukee establishment, reported: "McCarthy's strength—and McMurray's weakness—in Milwaukee county, was the surprise of the election to Democratic leaders." Problems from both the Left and the Right had bedeviled the Democratic candidate. "The hapless McMurray," the newspaper concluded, "was caught 'in the middle' on the 'Communist' issue. He lost strength, not only with the anti-Communist element which had been voting with the New Deal since 1932, but with the 'radicals' who backed Edmund Bobrowicz on the Democratic ticket in the fourth district." In effect, a divided and embattled labor movement had undermined the Democratic campaigns for all Wisconsin offices.[112]

By nearly as large a margin, the eighty-four-year-old Republican Goodland handily defeated Democrat Daniel Hoan, the former Socialist mayor of Milwaukee, in the gubernatorial race. The *Milwaukee Journal* came to the "inescapable" conclusion that "the Progressives followed their leadership and voted for Republicans, including McCarthy." In the fifth congressional district, Charles Kersten, the Republican, soundly defeated Biemiller, the AFL candidate. The Republican victories dramatically symbolized the end of the Wisconsin Socialist and Progressive traditions.[113]

In the fourth congressional district, the Republican Brophy defeated the upstart CIO-PAC candidate Bobrowicz in a relatively close race. Brophy received 47,935 votes; Bobrowicz. 43,268. Wasielewski, the three-term incumbent. was a distant third with only 36,780 votes. The *Milwaukee Journal* characterized the fourth district campaign as "one of the hottest and most unusual campaigns" in Milwaukee. It dramatically symbolized the tortuous process of Wisconsin's political realignment. "The campaign," the newspaper observed, "cast Wasielewski, the Democratic incumbent, as an Independent, against Brophy a former Socialist and Progressive who became a Republican last spring in the merger of the Republicans and Progressives, and Bobrowicz, a Communist running under the banner of the Democrats without the party leaders' blessing." It brought out over 130,000 voters, a record number for a Milwaukee off-year election. Brophy's strength was in West Allis and West Milwaukee, two areas affected by the picket line violence, and Wauwatosa, a Republican residential suburb. Bobrowicz's strength was in Cudahy and South Milwaukee, two ethnic and working-class suburbs. He also carried five of the district's "strongly Polish" wards. According to William G. Rice, the Democratic congressional candidate for Madison, "Bobrowicz came closer to election than any other Democratic Congressional candidate in Wisconsin." Milwaukee voters, he added, considered the Communist charges "either untrue or irrelevant."[114]

In the Wisconsin senate, Milwaukee voters returned all of the incumbents, three Democrats and one Republican, to office. Robert Tehan, who had figured prominently in the Bobrowicz affair, won by the narrowest margin. In the Wisconsin assembly contests, the Democrats also suffered some significant defeats. Charles Greene, the Milwaukee and Wisconsin Democratic leader, lost a close race to his Republican opponent. Five CIO-PAC-endorsed union candidates won assembly seats and five lost. Three CIO-PAC assembly candidates who the press identified as Communists (including Local 248 members Emil Mattson and Charles Fisher) lost. A fourth loser, John Killian, publicly had supported Bobrowicz's campaign. All in all, the Milwaukee Republicans took two seats from incumbents, Fisher and Green, and gained three more seats in other uncontested races.[115]

In an election postmortem, a *Milwaukee Journal* editorial analyzed the role of labor in the national and local elections. "All over the nation," it observed, "the people vented their wrath at Labor's spokesmen. Moderates as well as radicals went down." The formerly "strident and boastful" robust CIO-PAC, the editorial added, "flattened out completely this time. Its 'Jimmy Higgins' house to house campaign, its pamphlets, its radio broadcasts availed nothing. It neither 'purged' its opponents nor elected its friends. Many of its bitterest enemies won reelection by tremendous margins." In sum, the political mood of the nation and Milwaukee took a decisive turn toward social and political conservatism.[116]

In the 1946 election, conservative AFL leaders and militant CIO leaders shifted labor's political loyalties and altered the alignment of political forces. Progressives went into the Republican party. Old-guard Socialists went into either the Democratic or the Republican parties. In effect, fear of the Left in the Democratic Party drove conservative AFL and CIO labor leaders toward the Republicans. Moreover, in the campaign, the specter of Communism loomed large and resulted in considerable Red-baiting of left and liberal candidates. The result was a stunning victory for Joseph McCarthy and other Republicans.

# 7

## THE UNMAKING OF MILITANT UNIONISM II: UAW POLITICS AND THE RED SCARE, 1946–1950

The October strike violence and the November defeat of the CIO candidates in the Milwaukee general election signaled a major turning point in the long Allis-Chalmers strike. The two events marked the beginning of the end for the militants in the local. In November and December 1946, the UAW renewed its campaign against the Allis-Chalmers corporation on the picket lines. At the same time, however, national UAW politics—specifically, the factional dispute between Walter Reuther and R. J. Thomas—increasingly influenced the intense contest over management rights. The press charges of Communism, the deep factionalism within the Milwaukee and the Wisconsin CIO organizations, the debacle of the CIO foray into the Milwaukee and Wisconsin elections, and the internal UAW divisiveness weakened the Allis-Chalmers workers in their struggle for higher wages, union security, and grievance resolution.

In February and March 1947, the drama of the Allis-Chalmers strike moved to the national political stage. Three congressional committees, the Senate Labor and Public Welfare Committee, the House Education and Labor Committee (HELC), and the House Un-American Activities Committee (HUAC), took testimony and investigated the Allis-Chalmers strike and UAW Local 248. Chaired by Representative Fred Hartley, the House sponsor of the Taft-Hartley Act, the HELC heard the testimony of company and union officials. The committee looked forward to amending the National Labor Relations Act, which management conservatives believed tilted the balance of federal power toward labor unions. At the hearings, Harold Story led top Allis-Chalmers officials and R. J. Thomas led Local 248 leaders. Two freshmen congressmen, John Kennedy and Richard Nixon, sat on the HELC and interrogated union leaders about their alleged Communist activities. In addition, HUAC, which had recently gained prominence in the anti-Communist atmosphere of the new Cold War America, heard the testimony of three Local 248 opposition leaders. By March 1947, the combined weight of UAW factionalism and the Red Scare had broken the will of Allis-Chalmers strikers.

During the week of the election, the secretary of labor had once again attempted to mediate the Allis-Chalmers dispute. But the CIO's political failure had strengthened management resistance to Local 248 demands. Although Allis-Chalmers president Geist had reluctantly agreed to participate in another round of negotiations, he had asserted: "it must be understood that Allis-Chalmers will at no time negotiate while there is illegal picketing."[1]

The UAW also resolved to continue the long and difficult strike. In letters to all UAW locals, George Addes, the UAW secretary-treasurer, and Joseph Mattson, the regional director for Wisconsin, decried the Allis-Chalmers "union-busting campaign." They proclaimed: "[T]he *real* issues in dispute" were wages, a "workable" grievance procedure, and union security. UAW Local 248, they added, "offered to submit all issues to arbitration. The company's reply has been an outright refusal coupled with an intensification of their red-baiting campaign." Addes and Mattson charged that, in the John Sentinel series, the *Milwaukee Sentinel* "seeks to leave in the minds of the Wisconsin public the impression that *every* officer and *every* committeeman of our Allis-Chalmers Local No. 248 'is a Communist or subservient to the Communist Party.' "[2]

Two days later, the two UAW leaders reported on the Allis-Chalmers strike to the UAW Policy Committee. At the UAW meeting, the Policy Committee assigned Vice President R. J. Thomas to oversee the walkout. It also agreed to publicize the strike through a "radio program, publicity, setting up Citizens' Committee, etc." and to increase UAW financial and other aid for the West Allis strikers. In a press release, the UAW committee reaffirmed "its complete support of the striking Allis-Chalmers workers and we strongly condemn the refusal of this company to negotiate in good faith."[3]

With the assignment of Thomas, the Milwaukee strike became the arena for renewed factional politics. After Homer Martin bolted the CIO for the AFL, R. J. Thomas directed the UAW-CIO from 1939 to 1946. Along with George Addes, Thomas led the UAW with the support of its left faction, which worked closely with UAW Communists. In March 1946, Walter Reuther, a rising force within the UAW since the 1939 General Motors tool and die strike, finally challenged Thomas and won the UAW presidency. During the 1945–1946 General Motors strike, the left-wing United Electrical, Radio, and Machine

Workers Union (UE), had undercut Reuther's wage strategy by accepting a lower CIO wage package, which then became the pattern for postwar collective bargaining. Subsequently, Reuther made labor and Communism an important issue in his quest to maintain his hold on the UAW.[4]

In his hard-fought UAW campaign for the presidency, Reuther's slogan was "Against Outside Interference," an allusion to Communist influence or domination in some UAW locals. Although he never challenged a UAW member's right to be a Communist, Reuther severely questioned Communist interference with the basic principles of American trade unionism. For Reuther, the main issues were Communist policies supporting wartime piecework and incentive pay, endorsing a wartime draft-labor law, and encouraging UE treachery during the GM strike. Within the UAW, Reuther's supporters were a mixed coalition of Catholics, Socialists, anti-Stalinists, and conservative unionists.[5]

In a bitterly contested and tight race, Reuther narrowly defeated Thomas (by 124 votes out of over 8,700 cast) in the election for the UAW presidency. In the end, the difficult contest was a test of Reuther's personal popularity and not necessarily of his broader anti-Communist policies. Despite the loss of the presidency, the left-center Thomas-Addes coalition still won considerable support at the 1946 UAW convention. The UAW delegates elected Addes as secretary-treasurer, Thomas as first vice president, and Richard Leonard, another Thomas ally, as second vice president. Moreover, Thomas's allies controlled the UAW executive board by a two-to-one margin. Although Walter Reuther was UAW president, he would have a delicate and difficult one-and-one-half years governing the factionalized auto workers' union.[6]

Since Reuther's victory was not decisive, he remained vulnerable to a possible challenge from the UAW Left at the next national convention. Throughout the Allis-Chalmers strike, the Reuther and Thomas factions vied for the favor of local union members. When given the hard choice of a director for the troublesome strike of a left union against an immovable management, Reuther allowed his rival Thomas to oversee the impossible situation. With the difficult assignment, the former UAW president could easily stumble and lose support. And stumble he did as the Allis-Chalmers strike increasingly became a contentious issue in the UAW's postwar factional struggles.

Given Reuther's weak position and Thomas's dominant influence, the UAW Policy Committee strongly endorsed the cause of the Allis-Chalmers strikers. Reuther privately supported the conservative Milwaukee and Wisconsin CIO dissidents but could not publicly disavow the Allis-Chalmers strikers. After the November elections, Milwaukee

CIO unions pledged "mass support" for the Allis-Chalmers strike and established a committee to implement strike support activities. The CIO unions were a mix of conservative and radical CIO union leaders from the steel, electrical, brewery, packinghouse, and autoworker unions.[7]

After two more weeks of abortive negotiations, Leo LaMotte, a Thomas aide, criticized "the defiant and arrogant attitude of the Allis-Chalmers negotiating committee." Despite the national UAW presence, company officials charged that Thomas and other union negotiators were " 'Reds,' too." In frustration, the special federal conciliator called for a recess in the mediation sessions. He claimed that he was "unable to find any basis upon which the two sides could compromise."[8]

When federal mediation failed, Milwaukee workers again returned to the streets to defend the Allis-Chalmers strikers. At the end of November, Thomas appealed to all Milwaukee UAW and CIO locals for mass action on the West Allis picket lines. Even the national CIO president Philip Murray called for "all-out assistance," and the national CIO Executive Board endorsed the strikers' cause. Thomas called for a half-day demonstration by 20,000 Milwaukee CIO members. On Monday, November 25, the whole West Allis community tensely awaited the expected mass picket line. In the morning, only 150 pickets at the plant greeted the same number of police officers, but, at noon, the large Seaman Body UAW Local 75 planned to "take a holiday." Workers from several other large firms, including Sterling Motor Trucks, Lindemann and Hoverson, Wisconsin Motors, and Pressed Steel Tank also planned to take work holidays. By early afternoon, thousands of CIO picketers had appeared at the Allis-Chalmers gates. Around three thousand Local 75 members quit work and joined the Allis-Chalmers picket line. The picket signs also indicated the presence of conservative CIO steelworker and brewery worker locals. While the press and police counted anywhere from three thousand to six thousand picketers, Thomas "estimated as many as 10,000 pickets at one time and a total of 20,000." Sixteen union picketers were arrested in violent clashes with the police and fourteen, including the Local 75 president, were later charged with unlawful assembly and riot.[9]

Two weeks later, the Milwaukee CIO mobilized a second mass demonstration to support the Allis-Chalmers strikers. Once again, the right-wing CIO locals filled the Local 248 picket lines. Moreover, since the Seaman Body plant scheduled an operational shutdown, UAW leaders expected five thousand Local 75 members to participate in the UAW call for mass picketing. One conservative UAW leader proclaimed his support for the Allis-Chalmers workers' "struggle to win their strike for a decent contract and a living wage." Making a sharp distinction between Local 248 members and leaders, he added: "my call for all-out support for the membership of Local 248 in their strike in no way changes my attitude toward the leadership of Local 248."[10]

When the strike supporters massed at the Allis-Chalmers plant gates, the inevitable violence occurred. In the late afternoon, it flared when police inside the plant area "advanced upon the 500 pickets at the south gate and charged into the picket line to force open a path for the cars of employes waiting to leave the plant." The union claimed: "nearly 1000 cops and deputies charged the picket lines at the Hawley plant gates and beat the CIO demonstrators with blackjacks to open the lines and give cover to scabs who had been bottled up in the plant more than an hour." As fists began to fly, the *Milwaukee Journal* added, "The police and pickets at the other gates were attracted by the fight." In the "pitched" battle: "Rocks were thrown, officers' badges were torn and noses were bloodied in slugging fist fights." Once again, police attempted to arrest pickets who were in turn rescued by the infuriated crowd. In the struggle, "a score of persons were injured, including 11 peace officers, and two automobiles were burned."[11]

Fifty-five people, including two juveniles, were arrested. The fifty-three arrested adults represented several Milwaukee CIO unions, including Seaman Body, Allis-Chalmers, Wisconsin Motors, Pressed Steel Tank, Harnischfeger, and International Harvester workers. The arrested picketers included the UAW Local 75 president and the driver of the union sound truck. After forty-eight hours in jail, the arrested workers "were booked on charges of 'unlawful assembly' and 'riot.' " When they were arraigned, their bail ranged from $250 to $1,000. Some CIO leaders then threatened a "state-wide work holiday" to support the arrested picketers, but were overruled and a CIO general strike never materialized.[12]

In mid December 1946, Milwaukee's labor factionalism spilled over into the Wisconsin CIO convention. Through November and early December, the rightist CIO leaders continued to hold caucuses and meetings in a bid to repeat their Milwaukee CIO council victory at the state level. From December 13 to 15, 450 CIO delegates gathered for a long and contentious weekend in Wausau. The left-right CIO struggles in the streets, at the polling booths, and in the union halls continued in the selection of convention delegates. Obviously, Local 248's left-wing leadership and the Allis-Chalmers strike were important issues at the rancorous convention.[13]

During the first sessions, the CIO radicals and conservatives worked hard on the rules for voting and seating delegates. At the convention, national and regional CIO leaders, including John Brophy, the head of

CIO councils, Thomas, the UAW vice president and also a CIO vice president, and others from the automobile, clothing, packinghouse, and electrical workers' unions, marshaled their representatives and delegates. Robert Buse, the leftist Wisconsin CIO president and convention chair, consistently outraged the conservative delegates with his rulings. On several key issues, Brophy ruled in favor of the right-wing faction. After the CIO conservatives won important victories on voting procedures and seating delegates, the Left attempted a face-saving compromise for the election of state CIO officers. In order to "avoid a showdown" between Left and Right, one newspaper reporter noted, the Left "would call for sacrificing Robert Buse, incumbent left wing president" in order "to save Mel Heinritz, state CIO secretary." As the only salaried union position, the secretaryship was the more important of the two state CIO offices. The compromise candidate for CIO president was Herman Steffes, the recently arrested president of UAW Local 75.[14]

R. J. Thomas played a controversial public role in his support of the Allis-Chalmers union leaders and strikers. He vigorously caucused with both factions to arrange for an acceptable compromise on state CIO officers. On the last day, he dramatically appealed for state CIO support for the Allis-Chalmers strikers. Although Wisconsin CIO unionists were deeply divided over the Local 248 leaders, the plight of the rank-and-file strikers unified all delegates in their opposition to the intractable Allis-Chalmers management. Thomas proclaimed to the delegates: "I would like to see every local and every member surround that plant some morning, and if we can't keep those scabs out, we'll go in and take them out." He added, "I may get into trouble with the law for this, but I've been in jail before and I'm willing to go there again in the interests of the trade union movement." In the same vein, Robert Buse, the convention chair, declared: "We can't support these workers with motions and amendments. . . . Good men will be found on these picket lines, and that's all we ask."[15]

The UAW vice president's "inflammatory remarks" prompted outrage in the Wisconsin press and among public officials. For the *Milwaukee Sentinel*, Thomas's appeal indicated the "desperate state of the CIO United Automobile Workers strike against the Allis-Chalmers Manufacturing Co." In response to an inquiry about the UAW leader's speech, the Wisconsin assistant attorney general said that such action would violate the Allis-Chalmers injunction against mass picketing. In a similar response, the Milwaukee sheriff said, "I'd like to see him try it. What he likes and what he can get other people to do for him is another matter."[16]

Despite Thomas's impassioned appeal, the CIO rightists eventually duplicated their Milwaukee victory and won control of the Wisconsin

CIO Council. In their caucuses, they decided to reject compromise with the Left and to run their own full slate of state CIO officers. They supported Herman Steffes for president and ran John Sorensen, a West Allis steelworker, against Heinritz for secretary. Major Banachowicz, a Milwaukee hosiery worker, ran for vice president. When the CIO convention finally nominated officers, the *Milwaukee Journal* reported: "Robert Buse, left wing incumbent council president, in a surprise move declined nomination for reelection in favor of Herman Steffes." The remaining leftist slate included Mel Heinritz, who ran for secretary, and Malcolm Lloyd, a centrist UAW member, who ran for vice president.[17]

With Steffes unopposed for state CIO president, the major contest was between Heinritz and Sorensen for Wisconsin CIO secretary. The tally of ballots revealed a very tight race: Sorensen received 37,595 to Heinritz's 35,134 votes. In the other contested race, the centrist Lloyd defeated the official right-wing candidate for the state CIO vice president. Most important, the CIO conservatives captured fifteen of the twenty-three Executive Board seats. Since the union delegations selected these seats, the results indicated how deep Wisconsin labor conservativism ran. As the Christmas holiday season neared, the balance of Milwaukee and Wisconsin labor politics shifted further to the to the right. In January, the new state executive board selected Walter Cappel, an early leader of the conservative UAW caucuses, as the state CIO legislative representative, and Max Raskin, a Milwaukee attorney, as the CIO legal counsel.[18]

The 1946 Christmas season was a truly dismal one for Allis-Chalmers strikers. Two seasonal messages arrived in workers' mailboxes—one from the company and another from the union. Walter Geist emphasized a religious and corporate theme of social peace and harmony. "The message of peace and good will," he wrote, "is as real today as the night the angels sang it nearly 2000 years ago." After noting the survival of the "spirit of Christmas" through "wars and political and economic unrest," the Allis-Chalmers president appealed to his workers: "Let us in the light of His teaching find a way to establish a lasting and universal peace among nations and restore for our beloved America economic stability and prosperity for all of our people." The message was simple and conservative—an abiding faith in God and country would cure their mutual ills.[19]

A much longer letter from Robert Buse and the union Executive Board carried a more bitter and somber message for Local 248 members. Describing a brutal economic reality that undermined Geist's message of peace and goodwill, the embattled union leader wrote:

As a holiday message to you we had hoped to be able to announce that the strike has come to an end and the New Year will find you back at your job at higher pay and with new gains.

Unfortunately, we are not yet able to bring you these glad tidings. Instead of a heart, the Allis-Chalmers company has only a stone in its bosom. Instead of being moved by a spirit of giving that prevails during the Yuletide season, this heartless company sends you a blunt letter telling you that you will not get your vacation pay.

Like greedy old Scrooge, in Dickens' *Christmas Carol*, Allis-Chalmers does not believe in the Christmas spirit nor are they concerned with your welfare and needs.

The remainder of the union letter criticized tax rebates to Allis-Chalmers, repeated messages of support from other unions, castigated scabs and strikebreakers, reported on unfair labor practice charges filed against the company, and exhorted union members to hold solid for victory.[20]

After the Christmas and New Year holidays, developments in the Allis-Chalmers strike reflected the general conservative and rightward drift of UAW politics. In November 1946, another conservative challenge emerged from the West Allis shops. Walter Petersen created the Committee for the Repudiation of the Officers and Bargaining Agency of Local No. 248 (CROBA), which later became the Independent Workers of Allis-Chalmers (IWAC). Unlike Venne, who worked within the UAW, Petersen opted for independent unionism that avoided affiliation with either the CIO or the AFL. A highly skilled layout man in the Steam Turbine Department, Petersen led a workers' organization that carried a strong anti-CIO and almost antiunion message. Petersen, who had struggled against Local 248 leaders since 1939, also opposed the Communist connections of the Local 248 leaders. In early December, CROBA even advertised and endorsed a back-to-work movement of Allis-Chalmers workers. In the newspaper advertisement, CROBA declared: "We have returned to work after being taken to the cleaners by a bunch of Communists."[21]

In early December, Petersen sent an ultimatum to UAW president Walter Reuther, criticizing the "intolerable" situation and demanding "immediate and drastic action" against the Local 248 leaders. Claiming that more than two thousand members had repudiated the local leadership, he insisted on "an immediate election of new officers." Moreover, the CROBA leader demanded the reinstatement of suspended strikebreakers and a new WERB-supervised strike vote. "Unless such action is taken before Dec. 13, 1[9]46," Petersen threatened, "the Committee will consider that it has exhausted its remedy under the Union Constitution and will be forced to resort to the Labor Board for relief."[22]

In mid December, CROBA re-formed as Independent Workers of Allis-Chalmers and petitioned the WERB for a new representation election. At the time, the independent union claimed to represent a majority of Allis-Chalmers workers with 3,400 signed cards. In response to the IWAC call for a new election, Thomas declared, "The international union does not recognize scabs who are working in a strike bound plant." In early January, the WERB chair announced the Wisconsin labor board's decision to conduct another representation election on Sunday, January 26, at the Milwaukee auditorium. For the first time since the original 1938 NLRB election, Allis-Chalmers workers would voice their opinion on union representation.[23]

In response to the WERB announcement, Local 248 leaders followed a twofold plan of action. First, they attempted to challenge the Wisconsin labor board's authority to conduct a new election in the federal courts, arguing that federal labor law had precedence over state law. In federal court, Judge F. Ryan Duffy (Harold Story's brother-in-law) ruled against the union, and a federal appeals court upheld Duffy's ruling. The union leaders began an all out campaign to win the WERB election. They called for one thousand volunteer drivers with automobiles to carry scattered union voters to the polls. In a frantic appeal, they exhorted fellow unionists: "Remember the chips are down and the results of this election will determine who will win the strike. . . . The only question is: Will it be ended on the company's terms, or will it be ended on the union's terms—your terms?"[24]

In January 1947, a feud between Walter Reuther and R. J. Thomas erupted over the handling of the Allis-Chalmers strike and the IWAC petition for a new representation election. During the WERB election campaign, top CIO and UAW leaders secretly attempted to negotiate a strike settlement with Allis-Chalmers officials. After nine long months, over 36 percent of the Allis-Chalmers strikers returned to work. Faced with this grim situation, national CIO and UAW leaders realistically feared losing union representation in Wisconsin's largest firm. Just before the WERB election, Reuther met with Harold Story and other Allis-Chalmers officials in Milwaukee. Without the knowledge of Thomas or local union leaders, Reuther and John Brophy, CIO president Murray's personal representative, tried to negotiate a strike settlement. The proposed settlement would have completely capitulated to Allis-Chalmers demands. It called for removing Local 248 officers and establishing a CIO administrator until new elections for officers. Most important, Reuther and Brophy agreed to drop the principal demand for union security. According to one press account,

Thomas and Local 248 officials gave the Reuther-Brophy proposals "a cold shoulder."[25]

In an angry letter to Reuther and the UAW Executive Board, Thomas charged that the UAW president had undermined his efforts to lead the Allis-Chalmers strike and had violated UAW policies and procedures in his negotiations with Allis-Chalmers management. Thomas also claimed that Reuther permitted a "deliberate insult to [Local 248 president] Buse and to our union" at a meeting with corporate officials in the Milwaukee home of a Methodist minister. Moreover, Thomas asserted that Reuther had attempted to negotiate a secret deal behind the backs of the other UAW officers, the UAW Policy Committee, and the Local 248 officers.[26]

At the next UAW Policy Committee meeting, Thomas managed to hold together his left-center coalition and to call off further negotiations until after the WERB election. The "pro-Thomas forces," the *Milwaukee Journal* related, "reportedly told the meeting that the leadership of the striking local expected to win the bargaining agency vote by a majority of 'four to one.' " The *Milwaukee Sentinel* claimed that Thomas's faction "betrayed" the UAW president. "It is apparent," it concluded, "that the left wing faction opposes ending the strike at the present time for political reasons. Reuther, on the other hand, prefers to take no chances on losing one of the UAW's larger locals to an independent union." Despite intense UAW factionalism, Reuther presented a united UAW leadership to the press and public. "I want to say," he told reporters, "definitely and emphatically that the decision of the committee was unanimous."[27]

UAW Local 248 faced a major test in the WERB election. A *Milwaukee Journal* reporter offered an insightful assessment of the WERB election's significance. "To begin with," he observed, "the stakes in the election are much bigger than might be supposed at first glance." It would have "repercussions" for the strike and "in the top ranks of the International United Automobile Workers' union (CIO), the second largest labor organization in the country." Reuther and Thomas were "battling for control" of the UAW. On the one hand, Thomas wanted "a 248 election victory to lower Reuther's stock" among UAW leaders and to "pave the way . . . to recapture his job as president." On the other hand, the "agile Reuther . . . will have to do a lot of fast stepping to avoid getting caught in the middle, if Local 248 should win."[28]

Furthermore, the embattled Local 248 leaders confronted a formidable task in getting out the pro-UAW vote. While IWAC supporters were concentrated among the returned workers in the West Allis plant, UAW supporters were scattered in temporary jobs around the Milwaukee area. Nonetheless, the UAW local, the *Milwaukee Journal* observed, "showed its capacity for hard work in getting out the vote in the recent congressional elections." It added, "This willingness to get out and ring doorbells may stand the local in good stead in overcoming one of its election disadvantages." Despite their differences with Local 248 leaders, the conservative CIO locals "supported them in the election fight."[29]

The day before the election, Walter Petersen promised that, if victorious, IWAC would negotiate a swift end to the long Allis-Chalmers strike. "The strike," he declared, "has cost A-C workers over 20 millions in wages with a loss to the community of 80 millions. . . . Surely the facts are sufficient proof that Local 248 has mismanaged the strike." Confident of victory, Petersen promised that IWAC "will enter negotiations with the company in the spirit of true collective bargaining."[30]

UAW Local 248 won a tentative victory, receiving 4,122 votes compared to 4,015 for the IWAC. One hundred sixteen voters opted for no union. Fifty ballots were challenged. In fact, only thirty of the fifty challenged ballots would give a clear majority to the UAW local. Among the challenged ballots were those of Buse and Dombek, the union president and vice president, who had been fired for allegedly making libelous statements about the corporation. Since the independent union did not obtain the required majority of the voters, UAW Local 248 retained bargaining rights for all Allis-Chalmers workers.[31]

R. J. Thomas declared the WERB election a "victory" for UAW Local 248 and a "triumph for all organized labor." Despite overwhelming odds, he proclaimed, "the attacks of the company, the Milwaukee press, the Wisconsin employment relations board and certain minor clergymen, . . . the workers of Allis-Chalmers retained Local 248 as their bargaining agent." Thomas had reason to exult. The UAW local had overcome formidable obstacles: the nine-month strike's economic deprivation, the Red scare about Milwaukee and Wisconsin labor, and factionalism within the CIO, UAW, and UAW Local 248.[32]

The next day, Thomas fired the first public salvo against Reuther in his campaign for the UAW presidency. His "blistering attack," the *Milwaukee Sentinel* reported, removed "any doubt that the A-C strike has become an arena for Thomas and Reuther's battle over the UAW presidency." Apparently Thomas informed *Detroit Times* and *New York Times* reporters about his allegations against Reuther, even before Walter Reuther had received his letter.[33]

Reuther was infuriated. In a long letter to Thomas and a shorter one to all UAW locals, he claimed that Thomas had made absolutely no effort to discuss the complaints as recently as January 24. His "first hint of the synthetic storm" came at a recent Cleveland UAW educational conference when Thomas and his "political bloc" initiated "a lobby and bar-room whispering campaign. This campaign consisted of lies, slurs and insinuations to the effect that I had engaged in back-door dealing with the Allis-Chalmers Company without the knowledge of my fellow officers." Reuther charged that Thomas had made "hysterical quotations" to the press and "deliberate falsification of the facts." Reuther demanded that Thomas either retract his statements or file charges against him in accordance with the UAW constitution.[34]

The UAW president chastised Thomas for such criticism in this "period of growing reaction" against American labor. Recalling the UE actions in the long GM strike, he alluded to the similar left "political complexion" of the Allis-Chalmers UE, UAW, and Farm Equipment Worker locals. For the first time, he specifically criticized UAW Local 248, reiterating CIO president Murray's October warning to the UAW Executive Board: "if we did not clean up the mess created by the communist leadership of Local 248, we would be in grave danger of losing the strike." Reuther then publicly criticized Thomas's personal failure to live up to his union duties and responsibilities. At the Atlantic City CIO convention, he charged, Thomas stayed up late playing poker and missed two important morning meetings on the Allis-Chalmers strike.[35]

On the controversial secret Allis-Chalmers negotiations, the UAW president maintained that the national Policy Committee had authorized his contacts with Allis-Chalmers officials and that he had continuously reported back to the UAW committee on the status of negotiations. He also noted that he frequently consulted with Thomas on the "main items" of the Allis-Chalmers strike—"union security; wages; grievance procedure; and arbitration of disciplinary layoffs and discharges." Finally, Reuther claimed that he frequently spoke with Thomas about the Allis-Chalmers charges that the Local 248 leaders were not "democratically elected" and that a "lack of faith" caused a "grave split . . . in the union's ranks."[36]

The UAW president also responded to Thomas in a letter addressed to UAW Executive Board members. Once again, Reuther directly challenged the activities of Communists in the UAW. Stating his position on UAW Local 248, Reuther wrote:

> There are those in our union who hide behind the charge of redbaiting to escape from sober judgment and cold analysis of facts. I have not been, and am not now afraid of words. There are communists in our union and in our industry. I do not propose that they be driven from our union or from our industry. I do propose, however, that they shall not be allowed to utilize our union and its members for the prosecution of their alien ideology.

If some Allis-Chalmers workers wished to be Communist Party members, he told the UAW Executive Board members, "that is their business and their privilege. But when these employees propose to use our union for the furtherance of the interests and desires of the Communist Party, then it is our business."[37]

Evidently, Allis-Chalmers officials converted Reuther to their position on the Local 248 leaders, since the Allis-Chalmers research apparently provided many of the substantive facts for Reuther's charges. In a reference to the firm's pamphlet, "Principle Represented: Communist," Reuther noted that some Local 248 officers and shop leaders did sign the Communist Party's nomination petitions. Moreover, he added, "these petitions were circulated on the picket lines during a time when the union was fighting for its life." Although he again defended the political rights of union members, Reuther refused to permit "the destruction of the union" with the exercise of these political rights. "Why," he asked, "did they place this gigantic club in the hands of their management with which to beat our union to the ground?" The signing of the Communist petitions was a "colossal blunder and stupidity."[38]

Finally, Reuther directly challenged the members of Thomas's left majority on the UAW Executive Board. "I now demand," the UAW president declared, "that the International Executive Board remove the officers of Local 248 and authorize me to place an administrator over the local union in conjunction with [CIO] President Murray. If this is not done, your mechanical majority bloc on the Board shall stand indicted for the loss of that strike." Although it would take almost a year before the UAW Executive Board would finally accede to Reuther's demand, Reuther's response to Thomas's challenge made the Allis-Chalmers strike a central issue in the national UAW's left-right factional dispute.[39]

The struggle for the UAW presidency and against UAW Communists originated in the Milwaukee streets and union halls. Through the spring, summer, and fall of 1947, Reuther increased his public attacks against the left UAW coalition of Thomas and Addes. In June, the left coalition's failed attempt to merge the Farm Equipment Workers Union into the UAW was probably decisive in their eventual defeat. At the November UAW convention, Reuther finally consolidated his hold on the giant automobile workers union. By the fall, after months of bitter and unsuccessful factional struggle, the wearied and defeated Thomas and Addes allowed Reuther to run unopposed for the UAW presidency. The Reuther caucus's entire slate of officers, Reuther for president, Emil Mazey for secretary-treasurer, and John W. Livingston and Richard Gosser for the two vice presidents, all won. Most important, Reuther captured eighteen of the twenty-two Executive Board seats. In full control of the UAW, Reuther subsequently dismissed over one hundred left UAW members from staff positions.[40]

In mid February 1947, the swelling tide of state and national conservative reaction brought Allis-Chalmers officials and later Local 248 leaders to Washington to explain the Allis-Chalmers conflict. On February 14, Harold Story initially testified before the Senator Robert Taft's Labor and Public Welfare Committee. On February 24, he and several company officials appeared before the Hartley committee to testify about the strike. Their joint statement, which management later published for wide distribution, rested on the extensive and detailed Allis-Chalmers research of Communist literature, Milwaukee newspapers, and union newspapers from the 1920s to the 1940s.[41]

As the leading corporate spokesman, Story informed the Hartley committee that management testimony would present "a clear picture of the experience of Allis-Chalmers with communism in the form of the communistic leadership of local 248, UAW." His statement outlined the "destructive aims" of Communists in the American labor movement and the Communist connections of the UAW Local 248 leadership. Throughout, it criticized UAW Local 248 as "a tool of communism." It denounced the union's illegal picketing, limitations on the right to work, manipulation of government officials to threaten plant seizure, and undemocratic administration. His statement also praised the "sound" Allis-Chalmers industrial relations policy that met the Communist challenge and suggested legislative remedies to control Communist unions.[42]

In his opening statement, Story told the congressional committee:

> The greatest menace to our democratic form of government is the misuse of the tremendous power vested in labor unions in the hands of communistic union leaderships.
> What is the source of this tremendous union power? It is the control of essential services and industries which may be exercised by large unions.

Citing the recent coal, railroad, and maritime strikes as examples of the "paralyzing power" of large American unions, he argued that Communist unions were a "real threat to democracy because the communistic leaders are following the dictates of the Soviet Union whose aim is the destruction of our form of government."[43]

Sensitive to changing international events, Story in his testimony discovered the new Cold War and set the stage for an unfolding drama of international Communist conspiracy that reached into Wisconsin's largest industrial firm. He even referred to a recent

Communist-inspired French general strike. For the most part, he focused on the larger questions of Communist theories and practices, which did not directly touch on UAW Local 248. For his evidence on Communist aims, principles, and techniques, Story cited a long, mixed list of declarations from Communist theorists, programmatic statements, and publications, which dated back to the 1920s. Among those quoted, often far removed from UAW Local 248, were Lozovsky, Olgin, Bukharin, Lenin, and Browder.[44]

Story noted, however, that some of this literature was available in Communist bookstores throughout the United States. "Such ideas," he claimed, "are directly fed by Communist-led unions to their members through the medium of educational classes." He also charged that teachers from the Chicago Abraham Lincoln School, "formerly the Communist Workers School," conducted Local 248 educational classes. Furthermore, the Milwaukee Communist bookstore, he claimed, often had literature tables at the Local 248 educational meetings. "Thus," he concluded, "the program is worked up in Russia, is transmitted to the Communist Party headquarters, which, in turn, transmits it to its members who are heads of labor unions, who then transmit Communist doctrine to members in union meetings and 'educational' classes." Allis-Chalmers labor troubles, Story inferred, were thus a part of a larger international Communist plot. "By these means," he added, "the attempt is going on to radicalize and poison the minds of American workers."[45]

Other company officials added texture and detail to this account. Kenneth Haagensen, the firm's public relations director, identified the alleged Communists among the Local 248 officers and rank-and-file leaders. E. F. Ohrman, the vice president for manufacturing, next described the Allis-Chalmers history of the collective bargaining relationship with UAW Local 248 leaders. He emphasized the evenhanded management policies in contrast to the union's abuse of contract privileges, its program of violence, and its illegitimate strikes. John Waddleton, the Allis-Chalmers labor lawyer, testified about Local 248's illegal picketing and its interference with the right to work. A. K. Brintnall, the labor relations manager, discussed the undemocratic practices of the union leadership.[46]

Then Harold Story concluded with a summary of the Allis-Chalmers charges against UAW Local 248 and with recommendations for legislative remedies that would restrict Communist union leaders. The Communist Party, he believed, had "a well-conceived plan to undermine our democracy through application of certain techniques by communistic infiltration of the labor movement." The "communistic" Local 248 leadership was "faithfully and destructively applying Communist techniques in its relations with Allis-Chalmers." In the Reuther-Thomas contest for the UAW presidency, he maintained: "You have a quarrel between two leaders of that union, a quarrel which is resulting in a split in that organization . . . there is a group of Communists which [d]esires to support the activities of the Communist leadership of local 248." His obvious conclusion: "the menace of communism in the labor movement is general throughout the United States."[47]

Finally, Story provided specific legislative remedies to the House committee. Characterizing his proposals "as legislative weed killers of communist activities in the labor movement," he recommended an amendment to the NLRA that made "untruthful statements" an unfair labor practice. Since Communists made effective use of strikes to promote "class hatred," he called for an amendment to require "an affirmative strike vote of more than 50 per cent of . . . the bargaining unit." He even suggested specific language for strike ballots that would stop militant leaders from influencing workers to make rash strike decisions.[48]

Story also offered recommendations to ensure union democracy, to guarantee the right to work, and to restrict compulsory unionism. He wanted to allow minority unions to appeal to the NLRB to defend their workplace rights. He also desired legislative remedies to give "definite support to the right to work as a right equal in dignity to the right to strike." And he recommended "that contract clauses providing for compulsory unionism be declared against public policy and made illegal." Modeled along the lines of the 1939 Wisconsin Employment Relations Act, which Story had drafted, many of the corporate recommendations eventually found their way into the Taft-Hartley Act.[49]

Three days later, the House Un-American Activities Committee (HUAC) visited Milwaukee to uncover Communists in the Milwaukee labor movement. It heard testimony from three Local 248 opposition leaders, Leon Venne, Walter Petersen, and Floyd Lucia. Venne was the leader of the UAW opposition group and Petersen was the IWAC leader. Lucia was also an IWAC member and an Allis-Chalmers accountant who had moved from the sales department into the production shop in order to earn more money. Venne assured HUAC that Christoffel was a Communist. "It was through Harold Christoffel," he charged, "that several out-and-out Communists—and I would call them that—were injected into the local union." He estimated the UAW local contained five hundred "party members or good fellow travellers." Petersen gave an account of the Local 248 flying squadron's harassment and intimidation of strikebreakers. Lucia testified about Communist activities in his electrical control shop. He charged that in his shop, the Local 248 shop stewards and shop committeemen were either Communists or Communist sympathizers.[50]

A few days after HUAC's Milwaukee visit, Robert Buse, R. J. Thomas, and Harold Christoffel testified before the HELC in Washington. According to Christoffel, they expected to play their "trump card" with a union offer to arbitrate the long strike. In contrast to the welcoming reception given to the Allis-Chalmers officials and the UAW local's dissidents, the three UAW leaders faced something akin to an inquisition. Instead of a discussion of a strike settlement, the HELC wanted to hear about labor, Communism, and the Allis-Chalmers strike. Christoffel remembered, "We were the most surprised people when we got there." Robert Buse attempted to read testimony about the long history of contentious Allis-Chalmers labor-management relations. Although the HELC had allowed Allis-Chalmers officials to read their entire joint statement, it permitted the UAW leaders to read only abbreviated versions of their prepared statements.[51]

Taking the offensive, Buse charged that the Allis-Chalmers and J. I. Case strikes "resulted from the refusal of monopoly managements involved to bargain in good faith with their employees." In these strikes, the two firms refused "to accept the wholly equitable, sound, and American principle of arbitration." Both companies made a "deliberate decision to smash the chosen unions of their employees, first, through the provocation of strikes, and, second, through their refusal to settle those strikes upon any but their own arbitrary, unjust, and totally unacceptable terms." The public "assertions" of "Communist control," he said, "have been advanced by the Allis-Chalmers Co. purely in an effort to conceal its own despicable conduct."[52]

The feisty Buse then challenged both the Hartley committee and the Allis-Chalmers corporation. He derided the HELC effort "to enact legislation punishing labor" for management "crimes," which "were the responsibility of monopoly [and] would be destructive to the national interest and a perversion of simple justice." As for a possible strike settlement, Buse again offered the previous union proposal of "the just, equitable, and American method of arbitration." He even promised an immediate return to work if the committee members called on President Truman to establish "a fact-finding committee to investigate the merits of the parties' claim."[53]

But congressmen were not interested in a strike settlement. Rather they were interested in Communist subversion of American unions. When questioned about the signing of the Eisenscher nomination papers, Buse responded, "That is right, and I signed those nomination papers." He added: "I would like to explain that these nomination papers, along with other peoples' nomination papers, were circulated on our picket lines and everybody signed those nomination papers." Asked if he was a Communist when he signed the nomination papers, the union president answered: "I was not—and am not."[54]

With the exception of two Democrats, the other HELC members continued the hostile interrogation of the three UAW leaders. Charles Kersten, the new Republican from Milwaukee's fifth district, was the most aggressive. Both Buse and Christoffel suspected him of collaborating with Allis-Chalmers officials. Buse later recalled, "I often wanted to ask him how much the company paid him." Christoffel remembered that the HELC was "all cooked and dried." He added: "We could see the company guys screwing back and forth and talking to Kersten, the congressman at the time. Clearly, they had been working behind the scenes. . . . And, this was simply the culmination." At the HELC hearing, Kersten questioned Buse about his contacts with Eugene Dennis, Communist union stewards, and the distribution of Communist literature at union meetings.[55]

Harold Christoffel received the harshest treatment from HELC members. From the start, the legislators expressed their disdain and contempt for the young union veteran. Clare Hoffman, the Michigan Republican who led off the questioning, frequently raised argumentative points about union legislative recommendations, charges of corporate violence, and fact-finding proposals. He interspersed his questions with comments that strongly defended management rights. Christoffel's responses were often testy and sometimes long-winded. Then the conservative Republican asked a series of terse questions about Christoffel's membership in and associations with the Communist Party and Communist front organizations. Two days later, Christoffel was recalled. One Republican asked Christoffel about his military service in the Philippines, apparently suspecting Communist influence in demonstrations for the demobilization of the U.S. Army.[56]

Charles Kersten took up the hostile interrogation. He asked Christoffel about the Milwaukee Communist workers' school and whether or not he had met Eugene Dennis there. He inquired about Local 248's connection with the Abraham Lincoln School in Chicago and Sigmund Eisenscher's membership on the union educational committee. He also asked whether Christoffel knew Fred Blair, the Milwaukee Communist leader, and made other very specific inquiries about Christoffel's acquaintance with Communists and attendance at Communist meetings.[57]

Since the HELC apparently intended to obtain a perjury indictment against the former Local 248 president, Kersten hoped to trap Christoffel with the detailed questions. Aware of Louis Budenz's earlier public statements about Communists in the Allis-Chalmers UAW local, he shifted his questions to the 1941 defense strike. Two weeks earlier, Allis-Chalmers officials had brought Budenz to Milwaukee for a speech where the former *Daily Worker* editor asserted that the Communist Party ordered and Christoffel agreed to call the controversial 1941 strike. After reading a newspaper account of Budenz's allegation, Kersten asked:

> What do you have to say about that, Mr. Christoffel?
>
> MR. CHRISTOFFEL. Just a tissue of lies, completely. In 1941 the strike was called under the constitution of the union by a vote of the workers, because of the fact that the company had refused to deal with the workers as they should have been dealt with.
>
> MR. KERSTEN. You talked it over in New York, did you not?
>
> MR. CHRISTOFFEL. No, sir.
>
> MR. KERSTEN. You did not?
>
> MR. CHRISTOFFEL. No, sir; I talked it over in Detroit, I believe.
>
> MR. KERSTEN. Well, you talked it over with Mr. Budenz' committee, did you not?
>
> MR. CHRISTOFFEL. I certainly did not. I never saw the gentleman.
>
> MR. KERSTEN. You never saw Mr. Budenz?
>
> MR. CHRISTOFFEL. No, sir.[58]

Richard Nixon also was aggressive with the Milwaukee union leader. The freshman California Republican asked whether Christoffel knew of Communists or Communist Party sympathizers who were in union executive positions or were shop stewards or shop committeemen. To both questions, Christoffel answered: "Not to my knowledge." Nixon also asked another series of precise questions about Christoffel's associations with Communist front groups and about the union's resolutions on American involvement in World War II before, during, and after the Hitler-Stalin Pact and the invasion of the Soviet Union.[59]

Ten days later, the House Education and Labor Committee summoned Louis Budenz to testify about the Communist leadership of UAW Local 248. When Budenz identified himself, Charles Kersten commented that the HELC had subpoenaed the former Communist "in connection with the testimony of Harold Christoffel, who appeared here some 10 days ago and testified before this committee." After Budenz was sworn in, Kersten asked if Budenz knew Harold Christoffel. The former Communist replied: "I knew him quite well." Then, in response to carefully directed questions, Budenz recalled running into Christoffel at several Communist Party meetings. He concluded that he had met the Local 248 leader "in Milwaukee a number of times—on a number of occasions."[60]

The Wisconsin Republican then narrowed his focus to Budenz's Milwaukee speech about the 1941 defense strike. William Z. Foster,

Budenz told HELC members, "stood for the policy of snowballing strikes in order to stop all of the national defense, and also any aid to Britain." In the fall of 1940, Budenz, Eugene Dennis, and Ned Sparks, the Wisconsin Communist Party leader, often went to Meta Berger's home. "Eventually," he recalled, "we had a small group there. Mr. Christoffel and Sigmund Eisenscher and Fred Blair; there were a couple of others. I remember them distinctly," he recalled. "This meeting," Budenz continued, "followed several discussions . . . as to how to raise wage demands among the workers in order to bring about labor stoppages, and Allis-Chalmers had been considered because of the fact that Communists had such a strong control" and "a certain influence among the membership."[61]

During the discussion, Budenz testified, Eugene Dennis had mentioned that a strike "must be called at the Allis-Chalmers Co." The Local 248 president, the former Communist charged, mentioned "that there was friction with the A.F. of L. members and that there was possibility of making a move that would halt production." Asked whether Christoffel agreed "to carry out this strike," Budenz answered: "He did." Kersten later asked whether Christoffel and Buse were Communists; Budenz replied that he knew both Christoffel and Buse as Communist Party members.[62]

The day after Budenz's testimony, Allis-Chalmers officials sent Harold Christoffel a dismissal notice. They had already fired Local 248 president Buse and vice president Joseph Dombek for false statements against the company. In the dismissal notice, W. C. Van Cleaf, the industrial relations director, informed Christoffel that the reason for his termination was his "Communist activities." Van Cleaf specifically mentioned the Budenz HELC testimony about the "fraudulent" 1941 defense strike. "Your destructive activities," the Allis-Chalmers manager charged, "have caused inestimable harm to our employes, our company, and our country. Your discharge will prevent the continuation of such activities against our employes and our company."[63]

Two days later, the HELC sent a subcommittee, chaired by Kersten, to Milwaukee to obtain additional testimony and to tighten the noose of evidence around the necks of Christoffel and Buse. Before their arrival, Allis-Chalmers and *Milwaukee Sentinel* officials carefully laid the groundwork for the perjury charges against Christoffel, Buse, and possibly even R. J. Thomas. According to Hugh Swofford, who worked on the John Sentinel series, Allis-Chalmers, the *Milwaukee Sentinel*, and national, state, and local government officials attended meetings to assist the HELC subcommittee staff prepare the case against the UAW leaders. The group included Allis-Chalmers attorneys Story and Waddleton, Congressmen Kersten and Owens, a Department of Justice official, the HELC counsel, the *Milwaukee Sentinel* publisher Frank Taylor, its managing editor, and others. Swofford also remembered two strategy meetings among Allis-Chalmers, *Milwaukee Sentinel*, and government officials; a dinner that Story sponsored at the Milwaukee University Club; and a luncheon that Taylor held at the *Milwaukee Sentinel* offices.[64]

At these meetings, the HELC subcommittee refined its strategy for perjury cases against Christoffel and Buse. Using the Allis-Chalmers research files on Communism, Swofford compiled "an inch thick booklet typed on legal-size onion skin paper," which "included every allusion to any pro-Communist activity undertaken or pro-Communist expression contained in the minutes of the CIO County Council." Earlier Swofford and a conservative CIO leader broke into the Milwaukee CIO offices and microfilmed union records. Shortly after the HELC hearing, the page proofs of the Christoffel and Buse testimony "were forwarded to the Sentinel by the government printing office." At several meetings in Taylor's office, Harold Story, along with several Allis-Chalmers and *Milwaukee Sentinel* officials and employees, carefully read and analyzed the two union leaders' congressional testimony in order "to ferret out possible perjurious [*sic*] statements." After going through the record, Swofford added: "I finished the job, selecting a dozen points or so on which it might be possible to prove perjury against the A-C labor leaders." At the meetings, Story "mercilessly criticized my findings," Swofford claimed, to strengthen the government case against the union leaders. "The result of these meetings," he concluded, "was the dropping of any attempts to make perjury charges against Buse and concentrate on Christoffel."[65]

On March 17, the HELC subcommittee conducted its public hearings on the alleged Communist leaders in UAW Local 248. With a full complement of carefully selected local witnesses, it planned to solidify a perjury case against the Local 248 leaders. Two right-wing CIO leaders produced Milwaukee and Wisconsin records that refuted Thomas's and Christoffel's HELC testimony. In addition, the HELC subcommittee also subpoenaed Local 248 meeting minutes, correspondence, and financial records to prove the union's endorsement of Communist policies and financial support to Communist front organizations. Farrel Schnering, a former Wisconsin Communist, testified that Christoffel and his wife were Communists. Claire Merton, a Milwaukee Republican, testified that Christoffel and Milwaukee Communist leader Fred Blair "heckled" her at a local campaign rally. Adrian Merschon, an investigator of the Milwaukee Police Department's Red Squad, testified that Christoffel secretly met many times with Wisconsin Communist leader Ned Sparks. Merschon also presented the affidavit of Kenneth Goff, another former Wisconsin Communist, who claimed that Christoffel often met with Blair, Sparks, and Dennis.[66]

After the HELC members had returned to Washington, the *Milwaukee Journal* reported, "the committee members and their legal advisers are convinced they hit 'pay dirt' in the Milwaukee hearings, and that they are impressed by the vast amount of verbal and documentary evidence unearthed." The newspaper was "certain" that the House of Representatives would be asked to adopt a Kennedy motion for the Department of Justice to indict Christoffel and Buse for perjury. At the close of the hearings, one HELC member, Congressman Thomas Owens, noted that FBI director J. Edgar Hoover had recently said, "Communism was the greatest menace that we have in this country today." Although he initially doubted Hoover's claim, Owens commented that the Milwaukee hearings proved the existence of "such a nest of communism and of people who seemed to be inspired toward overthrowing our government." He concluded, "It is shocking. It certainly wakes me up. I hope that it awakens the American people to the danger that faces them." The Red Scare had arrived finally and fully in Milwaukee.[67]

Ultimately, the power and authority of the state legitimized the unmaking of the militant UAW local. Through February and March 1947, additional front-page headlines further undermined the union's position in the Allis-Chalmers strike. A month of Senate and House hearings fueled public speculation about the Communist domination of UAW Local 248 and the ten-month Allis-Chalmers strike. Two days after the hearings ended, Robert Buse futilely wired HELC chair Fred Hartley to ask for a full investigation "to include the company's activities in this strike." The Allis-Chalmers corporation, the union leader charged, used its $25 million tax rebate "to fight the union and force a long strike on its workers." Buse emphasized that more than eight thousand workers had voted to strike after two and one-half years of failed negotiations. And he noted that before and after the strike vote, the union had offered to submit the disputed issues to arbitration. If the HELC failed to investigate the Allis-Chalmers abuses, he could only conclude that the Hartley committee "served the interest of the Allis-Chalmers Co." and "had no intention of conducting the type of impartial inquiry it behooves a committee of your type to undertake."[68]

Despite the combative rhetoric, Local 248 and UAW leaders recognized that the end was near. The public hearings obviously devastated strike morale. During the Milwaukee HELC hearings, the UAW Executive Board once again conferred on the Allis-Chalmers strike. Three Local 248 leaders, Buse, Joseph Dombek, the vice president, and Fred McStroul, the recording secretary, attended the Louisville Executive Board meeting. For the UAW leaders, the hostile congressional interrogation of Thomas indicated a grave situation for the automobile workers union. During the UAW meeting, a newspaper account indicated possible union proposals "to break the stalemate" and end the strike. A Sunday Local 248 membership meeting, it added, would approve an end to the difficult strike. Although Thomas still did not endorse the plan, the strike's high $60,000 monthly cost and the negative publicity undermined his support on the UAW Executive Board. The UAW ordered the Local 248 leaders "to go home and end the strike."[69]

At the March 23 membership meeting, Buse and the other local union leaders finally recognized their defeat on the picket lines, in the press, and in the halls of Congress. More than half of the eleven thousand original strikers had already gone back to their jobs in the West Allis plant. Only twelve hundred Allis-Chalmers strikers attended the Sunday union meeting. In their report to the remaining strikers, Local 248 bargaining committee members cataloged the events that led to the bitter defeat—the corporate charges of "violence and anarchy," misuse of WERB authority, Red smear campaign in the Milwaukee press, back-to-work movements, mass arrests of pickets, contempt citations against twenty-six union officers and stewards, WERB collusion with corporate officials in an "illegal" representation election, and congressional witch-hunts among union leaders.[70]

After noting the need to break the stalemate, to continue court cases, and to organize for a new NLRB election, the Local 248 bargaining committee members reluctantly urged workers to return to the West Allis shops. "Because of the length of the strike," they reasoned, "we are sure everyone will agree that within the shop we will be able to win a decisive bargaining victory should another election be called. If, however, we remain outside, our forces will be scattered." In apparent defeat, the union leaders opted for a strategy of workplace struggle with management.[71]

In their appeal for a membership vote to return to the shops, the Local 248 leaders emphasized the need to retain bargaining rights, to eliminate company unionism, and to prevent sweatshop conditions in the West Allis plant. "IN VIEW OF THIS," the Local 248 bargaining committee report continued,

WE ARE FIRMLY COMMITTED THAT OUR FIGHT MUST BE CONTINUED INSIDE THE PLANT. . . . THE UNION WILL NEVER SURRENDER TO THIS ARROGANT AND DESPICABLE COMPANY. . . . WE WILL GO BACK WITHOUT A CONTRACT BEFORE WE WILL SIGN A SWEATSHOP AGREEMENT. WE WILL CONTINUE OUR FIGHT—NO MATTER HOW LONG IT TAKES—UNTIL WE WIN THE CONTRACT WE ARE ENTITLED TO— UNTIL THE COMPANY IS SOUNDLY THRASHED AND THE COMPANY UNION IS WIPED OUT OF EXISTENCE. THEN—AND ONLY THEN—WILL THIS STRIKE BE WON.

The beleaguered union leaders hardly sounded as though they had suffered a major setback.[72]

In a conciliatory gesture, the Local 248 leaders next urged unity and solidarity with the returned workers. "Once we are back in the plant," they pleaded, "there will not be two groups—strikers and non-strikers. As far as the union is concerned, there will be just one group—composed of all workers who want to unite to keep sweat-shop conditions out of the plant." By a margin of three to one, the twelve hundred striking union members accepted the bargaining committee proposal. After 329 long and bitter days, the Allis-Chalmers strike ended, but the union struggle continued on the shop floor.[73]

Allis-Chalmers officials immediately destroyed the union's strategy to reorganize and to rebuild the embattled UAW local. When the Allis-Chalmers strikers reentered the West Allis plant, W. C. Van Cleaf notified ninety-seven workers not to return to work. In addition to Robert Buse, the union president, Joseph Dombek, the vice president, and Harold Christoffel, the bargaining committee chair, ninety-four workers received a terse telegram: "PLEASE DO NOT REPORT FOR WORK. IN THE NEAR FUTURE YOU WILL BE ADVISED OF YOUR EMPLOYMENT STATUS AFTER YOUR CASE HAS BEEN CAREFULLY CONSIDERED UPON THE MERITS." In a press release, the corporation cited "disruptive acts" as the reason for the termination of the rank-and-file leaders. In addition to the three union officers, they dismissed a total of ninety-four workers, mainly union officers, shop stewards, committeemen, or strike activists. Although Allis-Chalmers officials later reconsidered several cases, eighty-one never returned to work.[74]

These vindictive dismissals eliminated the heart of the union local—its shop floor leadership. Four top union leaders—Buse, Dombek, McStroul, and Christoffel—and four of five bargaining committee members had been discharged. In the West Allis plant, 42 percent of the shop stewards were discharged and 29 percent quit or failed to return to work. Of the one hundred seventy-four shop committeemen, 14 percent were discharged and 29 percent quit. Many who quit left in the weeks just after the strike ended. At any rate, the higher the level of union leadership, the greater the company's vengeance.[75]

A UAW survey listed eighty-one discharged Allis-Chalmers workers, provided capsule biographies of them, and indicated the nature of their strike activities. Most were militant union pioneers, union members since 1937. At the time of the strike, they were not young and irresponsible workers. Their average age, which ranged from twenty-two to sixty-two, was almost forty-one years. They had also worked for the Allis-Chalmers firm for a number of years; the average length of service was 11.5 years. These fired workers were also committed union activists. Fifty-six, or 69 percent, had been arrested during the strike for blocking trains from entering the plant, picket line violence, or violations of court injunctions against mass picketing. Forty-six, or 57 percent, had been officers, bargaining committeemen, shop stewards, or shop committeemen. Thirty-nine, or 41 percent, actively served on the Allis-Chalmers picket line as daily picketers, picket captains, union kitchen workers, literature distributors, or union sound operators. And thirty, or 37 percent, had signed the Communist Party nomination papers.[76]

The dismissal of the union officers and rank-and-file leaders effectively destroyed the hope of a successful workplace struggle against management. Instead, it was the culmination of a long chain of events that resulted in the unmaking of the militant Allis-Chalmers UAW local. During the congressional investigations, Allis-Chalmers president Walter Geist published his account of "the Allis-Chalmers experience with a left-wing union" and discussed his views on the character of union leadership. According to Geist, "officers, stewards, and committeemen" were essential to "wholesome labor-management relations." The proper leaders were "capable, level-headed, American in outlook, and willing to work with foremen" toward "mutually beneficial" ends. For Geist, meddlesome, left-wing union representatives "stir[red] up storms" on the shop floor. The "crucial point," the Allis-Chalmers president concluded, was: "Will management retain control of the factories or will management let politically motivated union leaders drain away this control and substitute their own brand of rule or ruin?" For management, eliminating shop leaders was central to their retenting management rights at the workplace.[77]

But the Left died slowly at Allis-Chalmers. Despite the lost strike and dismissal of shop leaders, national and local UAW leaders decided to request a new NLRB representation election to demonstrate union strength in the West Allis plant. Earlier the U.S. Supreme Court invalidated the Wisconsin Employment Relations Board election, arguing that federal labor legislation superseded state labor law. Without a clear-cut decision on union representation, the relative strength of UAW Local 248 and the IWAC remained undecided. The UAW wanted a new election, a press release noted, "in order that negotiations can be resumed for reinstatement of the union contract and union conditions restored at the earliest possible moment."[78]

In July 1947, Local 248 leaders once again rallied union members for another march to the ballot box. For the UAW leaders, the principal reasons for another election were to obtain "a good union contract" and to re-create "a fighting union." They also wanted Allis-Chalmers workers to recognize "the Independent Union for what it is—a company union." They added that workers now saw "what working conditions are like without a contract and without grievance machinery."[79]

Three different unions competed to represent production workers in the sprawling West Allis plant—UAW Local 248, IWAC, and UAW-AFL. The latter was the Homer Martin UAW group that had returned to the craft federation. The main contest, however, was between the UAW and IWAC. In its campaign literature, Local 248 leaders stressed the recent advantages of CIO unionism, including the benefits of recognition, a grievance procedure, seniority, improved vacations, and higher wages. They also derided the IWAC leaders as antiunion agents of the Allis-Chalmers corporation. Walter Peterson, the IWAC president, they noted, "SCABBED" during the 1941 strike and was "ONE OF THE FIRST" to return to work in the 1946 strike. Other IWAC leaders were "money hungry" or "eager beaver" rate busters, close associates of foremen, or even former foremen.[80]

For the IWAC leaders, the fundamental issue was the Red leadership of the UAW local. One IWAC leaflet stressed the Communist domination of UAW Local 248 and proclaimed the goal "TO CLEAN OUT THE LABOR WRECKING COMMIES AND THEIR FELLOW TRAVELERS, WHO DOMINATE AND CONTROL LOCAL 248." Criticizing some of the top UAW leadership, the IWAC intended to "GET AWAY FROM SUCH MEN AS THOMAS . . . [and others], WHO BACK CHRISTOFFEL AND HIS BOYS, NOT BECAUSE OF REAL UNIONISM, BUT BECAUSE BIRDS OF A FEATHER FLOCK TOGETHER."[81]

The July 17 NLRB election attracted the intense interest of all factions among Allis-Chalmers workers. Within the UAW, both right- and left-wing factions submerged their differences and supported a vote for UAW Local 248. The IWAC offered a choice for anti-Communist conservative industrial unionism. The UAW-AFL offered a choice for a return to conservative craft unionism. The *Milwaukee Journal* anticipated "more than 90%" of the eligible workers would participate in the balloting vote, an unusually high turnout. In some Allis-Chalmers departments, 100 percent of the workers voted. "Many employes on vacation," the newspaper reported, "were coming back to cast their votes, including one who was driving from his vacation spot near Eagle River, Wis. [a far north Wisconsin community]." Even the ninety-one discharged Allis-Chalmers workers cast their ballots in "challenge" boxes.[82]

UAW Local 248 won a large plurality of the eligible ballots. The final tally was: UAW Local 248—3,640; Independent Workers of Allis-Chalmers—1,913; UAW-AFL—1,581; no union—81; void ballots—34; and challenged ballots—247. Despite almost impossible odds, the large plurality demonstrated a substantial, though partial, victory for the beleaguered UAW local. Many, however, voted for the conservative IWAC or UAW-AFL, and many UAW members voted for Reuther's more conservative unionism. If the UAW local had won ninety-two of the challenged ballots, which included those of the discharged shop leaders, it would have received a clear majority in the NLRB election. Still, UAW Local 248 retained the right to represent Allis-Chalmers workers. The Milwaukee NLRB office planned a quick decision on the challenged ballots. But the UAW's unfair labor practice charges on the fired Allis-Chalmers workers complicated a speedy final resolution of the NLRB election. "We won the [NLRB] election," Buse later recalled. "We lost everything else though."[83]

Although R. J. Thomas proclaimed a victory for the embattled UAW local, Reuther firmly held the reins of UAW power, consolidated his center-right coalition, and eventually appointed an administrator to direct UAW Local 248. In early December 1947, a disheartened Robert Buse appeared before the UAW Executive Board to report on the status of Local 248 since the NLRB election. He told the UAW leaders that his UAW local was a defeated and decimated labor organization. It had lost its important cadre of shop floor leaders. It could not obtain recognition from Allis-Chalmers officials. It had lost large numbers of members. Before the 1946 strike, around eight thousand members were on dues checkoff; in June 1947, only three hundred members paid their union dues. Buse said, "We were able to work it up a little, but you see what happens, as soon as a guy gets active in the shop, he is nailed." Although over thirty-six hundred workers had voted for the UAW local in the NLRB election, the UAW local now had a meager six hundred dues-paying members. Buse's account appalled Reuther and UAW Executive Board members.[84]

In order to remedy the situation, Reuther recommended a "clean slate" with the "power" of the national UAW behind a new organizational drive. Reuther, along with the top UAW officers and the Wisconsin regional director, recommended four steps: (1) appointing an administrator; (2) protecting UAW property and funds; (3) creating a broad organizing committee of Milwaukee CIO locals to rebuild the UAW local; and (4) granting the administrator control over UAW financial aid to the local. To facilitate the reorganization of the UAW local, Reuther asked for waiving initiation and reinstatement fees for the organizational campaign, providing full support to over one hundred discharged workers and to the jailed strikers, and working for NLRB certification. The reason for the draconian proposals, Reuther said, was that "a powerful local union had been destroyed." The UAW executive board approved the Reuther recommendations and appointed regional director Pat Greathouse as Local 248 administrator.[85]

In Milwaukee, Local 248 leaders apparently learned about a possible administrator the day before Buse's meeting with the UAW Executive Board. On November 30, Harold Christoffel and two other officers acted to retain control of $15,000 in union funds and union records. In their eyes, the current situation seemed to repeat the UAW factionalism almost a decade ago when Homer Martin had appointed an administrator and tried to take over the Milwaukee UAW local. For three days, they moved the funds and records "from bank to bank and home to home." Ten days later, a Milwaukee judge ordered the Local 248 leaders to turn over the union's funds, records, and offices to the UAW administrator. In 1949, the UAW convention expelled Christoffel, Buse, and eight former local union officers and trustees for mishandling union funds and records and for improper handling of UAW strike support funds.[86]

A few days after the UAW took over the Allis-Chalmers local, Walter Reuther publicly inaugurated his anti-Communist campaign. In a keynote address to the tenth annual Wisconsin CIO convention in Milwaukee, the UAW president proclaimed that the Allis-Chalmers UAW local "was a black spot on the whole CIO, in Wisconsin, and Milwaukee, in particular." After noting recent support from the national CIO, he declared his new UAW attitude toward the militant UAW local and urged Milwaukee labor to put "its own house in order."[87]

To the cheers of Wisconsin CIO delegates, Reuther proclaimed: "In the Allis-Chalmers situation, we lost the local union, we lost our collective bargaining contract, and we lost our bargaining rights. . . . But we lost there because there were people in leadership positions in that local who put loyalties outside of their union, outside of the rank and file, and outside of this country, above the loyalties to the membership in the union and their country. That is why we lost." Now supported by a center-right coalition of UAW officers and Executive Board members, Reuther declared to Wisconsin CIO unionists, "we are never going to permit the membership of any local to be betrayed as we believe the membership in Local 248 was betrayed in that situation." The UAW president then promised to rebuild the Allis-Chalmers local, negotiate an agreeable union contract, reinstate the discharged workers, and conduct democratic elections in the local.[88]

Despite the UAW president's promises, it took a long time to rebuild the largely destroyed local. Notwithstanding the absence of "Red" leaders, Allis-Chalmers officials continued to fight the union. In contract negotiations, Pat Greathouse, the conservative UAW administrator, did not fare much better than the union militants. For six months he attempted to negotiate a union agreement for Allis-Chalmers workers, finally signing a severely truncated one in June

1948. It offered few provisions for union security or membership stability. The short labor-management agreement contained provisions for union recognition, no strikes or lockouts, a union checkoff, union duties and privileges, and a "complaint procedure," not a formal mechanized grievance mechanism. In the union "duties and privileges" section, the UAW local and its members agreed not to "intimidate or coerce" workers or to engage in unsanctioned union activities. This included noninterference with "the orderly operation of the plant," the solicitation of membership only before and after shifts and during the lunch period, and the posting of "noncontroversial" union notices on glass-enclosed bulletin boards.[89]

The negotiated complaint procedure thoroughly gutted the union's former grievance process. The significant term "complaint" downplayed any notion that Allis-Chalmers workers could even have grievances against the benevolent corporation. In fact, the new agreement defined a complaint as "an individual problem relating to his work as distinguished from a matter properly the subject of collective bargaining." No longer would Allis-Chalmers officials allow strategic grievances to establish general principles for large numbers of workers. For worker representation on the shop floor, the complaint procedure permitted only departmental stewards, divisional chief stewards, and a nine-member shop committee. Without departmental subdivisions of shop committeemen, the Allis-Chalmers complaint procedure reduced the dense worker representation on the shop floor. In the larger departments, a single shop steward now represented two hundred, three hundred, or even four hundred workers.[90]

The new conservative Reutherite leaders faced the same difficult problems as their more militant Red predecessors. At an August 1948 membership meeting, for example, Joseph Glynn, the new Local 248 president, reported on negotiations, "the issue of arbitration was one of the main stumbling blocks, especially in its relation to grievances." Pat Greathouse, the recent administrator, supported the local president: "the Company has deliberately not bargained in good faith." He then listed other problem areas: arbitration of disciplinary discharges, policies for transfer and promotion, company control of setting rates, reopening of the contract for wages, management's desire to supervise the strike vote, reinstating discharged workers, and wages. On arbitration, a frustrated Greathouse declared: "All other area contracts have an arbitration clause such as we desire and which Allis-Chalmers will not establish." In effect, despite a new union leadership, the old Allis-Chalmers labor policies persisted.[91]

After months of difficult contract talks, Local 248 and Allis-Chalmers negotiators finally emerged with a new agreement in December 1948. It covered only thirty-six hundred of the Allis-Chalmers workers; the

*Milwaukee Journal* labeled it the "miracle on S. 70th st." "The contract," the newspaper reported, "symbolizes the end to a period of labor turmoil which included a bitter 11 month strike and the wrecking and rebuilding of [L]ocal 248." At the union ratification meeting, two members of the bargaining committee recommended the agreement's rejection because it did not contain a general wage increase. Moreover, they protested that it also did not contain a maintenance of membership clause, more liberalized vacation plan, or provision for the arbitration of all worker grievances. "The dissenters," the newspaper observed, "received considerable support from the floor." Nonetheless, Local 248 members reluctantly voted to accept the new Allis-Chalmers contract.[92]

Inside the front cover of the published 1948–1949 agreement, a cartoon demonstrated the Allis-Chalmers vision of the labor-management relationship. It depicted two donkeys tied together with a rope around their necks and two haystacks. In two frames, the donkeys tugged and strained to reach the separate haystacks. With puzzled stares, they finally recognized the rope that bound them together. In the final two frames, the cooperating donkeys devour one haystack and begin to eat the other. The obvious message: labor and management were tied to each other and needed to cooperate to achieve mutual success.[93]

In February 1949, Charles Schultz won an uncontested election to become Local 248 president. Probably the weak agreement generated membership opposition and undermined support for the previous union president. One month later, Schultz and Tony Audia, a UAW international representative, wrote a letter to President Harry S. Truman, castigating Harold Story for his recent congressional testimony in favor of the Taft-Hartley Act. In the early union years, they wrote Truman, "certain elements succeeded in infiltrating" the West Allis plant because "management's attitude provided the ideal breeding grounds for Communism." The Allis-Chalmers firm, Schultz and Audia charged, "was highly responsible for the development of subversive leadership." Although the Communist leaders played into management's hands in the 1946 strike, they claimed, "there were some basic issues involved that under normal circumstances would justify strike action." Even the new leaders, they wrote Truman, "found it unusually difficult to negotiate a contract with the Allis-Chalmers management." The current contract issues, they concluded, "were the same basic issues that have been in controversy over the period of many years."[94]

Intractable management plagued successive Local 248 leaders. In the 1949 contract negotiations, the "big three issues," Schultz said, were "the right to strike, full arbitration, and [the] Union Shop." These disputed issues had a painfully familiar ring to Allis-Chalmers union members. During one union meeting, Schultz characterized company negotiators as "vicious diplomats" who "appeared to be gentleman and scholars." At a membership meeting, local union members nervously authorized a strike to support union negotiators. Later, Schultz complained to shop stewards that, although the reorganized union proved "that we were not Communists," union negotiators still got nowhere with management. "Now they no longer have that complaint before them," he said, "and they are still unyielding." Despite the strike vote, the disheartened and demoralized Allis-Chalmers workers had little fight in them and accepted a weak contract.[95]

Throughout the contract negotiations, Schultz vented his frustrations with both union members and with management negotiators. UAW Local 248, he told shop stewards, was "a paper union of 4700 members with no fighting spirit." He asked: "can we exist with the present green book [i.e., contract] for the next 30 months, or must we do something about it?" The UAW local faced a dilemma. Schultz claimed, "it would take five years to build up the union to where it was before." At the same time, he said, "we cannot sign an inferior contract because other unions will have to do so." In the end, union leaders, negotiators, and members accepted an inferior agreement.[96]

In 1950, Allis-Chalmers officials dramatically reversed their long-standing open shop labor policy. By this time, UAW Local 248 had rebuilt its rank-and-file base. Management's continued opposition even to the conservative union could mean another long, costly strike. Although not as generous, the new Allis-Chalmers contract was similar to the 1950 General Motors contract, the famous "Treaty of Detroit." It contained the UAW's lucrative postwar settlements, which connected responsible unionism to higher wages and benefits. Its monetary provisions included a three-cent-per-hour general wage increase plus adjustments for skilled workers, improved life and health insurance plans, and longer vacations for senior employees. Unlike other UAW contracts, it did not provide for cost-of-living adjustments. As David Brody noted for other UAW settlements, the new Allis-Chalmers agreement recognized the "permanent presence" of the UAW local but protected the "essentials of managerial authority."[97]

In early June, Walter Geist issued a statement to the national and local UAW negotiators. The "infiltration of a notorious Communist and his satellites," Geist noted, "prevented normal development and, instead, made collective bargaining merely an instrument for communist-inspired strife and destruction." Since a union shop would permit "kangaroo courts" for "a coercive domination of our employees" and would also "undermine management's control of Company operations," the Allis-Chalmers president reasoned, his firm had staunchly resisted the repeated Local 248 demands for a union shop. The Taft-

Hartley Law, he added, made "possible the consideration of a modified union shop" provision. Moreover, a recent NLRB decision, which ruled that the Allis-Chalmers corporation did not have to "rehire" the workers of the old "communistic clique," created "an atmosphere . . . conducive to the achievement of a constructive relationship between the union and the company."[98]

Geist then proposed a settlement that would "give proper consideration to the Union's fears and the Company's traditional policy as to freedom of employe action." Any solution for the "entirely different" situation, Geist claimed, should consider three groups—new workers, workers who were not union members, and workers who were union members. Since Allis-Chalmers officials consistently promised workers that union membership or nonmembership "was a matter of free choice," the "only solution" that fulfilled labor and management requirements would contain: (1) "the majority vote of all employes in the bargaining unit"; (2) the condition that new workers would "be required, . . . to become and remain union members"; (3) old workers would not be required to join the union; (4) present union members would be required to remain members unless they chose to resign in a five-day escape period; and (5) the only reason for discharge would be the "non-payment of initiation fees and monthly dues." After many years of workplace struggle, management voluntarily offered Allis-Chalmers workers a union security clause.[99]

To be sure, Geist expected important concessions from Local 248 negotiators. The final contract contained a "mutual securities clause" and guaranteed the right to work. Most important, union negotiators accepted a "democratic processes" clause with novel provisions for conducting union elections and strike votes on company premises. Moreover, Geist later extracted important concessions on the wages of women workers. Although female workers had a separate seniority group in the 1948–1949 and initial 1950 contracts, they received the same starting as male workers. In a 1951 modification, union negotiators agreed to a male starting wage of $1.19 per hour and a female one of $1.09. In effect, the formerly proud and independent UAW local acceded to management oversight of its internal affairs and later surrendered the important principle of wage equity for men and women.[100]

Geist called the five-year agreement "a second miracle on South 70th Street." After the signing of the contract, Walter Reuther wired the Local 248 president, "Congratulations on the gains achieved in your new contract. You have proved, by winning pensions, hospital-medical insurance, higher wages and union shop, improved vacations, strengthened grievance procedure and seniority provisions, that Allis-Chalmers workers can march forward in the true tradition of the UAW-CIO." The Allis-Chalmers contract was "a significant victory for the entire community" and "a ringing affirmation of the fact that clean, democratic, American unionism is labor's best weapon for winning a better life."[101]

Despite more conservative UAW representation, major problems persisted in subsequent Allis-Chalmers contract negotiations. Even after the "second miracle of 70th street," the collective negotiations between Allis-Chalmers and UAW Local 248 remained acrimonious and difficult. In 1955, a UAW vice president, Leonard Woodcock, and his administrative assistant, Douglas Frazer, led the collective bargaining team for UAW Local 248. When negotiations failed, they asked for and received a unanimous strike vote to strengthen the union position. In his appeal to six thousand union members, Woodcock criticized the "democratic processes" clauses that gave management the authority to oversee union elections. The union members, the *Milwaukee Journal* reported, gave the "biggest roars" when he called for the union shop and condemned "the 'unique clauses born of communist domination.' " Ralph Koenig, the Local 248 president, "urged members to back up demands which will make them 'no longer second class citizens in labor affairs.' " Faced with a possible strike, the two sides eventually compromised on a new three-year contract.[102]

In 1959, seven thousand Local 248 members struck for seventy-seven days, a day longer than the 1941 defense strike. At the union meeting for contract ratification, Edward J. Merton, the Local 248 president, proclaimed this was "the first time we have won a strike against Allis-Chalmers." The strikers, he added, returned to work "as human beings, not beaten men." Through Merton's speech, angry strikers repeatedly shouted: "What about the scabs?" Referring to the one hundred or so strikebreakers and to Merton's comments that the union members would judge them, many shouted: "Fine 'em!" or "Throw them out of the union." For the most part, the strike settlement dealt with monetary issues, such as wages and pension, health, and supplemental unemployment benefits. Subsequently, Local 248 members fined the strikebreakers as much $100 for breaking union discipline. In a subsequent Supreme Court case, the UAW successfully defended the right to use fines to discipline union members.[103]

In 1962, after the expiration of the two year contract and months of negotiations, Local 248 members conducted the "shortest, most peaceful strike in the history of bargaining between the United Auto Workers and the Allis-Chalmers Manufacturing Co." Although the bargaining committee's minority report called for "greater gains in job security," union president Charles Schultz again emphasized economic issues in the agreement that settled the six-day strike. In the passionate debate for ratification, one disheartened worker pleaded: "Our people are sick and tired of strikes. We've gone out and hit our heads against a brick wall too often. . . . Other workers have their mortgages paid off but we haven't, because we're always on the bricks." Once again, the union members decided to fine strikebreakers.[104]

Every two or three years after 1962, when the union contract expired, Allis-Chalmers officials almost always forced a short, or sometimes long, strike in their several different plants. Gradually, the UAW brought the firm into line with the national pattern for the agricultural implement industry. As Allis-Chalmers entered the 1960s, however, its antiunion heritage resulted in severe financial troubles. Eventually, poor management decisions eroded the vitality of Wisconsin's largest industrial establishment and disrupted the lives of thousands of Allis-Chalmers workers.

# 8

## CONCLUSION

The Cold War against American labor began in the midst of the labor factionalism and the conservative assault on UAW Local 248. As national director of CIO councils, John Brophy was at the center of the CIO's postwar struggle against Communists. In his autobiography, he asserted: "The decisive battle with the Communists was fought in Wisconsin in the Allis-Chalmers strike of 1947." During the 1946–1947 strike, national CIO leaders recognized the public relations problem of having Communists in their union. It surfaced in the power struggles within the Milwaukee and Wisconsin CIO councils and the United Automobile Workers Union and in the HELC and HUAC hearings. The Allis-Chalmers fight, Brophy recalled, "helped to convince Murray that the time was at hand for the campaign against the Communists, which he carried through successfully during the next two or three years." In 1946, the Milwaukee and Wisconsin CIO councils shifted into the hands of labor conservatives. In 1947, the federal government began its attack on Communist and other leftist labor leaders. In 1947 and 1948, the large CIO unions, such as the UAW, continued the assault, consolidating center-right or right coalitions against the leftist leaders. In 1949, the CIO expelled the United Electrical Workers' and Farm Equipment Workers' unions and investigated nine other left unions. In 1950, it expelled the nine other unions. The expulsions tamed the CIO and prepared the way for its merger with the AFL in 1955. Without its militant left, the CIO, though socially a bit more progressive than the AFL, mirrored the political and economic conservativism of its former foe.[1]

The domestic Cold War had important implications for the future of the American labor movement. To be sure, some Local 248 leaders may have been Communists. If they were, the Allis-Chalmers tradition of antiunionism and the economic scars of the Great Depression certainly shaped their social, economic, and political outlook. Or they may well have simply worked with Communists to accomplish their main objective of building an industrial union in the West Allis plant. Since the traditional Milwaukee Left, that is, the Socialist Party, was so closely connected to the craft union old guard, the young Turks and shop veterans could move only further to the Left to secure advice on their vision of industrial unionism. Moreover, the New Deal coalition eroded the social base of the once powerful Milwaukee Socialist Party. Until the 1930s, industrial unionism was the program of the far Left, namely, the Industrial Workers of the World, which markedly declined after World War I, and the small Communist Party became a rising voice in the depression decade.

Through the Great Depression and into the war years, the militant leftists were indeed successful unionists. As in Allis-Chalmers, they succeeded where the venerable craft unionists failed in the hostile environment of the large mass-production industries. They succeeded among workers divided by race, gender, ethnicity, and skill levels. At Allis-Chalmers, these aggressive unionists united skilled and production workers, several ethnic groups, men and women, and blacks and whites into one big union to fight an arrogant and paternalistic management. They bargained collectively, obtained contracts, created systems of shop floor representation, and forcefully challenged managerial authority at the workplace. With their alternative vision of militant industrial unionism, they challenged the conscience and assumptions of the American labor movement.

In the post–World War II era, the political terrain shifted suddenly under the feet of labor's Left. For depression-era industrial unionists, the Communist Party's Popular Front policies offered an opportunity to pursue their labor union objectives. For a short time, the labor strategies of the industrial unionists and the Communist Party coalesced. Whether actual Party members or not, the leftist unionists apparently received organizational talent and tactical advice from Communist leaders and gave them a sometimes loose, sometimes firm, loyalty in the form of sympathetic union resolutions or contributions in support of Communist front organizations. To be sure, some had a difficult relationship with the Communist Party during the heyday of the Popular Front, through the Hitler-Stalin Pact, the Soviet-American alliance, and the emerging Cold War. But these issues were far removed from the day-to-day struggle of union building. Nonetheless, the Achilles' heel of labor's Left was its connection to the Communist Party, the political institution of a foreign power. With the postwar emergence of the United State and the Soviet Union as bipolar global powers, the leftist labor leaders, especially the Communists, were extremely vulnerable to charges that they were agents of a foreign government and threats to national security.

The Allis-Chalmers case connects two important explanations for the weakened state of the contemporary American labor movement. Some have argued that the purge of the Left seriously undermined a vigorous, militant, and progressive labor movement. More recently, others have argued that unions underestimated the antiunionism of corporate America. In fact, both factors were important in shaping modern American unionism.[2]

An often forgotten theme in Selig Perlman's *A Theory of the Labor Movement* is the considerable power of modern capitalism. Originally published in 1928 to validate American business unionism, Perlman's classic work, interestingly, reappeared in 1949, in the midst the conservative reaction against militant unionism. According to Perlman: "Three dominant factors . . . in recent labor history" were the suspect role of intellectuals, the "job consciousness" of American workers, and the "demonstrated capacity . . . of the capitalist group to survive." Captialism, Perlman argued, was not simply an economic and political arrangement where one class owned "the means of production, exchange, and distribution"; it was "rather a social organization presided over by a class with an 'effective will to power.' " The capitalist class "defend[ed] its power against all comers" and "convinced other classes that they alone, the capitalists, know how to operate the complex economic apparatus of modern society upon which the material welfare of all depends." Against the background of an assertive unionism, this "effective will to power" entailed the fierce defense of management's right to control the workplace.[3]

Under the guidance of men like Harold Story and Lee H. Hill, the Allis-Chalmers Manufacturing Company helped to reshape the American labor relations environment. According to Howell Harris, Allis-Chalmers was one of many important "center firms" that possessed and acted on a broad management vision to contain militant unionism. Along with other "industrial realists," it fiercely resisted labor's domination of the shop floor along two fronts: the one a basic "contest for power," and the other a more "complex struggle for moral authority." Influencing labor, the public, and the state and relying on their "practical conservatism" and "tactical flexibility," these industrial realists, Harris observed, "helped reorientate the climate of public opinion and public policy toward organized labor; they stabilized workplace and contractual relations on terms they were willing to accept; and they confined unionism to already-organized sections of the workforce."[4]

Using their significant economic and political power, Allis-Chalmers officials mobilized conservative workers, public opinion, and local and national authorities and engineered the purge of labor's Left. As the world war ended, they compiled their substantial research files on labor and Communism and forced Allis-Chalmers workers to take a long strike to maintain union conditions. During the 1946–1947 strike, although initially on the defensive, they recaptured the initiative with the John Sentinel and other exposés on Communists in the Milwaukee and Wisconsin CIO. Just before the fall election, they inaugurated a violent back-to-work movement, discrediting labor and its candidates and consolidating a growing popular mood of political conservativism. They encouraged opposition union movements within and outside the UAW, even managing to get Reuther involved in the delicate strike negotiations. They arranged for Budenz's speech in Milwaukee and used his charges as reasons for HELC and HUAC investigations of Local 248 leaders. They even coordinated and planned the HELC strategy against the militant unionists. And all of this simply constituted the documented record, and not the possible informal telephone conversations or personal contacts, of the Allis-Chalmers campaign against aggressive unionism.

In the late 1950s, Richard Lester developed the "union maturity thesis" to explain the taming of militant CIO unionism. "Many, especially the newly formed industrial unions," he argued, "have been shedding youthful characteristics in the process of settling down or 'maturing.' " In essence, American unions underwent a natural internal process of bureaucratic aging and moved from youthful rebellion to mature responsibility. Although he qualified his argument, Lester implied that internal processes—the centralization of functions and control, the alteration in top leadership, and the decline in militancy—were the principal causes of union maturity. With internal change, new types of union leaders emerged: "the oratorical agitators are superseded by the skillful managers."[5]

In 1940, Don D. Lescohier, a Wisconsin school labor economist and Allis-Chalmers consultant, similarly characterized Christoffel as the "particular type of man" for the early organizational phase of unionism. Such a leader, Lescohier wrote, was "aggressive, if not militant, indominatable [sic], courageous, a good bluffer." He was "not business minded," but "conflict minded." He saw "himself as the leader of a cause"; he saw "the company as a fort to be captured." Over time, he believed, a more mature leader could emerge to lead the militant UAW local.[6]

For both Lester and Lescohier, labor unions simply grew out of their immature organizational stage. The two analysts failed to consider the external influence of powerful economic and political forces.

The rebellious youngster never had the opportunity to mature. Instead, several powerful institutions severely disciplined it. And they certainly did not spare the rod and spoil the nonconformist child.

Nonetheless, the leftist CIO union leaders articulated an alternative vision of American unionism—a vision of militant industrial unionism. In 1948, sociologist C. Wright Mills described the social and political framework of the postwar American labor movement. He outlined the "main drift" of union bureaucratization where the union leaders, the "new men of power," served as a "shock absorber" between the corporate bureaucracies and the rank-and-file union members. On the other hand, Mills defined the "alternative" of labor's Left. "The unions, in the left's view," Mills observed, "should seek to establish a worker's control over the social process of work. The means that in every workshop . . . the unionized workers would continually strive to encroach upon the functions now performed by the owners of industry and their appointed managers." In the leftist challenge to management, he added, "The only limits to this encroachment are set by the union's power." As with the leftist Local 248 leaders, the shop steward system and the grievance process, Mills concluded, were the mechanisms for the assertion of workers' control and the challenge of management rights.[7]

In the early 1980s, Harold Christoffel and Robert Buse struggled to express their alternative concept of leftist unionism. Asked about his most important accomplishments, Buse responded, "The most important thing was that it brought a feeling of freedom to the guy in the shop." The former union president also said, "I think that it's more important to a worker in the shop to be able to express himself freely to his boss than money or anything else. That's the best working condition that you can have. And, that's what we did at Allis-Chalmers." In addition to improved wages and working conditions, Buse believed that UAW Local 248 brought rank-and-file workers "self-respect." Christoffel answered similarly, "I think that the idea of having a union, of having somebody represent you, of being able to hold your head high . . . It's this dignity, the workers' dignity, which is just as important [as money], or maybe more important, many times [more important]." Although both accepted the economic goals of traditional unionism, their alternative vision also incorporated a strong sense of worker empowerment and social equality.[8]

For Christoffel, the early "CIO put an entirely different complexion on unionism." For example, since white, male workers dominated the West Allis plant, a more "politic" union leader could easily disregard the needs and concerns of female and black workers. Nonetheless, the two union leaders frequently discussed their efforts to achieve racial and gender equity on the shop floor. When questioned about the Local 248 Women's Auxiliary, Christoffel noted: "We tried to bring the women together with the men [in the union]." A separate organization, he added, "didn't jibe with unity." Discussing black workers, Robert Buse proudly recalled "put[ting] an end" to discriminatory job practices. During the 1946–1947 strike, he remembered, these union policies paid "great dividends." He concluded: "I don't think that there were any colored guys that scabbed, none that I know of, because they knew that we fought for them." However, their progressive positions may well have contributed to the succession of conservative and independent union groups in the Allis-Chalmers shops. Moreover, a genuine accommodation to the needs and concerns of female and black workers remains a deep problem for the American labor movement.[9]

Finally, the two former Local 248 presidents were very critical of the Cold War CIO. Buse implicitly criticized the CIO's new men of power: "I don't think much of the CIO no more. . . . It's gotten respectable." Christoffel underscored the elimination of the Left's alternative vision: "The worst thing that happened to labor was the ostracizing and the cutting off of the left of the labor movement." The Cold War purge, both asserted, removed a talented and socially conscious core of rank-and-file labor leaders.[10]

Depending on their different social experiences, the main social actors faced very different futures. Even though Harold W. Story retired as Allis-Chalmers vice president in 1957, Milwaukee journalist Bob Riordan noted that he "kept right on going with a whole array of extracurricular activities" in numerous public and private organizations. "Still hungry for something to do," Riordan noted, the seventy-two-year-old Story "accepted an appointment to fill a vacancy on the Milwaukee School Board [MSB] in 1962—and then got himself elected in his first political venture of his career."[11]

As a school board member in 1963–1964, Harold Story, who fought the social revolution in American industry, reappeared to resist the mid twentieth century's second great social revolution—the civil rights movement. The "gruff, white-haired attorney with a penchant for legalism," Frank Aukofer, a Milwaukee journalist, noted, headed the MSB's new Committee on Equality of Educational Opportunity. Two weeks after receiving an NAACP report on the de facto segregation of Milwaukee public schools, Story responded: "As I read their report, it would abolish the neighborhood school system as it operates here." From this point on, the "preservation of the neighborhood school system at all costs," Aukofer wrote, "became the guiding principle of the majority of the special committee and the majority of the school board." By April 1964, Story had "slammed the door on the civil rights integration proposals" for Milwaukee. Although he recommended the loosening of student transfer policies, Story refused to act forcefully to promote racial integration of the Milwaukee school system. His response energized Milwaukee's black community for several years and resulted in community protests and boycotts of the public school classes. In 1976, over a decade later, Federal Judge John W. Reynolds finally issued a court order that called for the eventual end of desegregation in the Milwaukee public schools.[12]

A year later, when Story died, the *Milwaukee Journal* reported that he had "achieved note in a career as a labor-management relations leader that spanned the modern labor movement." The former Allis-Chalmers vice president, it continued, "was honored by numerous organizations for his civic work throughout his career."[13]

Walter Reuther was one of the "new men of power," who "matured" in the Cold War era. A Socialist in the 1930s, Reuther aspired to lead the UAW and the American labor movement. Although a smart and dedicated trade unionist, he never possessed an affinity for the gritty world of trade union life. Unlike an R. J. Thomas, whose rank-and-file popularity rested on all-night card games and drinking bouts, Reuther, one biographer noted, "lacked the common touch" but had the positive qualities of "hard work, self-discipline, oratorical creativity, and leadership talents."[14]

Although socially more progressive than the other new men of power, Reuther, the ex-Socialist, used the rising Cold War anti-Communist feeling in his struggle to gain the UAW presidency. Opposing Thomas's left-center coalition, he fashioned a center-right one to capture the UAW's top office in 1946. After the factional disputes with Thomas and the Executive Board, he chose the slogan "Teamwork in the leadership and solidarity in the ranks" in his campaign to extend his control over the UAW convention. Anti-Communism was also an important theme in his effort to solidify his control over the UAW. At the time, John DeVito, a weak opposition candidate for the UAW presidency, decried Reuther's tactics as "the best job of Red-baiting and fear psychology that I ever saw in my life." He told hostile UAW delegates, "Reuther has so many progressives and liberals scared, if they get up to talk against him they are afraid they might be labeled a Communist."[15]

"Teamwork" and "solidarity," however, meant UAW unity. It also implied UAW conformity. From 1947 on, Reuther ruled a one-party political machine that nonetheless bore progressive social and political overtones. In 1952, as leader of one of the nation's largest and most influential industrial unions, Reuther succeeded Philip Murray as head of the CIO. After George Meany replaced William Green as AFL president, both men conducted successful negotiations on the merger of the AFL and CIO in 1955. Meany served as its president and Reuther as its vice president. Possibly aspiring to the AFL-CIO presidency, Reuther chafed under Meany's more conservative leadership. By the mid-1960s, the two leaders divided over the issues of war, civil rights, and labor's future. In 1968, Reuther pulled the UAW out of the AFL-CIO. In May 1970, Reuther, his wife, and two others died in an airplane crash while visiting the construction site of Black Lake, the future UAW educational center in Northern Michigan. His untimely death removed him from the American labor scene.[16]

In contrast, Christoffel, Buse, and other rank-and-file union leaders suffered through tough times. During the postwar Red Scare, in June 1947, the House Education and Labor Committee recommended Harold Christoffel's indictment for perjured testimony. In March 1948, after four and one-half hours of deliberation, a federal jury in the District of Columbia ruled that Christoffel "lied" under oath when he said "that he was not a Communist, had never been connected with Communist activities and was not acquainted with certain state Communist leaders." Subsequently, Christoffel's attorneys appealed his conviction to the U.S. Supreme Court on the technicality of a committee quorum during his testimony. After the highest court upheld the Christoffel appeal, federal authorities retried the Milwaukee labor leader. In March 1950, a federal judge sentenced the former Local 248 president to a term of two to six years in federal prison. In June 1953, after further appeals, Christoffel served three years in the Lorton reformatory and later the Terre Haute federal penitentiary.[17]

Released in 1956, Christoffel returned to Nashotah, Wisconsin, a small town west of Milwaukee, and attempted to rebuild his life. Capitalizing on his craft skills, he survived as an electrical contractor. But in the eyes of the next generation of Wisconsin CIO leaders, Christoffel was a pariah. They had built their careers on ousting the Left from the Wisconsin labor movement. Still, even after personal hard times, Christoffel remained at ease with his life. When an interviewer inquired about Local 248's support for Communist Party organizations, Christoffel replied: "We did what we thought was right." After years of reflection, he could still add: "To hell with the nickel. I am interested in much more than that. I want to make a better world. . . . You've gotta move forward. You can't be afraid of labels or anything else."[18]

Although the HELC originally planned to indict him, Robert Buse escaped the difficulties that Christoffel confronted—the successive rounds of fund-raising, legal briefs, and court appearances. However, a Milwaukee area blacklist of Allis-Chalmers strikers restricted his economic opportunities. For a while, he worked as a field representative for the Farm Equipment Workers Union, organizing cannery workers. He later worked for the United Electrical Workers Union, but he quit when the UE wanted him to relocate in Michigan. For a short time, he worked for the Milwaukee Road with the building and bridges department. But the blacklist followed him. After the Milwaukee Road's main office received his social security number, the foreman informed Buse: "I gotta lay you off." Nonetheless, with his interpersonal and organizational skills, Buse later obtained employment as a foreman for the Blackhawk Tannery and then worked for the Greenfield Parks and Recreation Department. Although his life later stabilized, Buse recalled, "My wife gets awful mad at me, because we had it pretty tough."[19]

The fired rank-and-file union leaders also had "pretty tough" times. In 1950, Max Raskin, a UAW attorney, described the "typical case" of Walter Fleischer, one of the discharged shop leaders. When dismissed in 1947, Fleischer was fifty years old and had been a union member for ten years. He had worked with the Allis-Chalmers firm for sixteen years. According to Raskin, he held no union office and "was never disciplined during the entire course of his employment." In the 1946 strike, Raskin noted, his "only activity . . . was serving on the picket line occasionally." He was never arrested or charged with any violation of the law. No one ever even warned him of "any misconduct" for his picket line duties. His name did not appear as a signer of the Eisenscher Communist Party nomination papers. "He is entirely unaware of the reason for his discharge," Raskin concluded, "except that it be the discriminatory conduct on the part of the company."[20]

After the 1946–1947 strike broke out, Fleischer, a tractor shop assembler, faced a strong Milwaukee area blacklist for Allis-Chalmers strikers. "I was refused work several places," he responded to a union survey, "after I made out a form showing I worked so many years at Allis-Chalmers." After eight months of unemployment, he found work only as a sheet metal helper. In November 1947, Fleischer reported using up all his personal savings and working for only nine of seventeen months since the strike began. His dire economic straits forced him to borrow $800 from friends to pay taxes and to prevent the loss of his home. Seventeen months after the strike had started, he plaintively wrote, "I am still struggling to pay off [my debts] which is very hard in these times of everything so high."[21]

Three years later, Walter Fleischer's situation was even worse. One of his children, probably his daughter, desperately wrote to the Local 248 president, pleading, "Please help us out. Father being one of the 91 discharged some years back says he is positive Allis Chalmers has black balled him so as no matter where he works they always tell him to go after he has been there 30 or 90 days." Since his discharge, Fleischer "had about 50 jobs in all these years." His foremen, the daughter claimed, were "so satisfied with his work." Recently, Fleischer found a second-shift job at the Harnischfeger company. For the first time, the pay was good and he enjoyed the work. After the sixty-day probationary period, the foreman discharged him. As a result, the despairing daughter wrote, "he is so thin and despondent [and] says he will look around to see if he can get a gun and blow his brains out. [He] says he can't take it any longer."[22]

The Allis-Chalmers worker's daughter also described the family's desperate plight: "we have suffered so much." Her mother had recently returned from the hospital for the third knee operation in four years. Her father, she wrote, "remortgaged our Home 3 times in 5 years to keep from losing it." As winter approached, "we can only afford one ton of stoker coal at a time we are always so low in funds." Despite the hard times, "he still says Local 248 is his union." The daughter wondered whether the Local 248 president could assist them to obtain the help of an attorney, the governor, or a congressman, or whether he could use his influence with the CIO steelworkers' union to regain the Harnischfeger position. "He did no crime," she desperately appealed, "why should he be made to feel as if he was a criminal [when] all he asks is the right to work."[23]

From the 1960s on, Allis-Chalmers was a troubled firm. The elimination of militant unionism never resolved its difficult economic problems. Always third or fourth in its major product markets, the Wisconsin corporation had to struggle to survive in an extremely competitive economic environment. By this time, the market for the big stuff and agricultural equipment had shifted to Europe and to the developing Third World. In the 1960s, the Milwaukee firm confronted federal charges against major electrical producers for fixing prices and markets, large research and development costs for new products for different markets, sizable modernization expenses for the aging West Allis plant, and costly takeover bids from larger corporations.[24]

In 1968, David Scott became the first president hired from outside Allis-Chalmers to administer the troubled enterprise. According to corporate historian Walter Peterson, the Allis-Chalmers defense from takeover bids resulted in "the hemorrhaging of assets and income." Consequently, Scott needed "to cauterize areas in which the company was inefficient and non-competitive." He sold off unprofitable assets and acquired new ones, often abandoning traditional Allis-Chalmers strengths. In order to compete effectively in world markets, he acquired foreign enterprises and entered into transnational licensing arrangements and joint ventures. Foreshadowing corporate deindustrialization policies of the 1970s and 1980s, he also ran away from the skilled and unionized West Allis work force and constructed new facilities in the South and other parts of the world. By the mid-1970s, Peterson concluded, "Allis-Chalmers recovered from the crisis of the late sixties, and Scott reported in 1976 that their problems were behind them." Although net income, shareholder earnings, and total sales all rose, economic difficulties continued to plague management. The full effect of the first oil crisis of the early 1970s, the second oil crisis of the late 1970s, and the Reagan recession of the early 1980s devastated the midwestern industrial economy and the Allis-Chalmers firm. Through twelve years of David Scott's tenure as president, the West Allis work force declined from twelve thousand in 1968 to fewer than three thousand in 1980.[25]

By 1980, the Allis-Chalmers Corporation faced major financial problems. At the time, Scott blamed the UAW for the Allis-Chalmers misfortunes. He told stockholders: "We've either got to get away from the UAW or get out of the business." Refusing to consider failed corporate policies, Scott returned to the Allis-Chalmers legacy of antiunionism and criticized the UAW's high wage and benefits package and continued to lay off workers. In the end, he could not run from the UAW, and he eventually retired. In 1987, after Scott left, Allis-Chalmers reached the end of the road. The West Allis plant, formerly Wisconsin's largest industrial site, was an empty shell. Its work force declined to a skeleton staff of only 480 workers. In June 1987, corporate officials reorganized under Chapter 11 of the U.S. Bankruptcy Code. Five months later, they decided to merge the firm's various units and to sell all Allis-Chalmers assets. They also abandoned their financial commitments to workers' pension funds, creating the largest pension liability to the U.S. Benefit Guarantee Corporation up to that date.[26]

Today, the West Allis site is a painful manifestation of rustbelt deindustrialization. It shows the transition from an industrial to a service economy and from a high-wage union work force to a low-wage nonunion one. Most of the original buildings have been razed, and the ground has been leveled. Some buildings have become an industrial park, hoping to lure new seed industries to the Milwaukee area. The remaining structures have been converted into a West Allis shopping mall.

In 1984, a new generation of rank-and-file militants, emerging from the social radicalism of the 1960s, took over leadership positions in UAW Local 248. For three difficult years, they attempted to revitalize their weakened union with an innovative campaign against the troubled firm. They also organized Local 248's Fiftieth Anniversary Celebration for several hundred retired and active union members in the spring of 1986. The younger generation also invited Harold Christoffel, the local's founding president. Isolated and ignored for almost forty years, Christoffel finally returned to his roots. At the union dinner, Don Weimer, a Local 248 bargaining committeeman, recalled that Christoffel received "a warm ovation from both generations, including many of his former adversaries."[27]

# NOTES

## Abbreviations

| | |
|---|---|
| ACMC | Allis-Chalmers Manufacturing Company. |
| ACMCC | Allis-Chalmers Manufacturing Company Collection, MCHS. |
| ACMCC (Peterson) | Allis-Chalmers Manufacturing Company Collection, Walter F. Peterson Research Papers, MCHS. |
| *ACWU News* | *Allis-Chalmers Workers' Union News* |
| ALHUA | Archives of Labor History and Urban Affairs, Walter P. Reuther Library, Wayne State University, Detroit, Mich. |
| *CIO News* | *Wisconsin CIO News: Local 248 Edition.* |
| DDLP | Don D. Lescohier Papers, SHSW. |
| FJHP | Francis J. Haas Papers, Catholic University of America, Washington, D.C. |
| FMCS | Federal Mediation and Conciliation Service. |
| FTC | Federated Trades Council. |
| GAP | George Addes Papers, ALHUA. |
| *HELC Hearings* | House of Representatives, *Hearings before the Committee on Education and Labor . . . Bills to Amend and Repeal the National Labor Relations Act, and for Other Purposes* (Washington, D.C., 1947). |
| *HUAC Hearings* | House of Representatives, *Hearings before the Committee on Un-American Activities . . . February 27, 1947.* (Washington, D.C., 1947). |
| HWSC | Harold W. Story Collection, MCHS. |
| HWSP | Harold W. Story Papers, MARC. |
| IAM Dist. 10 Papers | International Association of Machinists, District 10, Papers, SHSW. |
| IAM Papers | F. Allis-Chalmers, Microfilm Reel No. 142, International Association of Machinists Papers, SHSW. |
| *Joint Statement* | Allis-Chalmers Manufacturing Company, *Joint Statement of A. K. Brintnall . . . , K. W. Haagensen . . . , E. F. Ohrman . . . , J. L. Waddleton . . . , and Harold Story, Vice President, before the House of Rep-* |

|  |  |
|---|---|
|  | resentatives Committee on Education and Labor, February 24, 1947 ([West Allis], [1947]). |
| JWGP | John W. Gibson Papers, F. Labor—Allis-Chalmers, 1945–1948, Box 17, John W. Gibson Papers, Harry S. Truman Library, Independence, Mo. |
| LAC Ruling | Labor Advisory Committee Ruling, F. 1937–1938 Co Ans 1–100, Box 1, UAW Local 248 Papers. |
| MARC | Milwaukee Area Research Center of SHSW, Golda Meir Library, University of Wisconsin–Milwaukee, Milwaukee, Wis. |
| MCHS | Milwaukee County Historical Society, Milwaukee, Wis. |
| MCIUCP | Milwaukee County Industrial Union Council Papers, MARC. |
| MEBM | Minutes of Executive Board Meeting, Box 13, UAW Local 248 Papers. |
| *MJ* | *Milwaukee Journal* |
| MMM | Minutes of Membership Meeting, Box 13, UAW Local 248 Papers. |
| MPL | Milwaukee Public Library. |
| *MS* | *Milwaukee Sentinel.* |
| MSCM | Minutes of Stewards' and Committeemen's Meeting, Box 13, UAW Local 248 Papers. |
| NDMB | National Defense Mediation Board. |
| NLRB | National Labor Relations Board. |
| "NLRB Testimony" | Box 10, Series 11, NLRB Transcripts and Exhibits, 1935–1948, RG 25. |
| NWLB | National War Labor Board. |
| "NWLB Documents" | ACMC, "Documents I–III; V–XXII Included with Statement before a Panel of the National War Labor Board," July 6, 1942, F. WLB 42 Docs, Box 11, UAW Local 248 Papers. |
| "NWLB Hearing" | "Proceedings of the National War Labor Board," Box 11, UAW Local 248 Papers. |
| "NWLB Statement" | ACMC, "Statement of the Allis-Chalmers Manufacturing Company in Negotiations with Local 248, UAW-CIO, before a Panel of the National War Labor Board," July 6, 1942, SHSW. |
| OHFC | Otto H. Falk Collection, MCHS. |
| "Resume" | "Resume of Pertinent Phases of Allis-Chalmers Labor History Depicting Destructive Effect of Communist Control of Labor Organization," c. 1950, Box 1 ACMCC (Peterson). |
| RG 25 | Record Group 25, Records of the National Labor Relations Board, National Archives, Washington, D.C. |
| RG 174 | Record Group 174, Records of the Department of Labor, National Archives, Washington, D.C. |

RG 202              Record Group 202, Records of the National War La-
                    bor Board, National Archives, Suitland, Md.
RG 280              Record Group 280, Records of the Federal Media-
                    tion and Conciliation Service, National Archives,
                    Suitland, Md.
SHSW               State Historical Society of Wisconsin, Madison,
                    Wis.
Swofford Affidavit  Hugh Swofford, Affidavit, January 23, 1950, F. 15,
                    Box 7, Nat Ganley Papers, ALHUA.
UAW Local 248 Papers  UAW Local 248 Papers, ALHUA.
WLOHP              Wisconsin Labor Oral History Project, SHSW.
"WLRA Clippings"    "Clippings: Wisconsin Labor Relations Act," F. Wis-
                    consin Labor Legislation, 1930s, Wisconsin Legis-
                    lative Reference Bureau Microfilm, Golda Meier
                    Library, University of Wisconsin–Milwaukee.
WSFLP              Wisconsin State Federation of Labor Papers,
                    SHSW.
WSIUCP             Wisconsin State Industrial Union Council Papers,
                    SHSW.
WPRP               Walter P. Reuther Papers, ALHUA.


## CHAPTER 1. Introduction

1.    *MS*, September 23, 1946.
2.    *Ibid.*, September 23–November 21, 1946.
3.    Dale Treleven, "Harold Christoffel Interview," January 21, 1982, WLOHP, SHSW.
4.    For biographical information on Harold Story, see *Wright's Directory of Milwaukee* (Milwaukee, 1880–1945); *Who's Who in Commerce and Industry* (Chicago, 1951); *MS*, July 6, 1957; ACMC, Press Release, July 9, 1957; and Bob Riordan, "Harold Story Birthday Celebration, 1970," Box 3, and F. Harold W. Story, Clippings—Personal, Box 2, HWSC.
5.    *Wright's Directory* (1910–1921); *Who's Who*; and Riordan, "Story Birthday."
6.    *Wright's Directory* (1930–1940); ACMC, "Press Release," July 9, 1957; and Riordan, "Story Birthday."
7.    For biographical information on Harold Christoffel, see *Wright's Directory of Milwaukee* (Milwaukee, 1900–1945); *Wisconsin CIO News*, February 21, 1938; *CIO News*, July 21, 1941; ACMC, "Harold Christoffel Employment Application, Duplicate," Box 31, ACMCC; Treleven, "Christoffel Interview."
8.    *Wright's Directory* (1919–1925).
9.    *Wright's Directory* (1919–1925); *Wisconsin CIO News*, February 21, 1938; and *CIO News*, July 21, 1941.
10.   Treleven, "Christoffel Interview"; *Wisconsin CIO News*, February 2, 1938; and *CIO News*, July 21, 1941.
11.   *CIO News*, July 21, 1941.
12.   Max M. Kampelman, *The Communist Party vs. the CIO* (New York, 1957), 26. For discussions on the issue of Communism and UAW Local 248, see Robert W. Ozanne, "The Effects of Communist Leadership on American Trade Unions" (Ph.D. dissertation, University of Wisconsin, 1954), 185–324; Thomas W. Gavett, *Development of the*

*Labor Movement in Milwaukee* (Madison, 1965), 161–165, 176–197; Bert Cochran, *Labor and Communism: The Conflict That Shaped American Unions* (Princeton, 1977), 166–176, 184–189, 272–275; Roger Keeran, *The Communist Party and the Auto Workers Unions* (Bloomington, 1980), 212–215, 266–278; Robert W. Ozanne, *The Labor Movement in Wisconsin: A History* (Madison, 1984), 79–102; and Martin Halpern, *UAW Politics in the Cold War Era* (Albany, 1988), 173–183. For the new labor histories of Communist or left union locals, see, e.g., Bruce Nelson, *Workers on the Waterfront: Seamen, Longshoremen, and Unionism in the 1930s* (Urbana, 1988); and Joshua B. Freeman, *In Transit: The Transport Workers Union in New York City, 1933–66* (New York, 1989). See also Nelson Lichtenstein et al., "An Exchange: Labor and Communism," *Industrial Relations* 19 (Spring 1980): 119–139.

13.  Harold Christoffel, *HELC Hearings* 4 (March 3, 1947); Robert Buse, *HELC Hearings* 4 (March 1, 1947): 1982; Treleven, "Christoffel Interview"; and Dale Treleven, "Robert Buse Interview," February 4, 1982, WLOHP.

14.  Swofford Affidavit, 1, 13–14, 17–19, 20–23, and 28–31; Christoffel, *HELC Hearings*, 2078–2142, passim; Louis F. Budenz, *HELC Hearings* 5 (March 13, 1947): 3603–3623, passim; HELC Subcommittee, "Congressional Hearing on Communistic Influences in Labor . . . ," Transcript, March 17, 1947, Box 3, WSIUCP; and *MJ*, March 5, 1947.

15.  *MJ*, February 16 and 17, 1947; Swofford Affidavit, 23–24; *MS*, February 17, 1947; Budenz, *HELC Hearings*, 3616, 3611–3612.

16.  Farrel Schnering, Affidavit, June 21, 1939, in *Journal of Proceedings of the Sixty-Fourth Session of the Wisconsin Legislature* (Madison, 1939), 1695; Farrel Schnering, HELC Subcommittee, "Congressional Hearing," March 17, 1947, 96, 98–99; and *MJ*, March 20, 1947, and June 9, 1939.

17.  Kenneth Goff, cited in *Journal . . . Wisconsin Legislature*, 2193–2194 and 2193–2193, and *MJ*, April 10, 1941.

18.  Ozanne, "Communist Leadership," 221.

19.  Dale Treleven, "Sigmund Eisenscher Interview," January 26, 1982, WLOHP; *MJ*, June 9, 1939, and April 10, 1941; Catherine Coberly "Walter Uphoff Interview," December 8, 1982, Wisconsin Democratic Party Oral History Project, SHSW.

20.  Swofford Affidavit, 20–21, and ACMC, *Joint Statement*, passim.

21.  "Oral Statement of Harold W. Story . . . before U.S. Senate Committee on Labor and Public Welfare, Friday, February 14, 1947," F. Misc. Labor: 1947–1950, Box 31, ACMCC; ACMC, *Joint Statement*, passim; Swofford Affidavit, 10; [William J. McGowan], "Resume of Pertinent Phases of Collective Bargaining at West Allis Works," typescript, c. 1950, Box 31, ACMCC; and [William J. McGowan], "Resume of Pertinent Phases of Allis-Chalmers Labor History Depicting Destructive Effect of Communist Control of a Labor Organization," mimeographed, c. 1950, Box 1, ACMCC (Peterson).

22.  ACMC, *Joint Statement*, 7–9, 39–45.

23.  Treleven, "Eisenscher Interview."

24.  Peggy Dennis, *The Autobiography of an American Communist: A Personal View of a Political Life, 1925–75* (Berkeley, 1977), 93, 95; John Blair to Peggy Dennis, June 19, 1967, F. Book 1, 1935–1937, Box 1, Peggy Dennis Papers, SHSW; Treleven, "Eisenscher Interview" and "Christoffel Interview."

25.  Treleven, "Eisenscher Interview."

26.  Halpern, *UAW Politics*, 339; and Robert Buse statement in "Chronological Background of the Circumstances in Local 248," July 6, 1949, 20, F. 27, Box 238, WPRP.

27.  Treleven, "Christoffel Interview."

28.  Treleven, "Buse Interview."

29.  Treleven, "Christoffel Interview."

30.  Story, "Oral Statement."

31.  Ozanne, "Communist Leadership," 185–324, passim.

32. Ibid., 252.

33. Ibid., 185. On the foreign policy stance of UAW Local 248, see *CIO News*, 1937–1945, and MMM, 1937–1945.

34. Ozanne, "Communist Leadership," 317.

35. Ibid., 312–313.

36. Steven Rossworm, "A Betrayal of Isaiah's Promise: Labor Priests, Labor Schools, the ACTU and the Expelled Unions," September 15, 1989, unpublished paper presented at Chicago Area Labor History Group, Newberry Library.

37. Elizabeth Fox-Genovese and Eugene D. Genovese, *The Fruits of Merchant Capital: Slavery and Bourgeois Property in the Rise and Expansion of Capitalism* (New York, 1983), 179–180.

## CHAPTER 2. The Making of Militant Unionism I

1. Philip Scranton, "Diversity in Diversity: Flexible Manufacturing and American Industrial Development, 1880–1930," 25, unpublished Paper, 1990 (copy in author's possession).

2. Gerd Korman, *Industrialization, Immigrants, and Americanizers: The View from Milwaukee, 1866–1921* (Madison, 1967), 41–51; and Walter F. Peterson, *An Industrial Heritage: Allis-Chalmers Corporation* (Milwaukee, 1978), 78.

3. Peterson, *Industrial Heritage*, 7–16, 18, 48–49, 70, 78, 89, 91; and Stephen Meyer, "Technology and the Workplace: Skilled and Production Workers at Allis-Chalmers, 1900–1941," *Technology and Culture* 29 (October 1988): 840–842.

4. Peterson, *Industrial Heritage*, 102, 104–105.

5. Daniel Nelson, *Managers and Workers: Origins of the New Factory System in the United States, 1880–1920* (Madison, 1975), 22–23; and Meyer, "Technology and the Workplace," 842–844.

6. Alfred D. Chandler, *The Visible Hand: The Managerial Revolution in American Business* (Cambridge, Mass., 1977), 241.

7. "The General Scheme of the New Milwaukee Plant of the Allis-Chalmers Company," *American Machinist* 25 (June 12, 1902): 841; "The Great West Allis Plant," *Machinery* 9 (February 1903): 286–288; and "Shop Dimensions at the Plant of the Allis-Chalmers Co., Milwaukee, Wis." *Engineering News* 56 (July 12, 1906): 28–30.

8. "Shop Dimensions," passim; and Peterson, *Industrial Heritage*, 110–111 and 129–132.

9. "Great West-Allis Plant," 288–289; Allis-Chalmers Co., *Works and Products of the Allis-Chalmers Co.* (Milwaukee, 1911), passim; ACMC, *Eighty-Eight Years of Progress: Allis-Chalmers* ([Milwaukee], 1935), 10.

10. Peterson, *Industrial Heritage*, 167, 169–175.

11. R. A. Crosby, "The Allis-Chalmers Tractor Division," Box 3, ACMCC (Peterson); ACMC, *Progress*, 7; Peterson, *Industrial Heritage*, 217, 231, 296–298.

12. Crosby, "Tractor Division"; and ACMC, *Progress*, 7.

13. ACMC, *Sales Bulletin* (November 1920, November 1921, and February 1924), Box 3, ACMCC (Peterson); Peterson, *Industrial Heritage*, 241–245.

14. ACMC, *Sales Bulletin* (November 1928 and November 1929); and Joseph Geschelin, "After Twenty-Three Years," *Automotive Industries* 79 (September 3, 1938): 282, 284.

15. Watson, "All-Modern Equipment Produces Allis-Chalmers Tractor," *American Machinist* 72 (March 13, 1930): 436–437. See also Frank J. Oliver, "Special-Purpose Equipment for Accurate Tractor Parts," *American Machinist* 72 (March 13, 1930): 458–462.

16. Geschelin, "After Twenty-Three Years," 282, 284.

17. Peterson, *Industrial Heritage*, 79–81, 116–118; Ozanne, *Labor Movement*, 6–11; Gavett, *Labor Movement*, 57–65.

18. David Montgomery, *The Fall of the House of Labor: The Workplace, the State, and American Labor Activism, 1865–1925* (New York, 1987), 26. On the culture of unionism, see also Montgomery, *House of Labor*, 170–213, and *Workers' Control in America: Studies in the History of Work, Technology, and Labor Struggles* (New York, 1979), 9–31; and Jeffrey Haydu, *Between Craft and Class: Skilled Workers and Factory Politics in the United States and Britain, 1890–1922* (Berkeley, 1988), 26–88.

19. Montgomery, *Workers' Control*, 11–14.

20. Montgomery, *House of Labor*, 204; and *Workers' Control*, 15–27.

21. Haydu, *Craft and Class*, 26–29, 59.

22. Ibid., 29; Mark Perlman, *The Machinists: A New Study of American Trade Unionism* (Cambridge, Mass., 1962), frontispiece; Montgomery, *House of Labor*, 215.

23. Haydu, *Craft and Class*, 50–51, 30, 41; and Montgomery, *House of Labor*, 55–56.

24. Montgomery, *House of Labor*, 212; and Haydu, *Craft and Class*, 29, 30, 54.

25. Harold M. Groves, "Early Unions in the Machinists' Craft and Their Influence," *Machinists' Monthly Journal* 38 (December 1926): 563, and "The Machinist in Industry: A Study in the History and Economics of His Craft" (Ph.D. dissertation, University of Wisconsin, 1927), 77–78.

26. Groves, "Machinist," 78–79.

27. Montgomery, *House of Labor*, 260–262; Haydu, *Craft and Class*, 78–79; Perlman, *Machinists*, 25–28; Selig Perlman and Robert Taft, *History of Labor in the United States, 1896–1932* 4 (New York, 1935): 115.

28. Montgomery, *House of Labor*, 265–269; Haydu, *Craft and Class*, 83–84; and Perlman, *Machinists*, 26–27.

29. Peterson, *Industrial Heritage*, 102–105; *MJ*, May 18 and 20, 1901; Gavett, *Labor Movement*, 121; and Ozanne, *Labor Movement*, 26–28.

30. Peterson, *Industrial Heritage*, 102–105; *MJ*, May 18 and 20, 1901; Gavett, *Labor Movement*, 121; and Ozanne, *Labor Movement*, 26–28.

31. *MJ*, May 18 and 20, 1901.

32. *MJ*, May 30, 1901.

33. Perlman, *Machinists*, 27–28; Peterson, *Industrial Heritage*, 117–119; and Ozanne, *Labor Movement*, 27–28.

34. Perlman and Taft, *History of Labor*, 110–114; F. T. Stockton, "The International Molders Union of North America," *Johns Hopkins University Studies in History and Political Science* 39 (1921—1922): 186–187; and Mary Loomis Strecker, "The Founders, the Molders, and the Molding Machine," *Quarterly Journal of Economics* 32 (February 1918), 283.

35. Stockton, "Molders Union," 186–187; Strecker, "Molding Machine," 289, 297–298; and A. O. Backert, "The Introduction of Molding Machines in Foundries," *Transactions of the American Foundrymen's Association* 25 (1917): 713.

36. Perlman and Taft, *History of Labor*, 112; and Stockton, "Molders Union," 194.

37. Stockton, "Molders Union," 194; Perlman and Taft, *History of Labor*, 113; and Strecker, "Molding Machine," 295.

38. Strecker, "Molding Machine," 301.

39. *MJ*, May 1 and 2, 1906; and *MS*, May 2, 1906.

40. *MS*, May 4, 8, and 9, 1906; and *MJ*, May 4, 1906.

41. *MS*, May 16 and 24, 1906; Ozanne, *Labor Movement*, 31; Edwin Witte, "A Review of the Labor Situation in the Metal Trades Industry . . . June 23, 1916," F. Labor History—Wisconsin Labor Movement, Box 125, Edwin Witte Papers, SHSW; and Strecker, "Molding Machine," 302.

42. *MJ*, May 26, 1906 and Peterson, *Industrial Heritage*, 120–121.

43. Ozanne, *Labor Movement*, 31.

44. John P. Frey, *History of a Criminal Conspiracy to Defeat Striking Molders* (n.p., n.d.), 3.

45. Montgomery, *Workers' Control*, 95, 98, and 99.

46. Untitled clippings, May 15 and 17, 1915, and August 31, 1915, F. Allis-Chalmers, 1901–1934, Industrial Clipping File, MCHS.

47. Untitled clippings, May 17 and August 31, 1915.

48. Ozanne, *Labor Movement*, 56; Jacob Friedrich, "NLRB Testimony," July 23, 1937, p. 1606; and *MS*, July 25, 1916.

49. *MJ*, July 18, 1916.

50. *MJ*, July 19, 21, 22, 24, 25, 26, and 27, 1916, and September 18, 1916.

51. On corporate paternalism and welfare capitalism, see David Brody, *Workers in Industrial America: Essays on the Twentieth Century Struggle* (New York, 1980), 48–81; and Irving Bernstein, *The Lean Years: A History of the American Worker, 1920–33* (Boston, 1972), 144–189.

52. Harold W. Story, "Outline for U.W. Seminar, Madison, Wis." January 6, 1948, Box 3, HWSC; and Harold Christoffel, *HELC Hearings*, 2079.

53. Harold Story, "A Plan for Industrial Peace," address before Joint Hearing of Wisconsin legislature, January 28, 1937, Box 3, HWSC.

54. Ibid.

55. Peterson, *Industrial Heritage*, pp. 76–78, 121, 193–194, 219–220, 289–290.

56. "Allis-Chalmers: America's Krupp," *Fortune* 29 (May 1939): 53, 55.

57. Ibid., 55–56.

58. Ibid., 57, 58, and 148.

59. Harold Story, "NLRB Testimony," July 12, 1937, p. 11.

60. Ibid., pp. 35–35, 37.

61. William Watson, "NLRB Testimony," July 12, 1937, pp. 110 and 116; and Hugo Liebert, "NLRB Testimony," July 13, 1937, pp. 303–304.

62. Christoffel, "NLRB Testimony," July 15, 1937, pp. 564–565.

63. NLRB, *Decisions and Orders of the National Labor Relations Board* 4 (Washington, 1938): 167; and George Geiger, "NLRB Testimony," July 19, 1937, p. 897.

## CHAPTER 3. The Making of Militant Unionism II

1. Gavett, *Labor Movement*, 152–153; and Peterson, *Industrial Heritage*, 283.

2. Unidentified clipping, December 4, 1930, Box 1; and *Allis-Chalmers Worker* (March 1932), Box 2, OHFC; Treleven, "Christoffel Interview" and "Buse Interview."

3. Jacob Friedrick, "NLRB Testimony," July 23, 1937, p. 1648; and Gavett, *Labor Movement*, 137, 138, 151.

4. Unidentified clipping, December 4, 1930, and *Allis-Chalmers Worker* (March 1932); and leaflet, "Fellow Workers! Employed! Unemployed! Support and Join the Hunger March to Allis-Chalmers!" Box 2, OHFC.

5. Friedrick, "NLRB Testimony," 1648–1650. For the leaflets for Metal Trade Council's organizational campaigns, see Box 2, Box 4, and "Allis-Chalmers Manufacturing Company Statement of Policy under the National Industrial Recovery Act," December 14, 1934, Box 9, IAM Dist. 10 Papers.

6. "Combatting the Industrial Recovery Act in Milwaukee," *Party Organizer* 6 (July 1933): 16–17.

7. Story, "The Modern Labor Problem from an Employer's Viewpoint," July 18, 1935; "Outline for U.W. Seminar, Madison, Wis." January 6, 1948, and "House

Couunsel—Retained Counsel," Speech, 1957, Box 3, HWSC; and Watson, "NLRB Testimony," July 12, 1937, p. 139.

8.    Story, "NLRB Testimony," July 12, 1937, p. 53.

9.    French, *The Shop Committee in the United States* (Baltimore, 1923), 9–10, 60–65.

10.    Senate, *Report of the Committee on Education and Labor: Violations of Free Speech and Rights of Labor: Industrial Espionage*, Report No. 46, Part 3 (Washington, 1937), 80.

11.    WAWC, Minutes of Special Meeting, October 2, 1934, and August 16, 1934–June 17, 1935, Box 9, IAM Dist. 10 Papers; ACMC, *Works Council* (West Allis, December 1934), passim; Christoffel, *HELC Hearings*, 2079–2080; Story, "NLRB Testimony," 176–177; and *ACWU News*, December 10, 1937.

12.    ACMC, *Works Council*, passim.

13.    Watson speech, February 21, 1934, cited in "Resume," 71.

14.    Christoffel, *HELC Hearings*, 2079–2080; Story, "The Labor Trend from an Employer's Viewpoint," Box 3, HWSC; and Story, "NLRB Testimony," 176–177.

15.    ACMC, *Works Council*, 11–12; Christoffel, *HELC Hearings*, 2079–2080; and Francis Kreps to Otto Jirikowic, October 8, 1934, Box 9, IAM Dist. 10 Papers.

16.    Story, "NLRB Testimony," 176; and "Resume," 71.

17.    WAWC, minutes of meetings, August 15, 1934–June 17, 1935.

18.    Story, "NLRB Testimony," 177 and 212, and "Modern Labor Problem"; and Christoffel, *HELC Hearings*, 2080 and 2079.

19.    *ACWU News*, December 10, 1937; Peter Gencuski, "NLRB Testimony," July 27, 1927, p. 1943; and Christoffel, "NLRB Testimony," 335.

20.    Julius Blunk, "NLRB Testimony," July 22, 1937, pp. 1542, 1541; *ACWU News*, March 11, 1938; and Gencuski, "NLRB Testimony," 1942.

21.    *ACWU News*, March 11, 1938, and December 10, 1937; and "Resume," 74.

22.    *ACWU News*, December 10, 1937, March 11, 1938, and August 2, 1937, and "Resume," 74.

23.    Frank Bolka, "NLRB Testimony," July 17, 1937, pp. 755, and 737–753 passim, 755; and Otto Jirikowic to H. F. Nickerson, October 12, 1934, Box 9, IAM Dist. 10 Papers.

24.    Bolka, "NLRB Testimony," 755.

25.    *ACWU News*, December 10, 1937; John Rucich, "NLRB Testimony," July 28, 1937, pp. 2170–2173; and Michael Boblin, "NLRB Testimony," July 20, 1937, pp. 989–991.

26.    *ACWU News*, December 10, 1937.

27.    Story, "NLRB Testimony," 229–231.

28.    *ACWU News*, December 10, 1937, and "Resume," 71–72.

29.    Story, "Modern Labor Problem;" ACMC, "Statement of Policy," December 14, 1934; Notes for Negotiations, October 20 to December 3, 1934, Box 9, IAM Dist. 10 Papers; "Agreement," c. late 1934, Box 10, Series 11, RG 25; "Resume," 71–72; *ACWU News*, December 10, 1938; and *CIO News*, June 25, 1938.

30.    ACMC, "Statement of Policy"; and Story, "Modern Labor Problem," 8.

31.    ACMC, "Statement of Policy."

32.    Ibid.

33.    *ACWU News*, December 10, 1937; and *CIO News*, June 25, 1938.

34.    Dennis, *American Communist*, 88–89, 92–93.

35.    John Blair to Peggy Dennis, June 19, 1967, F. Book 1, 1935–1937 Wisconsin, Box 1, Peggy Dennis Papers, SHSW; and "Nominate and Elect Fighting Workers—June 4th & 11th," Box 9, IAM Dist. 10 Papers.

36.    *ACWU News*, December 10, 1937; *CIO News*, June 25, 1938; Otto A. Jirikowic to Max Babb, August 14, 1935, Box 9, IAM Dist. 10 Papers.

37.    Story, "Modern Labor Problem."

38.    Ibid.

39.    Irving Bernstein, *The Turbulent Years: A History of the American Worker, 1933–1941* (Boston, 1971), 318–351.

40.   Unidentified clipping, March 25, 1934, Box 1, OHFC.

41.   "Resume," 76–77; and *ACWU News*, December 10, 1937.

42.   Handwritten notes of meeting, July 22, 1936, Max Babb to A.F. of L. Bargaining Committee, August 17, 1936, and Max Babb, "Rulings Relative to Company's Statement of Policy," August 18, 1936, Box 9, IAM Dist. 10 Papers.

43.   Harold Christoffel to Frank Morrison, F. Federal Letters, Box 6, UAW Local 248 Papers; MMM, August 18, 1936; and "Resume," 77.

44.   MMM, August 18, 1936 and September 12, 1936; and "Resume," 77.

45.   MMM, October 1, 1936.

46.   *ACWU News*, December 10, 1937; MMM, October 30, 1936; Christoffel to Morrison, January 15, 1937; and Otto A. Jirikowic to A. O. Wharton, November 28, 1936, Box 9, IAM Dist. 10 Papers.

47.   MMM, November 21 and December 19, 1936; and MEBM, November 8, 1936.

48.   O. A. Jirikowic to A. O. Wharton, December 31, 1936, and A. O. Wharton to William Green, February 25, 1937, IAM Papers, SHSW; and A. O. Wharton to O. A. Jirikowic, January 6, 1937, Box 9, IAM Dist. 10 Papers.

49.   MMM, January 14, 1937; and "Resume," 83.

50.   Christoffel to Morrison, January 15, 1937.

51.   Ibid.

52.   Ibid.

53.   Joseph Padway's comments during Christoffel, "NLRB Testimony," 405; and Thomas W. Gavett, "The Development of the Labor Movement in Milwaukee" (Ph.D. dissertation, University of Wisconsin, 1957), 338–340.

54.   MMM, January 23, 1937 and February 2, 1937; Gavett, "Labor Movement in Milwaukee," 338–340;" *CIO News*, June 25, 1938; and "Resume," 83–84.

55.   MSCM, February 21, 1937; MEBM, February 25, 1937; Peter Gencuski, "NLRB Testimony," 1941–1942; and MMM, February 28, 1937.

56.   MEBM, February, 28, 1937; and MMM, March 4, 1937.

57.   Jirikowic to Wharton, March 6, 1937, IAM Papers; Sidney Fine, *Sit Down: The General Motors Strike of 1936–1937* (Ann Arbor, 1969), 146, 209, and 322; and Paul Krakowski, "The Press Treatment of Wisconsin Labor" (M.A. thesis, University of Wisconsin, 1947), 59–62, 23.

58.   MEBM, March 11, 1937.

59.   Harold Christoffel to Homer Martin, March 9, 1937, F. Federal Letters, Box 6, UAW Local 248 Papers; and G. M. Bugniazet to A. O. Wharton, March 12, 1937, IAM Papers.

60.   Christoffel, "NLRB Testimony," 397 and 417; MEBM, March 14, 1937; MMM, March 14, 1937; and "Resume," 87.

61.   Julius Blunk to George Addes, May 28, 1937, F. Interna-tional Union, Box 1, UAW Local 248 Papers; and Blunk "NLRB Testimony," July 21, 1937, 1314, and 1548.

62.   Harold Story, "Sit-Down Strike—A Symptom," April 1, 1937, Box 3, HWSC; and Theodore Mueller, "Milwaukee Workers," Manuscript No. 14, MCHS.

63.   Harry A. Millis and Emily C. Brown, *From the Wagner Act to Taft-Hartley: A Study of National Labor Policy and Labor Relations* (Chicago, 1950), 40; "WLRA Clippings," passim; and "Resume," 86.

## CHAPTER 4. Consolidating the Union

1.   Treleven, "Buse Interview."

2.   Gordon M. Haferbecker, *Wisconsin Labor Laws* (Madison, 1958), 162; Darryl Holter, "Labor Law and the Road to Taft-Hartley: Wisconsin's 'Little Wagner Act,'

1935–45," *Labor Studies Journal* 15 (Summer 1990): 24–26; and "WLRA Clippings," passim.

3.     Story, "Industrial Peace."

4.     Ibid. Haferbecker, *Wisconsin Labor Laws*, 162–165; Holter, "Labor Law and the Road to Taft-Hartley," 26–34; and "WLRA Clippings," passim.

5.     "WLRA Clippings," passim.

6.     MMM, March 14, 1937; MEBM, March 14, 1937, and Christoffel, "NLRB Testimony," July 16, 1937, p. 693.

7.     Francis J. Haas, Memorandum on Allis-Chalmers Company . . . for Wisconsin Labor Relations Board, May 20, 1937, FJHP and F. Allis-Chalmers Manufacturing Co., I-52, 5/19/37, Box 1, Closed Labor Disputes, Wisconsin Employment Relations Board Papers, SHSW.

8.     MMM, May 23, 1937; and Story, "NLRB Testimony," July 13, 1937, 258.

9.     Christoffel, "NLRB Testimony," 553; and Story, "NLRB Testimony," 245, 297.

10.     "Agreement, 1938."

11.     Ibid.

12.     James A. Gross, *The Reshaping of the National Labor Relations Board: National Labor Policy in Transition, 1937–1947* (Albany, 1981), 45–48; and NLRB, "Case No. R-215," November 20, 1937, *Decisions and Orders of the National Labor Relations Board* 5 (1938): 159–177.

13.     NLRB, "Case No. R-215," February 8, 1937, *Decisions and Orders* 5 (1938): 158–164.

14.     *ACWU News*, January 7, 1938.

15.     MMM, January 9, 1938; *ACWU News*, January 21, 1938; and *CIO News*, May 14, 1938.

16.     *CIO News*, May 14, 1938; MSCM, May 22, 1938; and *CIO News*, June 11, 1938.

17.     MEBM, February 24, 1938; and MMM, March 1, 1938.

18.     MMM, April 9, 1938; *CIO News*, April 16, 1938; and MSCM, April 16, 1938.

19.     Bernstein, *Turbulent Years*, 388–431, and 682–703.

20.     Walter Galenson, *The CIO Challenge to the AFL: A History of the American Labor Movement* (Cambridge, 1960), 151–152; John Bernard, *Walter Reuther and the Rise of the Auto Workers* (Boston, 1983), 54–63; Martin Halpern, *UAW Politics in the Cold War Era* (Albany, 1988), 22–29; and Jack Skeels, "The Background to UAW Factionalism," *Labor History* 2 (1961): 158–181.

21.     Galenson, *CIO Challenge*, 161–165.

22.     Ibid.

23.     Harold Christoffel et al., to John L. Lewis, Telegram, July 20, 1938, and minutes of Trial Committee, undated, Box 1, MCIUCP; and *CIO News*, July 23, 1938.

24.     *CIO News*, July 23, 1938.

25.     Ibid.

26.     "Resume," 99–102; and *CIO News*, August 6, 1938.

27.     *CIO News*, August 6 and 13, 1938.

28.     "Resume," 102; and *MJ*, August 29, 1938.

29.     Galenson, *CIO Challenge*, 162–163; and *CIO News*, August 27 and September 3 and 10, 1938.

30.     Allis-Chalmers Manufacturing Company v 920 L88, 9/2/38, Box 1, Closed Labor Disputes, Wisconsin Labor Relations Board Papers, SHSW; and "Resume," 103.

31.     "Resume," 104; *MJ*, September 18, 1938; and MMM, September 22, 1938.

32.     "Resume," 103–104; *MJ*, September 18, 1938; *CIO News*, October 1, 1938; and MMM, September 22, 1938.

33.     MMM, September 22, 1938; and *CIO News*, October 1, 1938.

34.     "Resume," 104–106; MMM, October 25, 1938; and *CIO News*, October 15 and 19, 1938.

35.  MMM, November 13, 1938.

36.  MMM, March 19, 1939; "Resume," 107–108; and *CIO News*, December 19, 1938.

37.  "Resume," 108–109.

38.  MMM, April 16, 1939; and *CIO News*, April 10, 1939.

39.  Haferbecker, *Wisconsin Labor Laws*, 165–166; Edwin Witte, "Observations on . . . the Wisconsin Labor Relations Act," Box 196, Edwin Witte Papers, SHSW; Paul W. Glad, *The History of Wisconsin*, vol. 5 (Madison, 1990), pp. 536–537; and Ozanne, *Labor Movement*, 138–142.

40.  Haferbecker, *Wisconsin Labor Laws*, 166–167; "WLRA Clippings," passim; and Witte, "Observations."

41.  Haferbecker, *Wisconsin Labor Laws*, 166–167; "WLRA Clippings," passim; and "Harold Story: Biographical Notes, November 11, 1947," Box 2, HWSC.

42.  "WLRA Clippings," passim; and Haferbecker, *Wisconsin Labor Laws*, 166–169.

43.  Haferbecker, *Wisconsin Labor Laws*, 166–167. On active and inactive union members, see C. Wright Mills, *The New Men of Power: America's Labor Leaders* (New York, 1948), 36–38.

44.  Witte, "Observations."

45.  Charles B. Coates, "Drive for Closed Shop Is On," *Factory Management and Maintenance* 97 (August 1939): 30–32; MMM, November 19, March 19, and April 16, 1939; and MSCM, April 18 and May 2, 1939.

46.  MMM, March 19 and April 16 and 30, 1939; MSCM, April 18 and May 2, 9, and 15, 1939; and Carl Gill, Final Report, c. June 17, 1939, File No. 199–3681, RG 280.

47.  Gill, Final Report, c. June 17, 1939, Carl Gill to J. R. Steelman, June 19, 1939, and Carl Gill, Progress Report, May 25, 1939, File No. 199–3681, RG 280.

48.  O. A. Jirikowic to William Watson, June 3, 1939, IAM Papers.

49.  *MJ*, June 8, 1939.

50.  *MJ*, June 12, 1939; Gill, Final Report, c. June 17, 1939; and Gill to Steelman, June 19, 1939.

51.  *MJ*, June 13, 1939.

52.  Ibid., June 13, 14, and 15, 1939; Gill, Final Report, c. June 17, 1939; and Gill to Steelman, June 19, 1939.

53.  *MJ*, June 15, 1939; and Gill, Progress Report, May 26, 1939.

54.  Carl Gill to J. R. Steelman, June 12, 1939, File No. 199–3681; Gill, Final Report, c. June 17, 1939; Gill to Steelman, June 19, 1939; and *MJ*, June 18, 1939.

55.  "Resume," 123 and 125; and LAC Rulings, 166 and 167.

56.  "Resume," 124–125.

57.  Ibid., 129–130.

58.  Ibid., 131–132.

59.  J. F. Friedrick to John P. Frey, January 22, 1940, Box 1, IAM Dist 10 Papers.

60.  Ibid.

61.  O. A. Jirikowic to Joseph A. Padway, April 18, 1940, Box 1, IAM Dist. 10 Papers.

62.  MSCM, March 3 and 23, 1940; and MMM, March 26, 1940.

63.  "Resume," 139–143.

64.  MSCM, May 26, 1940; MMM, May 14, 1940; and John Leucke, Progress Report, April 18, 1940, File No. 199–3681A, RG 280.

65.  Leucke, Progress Report, April 22 and 23, 1940, and Final Report, April 29, 1940; and *CIO News*, May 6, 1940.

66.  Leucke, Progress Report, April 22 and 1940, and Final Report, April 29, 1940; and MMM, April 14, 1940. For the continuing factional strife in the West Allis plant, see MMM, May 28, June 8, August 18, and October 13, 1940, and MEBM, August 15, September 19, and October 7, 1940.

67.  Charles Heymanns, Report, August 31, 1940; and David Sigman, Report, September 7 and 30 and October 14, 1940, Box 5, WSFLP.

68. Sigman, Report, October 19, 1940.
69. Ibid., October 28, 1940; and David Sigman and Jacob Friedrick, FTC Organizational Letter, October 25, 1940, Box "Allis-Chalmers Pamphlets," MPL.
70. MMM, October 29, 1940.
71. *MJ*, March 20, 1941.
72. *MJ*, March 20, 1940; O. A. Jirikowic to Max Babb, October 31, 1940, and Max Babb to O. A. Jirikowic, November 6, 1940, Box 1, IAM Dist. 10 Papers.
73. *MJ*, March 20, 1940; Jirikowic to Babb, October 31, 1940; Babb to Jirikowic, November 6, 1940; and Grievances Nos. 550 and 557, "Subject Index of Grievances," Box 1, DDLP.
74. *CIO News*, December 30, 1940.
75. Ibid.; and Lloyd Garrison, Union Grievance No. 2, 6, 5, and 7, Box 11, UAW Local 248 Papers.
76. "Statement of Michael Bohacheff, October 29, 1941," IAM Papers.
77. O. A. Jirikowic to Max Babb, December 30, 1940, Box 1, IAM Dist. 10 Papers; *CIO News*, December 30, 1940, January 6 and 13, 1941; James P. Holmes to J. R. Steelman, December 21, 1940; and James P. Holmes, Preliminary Report, January 1, 1941, and Progress Report, January 6, 1941, File No. 196–4072, RG 280; and MEBM, December 30, 1940.
78. Holmes to Steelman, December 21, 1940.
79. Ibid.
80. Ibid.
81. Union flyer, "Meeting on Hit and Run Case," December 26, 1940, William Watson, Notice, December 27, 1940; and Harold Christoffel to Governor Julius Heil, December 26, 1940, Box 1, IAM Dist. 10 Papers.
82. MEBM, December 30, 1940; and Harold Christoffel to Max Babb, January 2, 1941, Box 1, IAM Dist. 10 Papers.
83. MSCM, January 5, 1941; and *CIO News*, January 13, 1941.
84. *MJ*, January 9 and 19, 1941.
85. Ibid., January 20 and 22, 1941; UAW Local 248 to All Allis-Chalmers Workers, January 22, 1941; and Union flyer, "The Allis-Chalmers Strike"; and Frances J. Haas, Progress Report, January 24, 25, and 26, 1941, File No. 196–4072, RG 280.
86. *MJ*, January 22, 1941.
87. Ibid.
88. Ibid., January 23, 24, 25, and 27, and February 2, 6, and 8, 1941; and Haas, Progress Report, February 5, 1941.
89. Clare Hoffman, Speech, *Congressional Record: House of Representatives*, January 29, 1941, pp. 353, 354; and *MJ*, February 1 and 14, 1941.
90. E. J. Cunningham, Memo, February 1, 1941 and Memo for the Record, February 1, 1941; and James P. Holmes to John R. Steelman, February 3, 1941, F. 196–4972, RG 280; Haas, Progress Report, February 5, 1941; and *MJ*, February 3, 1941.
91. *MJ*, February 9, 1941.
92. Ibid., February 11, 1941.
93. Haas, Progress Report, February 11 and 13, 1941; and *MJ*, February 12, 1941.
94. "Washington Agreement," no date, F. 196–4072, RG 280.
95. Ibid.
96. Haas, Progress Report, February 15, 1941; and Hillman Statement, February 15, 1941, F. 196–4072, Rg 280.
97. Haas, Progress Report, February 17–23, 1941; Cunningham, Memo for the Record, February 19, 1941; Holmes to Steelman, February 21, 1941; and *MJ*, February 17, 1941.
98. Haas, Progress Report, February 24, 1941; and Max Babb to All Allis-Chalmers Workers, February 27, 1941, Box 1, IAM Dist. 10 Papers.

99.   Haas, Progress Report, February 28 and March 1–3, 1941.

100.   Ibid., March 5 and 8, 1941; and *CIO News*, March 10, 1941.

101.   Haas, Progress Report, March 5 and 8, 1941.

102.   *MJ*, March 13, 1941; and *CIO News*, March 17, 1941.

103.   *MJ*, March 13, 1941; and *CIO News*, March 17, 1941.

104.   *MJ*, February 17, 1941, and March 23 and 25, 1941; *CIO News*, March 24, 1941; and Haas, Progress Report, March 18, 1941.

105.   Otto A. Jirikowic to H. W. Brown, February 11, 1941; Meeting Announcement, February 24, 1941, Box 1, IAM Dist. 10 Papers; and anonymous worker's letter cited in Hoffman speech, January 29, 1941, p. 352.

106.   Robert W. Ozanne, *A Century of Labor Management Relations at McCormick and International Harvester* (Madison, 1967), 198–203; and *MJ*, March 23 and 24, 1941.

107.   *MJ*, March 18 and 25, 1941.

108.   Ibid., March 26, 1941; Haas, Progress Report, March 25 and 26, 1941; and Telegram, William Knudsen and Frank Knox to Max Babb, March 26, 1941; Telegram, Max Babb to Each Employee, March 27, 1941, and Telegram, Harold Story to John R. Steelman, March 27, 1941, F. 196–4072, RG 280.

109.   J. F. Friedrick, David Sigman, and O. A. Jirikowic to the Allis-Chalmers Employees, March 26, 1941, and O. A. Jirikowic to H. W. Brown, March 27, 1941, Box 1, IAM Dist. 10 Papers; and *MJ*, March 26, 1941.

110.   *MJ*, March 27 and 28, 1941; and *CIO News*, March 31, 1941.

111.   *MJ*, March 27, 1941.

112.   Ibid., March 28 and 30, 1941.

113.   Ibid., March 30, 1941.

114.   Ibid., March 28, 30, and 31, 1941; and *CIO News*, April 7, 1941.

115.   *MJ*, April 1, 1941; *CIO News*, April 7, 1941; and Cunningham, Memo for the Record, April 1, 1941.

116.   J. Edgar Hoover to Major General Edwin M. Watson, March 27, 1941, and April 1, 1941, Box 13, Office Files 407B, FDRL.

117.   Telegram, Julius P. Heil to the president, April 2, 1941, Box 13, Office Files 407B, FRDL.

118.   Final Report, September 9, 1941, File No. 196–4072; RG 280 and Transcript, "National Defense Mediation Board, April 5–6, 1941," Box 31, RG 202.

119.   "National Defense Mediation Board, April 5–6, 1941," 28–29.

120.   Ibid., 30–31.

121.   Ibid., 33–36 and 42.

122.   "The Company will maintain discipline," n.d.; "Hillman Statement," February 15, 1941; and "O.P.M. Formula for Settlement of Allis-Chalmers Dispute," n.d., File No. 196–4072A, RG 280 and NDMB; "Case No. 6, Allis-Chalmers Manufacturing Company and United Automobile Workers, C.I.O," n.d., Box 532, Series 6, RG 202.

123.   Telegram, Harold Story to Frances Perkins, April 10, 1941, F. 196–4072A, RG 280.

124.   Ibid.

125.   Ibid., April 15, 1941, F. 196–4072A, RG 280.

126.   Holmes, Progress Report, January 6 and 8, 1941; Cunningham, Memorandum for the Record, January 30, 1941; and Memorandum, Thomas F. Burns to Sidney Hillman, March 8, 1941, FJHP.

## CHAPTER 5. Challenging Management Rights

1.    Florence Peterson, "Settlement of Grievances under Union Agreements," *Monthly Labor Review* (February 1940), 3–4; French, *Shop Committee*, 9–10 and 61–62; and ACMC,

*Works Council*, passim; Al Nash, *The Union Steward: Duties, Rights, Status* (Ithaca, 1983), 1–4.
2.    Merlin D. Bishop, *Duties of the Shop Steward* (Detroit, 1937), 1–2.
3.    Workers Education Bureau, *The Shop Steward: An Outline of His Work in the Union* (New York, 1935), 2; and Bishop, *Shop Steward*, 5–6.
4.    Bishop, *Shop Steward*, 5, and 7–8.
5.    *United Automobile Worker*, November 12, 1938, Bishop, *Shop Steward*, 6; and J. H. Wishart, *How to Win with the Union* ([Detroit], [c. 1940]), 19.
6.    Frank Bolka, "NLRB Testimony," July 16, 1937, 752; Otto A. Jirikowic to Max Babb, August 14, 1935; Max Babb, "Rulings Relative to Company's Statement of Policy," July 13, 1936; Harold Christoffel to Max Babb, December 8, 1936, Box 1, IAM Dist. 10 Papers; MMM, August 18, September 12, October 1, October 30, and November 10, 1936; MEBM, October 21, 1936.
7.    MEBM, January 18 and 25, 1937; and MSCM, February 21 and March 9, 1937.
8.    Blunk, "NLRB Testimony," July 22, 1937, 1512–1513.
9.    Ibid., 1513.
10.    "Agreement, 1937."
11.    Wishart, *How to Win*, 8–9.
12.    Christoffel, "NLRB Testimony," 1937, 378, and 395–396; "WLRA Clippings," passim; and Gavett, "Development of Labor Movement, 331–335.
13.    Michael Boblin, "NLRB Testimony," July 20, 1937, p. 998; and Harold Schuelke, "NLRB Testimony," July 20, 1937, p. 1079.
14.    Walter Miller, "NLRB Testimony," July 20, 1938, 1111–1113, 1126.
15.    Blunk, "NLRB Testimony," 1513, 1514.
16.    *ACWU News*, September 30, 1937.
17.    Blunk, "NLRB Testimony," 1555, 1515–1516, and 1555.
18.    Neil W. Chamberlain, *The Union Challenge to Management Control* (New York, 1948); Howell John Harris, *The Right to Manage: Industrial Relations Policies of American Business in the 1940s* (Madison, 1982); James B. Atelson, *Values and Assumptions in American Labor Law* (Amherst, 1983), 111–135; Brody, *Workers in Industrial America*, 177–181, 197–203, 206.
19.    LAC Ruling nos. 1–194; and "Subject Index of Grievance Rulings, 1–2,500," Box 1, DDLP.
20.    LAC Ruling nos. 1–16.
21.    Ibid., nos. 12, 14, 8, 18, 18, 20, 23, 35, 37, and 39.
22.    Ibid., no. 43.
23.    "Subject Index."
24.    Julius Blunk to Mr. Seehafer, January 31, 1938, and Julius Blunk to George Nordstrom, February 2, 1938, F. General Correspondence, 1938, Box 1, UAW Local 248 Papers.
25.    LAC Ruling nos. 70–75.
26.    Ibid., nos. 87–95.
27.    Ibid., no. 138.
28.    Ibid., no. 177.
29.    Peterson, *Industrial Heritage*, 242, 244–245, 263–263, and 272–273; Allis-Chalmers Workers' Union to United Automobile Workers of America, October 29, 1937, F. International Union, 1937–1938, Box 1, UAW Local 248 Papers; and LAC Ruling nos. 63 and 59.
30.    H. E. Ladwig to Harold Christoffel, March 1938, LAC Ruling no. 63.
31.    *Forward with Local 248 UAW-CIO* (West Allis, c. 1940) in Vertical File: UAW Locals, ALHUA.
32.    Ibid.
33.    Ibid.

34.   Don D. Lescohier, "The Closed Shop and Seniority," pp. 28a, 67a, and 76–77, Box 1, DDLP.

35.   Lloyd Garrison, "Union Grievance," No. 3, FJHP; O. J. Jirikowic to H. W. Brown, March 27, 1947; H. F. Nickerson to H. W. Brown, September 15, 1941; H. W. Brown to O. J. Jirikowic, July 20, 1941, IAM Papers; MEBM, April 28, 1941; and James P. Holmes, Progress Report, April 16, 1941, File No. 196–4072A, RG 280.

36.   Garrison, "Union Grievance," Nos. 1 and 3.

37.   Ibid., No. 3.

38.   Ibid., No. 3.

39.   Nelson Lichtenstein, *Labor's War at Home: The CIO in World War II* (New York, 1987), 73.

40.   Alberta Price Johnson, "From Mill Stones to Atom Smashers," vol. 4, pt. 1, unpublished manuscript, 5 and 125, Box 1, ACMCC (Peterson); Hugo Liebert, "NLRB Testimony," July 13, 1937, 301–304; James M. Holmes, Preliminary Report, December 18, 1941, File No. 196–8341, RG 280; "NWLB Statement," 17; and ACMC, *Women: Safe at Work at Allis-Chalmers* ([West Allis], 1942), 3 and 20–24. See also *We of Allis-Chalmers*, vol. 3 (April and October 1943); and *Supercharger News*, July 23 and November 24, 1944.

41.   John E. Johnson to G. L. Patterson, Memorandum, July 11, 1942, Case No. R-4131, NLRB Case Files, RG 25; Harold Christoffel to Richard Frankenstein, May 11, 1943, F. International Union, 1943, Box 2, UAW Local 248 Papers; and James A. Despins, Final Report, September 26, 1944, Case No. 445–4479, RG 280.

42.   Johnson, "Mill Stones," 132, 130, 135, and 136.

43.   Ibid., 130–131, 133–134, 282, and 284; and ACMC, *Recreation* ([West Allis], 1945).

44.   ACMC, *Women*, 1.

45.   Ruth Milkman, *Gender at Work: The Dynamics of Job Segregation by Sex during World War II* (Urbana, 1987), 4–7; and ACMC, *Women*, 14.

46.   ACMC, *Women*, 10 and 15; and Johnson, "Mill Stones," 133.

47.   ACMC, *Women*, 1 and 6.

48.   *CIO News*, October 26, 1942, and November 16, 1942.

49.   Joe William Trotter, *Black Milwaukee: The Making of an Industrial Proletariat, 1915–1945* (Urbana, 1985), 149 and 150.

50.   Ibid., 164, 170, and 167.

51.   Johnson, "Mill Stones," 5, 400, and 282; *We of Allis-Chalmers*, vol. 5 (October 1945); and *CIO News*, February 5, 12, and 26 and June 18, 1945.

52.   Julius Blunk to James H. Sieg, July 10, 1937, F. District Council, 1937–1938, Box 1, UAW Local 248 Papers; and Trotter, *Black Milwaukee*, 175.

53.   MMM, September 14, 1941; MEBM, December 2, 1941; Harold Christoffel to R. J. Thomas, June 16, 1943, F. Int'l U 1943; and Harold Christoffel to Supercharger News, July 19, 1943, F. General Correspondence, 1943, Box 2, UAW Local 248 Papers.

54.   Trotter, *Black Milwaukee*, 173 and 165–175.

55.   Treleven, "Christoffel Interview"; and Fred McStroul, "NWLB Hearing," February 12, 1945, 64, Box 11, UAW Local 248 Papers.

56.   Lee H. Hill, *Developing a National Labor Policy* (New York, 1945); Lee H. Hill and Charles R. Hook, *Management at the Bargaining Table* (New York, 1945); and Lee H. Hill, *Pattern for Good Labor Relations* (New York, 1947).

57.   Arthur K. Brintnall, "How Our Discipline Control Board Dispenses Justice," *Factory Management and Maintenance* 101 (October 1943): 104–105; and ACMC, *A Word . . . on the Discipline Control Board* (West Allis, no date), passim.

58.   Lee Hill, "NWLB Hearing," February 13, 1945, 191 Box 11, UAW Local 248 Papers; and "Agreement, 1943."

59.   Hill, "NWLB Hearing," February 13, 1945, p. 162; and Brintnall, "Discipline Control Board," 104–105.

60. Brintnall, 104–105.

61. ACMC, *Discipline Control Board*, 7.

62. For the photograph, see Brintnall, "Discipline Control Board," 104–105.

63. ACMC, *Discipline Control Board*, 2; and "NWLB Statement," 17.

64. ACMC, *Discipline Control Board*, 3–4.

65. Ibid., 4–5.

66. "Agreement, 1943"; and ACMC, *Discipline Control Board*, 5 and 6.

67. ACMC, *Discipline Control Board*, 6–7.

68. Brody, *Workers in Industrial America*, 201–208; and Lichtenstein, *Labor's War at Home*, 178–181.

69. Sumner H. Slichter, *Union Policies and Industrial Management* (Washington, 1941), 1 and 578.

70. Joel Seidman, *American Labor from Defense to Reconversion* (Chicago, 1953), 80–81; and Lichtenstein, *Labor's War at Home*, 71.

71. Lichtenstein, *Labor's War at Home*, 51, 71.

72. NWLB, "Case No. 211," March 30, 1943 *War Labor Reports* 7 (1943): 312–315, 302; John F. Eaton, "Daily Report of Hearings," July 8 and 10, 1942; "Memorandum for the Panel," July 6, 1942, F. 2338-AC (#)2, Box 142; and "Union Brief," F. 2338, Box 144, RG 202.

73. "NWLB Statement," 36, 40–53.

74. Ibid., 54–67.

75. NWLB, "Case No. 211," March 30, 1942, pp. 321, 325, 349, 299–300, 300–302; and NWLB, "Public Hearing," February 5, 1943, F. 2338, Box 678, RG 202.

76. NWLB, Case No. 211, March 30, 1942, pp. 301 and 300.

77. NWLB, Case No. 211, March 30, 1942, p. 325; and William H. Spohn, "Referee Decision No. 109," Box 11, UAW Local 248 Papers.

78. *CIO News*, June 15, 1942.

79. Ibid.

80. Ibid.

81. Ibid., August 3, 1942.

82. "NWLB Document," 203.

83. Ibid., 204–205.

84. *CIO News*, January 18, 1943.

85. Industrial Relations Review Board, "Review of Grievance No. 1823," January 6, 1942, Box 11, UAW Local 248 Papers.

86. Ibid.

87. Leo Teplow, "Review of Grievance No. 1897," December 30, 1942, Box 11, UAW Local 248 Papers.

88. Walter T. Fisher, "Referee Decision—Grievance No. 58: Stoppage in the Brass Foundry," January 26, 1943, Box 11, UAW Local 248 Papers.

89. Ibid.; and *CIO News*, January 18, 1943.

90. Fisher, "Referee Decision—Grievance No. 58."

91. Ibid.; and *CIO News*, January 18, 1943.

92. Fisher, "Grievance No. 56," January 18, 1943.

93. Fisher, "Referee Decision—Grievance No. 57," January 29, 1943.

94. Fisher, "Referee Decision—Grievance No. 58."

95. Ibid.; and "Supplementary Decision by Referee in Grievance No. 58," January 26, 1943.

96. *CIO News*, January 25, 1943.

97. *CIO News*, February 1, 15, and 22, 1943; and MSCM, February 2, 1943.

98. "Union Brief," F. Resignation of Referee and F. Spohn Preliminaries, Box 11, UAW Local 248 Papers.

99. Spohn Referee Decisions in Box 11, UAW Local 248 Papers.

100. Spohn, "Referee Decision No. 67."
101. Spohn, "Referee Decision No. 93."
102. Spohn, "Referee Decision No. 48."
103. Garrison, "Decision Number 49," Box 11, UAW Local 248 Papers.
104. "Conciliation Proceedings," June 3, 1946, pp. 56, 80–81, Box 6, UAW Local 248 Papers.
105. Spohn, "Referee Decision No. 86."
106. Ibid.
107. "NWLB Statement," 18.
108. Ibid., 18–20.
109. Spohn, "Referee Decision No. 104."
110. Ibid.
111. NWLB, "Transcript of Proceedings," February 13, 1945; "Conciliation Negotiations," June 20, 1946, Box 6, UAW Local 248 Papers; "Appendix B, National War Labor Board Report and Recommendation," c. December 1945, Case No. 111–9878D, RG 202; Union Notes, Negotiations, March 19, 1946, F. Conciliation, M-A, Box 12, UAW Local 248 Papers.
112. Sid Lens, "The Meaning of the Grievance Procedure," *Harvard Business Review* 26 (November 1948): 713.
113. Ibid., 716 and 718.
114. Ibid., 721.

## CHAPTER 6. The Unmaking of Militant Unionism I

1. MMM, January 11, February 8, March 14, April 11, May 9, 1944; MSCM, February 1, February 15, April 18, 1944; "Official Ballot for Executive Officers" and "To the Allis-Chalmers Workers' Union Local # 248," February 21, 1944, F. 1944—Election Committee, Box 3, UAW Local 248 Papers; Alvin Tarman to R. J. Thomas, November 26, 1944; Harold Christoffel to Alvin Tarman, May 17, 1944, F. 15; and F. 14, Box 76B, GAP.
2. MMM, May 9, 1944; Tarman to Thomas, November 26, 1944; and Christoffel to Tarman, May 17, 1944.
3. Tarman to Thomas, November 26, 1944; and Petition to Robert Buse, June 3, 1944, F. 15, Box 76B, GAP.
4. MSCM, June 13, 1944; MMM, June 13 and July 11, 1944; and Tarman to Thomas, November 26, 1944.
5. Tarman to Thomas, November 26, 1944; and MMM, August 8, 1944.
6. Arthur H. Pearson, Progress Report, March 30, 1944, and May 2, 1944, File No. 445–1466, RG 280.
7. *CIO News*, July 17, 1944.
8. Ibid.
9. NWLB, Recommendation, Case No. 111–9878-D [December 19, 1945], F. War Labor Board, Box 12, UAW Local 248 Papers.
10. NWLB, Recommendation [December 1945].
11. NWLB, "Dissenting Opinion of Industry Member," Case No. 111-9878-D, December 19, 1945, File No. 111-9878-D, Box 3222, RG 202.
12. Seidman, *American Labor*, 217–218.
13. UAW Research Department, "Allis-Chalmers Manufacturing Company," August 23, 1946, F. Leaflets, Letters, 1946–1947, Box 3, Local 248 Papers. For other accounts of the 1946–1947 strike, see Cochran, *Labor and Communism*, 272–275; Keeran, *Communist Party*, 266–278, and Halpern, *UAW Politics*, 173–183.

14. UAW Research Department, "Allis-Chalmers."
15. Ibid.
16. Walter Geist to "All the Men and Women of Allis-Chalmers," January 23, 1946, Box 1, DDLP.
17. Spohn, "Referee Decision No. 107."
18. Ibid.
19. Ibid.
20. Spohn, "Referee Decision No. 116"; and *CIO News*, February 8, 1946.
21. Spohn, "Referee Decision No. 116."
22. Ibid.
23. *CIO News*, February 8, 1946.
24. Robert Buse, "NWLB Hearing," January 15, 1945, p. 85; and February 13, 1945, pp. 122 and 147.
25. Hill and Hook, *Management*, 60, 73, and 219.
26. Walter Geist to "ALL THE MEN AND WOMEN OF ALLIS-CHALMERS," February 11, 1946, DDLP.
27. Ibid.
28. Geist to Allis-Chalmers Workers' Union, February 25, 1946; Geist to "ALL EM-PLOYES OF THE WEST ALLIS WORKS," March 5, 1946; and Geist to "ALL THE MEN AND WOMEN OF ALLIS-CHALMERS," March 21, 1946, Box 1, DDLP; and F. Conciliation, M-A, Box 12, UAW Local 248 Papers.
29. Robert Buse to Allis-Chalmers Workers and Their Families, c. April 24, 1946, F. Leaflets, Ads, Etc., Box 3, Local 248 Papers.
30. *MJ*, April 29, 1946.
31. Ibid.
32. Ibid., April 29 and 30, 1946.
33. Ibid., April 30, 1946; and Robert Buse, "Union Statement on the Strike," F. 7, Box 37, WPRP.
34. *MJ*, April 30 and May 1, 1946.
35. Ibid., May 1, 1946.
36. Ibid.
37. Ibid., May 3 and 4, 1946.
38. Undated clipping, JWGP.
39. Telegram, Walter Geist to Lewis B. Schwellenbach, May 30, 1946, JWGP.
40. Walter Geist to Lewis B. Schwellenbach, May 31, 1946, JWGP.
41. Lewis B. Schwellenbach to Harold D. Smith, June 4, 1946; and Lewis B. Schwellenbach to the president, June 4, 1946, JWGP.
42. "Conciliation Negotiations, June-July," Box 6, UAW Local 248 Papers.
43. *MJ*, June 19, 1946; and Telegram, Walter Geist to Lewis B. Schwellenbach, June 17, 1946, JWGP.
44. Draft Press Release, "President Orders Seizure of Farm Implement Plants," c. June 21, 1946; and Arthur Krock, *New York Times*, c. July 10, 1946, JWGP.
45. Frank R. Kent, *Evening Star*, July 29, 1946, JWGP.
46. *MJ*, August 12, 1946.
47. Chester Manly, *Chicago Tribune*, c. August 13, 1987, JWGP.
48. Walter Geist to "All Employees at West Allis Works," August 5, 1946, Box 1, DDLP.
49. Brody, *Workers in Industrial America*, 217–226; and James C. Foster, *The Union Politic: The CIO Political Action Committee* (Columbia, Mo., 1975), 66–94.
50. Thomas C. Reeves, *The Life and Times of Joseph McCarthy: A Biography* (New York, 1982), 69–108; David M. Oshinsky, *Senator Joseph McCarthy and the Labor Movement* (Kansas City, 1976), 1–33; and William F. Thompson, *The History of Wisconsin*, vol. 6 (Madison, 1988), pp. 449–466.

51.    Reeves, *McCarthy*, passim.; Oshinsky *McCarthy*, passim.; and Thompson, *Wisconsin*, passim.

52.    Reeves, *McCarthy*, passim.; Oshinsky *McCarthy*, passim.; and Thompson, *Wisconsin*, passim.

53.    *CIO News*, August 2, 1946.

54.    *MJ*, August 14 and 15, 1946; and *Daily Picket*, August 9, 15, 22, and 24, 1946.

55.    *MJ*, August 14, 1946; and *CIO News*, August 16, 1946.

56.    *MJ*, August 16, 1946; and Thaddeus Wasiliewski to Regina and Gene Wasielewski, August 16, 1946, F. Correspondence, 1946, Box 1, Thaddeus F. B. Wasielewski Papers, MARC.

57.    Swofford Affidavit, 7–8; Pat Greathouse to Walter Reuther, June 14, 1946, and c. August 3, 1946; and "Policy Statement of UAW-CIO Progressive Caucus of Region #4," F. 1, Box 212, WPRP.

58.    Swofford Affidavit, 8.

59.    *MS*, September 2, 1946.

60.    *MJ*, September 5, 1946.

61.    *MS*, September 19, 1946.

62.    *MJ*, September 22, 1946.

63.    Ibid., September 23 and 24, 1946.

64.    See front-page articles in *MS*, September 23-November 21, 1946; and Swofford Affidavit, 7–10.

65.    *MS*, September 23 and 24, 1946.

66.    Ibid., September 25, 1946.

67.    ACMC, *Principle Represented: Communist* ([West Allis], [1946]).

68.    Buse, *HELC Hearings*, 1986; and Treleven, "Eisenscher Interview."

69.    Joseph Mattson to Walter Reuther, October 9, 1946, F. 8, Box 36, WPRP.

70.    Ibid.

71.    Leon Venne, *HUAC Hearings*, pp. 33, 37, and 40–41.

72.    Ibid., 45.

73.    Ibid., 45; and *MJ*, October 7, 1946.

74.    Telegrams, Leon Venne to Walter Reuther and Philip Murray, October 8, 1946, F. 8, Box 36, WPRP.

75.    *MS*, October 12, 1946.

76.    *MJ*, October 14, 1946; Venne to Reuther, November 8, 1946; and Venne to Local 248 UAWA, CIO, November 4, 1946, F. 9, Box 36, WPRP.

77.    *MJ*, October 9 and 10, 1946; and Gavett, *Labor Movement*, 185–189.

78.    *MJ*, October, 9, 10, 1946, 11, and 14, 1946; and *MS*, October 14, 1946.

79.    *MJ*, October 16, 1946.

80.    Ibid., October 17, 1946.

81.    Ibid.

82.    Ibid.

83.    Ibid., October 18, 1946.

84.    Thaddeus Wasielewski to Regina and Gene Wasielewski, April 16, 1946; *MJ*, August 21 and 23, 1946; and *Labor Views* (August 1946).

85.    *MJ*, August 16, 1946.

86.    Ibid., August 25, 1946.

87.    Ibid., September 13, 1946.

88.    Ibid., September 14, 1946.

89.    Ibid., September 14, 16, and 17, 1946.

90.    Ibid., September 25, 1946.

91.    Ibid., September 29 and 30, 1946.

92.    Ibid., October 2, 3, 5, and 6, 1946.

93.    Ibid., October 6, 15, and 16, 1946.

94.   *MS*, October 24, 1946.
95.   Ibid., October 24, 1946.
96.   *MJ*, October 17, 1946; and Kersten Campaign Literature, Box 1 Series 4, Charles J. Kersten Papers, Marquette University.
97.   *MJ*, October 18, 23, and 25, and November 3, 1946.
98.   Ibid., October 25, 1946.
99.   *MS*, October 7, 1946.
100.  *MJ*, October 28, 1946.
101.  Ibid.
102.  Ibid.
103.  Ibid., October 29, 30, and 31, 1946.
104.  Ibid., October 29, 1946.
105.  Ibid., October 31, 1946.
106.  Ibid., November 1, 1946.
107.  Ibid.
108.  Ibid., November 1 and 4, 1946.
109.  Ibid., November 4, 1946.
110.  Ibid., November 1 and 3, 1946.
111.  *MS*, November 11, 1946; and *MJ*, November 6, 1946.
112.  *MS*, November 11, 1946; and *MJ*, November 6, 1946.
113.  *MJ*, November 6, 1946.
114.  Ibid., November 6, 1946; and William G. Rice to Lewis B Schwellenbach, March 17, 1947, Box 183, RG 174.
115.  *MJ*, November 6, 1946.
116.  Ibid., November 13, 1946.

## CHAPTER 7. The Unmaking of Militant Unionism II

1.    Telegram, L. B. Schwellenbach to Walter Geist and Robert Buse, November 1, 1946; and Telegram, Walter Geist to Lewis B. Schwellenbach, November 2, 1946, Box 171, RG 174.
2.    George Addes and Joseph Mattson to All UAW-CIO Local Union Executive Boards and Members, November 4, 1946; Box "UAW Brochures, Newspaper Articles," MPL.
3.    [George Addes],"[N]otes from Nov 6 1946 [P]olicy [C]ommittee [M]eeting, not previously typed up" and "Policy Committee Meeting—Wednesday, November 6," F. 9, Box 36, WPRP; UAW Public Relations Department, Press Release, November 7, 1946, F. 18, Box 68, Donald Montgomery Papers, ALHUA; and *MJ*, November 8, 1946.
4.    John Barnard, *Reuther*, 109–113; and Jack Stieber, *Governing*, 7–13.
5.    Barnard, *Reuther*, 111–112; and Stieber, *Governing*, 10–11.
6.    Barnard, *Reuther*, 112–113; and Stieber, *Governing*, 10–11.
7.    *CIO News*, November 19, 1946.
8.    Ibid., November 22, 1946; and *MJ*, November 20 and 21, 1946.
9.    *MJ*, November 22 and 25, 1946; and *CIO News*, November 29, 1946.
10.   *MJ*, December 9, 1946; and Walter Cappel, Press Release, December 7, 1947, F. 10, Box 36, WPRP.
11.   *MJ*, December 11, 1946 and Local 248 Press Release (c. December 11, 1946), F. Press Releases, Box 3, UAW Local 248 Papers.
12.   *MJ*, December 11, 12, and 13, 1946; and Local 248 Press Release.

13.   *MJ*, December 13, 1946; *MS*, December 14, 1946; "Proceedings: Ninth Annual Convention: Wisconsin State Industrial Union Council," December 13–15, 1946, MARC.

14.   *MJ*, December 14 and 15, 1946; 1946; *MS*, December 14 and 15, 1946; John Brophy, *A Miner's Life* (Madison, 1964), 290–291; and Ozanne, *Labor Movement*, 90–94.

15.   Thomas, "WSIUC Proceedings," December 15, 1946; *MS*, December 14 and 16, 1946; and *MJ*, December 14 and 16, 1946.

16.   *MS*, December 16, 1946.

17.   *MJ*, December 16, 1946; and *MS*, December 16, 1946.

18.   *MJ*, December 16, 1946 and January 13, 1947; and *MS*, December 16, 1946.

19.   Walter Geist to All the Men and Women of Allis-Chalmers, December 19, 1946, Box 1, DDLP.

20.   Robert Buse to Members of Local 248, December 24, 1946, F. Local 248, Box 4, UAW Local 248 Papers.

21.   Walter Petersen, *HUAC Hearings*, 52–54; Walter Petersen to Walter Reuther, December 5, 1946, F. 11, Box 36, WPRP; and *MJ*, November 20, 1947.

22.   Petersen to Reuther, December 5, 1946.

23.   *MJ*, December 11 and 13, 1946, and January 10, 1947.

24.   Ibid., January 11, 1946.

25.   *MS*, January 20, 1947; and R. J. Thomas to Walter Reuther, January 26, 1947, F. 13, Box, 36, WPRP.

26.   Thomas to Reuther, January 26, 1947; *MS*, January 21, 22, and 24, 1947; and *MJ*, January 23 and 25, 1947; Walter Reuther to R. J. Thomas, undated copy, John Brophy to Walter Reuther, January 31, 1947, F. 13, and Ensworth Reisner to Walter Reuther, February 4, 1947, F. 9, Box 36, WPRP; and "EXHIBIT NO. 2 . . ," undated, F. 8, Box 10, R. J. Thomas Papers, ALHUA.

27.   *MS*, January 22–25, 1947; and *MJ*, January 23, 24, and 25, 1947.

28.   *MJ*, January 26, 1947.

29.   Ibid.

30.   Ibid.

31.   Ibid., January 27, 1947; and *MS*, January 27, 1947.

32.   *MJ*, January 27, 1947.

33.   *MS*, January 28, 1947; Thomas to Reuther, January 26, 1946; Reuther to Thomas, undated.

34.   Reuther to Thomas, undated; and Walter Reuther to All Local Unions, UAW-CIO, January 28, 1947, F. 13, Box, 36, WPRP.

35.   Reuther to Thomas, undated.

36.   Ibid.

37.   [Walter Reuther to UAW Executive Board,] Draft letter, undated, F. 13, Box 36, WPRP.

38.   Ibid.

39.   Ibid.

40.   Stieber, *Governing*, 10–14; and Barnard, *Reuther*, 113–117.

41.   R. Alton Lee, *Truman and Taft-Hartley* (Lexington, Ky., 1966); Story, "Oral Statement"; Story et al., *HELC Hearings*, vol. 3, 1335–1487; and ACMC, *Joint Statement* ([West Allis], [1947]).

42.   Story, *HELC Hearings*, 1337.

43.   Ibid., 1338.

44.   Ibid., 1337–1343.

45.   Ibid., 1343.

46.   Haagensen, *HELC Hearings*, 1344–1348; Ohrman, *HELC Hearings*, 1352 and 1353; Waddleton, *HELC Hearings*, 1356–1362; and Brintnall, *HELC Hearings*, 1369–1374.

47.   Story, *HELC Hearings*, 1375.

48. *Joint Statement*, 29–30.

49. Ibid., 30 and 31.

50. Leon E. Venne, *HUAC Hearings*, 34–37, 41–48; Walter Petersen, *HUAC Hearings*, pp. 50–51, 53–55, and Floyd D. Lucia, *HUAC Hearings*, 2–11, 20.

51. Treleven, "Christoffel Interview" and "Buse Interview"; and R. J. Thomas, Robert Buse, and Harold Christoffel, *HELC Hearings*, 2024–2047.

52. Buse, *HELC Hearings*, 1974.

53. Ibid., 1975–1976.

54. Ibid., 1982.

55. Treleven, "Buse Interview" and "Christoffel Interview"; and Buse, *HELC Hearings*, pp. 1982, 1984, and 1998–2001.

56. Christoffel, *HELC Hearings*, 2086–2101, 2104–2107.

57. Ibid., 2108–2111.

58. Ibid., 2112–2113 and 2115.

59. Ibid., 2123–2128.

60. Budenz, *HELC Hearings*, 3604, 3604–3605, and 3607–3608.

61. Ibid., 3610–3612.

62. Ibid., 3612, 3614, and 3615.

63. *MJ*, March 16, 1947.

64. Swofford Affidavit, 33 and 35.

65. Ibid., 28, 31, and 32.

66. HELC Subcommittee, "Congressional Hearing," March 17, 1947; "Swofford Affidavit," 24; and *MJ*, March 17–20, 1947.

67. *MJ*, March 20, 1947.

68. Ibid., March 21, 1947.

69. Ibid., March 18, 1947.

70. ACMC, "Memorandum No. 247," March 24, 1947, and "Report of the Bargaining Committee," March 23, 1947, F. 14, Box 36, WPRP.

71. "Report of the Bargaining Committee," March 23, 1947.

72. Ibid.

73. "Report of the Bargaining Committee," March 23, 1947; and ACMC, "Memorandum No. 247."

74. ACMC, "Memorandum No. 247"; and Max Raskin to General Counsel, National Labor Relations Board, July 18, 1950, F. 91, Box 8, UAW Local 248 Papers.

75. "Steward and Committeeman List of Local #248, UAW-CIO," c. December 1948, F. 91, Box 8, UAW Local 248 Papers.

76. Raskin to General Counsel, NLRB, July 18, 1950. For the signers of the Communist Party nomination papers, the names listed in the Raskin letter were compared to the names listed in the Allis-Chalmers pamphlet, *Principle Represented: Communist*.

77. Walter Geist, "The Allis-Chalmers Experience with a Left-Wing Union," *Factor Management and Maintenance* 105 (March 1947): 83.

78. Harold Christoffel to National Labor Relations Board, June 3, 1947; and Press Release, June 4, 1947, F. Press Releases, Box 3, UAW Local 248 Papers.

79. Press Release, June 4, 1947.

80. *MJ*, July 17, 1947; and "The CIO pays off," "50 Questions and Answers about Your Union," and "The Bad Penny Turns Up Again," F. Leaflets—NLRB Election 1947, Box 3, UAW Local 248 Papers.

81. "Yes, We Have Read It!" F. 9, Box 10, R. J. Thomas Papers, ALHUA; and "WHY WAS THE INDEPENDENT UNION FORMED?" F. 4, Box 1, Nat Ganley Papers, ALHUA.

82. *MJ*, July 17, 1947.

83. "Tally of Ballots," F. Local 248, Box 4, UAW Local 248 Papers; *MJ*, July 18, 1947; *MS*, July 18, 19, 1947; and Treleven, "Buse Interview."

84. "Regular Session, International Executive Board UAW CIO," December 1, 1947, MI, 600, 604, and 605, Box 1, UAW International Executive Board Papers, ALHUA.

85. "Regular Session," December 1, 1947, 614–617.

86. *MJ*, December 2, 1947; and International UAW Grievance Committee, "Case Number 6: Robert Buse, Harold Christoffel, et al. vs. Local Union 248," F. Charges Ulysses McQuittie, Box 3, UAW Local 248 Papers.

87. Walter Reuther, "Proceedings Wisconsin State Industrial Union Council Affiliated with C.I.O.," December 5–7, 1947, 342, MARC.

88. Ibid., 343–344.

89. "Agreement, 1948," F. Bargaining Negotiations, Box 4, UAW Local 248 Papers.

90. Ibid.

91. "Membership Meeting," Sunday, August 29, 1948, F. Membership Meeting, Box 3, UAW Local 248 Papers.

92. *MJ*, December 11, 20, 1948.

93. "Agreement, 1948–1949."

94. "Membership Meeting," February 6, 1949, F. Membership Meetings, 1949; and Charles Schultz and Tony Audia to Harry S. Truman, March 22, 1949, F. President of US, Box 3, UAW Local 248 Papers.

95. "Membership Meeting, September 7, 1949, Second Shift," F. Membership Meeting—1949 and Joint Council Meeting Minutes, September 12 and 26 and October 10, 1949, F. Joint Council Minutes, 9/48–12/49, Box 3, UAW Local 248 Papers; *MJ*, September 18, 1949; and *MS*, September 28, 1949.

96. "Executive Board Meeting of Wednesday, November 16, 1949," F. Executive Board Minutes, Box 3, UAW Local 248 Papers.

97. Brody, *Workers in Industrial America*, 184, 185, and 191–193; Nelson Lichtenstein, "UAW Bargaining and Shop Floor Conflict, 1946–70," *Industrial Relations* 24 (Fall 1985): 360–381; and ACMC, "Press Release," June 30, 1950, *The Next Five Years* ([West Allis], [1950]).

98. "Statement from Walter Geist," June 9, 1950, *The Next Five Years*.

99. Ibid.

100. "News Release," June 30, 1950; Walter Geist to the Men and Women of Allis-Chalmers, June 30, 1950; Walter Geist to the Men and Women of Allis-Chalmers, July 1, 1950, *The Next Five Years*; "Agreement, 1948–1949" and "Agreement, 1950–1955"; and "Memorandum of Agreement," October 4, 1951, F. 1950–1955 Contract Modifications, Box 4, UAW Local 248 Papers.

101. Telegram, Walter Reuther and John Livingston to Charles Schultz, July 30, 1950; and Telegram, Walter Reuther to Charles Schultz, F. Reuther, Walter, Box 4, UAW Local 248 Papers.

102. *MS*, August 4, 18, 1955.

103. Peterson, *Industrial Heritage*, 245; *MJ*, April 20, 1959; Steve Schlossberg to Officers, Board Members, and Staff, June 14, 1967, F. 2, Box 37, WPRP.

104. *MJ*, March 5, 1962; Peterson, *Industrial Heritage*, 345; *MJ*, February 27, 1968.

## CHAPTER 8. Conclusion

1. Brophy, *A Miner's Life*, 291 and 294.

2. Cochran, *Labor and Communism*, 315–322; Halpern, *UAW Politics*, 265–267; Harris, *Right to Manage*, 7–13; Kim Moody, *An Injury to All: The Decline of American Unionism* (New York, 1988), 24–40.

3. Selig Perlman, *A Theory of the Labor Movement* (New York, 1949), 4–8.

4. Harris, *Right to Manage*, 12, 10, 198, 204, and 67–70.

5. Richard A. Lester, *As Unions Mature: An Analysis of the Evolution of American Unionism* (Princeton, 1958), 21, 22.

6. Don D. Lescohier, "Report on Closed Shop and Seniority Policies on Collective Bargaining," April 10, 1940, 11, DDLP.

7. C. Wright Mills, *The New Men of Power: America's Labor Leaders* (New York, 1948), 224, 353.

8. Treleven, "Buse Interview" and "Christoffel Interview."

9. Treleven, "Christoffel Interview" and "Buse Interview."

10. Treleven, "Buse Interview" and "Christoffel Interview."

11. Bob Riordan, "Buck," 1970, Box 3, HWSC.

12. Frank Aukofer, *City with a Chance* (Milwaukee, 1968), 51.

13. *MJ*, October 30, 1977.

14. Barnard, *Reuther*, 109, 104–110.

15. Halpern, *UAW Politics*, 230 and Barnard, *Reuther*, 114–117.

16. Barnard, *Reuther*, 157–161, 195–198, and 212.

17. *MJ*, March 4, 1948, and July 17, 1956; *New York Times*, March 15, 1950; *MS*, July 17, 1956.

18. Treleven, "Christoffel Interview."

19. Treleven, "Buse Interview."

20. Max Raskin to General Counsel, National Labor Relations Board, July 18, 1950, F. 91, Box 8; and Max Raskin to Irving J. Levy, October 24, 1950, F. Raskin, Max, Box 4, UAW Local 248 Papers.

21. "Questionnaire on Financial States of the 91 Discharged Allis-Chalmers Workers," F. 91 Financial Forms, Box 4, UAW Local 248 Papers.

22. The Walter Fleischer family to Charles Schultz, September 1950, F. 91, Box 8, UAW Local 248 Papers.

23. Ibid.

24. Peterson, *Industrial Heritage*, 359–368.

25. Ibid. 397, 409, 371–409; and *MS*, May 17, 1980.

26. Peterson, *Industrial Heritage*, 359; *MJ*, November 9, 1980, and November 10 and November 15, 1987; and *MS*, November 10, 1987.

27. Author's telephone conversation with Don Weimer, February 12, 1991.

# INDEX

Abraham Lincoln School, 200, 203
Addes, George, 61, 181, 187, 188, 198
AFL-CIO: civil war, 15, 76, 103 (*see also* factionalism); merger, 220, 226–227. *See also* American Federation of Labor; Congress of Industrial Organizations
African-American workers, 38, 68, 120, 124–126, 142–143, 148, 224–225; craft union reaction to, 124; German and Polish reaction to, 124; numbers of, 124; management discrimination against, 143; union policy toward, 125; upgrading of, 125; unskilled, 125–126. *See also* Jamaican workers
All-American Women, 98
Allie Charmer, 122
Allis, Edward P., 17
Allis-Chalmers American Federation of Labor, 54
Allis-Chalmers Clubhouse, 35
Allis-Chalmers Federal Labor Union. *See* Federal Labor Union 20126
Allis-Chalmers Manufacturing Co., 11, 28, 31, 32, 33, 35, 191; anti-unionism, 97, 213–118; Communism file, 9; defense contracts in 1941, 92; divided management, 63; expansion of, 18–22; financial stability, 152–153; formation of, 17–18; labor policy of, 49–50; largest Wisconsin corporation, 2; number of workers, 38; plant closing, 230; power of, 222–223; problems with conservative UAW, 218–219; products, 17, 19, 36; reaction to NLRA, 53; tax breaks, 152–153, 207; troubled firm, 229–230; wartime profits, 152
*Allis-Chalmers Worker*, 40
*Allis-Chalmers Workers' Union News* (*ACWU News*), 45, 46, 55, 68

Allis Mutual Aid Society, 35
American-born workers, 29, 31, 35
American Federation of Labor (AFL), 11, 12, 13, 15, 16, 22, 23, 26, 33, 38, 39, 45, 48, 52, 53, 55, 61, 64, 68, 86, 87, 89, 97, 119, 164, 165, 178, 185, 205; back-to-work movement during 1941 strike, 98–99; business agents, 48, 49; craft unions, 66, 86; FLU, 59; industrial unionism, 54, 83; initiation fees, 46; membership, 49; Metal Trades Council, 41; Metal Trades Department, 83; old guard, 63; organization of Allis-Chalmers, 40, 83–84, 85–88; reaction to WERA, 77; Socialists, 10; and strike of 1939, 79–80; style of unionism, 62; system of representation, 109. *See also* International Association of Machinists; International Brotherhood of Electrical Workers; International Molders' Union; United Automobile Workers Union–American Federation of Labor
Americanism, 34, 138
American Plan, 17, 34
American Workers for Defense (AWD), 98, 119
America's Krupp, 35
anti-unionism, 7, 15, 16, 17, 26, 28, 30, 34, 87, 88, 98, 119, 187, 213, 222
apprenticeship, 5, 35
arbitrator, *see* impartial referee
Audia, Tony, 215
auto workers, 166, 173, 189
AWD, *see* American Workers for Defense

Babb, Max, 4, 49, 50, 56, 66, 72, 85, 90, 91, 93, 95, 96, 98, 99
back-to-work movement, 80, 96–98, 100, 119, 179